Peer Relationships
and Adjustment
at School

A volume in
Adolescence and Education
Tim Urdan, *Series Editor*

Peer Relationships and Adjustment at School

edited by

Allison M. Ryan
University of Michigan, Ann Arbor

Gary W. Ladd
Arizona State University

≡IAP

INFORMATION AGE PUBLISHING, INC.
Charlotte, NC • www.infoagepub.com

Library of Congress Cataloging-in-Publication Data

Peer relationships and adjustment at school / edited by Allison M. Ryan, Gary W. Ladd.
    p. cm. – (Adolescence and education series)
 Includes bibliographical references.
 ISBN 978-1-61735-807-4 (pbk.) – ISBN 978-1-61735-808-1 (hardcover) – ISBN 978-1-61735-809-8 (ebook) 1. Student adjustment. 2. Interpersonal relations in adolescents. I. Ryan, Allison M. II. Ladd, Gary W., 1950-
 LB1139.S88P44 2012
 371.93–dc23

                                        2012006588

For Joe, Ella and Jack
—Allison Ryan

For Becky, Karen, and Marion
—Gary Ladd

CONTENTS

PART II

PRACTICES AND INTERVENTIONS THAT SUPPORT POSITIVE PEER RELATIONSHIPS AT SCHOOL

CHAPTER 1

PEER RELATIONSHIPS AND ADJUSTMENT AT SCHOOL

An Introduction

Allison M. Ryan

Students and parents streamed towards the schoolhouse doors and clustered in a group on the steps. Anticipation marked their faces as they approached the crowd and made their way to the front. Students emerged every few moments—some with elation and excitement, others with uncertainty and a few with disappointment. There were high fives among some students. Other students were consoled by their parents and friends. Some parents beamed as if they had won the lottery. Other parents looked frustrated.

What was going on? It was only days before the school year began and the principal had just posted the class lists at the elementary school my children attended. Not too far away at the middle school a similar scene was unfolding with parents and students learning their team assignments within their grade. In the United States it is typical each year when children move to the next grade level that they are reassigned to a new class with a differ-

Peer Relationships and Adjustment at School, pages 1–7
Copyright © 2012 by Information Age Publishing

ent teacher and peer group. At the middle school level they are assigned to a team within their grade that has its own set of teachers and students with whom they will have classes for the year.

As I watched this scene unfold, it was interesting to me to see the focus of both the students and parents on peers. Everyone wanted to know who their teacher would be, but they also wanted to know which peers would be in their class. Emotions ran high and ranged from glee at being with close friends to sadness at being separated from friends. Parents could be heard talking about their pleasure that their child was with peers that they got along with well or were good role models. Other parents were relieved that their child was not with a peer who had caused problems the previous year. Some parents were visibly upset that a problematic peer relationship had not been taken into consideration in placing two children in the same class again. Parents and students alike seemed highly attuned to the fact that the peers in their classes would matter a great deal for their school experience.

Theory and research to date has not fully explicated how and why peer relationships matter for adjustment at school. It is the aim of our book to advance our understanding of peer relationships and students' adjustment at school. The focus is on students' social and academic adjustment at school. This is important because historically, there has been more attention to peers as the key influence on students' social development and teachers and parents as the key influence on students' academic development (Juvonen & Wentzel, 1996; Ladd, 2005; Ryan, 2000). There is increasing evidence that peer relationships play a crucial role in academic adjustment (e.g., Altermatt & Broady, 2009; Buhs, Ladd, & Herald, 2006; Gest, Ruilson, Davidson, & Welch, 2008; Hamm, Schmid, Farmer, & Locke, 2011; Kindermann, 2007; Ryan & Shim, in press; Wentzel, 2009). Students' academic and social adjustment is intertwined, and peers matter in important ways for academic as well as social adjustment. Our goal was to bring together an array of respected scholars to examine the varied and complex ways in which peers influence students' beliefs and behaviors in the school context. We invited scholars who study peers and adjustment from elementary through high school, with a special focus on adolescent issues. We received a rich set of chapters that collectively contain a variety of conceptualizations of peer relationships and adjustment at school.

THEMES OF THE VOLUME

The chapters in this volume reflect several broad themes. First, attention to the multifaceted and complex nature of peer relations is necessary for a full understanding of peer relations and adjustment at school. A perusal of the chapters highlights the broad array of types of peer relationships that students engage in at school. Students work with classmates, interact in groups, and form friendships. Transcending specific interactions and relationships, students experience different levels of acceptance and varying reputations among their peers. Ladd, Kochenderfer-Ladd, Visconti, and Ettekal consider peer relations in regard to teacher-prescribed peer collaboration partnerships in the classroom (e.g., small group work or collaborative learning). They examine the types of social skills or behavioral competencies that children must possess to work effectively with peers in the classroom. Kindermann and Skinner focus on the nature of students' close friendships and peer groups. They consider how both types of peer relations operate together in students' lives and matter for adjustment at school. Cillessen and van den Berg draw attention to the difference between peer acceptance and popularity. They discuss the varying implications of peer acceptance and popularity for students' academic and social development.

Second, attention to the explanatory mechanisms, or processes underlying peer influence, is needed for a full understanding of peer relations and adjustment at school. Across the chapters the processes by which peers promote or hinder students' engagement, learning, and achievement are given much consideration. Wentzel, Donlan, and Morrison describe how peers provide important supports in the form of expectations, instrumental help, emotional support, and safety which matter for social and academic outcomes at school. Modeling, direct communication, peer monitoring, and emotional support are presented as processes that are central to understanding how peers provide such support for adjustment. Altermatt also provides an insightful discussion of the processes of peer influence. In her chapter, she argues that attention to discourse with peers provides a critical window to document and better understand how such processes unfold among students. As pointed out by Ryan, Jamison, Shin, and Thompson, the social goals that students have for their peer relationships play an important role in understanding the processes that unfold within peer relationships.

Third, attention to how peer relations develop within the classroom context and in relation to different teacher practices or curricular programs is a promising avenue for educators to guide students' peer relationships and support school adjustment. The social context matters for the nature and quality of relationships that students have with one another. Teachers create communities within their classroom that concern norms and values for not only learning but student relationships as well. Programs or specialized curriculum at the individual, class, or school level can influence peer relationships and adjustment at school. In the chapter by Hughes as well as the chapter by Wentzel, Donlan, and Morrison, the authors discuss classroom level processes, namely teachers' interaction and strategies that impact children's social lives. Hughes reviews several interventions that target teacher's social–emotional practices and have been shown to improve students' social competencies. In two of the chapters (see Lochman, Boxmeyer, Powell, Barth, and Barker; and Salmivalli, Garandeau, and Veenstra), we see how programs designed to alleviate peer relation problems (aggression and bullying) facilitate school adjustment via improvements not only in the targeted social behavior but academic outcomes as well. In the Hamm, Hoffman, and Farmer chapter, we see how a program can support teachers in taking an active role in developing positive peer cultures around effort and achievement during early adolescence.

OVERVIEW OF THE CHAPTERS

We divided the book into two sections. The first set of chapters focus on the nature of peer relationships at school, linkages between peer relationships, and different aspects of school adjustment as well as examination of the underlying processes that explain such linkages. The second set of chapters also explores such issues but contains a primary focus on what might be done in classrooms and schools to better support positive peer relationships and diminish peer problems and thus promote students' school adjustment.

Part I. Peer Relationships: Nature, Processes, and Implications for School Adjustment

Ladd, Kochenderfer-Ladd, Visconti, and Ettekal discuss the importance of children's ability to interact in a constructive manner with classmates in three regards: participation or engagement in classroom activities, academic learning, and scholastic achievement. They provide an overview of conceptual frameworks that have guided research on children's classroom peer relationships and evidence for how such relationships are related to academic engagement, learning, and achievement. They review work on important interpersonal determinants of classroom peer relationships. They delineate the social skills or behavioral competencies children need to forge such classroom peer relationships. They consider teacher-prescribed peer collaboration partnerships whose success depends on social skills and social relationships. They present a framework for this understudied aspect of classroom peer relations and preliminary findings from studies to identify skills children need to succeed in peer-mediated learning activities.

Kindermann and Skinner focus on the nature of peer groups and friendship networks. They point out that researchers tend to focus on friends or groups and rarely consider the role of both types of relationships simultaneously. They offer a tensegrity metaphor to illustrate how friends and peer groups co-exist and operate in children and adolescents' lives. Peer influence from different relationships may have similar effects but combine in powerful ways that matter for school adjustment. They report results of a study concerning sixth grade students' friends and peer groups.

Wentzel, Donlan, and Morrison provide a review of linkages between peer relationships and school adjustment and then focus on the mechanisms of peer influence. They aptly note that more research is needed in regards to understanding how and why peer relationships might contribute to students' adjustment at school. They examine the different kinds of support that peers provide for students at school and the processes of peer influence that underlie such support. They conclude with a discussion of the role of the teacher and school context in peer relationships at school.

Altermatt takes up a similar focus on mechanisms of peer influence in her chapter and argues that attention to achievement-related discourse with peers provides critical insights. To illustrate her point, Altermatt reviews work on peer discourse, externalizing and internalizing symptoms and then discusses in more depth research on peer discourse and school adjustment. Discourse with peers highlights how modeling, expectancy socialization, informational and emotional support underlie peer influence.

Cillessen and van den Berg consider another important facet of the social world at school: popularity. They discuss popularity and peer acceptance as indicators of two different ways to be socially successful or competent in the peer group, each with their own developmental trajectories. They note that while popular students are seen as attractive and cool, they are not all well-liked or doing well in school. They conclude with a discussion of implications and some results from an intervention study that focused on improving peer relationships in the classroom.

Ryan, Jamison, Shin, and Thompson draw attention to students' social motivation in relation to their peer relationships and school adjustment. They present a model of social achievement goals that distinguishes different social strivings students might have at school. They synthesize results of their research showing that individual differences in social goals have implications for students' social adjustment. They conclude with a discussion of educational implications.

Part II. Practices and Interventions that Support Positive Peer Relationships at School

Hughes considers teachers as chief architects of the classroom context who exert much influence on students' peer relationships at both the individual and classroom level. With a developmental system perspective, she reviews research on those teacher interactions and strategies that impact students' social lives in classrooms. She discusses the different processes by which teachers affect peer relationships. Hughes notes that such knowledge could inform teacher preparation and professional development efforts to build teacher–student relationships to promote students' school adjustment.

Hamm, Hoffman, and Farmer also consider the teacher's role but in relation to adolescent peer cultures. They examine how intentional and unintentional instruction, management, and relational practices matter for the peer cultures that develop in classrooms and schools. They describe their intervention, Project SEALS (Supporting Early Adolescent Learning and School Success), and summarize some of the effects of SEALS from a series of randomized control trial experiments conducted in rural schools. Their results indicate the need for teachers to be able to coordinate academic, behavioral, and social aspects of classrooms to facilitate positive peer culture and diminish problematic peer cultures around effort and achievement at school.

Lochman, Boxmeyer, Powell, Barth, and Barker describe their school-based program Coping Power that was designed to address social cognitive deficiencies that contribute to aggressive children's problems. They review their research showing the effectiveness of Coping Power to reduce aggressive and antisocial behaviors. They then discuss newer findings indicating the effectiveness of Coping Power in regards to improving academic outcomes.

Salmivalli, Garandeau, and Veenstra describe their school-based program KiVa that was designed to diminish bullying behavior and widely implemented in Finnish comprehensive schools. They report evaluations of their program that indicated that anti-bullying interventions are valuable not only because they benefit a relatively small minority of victims who frequently suffer from bullying, but also because they increase the well-being, school motivation, and possibly even academic performance of a much wider group of students.

CONCLUSION

Taken together, the chapters in this volume advance our knowledge of peer relations and school adjustment. Collectively, they highlight the multifaceted nature of peer relations at school and move the field toward more complex conceptualizations of how and why peers matter for adjustment at school. They provide important insights into how educators can capitalize on the power of peers and promote adjustment at school. It is hoped that they stimulate new ideas and directions for research.

REFERENCES

Altermatt, E. R., & Broady, E. F. (2009). Coping with achievement-related failure: An examination of conversations between friends. *Merrill-Palmer Quarterly, 55*(4), 454–487.

Buhs, E. S., Ladd, G. W., & Herald, S. L. (2006). Peer exclusion and victimization: Processes that mediate the relation between peer group rejection and children's classroom engagement and achievement. *Journal of Educational Psychology, 98*, 1–13.

Gest, S. D., Rulison, K. L., Davidson, A. J., & Welsh, J. A. (2008). A reputation for success (or failure): The association of peer academic reputations with academic self-concept, effort, and performance across the upper elementary grades. *Developmental Psychology, 44*, 625–636.

Hamm, J. V., Schmid, L., Farmer, T. W., & Locke, B. (2011). Injunctive and descriptive peer group norms and the academic adjustment of rural early adolescents. *Journal of Early Adolescence, 31*, 1–33.

Juvonen, J., & Wentzel, K. (1996). *Social motivation: Understanding children's school adjustment.* New York, NY: Cambridge University Press.

Kindermann, T. A. (2007). Effects of naturally-existing peer groups on changes in academic engagement in a cohort of sixth graders. *Child Development, 78*, 1186–1203.

Ladd, G. W. (2005). *Children's peer relationships and social competence: A century of progress.* New Haven, CT: Yale University Press.

Ryan, A. M. (2000). Peer groups as a context for the socialization of adolescents' motivation, engagement, and achievement in school. *Educational Psychologist, 35*, 101–111.

Ryan, A.M. & Shim, S. S. (in press). Changes in help seeking from peers during early adolescence: Associations with changes in achievement and perceptions of teachers. *Journal of Educational Psychology.*

Wentzel, K. R. (2009). Peers and academic functioning at school. In K. H. Rubin, W. M. Bukowksi, & B. Laursen (Eds.), *Handbook of peer interactions, relationships, and groups* (pp. 531–547). New York, NY: Guilford.

PART I

PEER RELATIONSHIPS:
NATURE, PROCESS, AND IMPLICATIONS
FOR SCHOOL ADJUSTMENT

CHAPTER 2

CLASSROOM PEER RELATIONS AND CHILDREN'S SOCIAL AND SCHOLASTIC DEVELOPMENT

Risk Factors and Resources

Gary W. Ladd, Becky Kochenderfer-Ladd, Kari Jeanne Visconti, and Idean Ettekal
Arizona State University

Much of what we know about school as a context for children's learning and development stems from research on the academic challenges that youth face in classrooms. This is understandable because the primary mission of schooling is to ensure that children master academic skills and achieve scholastically. However, in classrooms, children are also confronted by a complex array of interpersonal challenges, some of which may have important implications for their educational progress. For example, instructional practices, learning activities, and other aspects of children's daily lives in

Peer Relationships and Adjustment at School, pages 11–49
Copyright © 2012 by Information Age Publishing
All rights of reproduction in any form reserved.

classrooms require that they possess age-appropriate social skills and know how to utilize them as a means of developing constructive relationships with classmates and teachers. It is conceivable, therefore, that not only the scholastic but also the interpersonal challenges that confront children affect their development and performance in school.

Because education is a social enterprise, it is surprising that investigators have tended to overlook interpersonal challenges and competencies as predictors of children's classroom learning and achievement. Beginning in the 1990s, however, researchers began to examine the premise that some interpersonal factors, such as children's social behavior in classrooms and their relationships with classmates and teachers, have an important bearing on their educational attainment (see Ladd, 1996, 2003, 2005; Perry & Weinstein, 1998). Much of what researchers have uncovered is consistent with the hypothesis that children's interactions and relationships with teachers and classmates have an effect on their engagement, learning, and achievement in classrooms. That is, considerable evidence underscores the importance of children's relationships with their teachers (see Kochenderfer-Ladd & Pelletier, 2008; Pianta & Steinberg, 1992; Troop-Gordon & Quenette, 2010), and an equally large body of findings attest to the importance of children's ability to interact and form constructive relationships with classmates. It is the latter of these two literatures that is the focus of this chapter. Our aim is to reflect on what has been learned about children's interactions and relationships with classmates as it pertains to three aspects of schooling: participation or engagement in classroom activities, academic learning, and scholastic achievement.

To achieve this purpose, we consider evidence from three allied research domains and organize the chapter accordingly. In the chapter's first section, we provide an overview of the types of classroom peer relationships that have received the greatest research attention, the rationales (i.e., frameworks, hypotheses) that have guided investigation of these relationships, and the discoveries that have emerged in recent years. Of particular interest is theory and data that elucidate how children's participation in various forms of classroom peer relationships is related to their academic engagement, learning, and achievement. Next, in the chapter's second segment, we review findings from research on the interpersonal determinants of classroom peer relationships. Of particular interest in this section are data that point to the types of social skills or behavioral competencies that children must possess to develop constructive social ties and avoid negative peer experiences with classmates.

Then, in the third section, consideration is given to another aspect of classroom peer relations that, although less well investigated, may be just as pivotal to children's school engagement, learning, and achievement: namely, teacher-prescribed peer collaboration partnerships (e.g., dyadic or group peer-mediated learning, or PML activities). Just as children's success in other types of classmate relationships depends on their social competence, the extent to which they profit from PML activities (i.e., relating effectively with learning partners, profiting from collaborative interactions) likely depends on the skills they bring to these tasks and the nature of the relationships they forge with work partners. Accordingly, in this section, we consider frameworks for research on this understudied aspect of classroom peer relations, and present preliminary findings from studies that have been undertaken to identify the skills children need to succeed in PML activities.

PEER RELATIONSHIPS AS A CONTEXT FOR SOCIAL AND ACADEMIC LEARNING

A common premise of socialization theories is that children learn most naturally and effectively within relationships (see Damon, 1984; Piaget, 1965; Vygotsky, 1978). Whether in relationships with parents, teachers, siblings, or peers, when partners are faced with common tasks or challenges, they often try to assist each other by taking on roles such as teacher, tutor, or collaborator. Moreover, balance or reciprocity in collaborative roles is more likely to occur in egalitarian (e.g., peer relationships) as opposed to hierarchical relationships (e.g., adult–child; see Ladd, 2005).

In classrooms, children are regularly in contact with classmates and have many opportunities to form ties or "partnerships" to work on school-related tasks. These ties are referred to as peer relationships because children and their classmates tend to be the same age. Because peers mature on similar timetables, develop similar interests and skills, and spend increasing amounts of time with each other during the school years (Larson & Richards, 1991), it has been theorized that classmates are in a unique position to influence children's engagement in learning, their school attitudes, and ultimately, their academic achievement (Hymel, Comfort, Schonert-Reichl, & McDougall, 1996). In fact, some scientists contend that the impetus for learning (e.g., motivational bases; see Kindermann, 2007; Wentzel, Barry & Caldwell, 2004), and the type of learning that occurs within peer relationships is unique relative to that which occurs with other socializers, such as parents, siblings, and teachers (see Furman & Robbins, 1985; Wentzel & Looney, 2007). In this sense, classroom peer relationships can be seen as an important context for children's social and scholastic learning in school settings. This premise is part of a larger "social learning hypothesis" that depicts peers as important and influential socializing agents and that attributes the bulk of peer influence to the interactions and experiences that children have within peer relationships (see Ladd, 2005, 2007).

Types of Classroom Peer Relations and Relational Influences

It has been proposed that not only the *types* of relationships children have with classmates, but also the *nature* of the interactions that transpire within these relationships, affect children's learning and achievement. Moreover, relational influences on learning may be either positive or negative in nature. Support for these propositions comes from evidence indicating that most children participate in multiple types of relationships with classmates, and the processes that are part of children's participation in these relationships are significant predictors of their scholastic engagement, learning, and achievement (see Fredricks, Blumenfeld, & Paris, 2004; Ladd, Herald, & Kochel, 2006; Perry & Weinstein, 1998).

In recent years, investigators who have examined how peer relations in classrooms are linked with children's educational performance have focused on three conceptually and empirically distinct types of relationships: friendships, acceptance or rejection by the peer group, and peer victimization (see Ladd, Kochenderfer, & Coleman, 1997). In general, friendship has been defined as a voluntary, dyadic form of relationship that often embodies a positive affective tie (Furman & Robbins, 1985; Howes, 1988), whereas peer acceptance/rejection has been defined as a child's relational "status" in a peer group, as indicated by the degree to which he or she is liked or disliked by group members (Asher, Singleton, Tinsley, & Hymel, 1979). Peer victimization, in contrast, has been defined as a form of relationship in which a subset of the peer group (e.g., one or several peers) frequently aggresses against specific children, particularly those who may be unable to stop the harassment (Perry, Kusel, & Perry, 1988). Implied in this definition is the assertion that "victims" are frequently the recipients of peers' aggression (Kochenderfer-Ladd & Ladd, 2001; Olweus, 1993; Perry et al., 1988).

The lines of investigation that show promise for elucidating how these relationships influence children's educational performance have been predicated on the assumption that children's relations with classmates immerse them in processes (e.g., participation vs. exclusion, support vs. conflict, receiving assistance vs. being ignored) that affect their learning and achievement in this context (e.g., level of school engagement; amount of learning, increases or decreases in their sense of worth, academic competence, etc.; see Ladd, 2003, 2005). Because peer relationships bring different processes to bear upon children and confer different provisions, it is likely that they vary in adaptive significance for school-related demands (see Ladd et al., 1997).

Classroom Friendships

Investigators have studied several aspects of classroom friendships including children's participation in a single close friendship, the number of mutual friends they have in their classrooms, the duration of these relationships, and features that reflect the quality of a friendship (see Ladd, 2005). Another key objective has been to identify the types of processes that occur in friendships that influence children's school engagement and achievement.

There is support for the hypothesis that classroom friends facilitate children's classroom participation because they provide instrumental (e.g., assistance with social or scholastic problems) and psychological support (e.g., emotional and/or physical security; Berndt, Hawkins, & Jiao, 1999; Ladd, Kochenderfer, & Coleman, 1996). Ladd et al. (1996) detected variability in the quality of the friendships that children formed as they entered school and found that youth who saw their friendships as offering higher levels of support and instrumental aid tended to view their classrooms as supportive interpersonal environments. Similarly, Wentzel (1998) found that children who felt supported by peers were more emotionally secure and engaged in the academic environment. It has also been shown that adolescents who have friends report higher levels of emotional well-being (Berndt & Keefe, 1995), which is linked to positive classroom behavior and academic achievement (Connell & Wellborn, 1991; Wentzel, 1998; Wentzel & McNamara, 1999).

Other data imply that friends can be motivators of school success by modeling socially acceptable behavior (Berndt et al., 1999). Findings indicate that youth who have classroom friends are more likely to engage in positive social interactions (Azmitia & Montgomery, 1993) and prosocial behaviors (Barry & Wentzel, 2006) than their friendless counterparts. Moreover, it may be the case that children align themselves with their friends' academic goals. In one study, preadolescents who viewed their friends as having high academic goals behaved in ways that helped promote their own academic achievement (Wentzel, Filisetti, & Looney, 2007).

However, not all of the processes that transpire between friends are supportive or positive. When children have been interviewed about their friendships, it is common for them to report instances of conflict, rivalry, and betrayal (e.g., see Berndt, 1986; Ladd et al., 1996; Parker & Asher, 1993; Youniss, 1980). Although only a few investigators have explored the relation between conflict in classroom friendships and children's school adjustment, the evidence implies that greater discord in friendships correlates with negative school attitudes and disruptive behavior. In one study, kindergartners who reported higher levels of conflict in their classroom friendships were less prone to like school or experience positive emotions during the school day than classmates who experienced lesser conflict in their classroom friendships (Ladd et al., 1996). In studies conducted with adolescents, Berndt and colleagues (Berndt & Keefe, 1995; Berndt, 1996) found that negative interactions between friends were associated with gains in classroom disruptiveness over the course of a school year.

Together, these studies suggest that having friends in the classroom and the features of these relationships may have an important bearing on children's success in school. Moreover, these findings suggest that friendships do not always have positive effects on children's adjustment. Thus, it is important to consider the quality of children's friendships, and not just the absence or presence of such relationships, when examining school adjustment.

Classroom Peer Acceptance and Rejection

A growing corpus of findings implies that, whereas acceptance by classmates facilitates children's learning and achievement, rejection has the opposite effect. A key hypothesis in research on rejection is that, when peers dislike persons within their group, they tend to act in rejecting ways towards these children (e.g., ignoring, excluding them from activities), and these behaviors mark specific children as disliked or rejected (Buhs & Ladd, 2001; Coie, 1990; Hymel, Wagner, & Butler, 1990). A likely consequence is that, the more children are seen as rejected, the more classmates exclude them from classroom activities, or minimize their roles and degrade their contributions in such activities. A related hypothesis is that peer rejection impairs school performance because, when children's participation is reduced or hindered, they are deprived of the interpersonal processes (e.g., peer support, tutoring, inclusion in study groups, etc.) that facilitate learning and achievement (see Buhs & Ladd, 2001; Buhs, Ladd, & Herald, 2006).

Consistent with expectations, data show that rejected children often become marginalized from the mainstream of peer activities (Ladd, Price, & Hart, 1990), become disengaged from classroom activities (Buhs & Ladd, 2001), and are excluded from participation by classmates (Buhs et al., 2006). Early peer rejection, occurring at school entry, predicts problems such as negative school attitudes, school avoidance, and underachievement during the first year of schooling and thereafter (Ladd, 1990; Ladd, Birch, & Buhs, 1999; Ladd & Burgess, 2001). Later, in the elementary years, peer rejection has been linked with loneliness (Parker & Asher, 1993), conduct problems (Ladd, 2006), lower emotional well-being (Ladd, 2006), and academic deficits (Ladd et al., 1997). Moreover, peer rejection during the school years has been linked with long-term problems such as dropping out of school, truancy, and underachievement (see Ladd, 2005; Parker & Asher, 1987).

Perhaps the most compelling corroboration for the rejection-limits-engagement hypothesis comes from a recent investigation conducted by Ladd, Herald-Brown, and Reiser (2008). These investigators traced children's movement in and out of classroom peer rejection across all of the grade school years and found that, regardless of whether children were rejected during the early or later years of grade school, longer periods of rejection were accompanied by lesser growth in classroom participation. The most serious patterns of disengagement were found for children who were continuously rejected throughout grade school. In contrast, children who moved out of rejection and toward acceptance by their classmates were more likely to show gains in classroom participation.

Other data imply that the effects of peer rejection on children's engagement or opportunities for participation in peer activities may be fairly pervasive within the school context. Disliked or rejected children appear to exhibit higher levels of disengagement not only in relatively structured activities that occur in classrooms (e.g., cooperative learning groups; see Furman & Gavin, 1989; Ladd et al., 2008), but also in relatively unstructured activities that occur outside the classroom (e.g., recess, playground periods; see Asher, Rose, & Gabriel, 2001; Ladd et al., 1990). For example, within the context of classroom peer activities (e.g., cooperative learning groups), disliked children are often the last to be chosen by peers for group work, and even when assigned to learning activities by teachers, these children may remain isolated (Blumenfeld, Marx, Soloway, & Krajcik, 1996).

Taken together, this evidence suggests that peer group rejection has adverse consequences for children's engagement and achievement in school. It appears that classroom peer rejection decreases children's opportunities to participate in classroom learning activities and makes it less likely that they receive social and scholastic support from classmates.

Classroom Peer Victimization

Efforts to identify and study victimized children in school contexts have expanded exponentially in recent years, due to educators' and parents' concerns about school violence and children's safety in school (see Kochenderfer-Ladd & Ladd, 2010; Ladd, 2005). Accruing evidence suggests that peer harassment is a relatively age-invariant phenomenon, occurring at all levels of schooling (see Kochenderfer-Ladd & Troop-Gordon, 2010), including the earliest school years (e.g., kindergarten and the primary grades; see Alsaker & Gutzwiller-Helfenfinger, 2010; Kochenderfer-Ladd & Wardrop, 2001; Ladd & Kochenderfer-Ladd, 2002). Moreover, school-based harassment and victimization has been linked with many forms of school maladjustment, including absenteeism, low GPA, poor academic readiness, and school avoidance (e.g., Iyer, Kochenderfer-Ladd, Eisenberg, &Thompson, 2010; Juvonen, Nishina, & Graham, 2000; Kochenderfer & Ladd, 1996; Ladd et al., 1997; Lopez & DuBois, 2005; Schwartz, Gorman, Nakamoto, & Toblin, 2005).

It has been proposed that peer victimization produces psychological distress in children, and, in turn, the psychological problems children develop as a result of peer victimization become the causes of their educational difficulties. Accordingly, Ladd et al. (1997) found that young children who were exposed to high levels of peer victimization displayed increases in school avoidance and loneliness in school. In a study where researchers followed first and third graders into second and fourth grade, results showed that peer victimization led to decreases in children's effortful control skills that, in turn, predicted lower school engagement and academic achievement (Iyer et al., 2010). Similarly, Schwartz et al. (2005) reported that, for a sample of third and fourth graders, victimization predicted increases in depression, which, in turn, forecasted gains in academic difficulties (i.e., GPA, achievement test scores) over a one-year period. With middle school children as well, evidence indicates that the link between victimization and school adjustment (i.e., GPA, absenteeism) is mediated by psychological symptoms (e.g., self-worth, loneliness, depression; Juvonen et al., 2000; Lopez & DuBois, 2005).

Results of these studies suggest that victims of peer harassment are at risk for academic difficulties, and that psychological problems are among the mechanisms underlying the relation between peer victimization and school maladjustment. Victimization, it would appear, has the potential to both provoke and exacerbate psychological ailments that may detract from children's engagement in learning and achievement in school.

Overall, studies of children's relations with classmates imply that peer relationships—particularly adverse ones—play an important role in both social and scholastic development. This evidence raises critical questions about the forms of competence children need to develop healthy peer relationships in classrooms. In the following section, we briefly review what is known about the social competencies and behaviors that are predictive of children's participation in these various types of relationships.

SOCIAL COMPETENCE: PREDICTORS OF CLASSROOM PEER RELATIONSHIPS

One of the principal reasons why children fail to develop supportive ties with classmates is that they lack the social competence to do so (see Ladd, 2005). Thus, one important objective for educators is to identify interpersonal competencies that children need to develop positive relationships with classmates and create educational strategies (e.g., instructional and curricular methods) that enable children to acquire and utilize these skills to form and maintain such ties. However, before educators can devise strategies that help children develop skill sets for classroom social tasks, they must possess a working definition of the concept of social competence and identify the types of skills that children need to relate effectively with classmates.

The term "social competence" came into being as researchers sought to understand the origins of children's success and difficulty in peer interactions and relationships (see Ladd, 2005). Competent children are seen as possessing specific abilities that allow them to perform certain tasks at a level that others would judge to be "effective" or "successful." Evidence suggests that children need fairly complex and diverse "skill sets" to be successful at tasks such as making friends, gaining entry into classroom activities, and becoming accepted members of their peer groups (see Coie & Kupersmidt, 1983; Gottman, 1983; Ladd, 2005). For this reason, researchers have tended to define social competence in task-specific terms and identify skill sets by contrasting the behaviors of children who do versus do not succeed at specific social tasks. Findings suggest that it is possible to identify some behaviors that are "competent" (i.e., associated with or anteceding successful social outcomes) and others that are "incompetent" (i.e., associated with ineffective or adverse social outcomes).

Most of the child behaviors that researchers have identified as forms of social competence or incompetence can be grouped into three categories, termed *prosocial behaviors* (e.g., friendly, cooperative interaction patterns), *antisocial behaviors* (e.g., aggression), and *asocial behaviors* (e.g., solitary play, onlooking, unoccupied behavior, etc.). Of these three classes of behavior, only prosocial behavior has been conceptualized as a form of social competence (see Ladd, 1999, 2005). In the following sections, we review the evidence linking prosocial behaviors to the development of positive classroom peer relationships before presenting findings linking social incompetence, specifically antisocial and asocial behaviors, to poor classroom relationships.

Social Competence: Prosocial Behaviors as Determinants of Positive Relationships

Prosocial behavior can be seen as one of the most important, if not essential, forms of social competence for many types of childhood social tasks. To illustrate, Gottman (1983) found that prosocial skills forecasted children's success at friendship formation. Similarly, Howes (1988) found that toddlers with cooperative play styles were more likely to maintain their friendships, and Berndt and Das (1987) reported that prosocial behavior predicted whether fourth graders would maintain or lose friendships over a school year. Children who act prosocially also have been found to demonstrate more success at becoming accepted by classmates (Ladd, Price, & Hart, 1988).

Educators value prosocial behaviors, such as sharing, cooperating, helping, and communicating, because they are a means of achieving order and harmony within social groups, and they serve as a way of creating equitable access to resources. Essentially, when children act prosocially, they are demonstrating respect, supporting others (instrumentally and emotionally), facilitating interpersonal engagement (inclusion rather than exclusion from interactions and activities), and in many cases, creating an interpersonal environment that is conducive to learning. Prosocial skills can be seen as prerequisites for learning and achievement because, to succeed in classrooms, children must interact and participate effectively with classmates in school activities (Finn, 1993; Ladd, Buhs, & Seid, 2000).

Social Incompetence: Behavioral Antecedents of Poor Classroom Peer Relationships

In contrast to prosocial behaviors, antisocial behaviors (e.g., aggression) have been construed as actions that harm others, deprive peers of important interpersonal resources (e.g., instrumental support, companionship), and create social costs for the perpetrator (e.g., censure by classmates, teachers). In classrooms, antisocial behaviors are discouraged because they are inimical to social norms and conventions and pose a threat to the safety and rights of individuals within the group.

In addition to being frowned upon by peers and adults, antisocial behavior has been linked with the occurrence and development of a broad array of maladaptive outcomes. There is substantial evidence showing that aggressive behavior correlates inversely with friendship and peer acceptance (e.g., Coie & Kupersmidt, 1983; Dodge, 1983; Ladd et al., 1988) and is predictive of increased risk for peer victimization (Kochenderfer-Ladd, 2003; Perry et al., 1988; Schwartz, Proctor, & Chien, 2001). For example, both confrontive and relational (i.e., attempts to damage another's relationships) forms of aggression have been linked to problematic friendships and peer rejection in boys and girls (Grotpeter & Crick, 1996), and aggressive children appear to have difficulty maintaining their friendships (Parker & Seal, 1996).

Similar to antisocial behavior, asocial behaviors have also been linked to problematic peer relationships. Children who engage in asocial behaviors tend to eschew contact with peers or act in ways that limit their contacts with classmates (e.g., seldom initiating interactions, failing to maintain interactions, etc.). Children prone toward certain patterns of asocial behavior, such as reticent or submissive behaviors (Rubin, Burgess, & Hastings, 2002; Schwartz, Dodge, & Coie, 1993) appear to be at greater risk for peer abuse (e.g., victimization). Schwartz and colleagues (1993), for example, found that boys who became passive victims exhibited submissive and incompetent interaction styles and became progressively more withdrawn over time. In classrooms, where social interaction is required as part of instruction, asocial behaviors not only interfere with relationship development (e.g., making friends), but also engagement in learning activities (e.g., failing to take part or fully participate in PML or other types of scholastic activities).

A 4th Classroom Peer Relations Context: Teacher-Prescribed Peer Partnerships

It is likely that the benefits of social competence extend beyond enabling children to develop and maintain friendships and peer acceptance among classmates. Classroom instructional practices often necessitate that children interact skillfully with classmates in dyadic or small-group activities; in such contexts, they must effectively collaborate to complete academic tasks. Further, in such activities, it is often necessary for children to work with classmates that they may not like or prefer not to have as partners. Thus, social competence is also an important prerequisite for children's participation in teacher-prescribed peer partnerships and work groups.

Educators recognize that student-to-student interactions can be an effective learning resource (Ladd et al., 1997; Piaget, 1926; Vygotsky, 1934/1986). Indeed, many forms of peer-mediated learning (e.g., collaborative or cooperative PML) are widely used in U.S. schools to increase student motivation, engagement, and "active" forms of learning (see Fuchs, Fuchs, Hamlett, Phillips, Karns, & Dutka, 1997; Ryan, Reed, & Epstein, 2004; Webb & Farivar, 1994). Moreover, evidence suggests that, as an instructional strategy, PML is effective for promoting many aspects of achievement and intellectual development for children of all ages (see Cohen, 1994). Thus, it is not uncommon for teachers to create opportunities for classmates to learn from each other, such as by having children work in investigative teams or collaborate on academic assignments or projects (Damon & Phelps, 1989; Fredricks et al., 2004; Johnson & Johnson, 2000; Ladd et al., 2006; Maheady, Mallette, & Harper, 2006; Perry & Weinstein, 1998; Slavin, 1995). In fact, nearly 80% of elementary school (and 62% of middle school) teachers use peer-mediated learning (PML) in their classrooms on a sustained basis (Puma, Jones, Rock, & Fernandez, 1993).

By assigning children to dyads or small groups to engage in PML tasks, teachers are, in effect, creating *temporary peer partnerships* and encouraging children to engage in social interactions that are intended to promote learning. Exactly what types of peer interactions are needed for learning to occur, and which benefit all participants (rather than just some participants), have not been well specified. Further, the task of specifying these processes is made more complex by the fact that competent and productive modes of interaction likely vary across tasks, academic domains, and students. At a more fundamental level, and perhaps of even greater concern, is the fact that PML activities are often implemented in classrooms with the assumption that children possess the competence (i.e., interpersonal skills) needed to interact collaboratively and productively (i.e., devise and engage in interactions that lead to learning) with their peer partners or group members. As we shall see, this assumption may be unfounded. That is, it may be erroneous to assume that all or even most children possess the skills to work harmoniously and productively with their classmates. Rather, it is probable that substantial individual differences exist in children's social readiness for PML activities and that many children are insufficiently prepared to interact with peer partners or group members in harmonious and productive ways (e.g., engage in modes of interaction that build collaborative partnerships and foster learning).

Evidence that might reflect on the hypothesis that children may be ill-prepared to work with peers in productive ways is scant. Although there is a sizable body of evidence on PML and its effects—with much of it attesting to its benefits (e.g., children who work collaboratively with classmates perform better academically than those who work independently; see Azmitia, 1988; Damon, 1984; Fawcett & Garton, 2005; Tudge, 1992; Tudge & Winterhoff, 1993)—the findings are not always consistent (Sharan, 1980). Further, insight into the mechanisms responsible for learning, and evidence that would explain why some children profit more from this instructional strategy than others, remains limited. At present, in their attempts to elucidate the mechanisms that underlie differential learning outcomes, researchers have tended to focus on structural variations in peer collaboration, such as modifications in the ways children are paired (e.g., varying group size or participant ability levels, using homogenous or heterogeneous skill level dyads; see Fawcett & Garton, 2005). However, it is also possible that some children do not fully benefit from PML activities because they lack the social competencies needed to collaborate effectively with their classmates.

Defining Social Competence in Peer Collaborative Academic Contexts

Little theory or evidence exists that stipulates the types of collaborative social skills that children need to work effectively within PML activities. Conceptually, it might be argued that social competence is task-specific; that is, children might need one set of skills to be successful at forming relationships with classmates (e.g., to acquire friendships, gain peer acceptance) and another repertoire to be effective at collaborating with classmates on academic tasks (e.g., work-related skills, tutoring skills, collaborative skills). Investigators who study young children, for example, have differentiated between "social" and "work" skills as a way of conceptualizing the types of social competencies that enable children to succeed within the social as opposed to the scholastic domains of schooling (see McClelland & Morrison, 2003; McClelland, Morrison, & Holmes, 2000). With this taxonomy, work-related skills refer to behaviors such as listening and following directions, cooperating with classmates, taking turns, staying on task, organizing work materials, being interested and involved in classroom activities, and focusing and paying attention to tasks. There is some evidence to suggest that these skills are positively associated with children's academic performance and school success (Foulks & Morrow, 1989; McClelland et al., 2000), and it is plausible that many of these same work-related skills are important for children to collaborate effectively with classmates.

Alternatively, it is possible that many of the same social skills that help children form positive peer relationships with classmates (e.g., making friends) also make them effective work partners for academic activities. For example, classmates may consider children who often act prosocially (e.g., cooperative, helpful) to be attractive not only as friends but also as work partners.

Unfortunately, speculation alone is insufficient to fully identify the forms of competence that children need to work effectively within and benefit from PML activities. To achieve a better understanding of this skill domain, there is a need to theoretically define and empirically document the social competencies that underlie effective collaboration in teacher-prescribed peer partnerships and groups. As a point of departure for both of these tasks, it could be useful to draw upon relevant theoretical and/or empirical literatures. Two such sources of information strike us as potentially useful. The first is theory pertaining to peer collaborative learning, and in particular, premises about the processes that are central to learning or that specify the types of interactions that collaborators must engage in for learning to occur. A second potential resource is the evidence obtained from investigators' attempts to devise and implement collaborative learning programs in classrooms.

THEORIES ABOUT COLLABORATIVE LEARNING AND FUNDAMENTAL COLLABORATIVE PROCESSES

Researchers who have attempted to define and study the collaborative learning processes have tended to work from perspectives articulated by Lev Vygotsky (1978) and Jean Piaget (1965, 1985). One reason these theorists have been influential is that their writings identify mechanisms within peer interactions that, if present, are hypothesized to promote learning.

Vygotsky

Broadly speaking, Vygotsky's theory describes the social context of learning as one in which less-skilled individuals engage in a series of social interactions with more-skilled persons, the latter of which use their expertise to help novices make forward progress within their "zone of proximal development" (Vygotsky, 1978). With an emphasis on scaffolding as a primary means of learning and development, Vygotsky's ideas have been commonly applied to the study of peer mentoring or peer tutoring, a specific learning context in which a less-skilled student is paired with a peer of a higher skill level (see Damon, 1984; Hogan & Tudge, 1999 for reviews). Considerable evidence has accrued to suggest that tutoring between two children of differing skill levels, with one being "expert" and the other "novice," does indeed lead to improved cognitive skills and greater generalization of knowledge to other tasks (Azmitia, 1988; Damon & Phelps, 1989).

Although this theory offers insight into the potential processes that are inherent in peer tutoring or mentoring, its application is less clear or relevant to the context of *peer*-mediated learning, or peer *collaboration*. It is debatable, for example, whether experts and novices are essentially "peers" in the sense of being persons who possess similar capabilities. Moreover, the instructional processes that occur when skilled persons tutor novices are more likely to be unidirectional (e.g., didactic) rather than collaborative. In view of this, concerns have been raised about the "fairness" of tutoring relationships for tutors—that is, it is not clear that mentors profit academically (or receive commensurate learning opportunities) when they are placed in the role of helping mentees learn what they already know.

In contrast, collaborative learning strategies are typically based on the assumption that work partners possess the same or similar skill levels in relation to assigned academic tasks (see Damon & Phelps, 1989). When the skill differential between two students is minor rather than major, it is not as likely that scaffolding becomes the primary process that drives peer interaction and learning. Instead, it is when classmates' skills are nearly commensurate, and no one student is expert, that group members tend to team up and work collaboratively. That is, collaborators approach problems as pairs or teams that are comprised of novices. In fact, research findings suggest that, particularly when tasks are difficult, group members tend to pool their knowledge and skills (Hill, 1982).

Piaget

Jean Piaget' theories and associated evidence have also influenced researchers' conceptions of peer collaboration. Piaget saw children as distilling knowledge, in the form of internal cognitive processes, from experience. Once formed, these processes could be applied or adapted by children to "learn" (construct meaning) from new experiences (Piaget, 1965).

In collaborative learning contexts, where children join forces to work as a team, it is possible to conceive of participants as co-constructing knowledge about common experiences (e.g., a shared task, joint problem solving) through processes that are both internal (each participant's thought processes) and interpersonal (e.g., interaction processes, such as discourse between partners). Thus, collaborative processes, such as discourse and joint problem solving, contribute to knowledge that is constructed at the individual level (e.g., learning in the child) because the interactions that occur between peers (e.g., joint discussions, sharing of ideas, conflict between partners, etc.) elaborate existing ways of thinking or perturb new forms of thought. Indeed, researchers have found that cooperative learning maximizes social cognitive development, as compared to individual or competitive learning environments (Johnson & Johnson, 1982).

As such, Piagetian theory is a relevant theoretical lens through which to understand the processes that lead to learning when agemates, or co-equals, work together to solve problems, complete assignments, and so on. Unlike Vygotsky's perspective, Piagetian theory does not assume or require the presence of a skill differential between collaborating peers, but rather provides a rationale for pairing peers (co-equals, novices) and encouraging them to work collaboratively to complete academic tasks. Thus, when academic group work is viewed from this perspective, collaboration can be seen as an interpersonal process that is conducted in the context of social relationships for the purpose of constructing shared understandings of a common experience or task (see Damon, 1984; De Lisi & Golbeck, 1999 for reviews).

At a more specific level, researchers working from Piaget's theory have emphasized the importance of three interrelated processes as components for peer collaboration. These are the co-construction of knowledge, exposure to perturbation or conflict, and conflict resolution.

Co-construction of Knowledge

Sullivan (1953) and others (e.g., Youniss, 1980) have argued that the co-construction of knowledge, or shared meaning, is the central and most important task of collaboration. This occurs when pairs or groups of children mutually engage in processes such as idea sharing, idea analysis and defense, plan-making or strategizing, idea testing or application, problem solving, and error analysis. Processes that enable collaborators to arrive at co-constructed solutions or products for academic activities may be task-focused (e.g., discussing how to complete the assignment, interpret instructions, find materials, apply formulas, etc.), or person-focused (e.g., deciding whose turn it is, who talks first, assigning partner roles, allocating workloads, etc.). For example, children working collaboratively must not only develop an understanding of their assignment, come to agreement about how to complete it, and obtain required products (e.g., correct responses to math problems), but they also negotiate interpersonal issues that impinge on task performance and completion (e.g., differences in individuals' communicative styles, personality traits, social reputations, and preexisting relationships).

Experiencing and Resolving Conflict

As group members work together on teacher-prescribed assignments (i.e., engage in learning or the co-construction of knowledge), numerous task and interpersonal challenges (perturbations) are likely to arise and confront collaborators (De Lisi & Golbeck, 1999; Piaget, 1985). In other words, because co-construction is an active interpersonal process, children are likely to experience conflict. The events that trigger conflicts may stem from task- or person-related events, interactions, or activities that occur within groups. Conflicts that arise between peer collaborators may have productive purposes, as when individuals disagree about how to approach a problem, propose differing solutions, and debate the accuracy of results or answers. However, conflicts can also be counterproductive to learning, particularly if disagreements discourage collaborative engagement by preventing members from working together or creating adverse interpersonal relations (e.g., cause members to dislike each other, attack or aggress against each other, demean each other's ideas or work, etc.). Often it is when conflicts escalate, become prolonged, or fail to achieve resolution that they disrupt collaboration, discourage partner participation, or halt work altogether and thereby circumvent learning and task completion.

Not surprisingly, research on peer collaboration suggests that conflict *resolution* is an essential element of the learning process (Johnson & Johnson, 1979; Smith, Johnson, & Johnson, 1981). Disagreements, once they occur, must be resolved in a way that allows partners or group members to re-engage intellectually and interpersonally (e.g., readdress the task and return to working with each other). Between collaborative partners, or group members, it appears important for children to actively seek equilibrium following the disruptions that conflicts introduce (see Moshman & Geil, 1998).

However, because experiencing and resolving conflict are ways children learn from their behaviors and make modifications to their future actions and strategies, it could be argued that such processes should not be ignored or minimized when using peer-mediated learning. In other words, conflict is to be expected within the unique dynamics of a group learning environment and, thus, it is important that children learn valuable conflict resolution skills to promote effective collaborations.

The Role of Social Skills

Relatively little attention has been devoted to children's social skills in theory and research on peer collaboration and learning in classrooms. Individual differences in the skills children bring to collaborative interactions are not central to Piaget's theory, and they are seldom mentioned by investigators who have implemented and evaluated collaborative and cooperative learning programs in classrooms. However, it stands to reason that social skills play a role in children's ability to engage in and profit from peer-mediated learning activities (Cohen, 1994). Unless children are able to relate and work effectively with agemates, it is not likely that they will be productive collaborators; that is, if children lack essential collaborative skills they are not prepared to respond to the academic (learning, problem solving) and interpersonal challenges (assisting, supporting partners; resolving conflicts, etc.) that are inherent in teacher-prescribed peer partnerships.

Because little is known about the specific skills children need to effectively engage in peer collaboration, researchers are faced with the challenge of identifying these skills. In particular, there is a need to document the types of skills that enable children to participate effectively in collaborative activities, and to develop instructional strategies that will enable children to acquire and become proficient at these skills.

Social Competence: Identifying Skills for Peer Collaboration

A logical first step toward identifying the skill sets that children need for peer collaboration is to map the interpersonal demands of prototypical collaborative tasks and determine whether these tasks call for specialized skills—that is, skills other than those known to be essential for positive peer relations. For grade-school children, collaborative tasks can be conceptualized (see Cohen, 1994) as academic assignments that are: (1) designed and prescribed by teachers, (2) undertaken by two or more classmates (i.e., dyads, small groups), and (3) performed with the expectation that all participants (each member of the dyad or group) will work together to achieve a collective goal or product (i.e., find a solution to a problem, obtain a correct answer, achieve consensus on a conclusion, etc.). Although the dynamic structure of collaborative assignments varies as a function of the task and participants (e.g., academic content, instructions, objectives, student cognitive and behavioral processes; see Cohen, 1994), process models typically specify both cognitive and social components. For example, Barnes and Todd (1977) proposed a model that contained multiple cognitive components (e.g., constructing meaning for the assigned task, devising a problem to work on, setting up hypotheses, gathering evidence) as well as multiple social processes (e.g., controlling progress, managing competition and conflict, providing mutual support). In another model (Vedder, 1985), collaborative tasks were conceptualized as including processes such as specifying goals, planning procedures, generating and selecting among alternative strategies, attempting solutions, revising plans, and so on. For purposes of illustration, a theoretical eclectic model of classroom peer collaboration based on the processes that have been proposed or investigated in past research is presented in Figure 2.1. For example, this model depicts the initial processes of a collaborative task including the formation of partnerships, clarification of the task goals and products, and preparation activities (e.g., procurement of materials) followed by a strategizing stage during which time partners plan how to achieve the group's goals. Once established, partners then put their plan into action and begin a cycle of evaluating, revising, and tracking their progress until the task is complete.

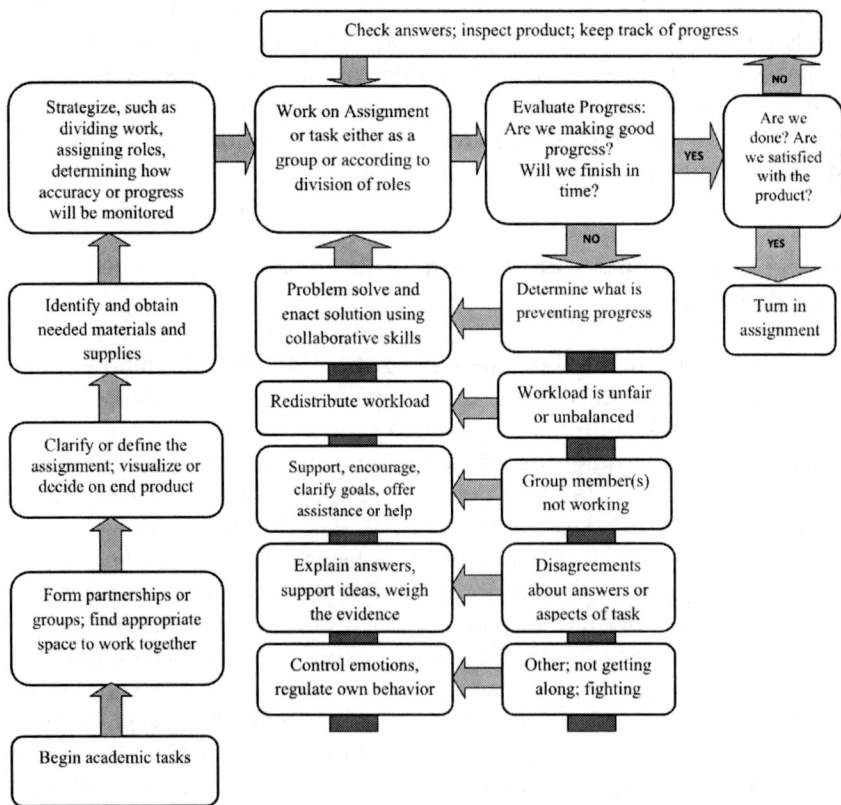

Figure 2.1 A model of collaborative processes for teacher-prescribed peer group activities.

However, as also illustrated in Figure 2.1, problems and issues may arise during the process that impede progress. When such perturbations arise, group members need to identify the problem and work together to determine a new course of action and re-engage in the activity. Common problems are depicted in Figure 2.1 to illustrate some of the issues that groups face, such as: (1) partners' perceptions of an unbalanced workload, (2) a group member who has stopped working (e.g., may have left the group, is goofing off, or may be refusing to work with others), (3) conflict, such as disagreements over answers or the next course of action for a project, and (4) fights about the task or personal matters. Solving such issues requires that group members posses specific collaborative skills and willingness to work together.

If it can be assumed that some, if not most, of the processes inherent in collaborative tasks are represented in Figure 2.1, then it may be worthwhile to speculate about the skill sets that children need to participate successfully in this peer context. As previously noted, it is possible that the skills that enable children to collaborate successfully on academic activities are the same as those needed to establish and maintain healthy peer relationships. Wentzel and Watkins (2002), for example, have argued that the behavioral styles that contribute to children's social status and peer acceptance are also likely to promote academic engagement and motivation. Similarly, Connell and Wellborn (1991) contend that relational skills, such as acting in a prosocial manner, regulating one's emotions and behaviors, and communicating effectively with others, are also fundamental for school achievement. Other investigators, particularly those who have researched cooperative learning strategies, have emphasized the importance of social as well as work-related skills, such as soliciting opinions, communicating explicitly, modifying viewpoints, and managing competition and conflict (Barnes & Todd, 1977). Insight into whether these assumptions are correct, or whether there are differences in the skills that children need to succeed as collaborators rather than friends or playmates, requires further investigation.

At present, at least two types of evidence appear pertinent to the task of generating hypotheses about the types of skills that grade-school children need to be effective collaborators in teacher-prescribed peer learning activities. The first is data that have accrued from prevention and intervention studies in which investigators attempted to manipulate (e.g., teach, train) skills that were expected to produce improvements in children's scholastic performance. Only a few such studies have been undertaken to ascertain whether specific social skills as exhibited during peer-mediated learning activities (e.g., cooperative learning activities) are associated with gains in children's achievement. Webb and Farivar (1994), for example, found that the nature of the interactions that occurred between students during cooperative learning activities affected the extent to which children benefited from those activities. Specifically, it was discovered that Latino and African

American children who were given specific instructions on communication skills and work-related helping skills performed better academically after participating in cooperative learning activities when compared to children who only received instructions in communication skills.

In another study, Fuchs and colleagues (1997) used an experimental design to compare the mathematics achievement of children who were assigned to three groups. In the first group, children participated in peer-mediated learning (PML), but before beginning their work, they received instructions about how to offer and request help from their partners. Children in the second group also participated in PML and received the same instructions as those provided to the first group but, in addition, they were taught to provide partners with task-relevant explanations and to adjust explanations to assist their partners with the assignment. The third group served as a non-PML control group and did not receive instructions about any work-related skills. Results not only showed improvements in math achievement for the two experimental groups, as compared to the control group, but children in the second experimental group evidenced larger math gains than those in the first group. Thus, the Fuchs et al. (1997) findings suggest that not only does PML improve children's achievement, but that instruction on collaborative skills enabled children to derive greater benefit from PML. Additional support for this conclusion can be found in a study by Mesch, Lew, Johnson, and Johnson, (1986). These investigators found that five learning-disabled adolescents made greater gains in achievement if they received social skill assistance while taking part in PML.

Findings from the aforementioned studies imply that there are at least three types of collaborative skills that help children form effective peer partnerships: (1) communication skills, (2) work-related helping skills, such as offering and requesting help, and (3) sharing task-relevant ideas or explanations. Other data that aid the identification of collaborative skills come from studies in which investigators have researched barriers to effective collaboration. Dion, Fuchs, and Fuchs, (2005), for example, found that many school-age children lack communication skills that are essential for PML activities. Other barriers to effective collaboration include peers' inability to establish common or shared goals for assigned academic tasks, and disparities in participants' engagement (i.e., one child less interested/engaged than others), persistence (i.e., one child stops working or gives up before others), and workloads (i.e., one child does more/less work than others). It is also not uncommon for work partners to disagree, fight, or disparage each other's work, all of which can serve as barriers to collaboration and task completion (see Weinstein, 1991 for a review). In such circumstances, it is not surprising that children's attempts to collaborate break down or become unproductive.

A second, perhaps less-utilized approach to skill identification is to sample persons who are directly involved in collaborative learning and utilize these participants as informants about collaborative skills. Potential strategies for identifying collaborative skill sets include: (1) observing and documenting the skills children use as they engage in collaborative learning activities, (2) asking children and their collaborative partners to describe behaviors or work habits that they utilize and/or value in workmates, and (3) asking teachers—that is, persons who regularly devise, implement, and observe collaborative activities—to specify, enumerate, or evaluate skill prerequisites, usage, and so on.

Although it has been rare for investigators to undertake this type of research, initial findings attest to the potential utility of this mode of inquiry. Prague (1989), for example, asked students to describe skills that they thought were useful when working with classmates on school work. The results pointed to several types of social skills that appear distinct from those typically reported by researchers who study other aspects of children's peer relations (e.g., friendship formation, peer group acceptance, etc.). Included among these were skills such as dividing the assigned work fairly, working effectively and efficiently, prompting responses from others, and thinking creatively. Similarly, when asking children what qualities make a classmate a good work partner, Kochenderfer-Ladd, Ladd, Visconti, and Ettekal (2010) found that children mentioned such collaboration-specific skills as staying on task, sharing ideas and suggestions with each other, listening, providing task-specific instrumental support, and working through disagreements. Such findings suggest that while existing research on social skills for peer relationships may provide a basis for understanding competencies that are essential for one type of interpersonal task (e.g., friendship making, peer acceptance), this data base may not fully represent the types of skills that children need to function effectively when collaborating with peers on academic tasks.

Mapping Collaborative Skill Sets in Grade-School Classrooms: Preliminary Findings from the 4R-SUCCESS Project

We have recently undertaken a three-year project to identify collaborative skills that can be taught to children as a means of improving their academic and social learning in teacher-prescribed peer partnerships. To be specific, our aim is to develop 4R-SUCCESS (4Rs = reading, 'riting, 'rithmetic, and relationships: Students Using Collaborative Curricula to Enhance Social-Scholastic Skills), a program that integrates teachers' coaching of collaborative skills into dyadic and small-group PML activities. Initial project aims and preliminary findings are described in the sections that follow.

Development of the 4R-SUCCESS program has been guided by several key objectives. One principal aim is to identify collaborative skills that are endemic to PML activities as implemented in grade school classrooms. As part of this goal, it is our intention to discriminate among the skills that children exhibit while engaging in PML activities, and document those that appear to play a beneficial role in collaborative interactions and products. Ultimately, our aim is to create a collaborative skill (CS) taxonomy— that is, to develop a catalog of skills that appear requisite for effective collaboration and partnerships in teacher-prescribed PML activities. Another principal goal is to formulate, based on the evidence used to construct the CS taxonomy, a collaborative skills curriculum for the 4R-SUCCESS program, and a delivery system (i.e., an instructional methodology) that is feasible and effective for teachers to use in grade school classrooms. Finally, it is of interest to determine whether implementation of the 4R-SUCCESS program in grade school classrooms will improve children's collaborative skills, enable children to form effective working relationships with peers (i.e., supportive, productive peer partnerships), and increase children's academic and social competence.

In the pages that remain, we present preliminary findings that address the project's initial aims: specifically, the identification of collaborative skills and the creation of the collaborative skill taxonomy. Our pursuit of this objective was based on the assumption that differences exist in the behaviors children display when collaborating with peers on teacher-prescribed assignments, and that it is possible to document behaviors that (1) are actually used by children during collaborative activities, and (2) are differentially preferred by collaborators (e.g., peer partners) and instrumental to the success of collaborators' efforts (e.g., achieving interactional harmony; making progress toward the completion of assignments, finding correct answers, learning, achievement, etc.). Further, we regarded the above-stipulated criteria as a basis for establishing the social validity of identified skills, and ultimately, the collaborative skill taxonomy. Thus, to document collaborative skills, and ensure their social validity, we sought to identify skills that were *actually utilized* by children in collaborative contexts (classroom PML activities) and considered *valuable* or important (i.e., desirable in a work partner) by peer collaborators (classmates within our targeted age groups).

Our search for collaborative skills began with informal observations of teacher-prescribed, dyadic peer collaborative activities within many third- and fifth-grade-school classrooms. From these data, our research team (Kochenderfer-Ladd et al., 2010) formulated seven preliminary skill categories that appeared to capture essential forms of collaborative behavior in teacher-assigned PML tasks. As shown in Table 2.1, the descriptive labels

TABLE 2.1 Percentages of Interviewed Children who Mentioned a Skill Reflecting the CS Domain

Collaborative Skill Domain	All Children (N = 113)	Girls (n = 56)	Boys (n = 57)
Staying on task	18.6	19.6	17.5
Understand others/perspective taking	3.5	3.6	3.5
Communication and listening	20.4	17.9	22.8
Cooperation and collaboration skills	26.5	23.2	29.8
Emotion and behavior regulation	11.5	8.9	14.0
Support (instrumental, social and emotional)	47.8	50.0	45.6
Solving disagreements and compromising	11.5	14.3	8.8
Relational qualities	27.4	24.6	30.4
Individual qualities	31.9	28.6	35.1
Task qualities	15.0	21.4	8.8
Other	8.0	8.9	7.0

assigned to these seven collaborative skill (CS) categories were as follows: (1) staying on task (i.e., perseverance, sharing task-related ideas), (2) understanding partners' perspective, (3) communication and listening skills, (4) cooperative and collaborative skills, (5) emotion and behavior regulation, (6) supporting partners (i.e., providing instrumental, social, and emotional support), and (7) solving disagreements (i.e., conflict resolution).

We then conducted individual, open-ended interviews with 113 (57 boys and 56 girls) children from ethnically diverse third through fifth grade classrooms to determine whether the proposed CS categories would be independently cited (i.e., authenticated; substantiated) by members of our target population (3rd through 5th graders). Within these one-on-one interviews, children were asked a series of open-ended questions, one of which was: "When you work in groups on schoolwork, what makes someone a good work partner?" Children were permitted to talk freely and gave an average number of three responses to this question (range = 1 to 7). Narrative responses to this question (and others not reported here) were reliably categorized by pairs of trained coders (91% M agreement) into a total of 11 categories, which included the 7 collaborative skills and four non-skill categories that were implied by the data: "relational factors" (i.e., being a friend, we like each other), "characteristics of the partner" (i.e., smart, cool), "task qualities," and "other" (see Table 2.1). Fully 82% of children's open-ended responses reliably fit into the seven CS categories, and the remaining 18% of responses were reliably classified into the remaining non-skill categories.

Further evidence of the social validity of the CS skill categories was obtained by asking third and fifth graders to rate the importance of these seven collaborative skills. The purpose of these data was to ascertain chil-

dren's perceptions of the value or importance of specific types of collaborative skills for contexts in which they worked with peers on academic tasks.
To obtain this information, we constructed a rating measure that contained
skill exemplars of each category, and asked children to rate each exemplar
on a 3-point scale, with scale points ranging from 1 (*not important*) to 3 (*very
important*). This instrument was administered to the same 113 children who
participated in open-ended interviews plus an additional 40 third and fifth
graders ($n = 153$; 48.9% boys).

Analyses of respondents' ratings (MANOVAs by grade and gender) are
presented in Table 2.2. As can be seen, the average of the ratings that children gave to skill exemplars from each of the CS categories ranged from
1.76 to 2.44 (score of 2 = *important*; 3 = *very important*), suggesting that children regarded each of these collaborative skills as a valuable partner characteristic. Although these ratings did not differ by grade level, significant
gender differences were found suggesting that girls valued some collaborative skills (e.g., communication, cooperation, emotion/behavior regulation) more than boys (see Table 2.2).

After establishing that children regarded skills belonging to each of the
seven skill categories as assets for a work partner, we sought to determine
whether third and fifth graders actually used these skills. We also attempted to determine whether skill usage was related to children's desirability
among classmates as work partners, and to their scholastic achievement.
To gather data on these additional markers of social validity, we asked third
and fifth graders to rate classmates' use of 11 skills representing exemplars
of the seven collaborative skills. To be specific, children rated (0 = *never*,
1 = *rarely*, 2 = *sometimes*, and 3 = *most of the time*) how often each of their classmates exhibited the eleven collaborative skill exemplars (see Table 2.3):
two items tapped communication, two items assessed emotion and behavior regulation, three items tapped distinct forms of support (instrumental,
social, and emotional) and all other skills were measured with a single ex-

**TABLE 2.2 Descriptive Statistics of Children's Ratings of Collaborative
Skill Importance**

Collaborative Skill Domain	All	SD	Boys	Girls	F	p
Staying on task	2.44	.62	2.40	2.48	0.64	NS
Understand others/perspective taking	1.82	.75	1.70	1.96	4.09	<.05
Communication and listening	2.07	.69	1.94	2.19	4.79	<.05
Cooperation and collaboration skills	2.25	.68	2.13	2.37	4.36	<.05
Emotion and behavior regulation	2.43	.60	2.31	2.56	6.33	<.05
Support (instrumental, social and emotional)	2.05	.65	1.97	2.12	1.90	NS
Solving disagreements and compromising	1.76	.56	1.66	1.84	3.26	NS

TABLE 2.3   Peer Ratings of How Often Classmates Use Collaborative Skills

Collaborative skill domain	Boys	Girls	F	p
Staying on task (work hard until done)	2.20	2.39	6.58	<.05
Understand others/perspective taking	2.24	2.39	4.32	<.05
Communication and Listening	2.11	2.25	4.01	<.05
Sharing Ideas (communication)	1.99	2.04	0.30	NS
Cooperation and collaboration (taking turns)	2.38	2.43	0.90	NS
Emotion Regulation	2.09	2.31	10.43	<.01
Behavior Regulation	2.30	2.47	5.43	<.05
Support (Instrumental)	2.15	2.25	1.62	NS
Support (Social)	1.78	1.84	0.52	NS
Support (Emotional)	1.99	2.10	2.49	NS
Solving Disagreements	1.98	2.05	0.93	NS

emplar. Children were also asked to rate how much they liked to work with each of their classmates (i.e., work partner desirability) using a five point scale (i.e., 1 = *not much*, 3 = *kind of*, and 5 = *a lot*), and achievement data were gathered from teachers. Analyses were conducted by dividing children into groups. First, children were assigned to one of three groups using work partner desirability as a criterion (groups = low, scores in bottom tertile; moderate, scores in middle tertile; or high, scores in top tertile). Next, children were assigned to one of three achievement groups using teacher-reported achievement scores as a criterion (i.e., low, middle, high tertiles).

Skill usage ratings were analyzed by grade and gender (MANOVA) and results are presented in Table 2.3. The overall pattern of means (grade effects were nonsignificant) suggests that children perceive their classmates as using all of the skills at least "sometimes" or more often during PML activities. Significant sex differences were found such that girls were rated higher than boys on 5 of the 11 collaborative skills: (1) staying on task, (2) understanding their partners' perspectives, (3) communicating and listening to their partners, (4) regulating their emotions, and (5) regulating their behaviors.

Additional analyses were performed to assess whether children who varied in their desirability as work partners (grouped as low, moderate, or highly preferred by classmates) differed in their use of collaborative skills, as rated by their classmates. Findings, as shown in Table 2.4, suggest that the persons children preferred as work partners (i.e., those in the "high" desirability group) were classmates who most often used each of the seven types of collaborative skills.

Likewise, analyses were undertaken to determine whether children who differed in achievement (grouped as low, moderate, or high achievers) varied in their use of collaborative skills, as rated by their classmates (see Table 2.5).

TABLE 2.4 Peer Ratings of Collaborative Skill Use of Children Rated High, Medium, and Low on Peer-Ratings of Partner Preference

Skill Category	Low	Moderate	High	F	p
Staying on Task	1.94[a]	2.31[b]	2.63[c]	46.97	<.001
Understanding others	2.00[a]	2.35[b]	2.60[c]	32.92	<.001
Communication and listening	1.81[a]	2.19[b]	2.53[c]	72.12	<.001
Cooperation and collaboration	2.11[a]	2.45[b]	2.65[c]	37.50	<.001
Emotion regulation	1.94[a]	2.26[b]	2.40[c]	17.81	<.001
Behavior regulation	2.14[a]	2.39[b]	2.59[c]	15.56	<.001
Support (Instrumental)	1.75[a]	2.28[b]	2.55[c]	57.34	<.001
Support (Social)	1.40[a]	1.88[b]	2.13[c]	41.74	<.001
Support (Emotional)	1.67[a]	2.07[b]	2.37[c]	58.85	<.001
Solving Disagreements	1.74[a]	2.05[b]	2.28[c]	26.90	<.001

Note: Means in each row denoted by different superscripts differ at $p < .05$ using Bonferroni post hoc tests.

TABLE 2.5 Teacher Reports of Children's Skill Use for Low, Moderate, and High Levels of School Achievement

Collaborative Skill Domain	Low	Moderate	High	F	p
Staying on task	1.66[a]	2.14[b]	2.64[c]	16.07	<.001
Understanding others	2.07[a]	2.40[ab]	2.59[b]	4.31	<.05
Communication and listening	2.04[a]	2.43[b]	2.73[c]	16.25	<.001
Cooperation and collaboration	1.93[a]	2.36[b]	2.59[b]	6.52	<.01
Emotion and behavior regulation	2.11[a]	2.47[b]	2.75[c]	13.99	<.001
Support	1.77[a]	2.18[b]	2.29[b]	5.89	<.01
Solving disagreements	1.93[a]	2.38[b]	2.69[b]	7.31	<.001

Note: Means in each row denoted by different superscripts differ at $p < .05$ using Bonferroni post hoc tests.

As was found for partner desirability, children classified as higher achievers were rated as using each of the seven types of collaborative skills more often than children who were members of the moderate and low achievement groups. Overall, these findings are consistent with the premise that children who use the identified collaborative skills frequently, as compared to those who do so less often, tend to be preferred work partners and higher achievers.

In sum, a critical first step in the development of 4R SUCCESS was to define and document children's collaborative skills, and evaluate their social validity—that is, determine the extent to which targeted skills are utilized by third and fifth graders, are important to children in these age groups, and are associated with children's academic success in school. Ensuring that the skills included in our collaborative taxonomy are socially valid increases the probability that teachers will implement 4R SUCCESS and that children who participate will profit from the program in meaningful ways. The findings obtained thus far suggest that seven types of collaborative skills are not only important to children and teachers, but also linked in positive ways with social and academic outcomes (partner preference, achievement). Finally, although not presented here, school comparisons showed that our findings were consistent across three different types of schools and student populations. These results imply that the skill domains represented in our taxonomy are relevant (i.e., socially valid) across diverse student populations.

SUMMARY AND CONCLUSIONS

Educational researchers have studied peer relations in school contexts primarily to learn about the origins of children's social difficulties and to gain insight into the effects that such difficulties might have on their school adjustment and performance (see Ladd, 2005; Parker & Asher, 1987; Rubin, Bukowski, & Parker, 2006). Although the causal proposition that problematic classroom peer relations undermine children's educational engagement and progress has not been definitively proven, it has received substantial empirical support. As illustrated in this chapter, adverse relations with classmates (e.g., peer rejection, victimization, friendlessness) and associated processes (e.g., exclusion from learning activities, harassment) predict not only the inception of school adjustment problems (e.g., negative school attitudes, school disaffection/disengagement, underachievement; Buhs & Ladd, 2001; Ladd, 1990), but also the growth (e.g., Kochenderfer-Ladd & Wardrop, 2001; Ladd et al., 1997; Ladd & Burgess, 2001) and the long-term trajectories of these problems (see Buhs et al., 2006; Ladd et al., 2008).

Shifting the Emphasis of School-Based Peer Relations Research: Identifying Classroom Peer Contexts, Tasks, and Experiences that Benefit Children

The question of whether classroom peer relations serve beneficial purposes for children in the school context has, by comparison, received far less investigative attention. We know very little, for example, about whether children's interactions and affiliations with classmates have positive effects on their development and achievement. Moreover, if children do profit from some aspects of their relations with classmates, we know even less about the types of interactions and relationship processes that might be responsible for such effects.

Erasing this void in our knowledge could prove useful from a scientific as well as an applied point of view. Scientifically, studies aimed at these objectives could help shift the "dysfunction-oriented" paradigms that dominate peer relations research today toward frameworks that emphasize positive development, competence, and well-being. Rather than continuing to ask questions such as "How do adverse peer relations foster social and scholastic dysfunction?" researchers could devote more effort to questions such as "What types of classroom peer processes promote children's social and academic competence and progress?" From an applied perspective, gaining a better understanding of the peer processes that enhance children's development in school contexts would be consistent with contemporary school improvement initiatives, and the resulting discoveries could have far-reaching implications (e.g., impact on educational policies, practices, and reforms). Educational researchers could embrace this challenge by investigating classroom peer processes that, theoretically, have the potential to improve grade school children's interpersonal and scholastic development.

Teacher-Prescribed Collaborative Learning Activities: A Beneficial Classroom Peer Context?

In the preceding pages, we have argued that investigations of classroom peer-mediated learning (PML) activities and, in particular, the collaborative processes involved in teacher-prescribed collaborative peer interactions and partnerships offer an opportunity to examine the peer interactions that promote healthy interpersonal and academic adjustment. PML activities, such as investigative teams, peer collaboration and tutoring, and competitive and cooperative learning groups (Damon & Phelps, 1989; Johnson & Johnson, 2000; Maheady et al., 2006; Slavin, 1995), are widely used methods in American schools—nearly 80% of teachers use some form of cooperative or collaborative peer learning in their classrooms (Puma et al., 1993). However, after decades of research on PML, it is clear that more has been learned about the outcomes of these activities (e.g., learning, achievement) than about the *social* processes that produce the effects (see Blumenfeld et al., 1996; Bossert, 1988; Cohen, 1994; Furman & Gavin, 1989; O'Donnell, 2006). Empirical documentation of the actual *peer processes* that occur within PML activities and the links between such processes and specific *social and scholastic outcomes* (e.g., gains in social and academic competence) remains limited (Bossert, 1988; Furman & Gavin, 1989; O'Donnell, 2006).

Proponents of PML have argued that peer processes (e.g., peer encouragement, helping, cooperation) are fundamental to many types of PML programs and activities and should, in theory, enhance not only children's academic learning but also their relations with classmates (e.g., improve friendships and peer group acceptance; Bossert, 1988; Johnson & Johnson, 1985). Empirical support for this proposition, however, is quite limited. There is some evidence to suggest that children benefit academically from hearing peers provide explanations for scholastic tasks during PML activities (Webb, 1985), and from teaching members of their groups (Peterson, Janicki, & Swing, 1981). Other data suggest that children become more prosocial as a result of participating in cooperative learning groups (Hertz-Lazarowitz, Sharan, & Steinberg, 1980). The latter findings, however, are countered by evidence indicating that peers do not always act prosocially toward each other or work to benefit other members of their groups; during group activities, for example, some children attempt to dominate others, seek to benefit themselves at others' expense, loaf instead of participating, ignore or exclude others from conversations, and so on (see Blumenfeld et al., 1996).

Thus, although it appears that PML has the *potential* to benefit children socially and scholastically, evidence suggests that children's experiences in this context are not always positive and that some participants profit from their interactions more than others. Although the reasons for this are likely complex, we have proposed that children's skills play a role in their ability to engage in and profit from PML activities. Unless children are able to relate and work effectively with agemates, it is not likely that they will be productive collaborators—that is, if children lack essential collaborative skills, they are not prepared to respond to the academic (e.g., learning, problem solving) and interpersonal challenges (e.g., assisting and supporting partners, resolving conflicts, etc.) that are inherent in teacher-prescribed peer partnerships.

Helping Children Benefit from Teacher-Prescribed Collaborative Learning Activities

If teacher-prescribed collaborative learning activities are potentially beneficial for children, then it makes sense to develop educational strategies that will ensure that all children derive maximum benefit from their participation in this peer context. In this chapter, we argue that educators can help children benefit maximally from classroom PML activities by identifying the types of skills they need to function effectively in this peer context and by helping children learn and become proficient at these skills. Our contention is based on the assumption that teacher-prescribed collaborative learning activities constitute a specific type of peer context (i.e., dyadic or small group teams) that is convened for a specific social/scholastic goal, such as the need to jointly complete an academic assignment, and that children need specific skills (i.e., collaborative skills) to adapt to this context and profit from their participation.

By extension of this logic, classroom peer contexts, depending on their organization and purposes, contain different types of interpersonal and academic demands and, thus, are best negotiated when children possess competencies that are well-suited or specific to that context. If we embrace this perspective, then it can be argued that an important investigative agenda for educational researchers is to identify the skills that children need to succeed in teacher-prescribed collaborative learning activities.

Our efforts to achieve this goal have been based on investigative strategies that are similar to those implemented in the past to identify requisite competencies for other types of contexts/tasks, including entering peers' ongoing play (e.g., peer group entry skills; see Putallaz, 1983), friendship making (e.g., friendship formation skills; see Gottman, 1983; Parker & Seal, 1996), and earning acceptance in new peer groups (e.g., group acceptance skills; see Coie & Kupersmidt, 1983; Dodge, 1983). As illustrated here, the skills we have identified thus far are not entirely redundant with those profiled for previously investigated peer contexts/tasks. These findings lend support to the hypothesis that, in part, the skills children need to succeed in and profit from teacher-prescribed collaborative learning activities are distinct from those needed in other types of peer contexts.

Directions for Future Research

It appears that much remains to be learned about teacher-prescribed collaborative learning activities as a specific type of peer context, and about the skills children need (i.e., collaborative skills) to fit into and profit from their participation in this context. To advance current knowledge in these domains, three wide-ranging investigative agendas can be identified. First, it will be important to understand how classroom collaborative activities differ in form, content, and goals, and how these variables affect children's participation and the skills they need to work with partners and profit scholastically. Likewise, descriptive and process-oriented research is needed to profile the types of demands (interpersonal and scholastic) this context confers on children, determine whether children need different skills when they collaborate with same- versus cross-sex partners, and document changes in skill repertoires as children mature. Second, more detailed information should be gathered on the types of peer processes that occur in different types of peer collaboration activities, and on the classroom peer-relational and academic outcomes that are associated with these processes. Third, those who develop and implement programs designed to prepare children for teacher-prescribed collaborative learning activities should consider whether the extent to which children profit from these activities depends on the skills they bring to this context. For example, Johnson and Johnson (1994) argue not only must students be taught social skills required for high quality collaboration, but they must also be motivated to use them if cooperative groups are to be productive. Further, some researchers contend that the effects of collaborative learning on children's social competence tend to be weak and heterogeneous because these activities do not overcome impediments such as children's problem behaviors and lack of social skills (Dion et al., 2005). Thus, to maximize the benefits learners derive from these instructional contexts, it may be necessary to devise and implement classroom practices that will prepare children for the social demands of collaborative learning activities. Finally, there is a need for educators to experiment with different types of teacher-prescribed peer contexts (e.g., dyadic, small group activities), tasks (e.g., cooperative, collaborative assignments), and processes (e.g., modes of interaction) as a means of discovering strategies that produce meaningful gains in children's social learning and academic achievement. Together, progress toward these objectives will yield not only a more comprehensive understanding of the social processes underlying children's collaborative learning, but also an empirical data base that can be used to create technology (e.g., curricula, instructional methodology, etc.) for promoting social and scholastic learning in the classroom peer context.

NOTE

Gary W. Ladd, School of Social and Family Dynamics & Department of Psychology; Becky Kochenderfer-Ladd, School of Social and Family Dynamics; Kari Jeanne Visconti, School of Social and Family Dynamics; Idean Ettekal, School of Social and Family Dynamics.

Portions of this chapter and many of the empirical studies cited here in that were published by the authors have been prepared with support from the National Institutes of Health (1-RO1MH-49223, 2-RO1MH-49223, R01HD-045906), the National Science Foundation (Grant #0318462), and the Institute for Educational Studies (R305A090386). Special appreciation is expressed to the children, parents, teachers, and schools that participated in these studies, and to those who assisted with data collection and analyses.

Correspondence concerning this article should be addressed to Gary W. Ladd, P.O. Box 853701, Arizona State University, Tempe, AZ, 85287-3701, email: gary.ladd@asu.edu.

REFERENCES

Alsaker, F. D., & Gutzwiller-Helfenfinger, E. (2010). Social behavior and peer relationships of victims, bully-victims, and bullies in kindergarten. In S. R. Jimerson,

S. M. Swearer, & D. L. Espelage (Eds.), *The handbook of school bullying: An international perspective* (pp. 87–99). Mahwah, NJ: Lawrence Erlbaum Associates.

Asher, S. R., Rose, A. J., & Gabriel, S. W. (2001). Peer rejection in everyday life. In M. R. Leary (Ed.), *Interpersonal rejection* (pp. 105–142). London, UK: Oxford University Press.

Asher, S. R., Singleton, L. C., Tinsley, B. R., & Hymel, S. (1979). A reliable sociometric measure for preschool children. *Developmental Psychology, 15,* 443–444.

Azmitia, M. (1988). Peer interaction and problem solving: When are two heads better than one? *Child Development, 59,* 87–96.

Azmitia, M., & Montgomery, R. (1993). Friendship, transactive dialogues, and the development of scientific reasoning. *Social Development, 2,* 202–221.

Barnes, D., & Todd, F. (1977). *Communication and learning in small groups.* London, UK: Routledge and Kegan-Paul.

Barry, C. M., & Wentzel, K. R. (2006). Friend influence on prosocial behavior: The role of motivational factors and friendship characteristics. *Developmental Psychology, 42,* 153–163.

Berndt, T. J. (1986). Children's comments about their friendships. In M. Perlmutter (Ed.), *Cognitive perspectives on children's social and behavioral development.* (pp. 189–212). Hillsdale, NJ: Erlbaum.

Berndt, T. J. (1996). Exploring the effects of friendship quality on social development. In W. M. Bukowski, A. F. Newcomb, & W. W. Hartup (Eds.), *The company they keep: Friendship in childhood and adolescence* (pp. 346–365). New York, NY: Cambridge University Press.

Berndt, T. J., & Das, R. (1987). Effects of popularity and friendship on perceptions of the personality and social behavior of peers. *Journal of Early Adolescence, 7,* 429–439.

Berndt, T. J., & Keefe, K. (1995). Friends' influence on adolescent's adjustment to school. *Child Development, 66,* 1312–1319.

Berndt, T. J., Hawkins, J. A., & Jiao, Z. (1999). Influences of friends and friendships on adjustment to junior high school. *Merrill-Palmer Quarterly, 45,* 13–41.

Blumenfeld, P. C., Marx, R. W., Soloway, E., & Krajcik, J. (1996). Learning with peers: From small group cooperation to collaborative communities. *Educational Researcher, 25,* 37–40.

Bossert, S. T. (1988). Cooperative activities in the classroom. *Review of Research in Education, 15,* 225–250.

Buhs, E. S., & Ladd, G. W. (2001). Peer rejection as antecedent of young children's school adjustment: An examination of mediating processes. *Developmental Psychology, 37,* 550–560.

Buhs, E. S., Ladd, G. W., & Herald, S. L. (2006). Peer exclusion and peer abuse: Processes that mediate the relation between peer group rejection and children's classroom engagement and achievement? *Journal of Educational Psychology, 98,* 1–13.

Cohen, E. G. (1994). Restructuring the classroom: Conditions for productive small groups. *Review of Educational Research, 64,* 1–35.

Coie, J. D. (1990). Toward a theory of peer rejection. In S. R. Asher & J. D. Coie (Eds.), *Peer rejection in childhood* (pp. 365–401). New York, NY: Cambridge University Press.

Coie, J. D., & Kupersmidt, J.B. (1983). A behavioral analysis of emerging social status in boys' groups. *Child Development, 54,* 1400–1416.

Connell, J. P., & Wellborn, J. G. (1991). Competence, autonomy, and relatedness: A motivational analysis of self-system processes. In M. R. Gunnar and L. A. Sroufe (Eds.), *Self processes and development. The Minnesota symposia on child psychology, Vol. 23* (pp. 43–77). Hillsdale, NJ: Lawrence Erlbaum Associates.

Damon, W. (1984). Peer education: The untapped potential. *Journal of Applied Developmental Psychology, 5,* 331–343.

Damon, W., & Phelps, E. (1989). Strategic uses of peer learning in children's education. In Berndt, T. J., & Ladd, G. W. (Eds.), *Peer relationships in child development* (pp. 135–157). Hoboken, NJ: John Wiley & Sons.

De Lisi, R., & Golbeck, S. L. (1999). Implications for Piagetian theory for peer learning. In A. M. O'Donnell & A. King (Eds.), *Cognitive perspectives on peer learning* (pp. 3–37). Mahwah, NJ: Lawrence Erlbaum Associates.

Dion, E., Fuchs, D., & Fuchs, L. (2005). Differential effects of peer-assisted learning strategies on students' social preference and friendship making. *Behavior Disorders, 30,* 421–429.

Dodge, K. A. (1983). Behavioral antecedents of peer social status. *Child Development, 54,* 1386–1399.

Fawcett, L. M., & Garton, A. F. (2005). The effect of peer collaboration on children's problem-solving ability. *British Journal of Educational Psychology, 75,* 157–169.

Finn, J. D. (1993). *School engagement and students at risk.* Washington DC: Department of Education, National Center for Educational Statistics.

Foulks, B., & Morrow, R. D. (1989). Academic survival skills for the young child at risk for school failure. *Journal of Educational Research, 82,* 158–165.

Fredricks, J. A., Blumenfeld, P. C., & Paris, A. H. (2004). School engagement: Potential of the concept, state of the evidence. *Review of Educational Research, 74,* 59–109.

Fuchs, L. S., Fuchs, D., Hamlett, C. L., Phillips, N. B., Karns, K., & Dutka, S. (1997). Enhancing students' helping behavior during peer-mediated instruction with conceptual mathematical explanations. *The Elementary School Journal, 97,* 223–249.

Furman, W., & Gavin, L. A. (1989). Peer's influence on adjustment and development: A view from the intervention literature. In T. J. Berndt & G. W. Ladd (Eds.), *Peer relationships in child development* (pp. 319–340). Hoboken, NJ: John Wiley & Sons.

Furman, W., & Robbins, P. (1985). What's the point? Issues in the selection of treatment objectives. In B. Schneider, K. H. Rubin, & J. E. Ledingham (Eds.), *Children's peer relations: Issues in assessment and intervention* (pp. 41–54). New York, NY: Springer-Verlag.

Gottman, J. M. (1983). *How children become friends.* Chicago, IL: University of Chicago Press.

Grotpeter, J. K., & Crick, N. R. (1996). Relational aggression, overt aggression, and friendship. *Child Development, 67,* 2328–2338.

Hertz-Lazarowitz, R., Sharan, S., & Steinberg, R. (1980). Classroom learning style and cooperative behavior of elementary school children. *Journal of Educational Psychology, 72,* 99–106.

Hill, G. (1982). Group versus individual performance: Are N + 1 heads better than one? *Psychological Bulletin, 91,* 517–539.

Hogan, D. M., & Tudge, J. R. H. (1999). Implications for Vygotsky's theory for peer learning. In A. M. O'Donnell & A. King (Eds.), *Cognitive perspectives on peer learning* (pp. 39–65). Mahwah, NJ: Lawrence Erlbaum Associates.

Howes, C. (1988). *Peer interaction of young children.* Chicago, IL: University of Chicago.

Hymel, S., Comfort, C., Schonert-Reichel, K., & McDougall, P. (1996). Academic failure and school dropout: The influence on peers. In J. Juvonen & K. R. Wentzel (Eds.), *Social motivation: Understanding children's school adjustment. Cambridge studies in social and emotional development* (pp. 313–345). New York, NY: Cambridge University Press.

Hymel, S., Wagner, E., & Butler, L. J. (1990). Reputational bias: View from the peer group. In S. R. Asher & J. D. Coie (Eds.), *Peer rejection in childhood. Cambridge studies in social and emotional development* (pp. 156–186). New York, NY: Cambridge University Press.

Iyer, R., Kochenderfer-Ladd, B., Eisenberg, N., & Thompson, M. (2010). Peer victimization and effortful control: Relations to school engagement and academic achievement. *Merrill-Palmer Quarterly, 56,* 361–387.

Johnson, D. W., & Johnson, R. T. (1979). Conflict in the classroom: Controversy and learning. *Review of Educational Research, 49,* 51–70.

Johnson, D. W., & Johnson, R. (1982). Healthy peer relationships: A necessity not a luxury. In P. Roy (Ed.), *Structuring cooperative learning experiences in the classroom: The 1982 handbook* (pp. 45–82). New Brighton, MN: Interaction Book Company.

Johnson, D., & Johnson, R. (1985). The internal dynamics of cooperative learning groups. In R. Slavin, S. Sharan, S. Kagan, R. Hertz-Lazarowitz, C. Webb, & R. Schmuck (Eds.), *Learning to cooperate, cooperating to learn* (pp. 103–124). New York, NY: Plenum Press.

Johnson, D., & Johnson, R. (1994). *Leading the cooperative school* (2nd ed.). Edina, MN: Interaction Book Company.

Johnson, D., & Johnson, R. (2000). Cooperative learning, values, and culturally plural classrooms. In M. Leicester, C. Modgill, & S. Modgill (Eds.), *Values, the classroom, and cultural diversity* (pp. 15–28). London, UK: Cassell PLC.

Juvonen, J., Nishina, A., & Graham, S. (2000). Peer harassment, psychological adjustment, and school functioning in early adolescence. *Journal of Educational Psychology, 92,* 349–359.

Kindermann, T. A. (2007). Effects of naturally existing peer groups on changes in academic engagement in a cohort of sixth graders. *Child Development, 78,* 1186–1203.

Kochenderfer-Ladd, B. (2003). Identification of aggressive and asocial victims and the stability of their peer victimization. *Merrill-Palmer Quarterly, 49,* 401–425.

Kochenderfer, B. J., & Ladd, G. W. (1996). Peer victimization: Cause or consequence of children's school adjustment difficulties? *Child Development, 67,* 1293–1305.

Kochenderfer-Ladd, B., & Ladd, G. W. (2001). Variations in peer victimization: Relations to children's maladjustment. In J. Juvonen & S. Graham (Eds.), *Peer harassment in school: The plight of the vulnerable and victimized* (pp. 25–48). New York, NY: Guilford Press.

Kochenderfer-Ladd, B., & Ladd, G. W. (2010). A child-by-environment framework for planning interventions with children involved in bullying. In E. M. Vernberg & B. K. Biggs (Eds.), *Preventing and treating bullying and victimization: Integrative and Evidence-based practices* (pp. 45–74). New York, NY: Oxford University Press.

Kochenderfer-Ladd, B., & Pelletier, M. (2008). Teachers' views and beliefs about bullying: Influences on classroom management strategies and students' coping with peer victimization. *Journal of School Psychology, 46,* 431–453.

Kochenderfer-Ladd, B., & Troop-Gordon, W. (Guest Eds.). (2010). Peer victimization: Contexts, causes and consequences. [Special issue]. *Merrill-Palmer Quarterly, 56,* 221–230.

Kochenderfer-Ladd, B., & Wardrop, J. L. (2001). Chronicity and instability of children's peer victimization experiences as predictors of loneliness and social satisfaction trajectories. *Child Development, 72,* 134–151.

Kochenderfer-Ladd, B. J., Ladd, G. W., Visconti, K. J., & Ettekal, I. (2010, June). *The social validity of the 4R Success collaborative skill taxonomy.* Poster presented at the meeting of the Institute of Education Sciences Annual Meeting, National Harbor, MD.

Ladd, G. W. (1990). Having friends, keeping friends, making friends, and being liked by peers in the classroom: Predictors of children's early school adjustment? *Child Development, 61,* 1081–1100.

Ladd, G. W. (1996). Shifting ecologies during the 5–7 year period: Predicting children's adjustment to grade school. In A. Sameroff & M. Haith (Eds.), *The five to seven year shift* (pp. 363–386). Chicago, IL: University of Chicago Press.

Ladd, G. W. (1999). Peer relationships and social competence during early and middle childhood. *Annual Review of Psychology, 50,* 333–359.

Ladd, G. W. (2003). Probing the adaptive significance of children's behavior and relationships in the school context: A child by environment perspective. In R. Kail (Ed.), *Advances in child behavior and development* (pp. 43–104). New York, NY: Wiley.

Ladd, G. W. (2005). *Children's peer relations and social competence: A century of progress.* New Haven, CT: Yale University Press.

Ladd, G. W. (2006). Peer rejection, aggressive or withdrawn behavior, and psychological maladjustment from ages 5 to 12: An examination of four predictive models. *Child Development, 77,* 822–846.

Ladd, G. W. (2007). Social learning in the peer context. In O. Saracho & B. Spodek (Eds.), *Contemporary perspectives on research on social learning in early childhood education* (pp. 133–164), Charlotte, NC: Information Age Publishing.

Ladd, G. W., Birch, S. H., & Buhs, E. S. (1999). Children's social and scholastic lives in kindergarten: Related spheres of influence? *Child Development, 70,* 1373–1400.

Ladd, G. W., Buhs, E., & Seid, M. (2000). Children's initial sentiments about kindergarten: Is school liking an antecedent of early classroom participation and achievement? *Merrill-Palmer Quarterly, 46,* 255–279.

Ladd, G. W., & Burgess, K. B. (2001). Do relational risks and protective factors moderate the linkages between childhood aggression and early psychological and school adjustment? *Child Development, 72*, 1579–1601.

Ladd, G. W., Herald, S. L., & Kochel, K. P. (2006). School readiness: Are there social prerequisites? *Early Education and Development, 17*, 115–150.

Ladd, G. W., Herald-Brown, S. L., & Reiser, M. (2008). Does chronic classroom peer rejection predict the development of children's classroom participation during the grade school years? *Child Development, 79*, 1001–1015.

Ladd, G. W., & Kochenderfer-Ladd, B. (2002). Identifying victims of peer aggression from early to middle childhood: Analysis of cross-informant data for concordance, estimation of relational adjustment, prevalence of victimization, and characteristics of identified victims. *Psychological Assessment, 14*, 74–96.

Ladd, G. W., Kochenderfer, B. J., & Coleman, C. C. (1996). Friendship quality as a predictor of young children's early school adjustment. *Child Development, 67*, 1103–1118.

Ladd, G. W., Kochenderfer, B. J., & Coleman, C. (1997). Classroom peer acceptance, friendship and victimization: Distinct relational systems that contribute uniquely to children's school adjustment? *Child Development, 68*, 1181–1197.

Ladd, G. W., Price, J. M., & Hart, C. H. (1988). Predicting preschoolers' peer status from their playground behaviors. *Child Development, 59*, 986–992.

Ladd, G. W., Price, J. M., & Hart, C. H. (1990). Preschoolers' behavioral orientations and patterns of peer contact: Predictive of peer status? In S. R. Asher & J. D. Coie (Eds.), *Peer rejection in childhood* (pp. 90–115). New York: Cambridge University Press.

Lopez, C., & DuBois, D. L. (2005). Peer victimization and rejection: Investigation of an integrative model of effects on emotional, behavioral, and academic adjustment in early adolescence. *Journal of Clinical Child and Adolescent Psychology, 34*, 25–36.

Maheady, L., Mallette, B., & Harper, G. F. (2006). Four classwide peer tutoring models: Similarities, differences, and implications for research and practice. *Reading & Writing Quarterly, 22*, 65–89.

Mesch, D., Lew, M., Johnson, D., & Johnson, R. (1986). Isolated teenagers, cooperative learning, and the training of social skills. *Journal of Psychology, 120*, 323–334.

McClelland, M., & Morrison, F. (2003). The emergence of learning-related social skills in preschool children. *Early Childhood Research Quarterly, 18*, 206–224.

McClelland, M., & Morrison, F., & Holmes, D. (2000). Children at risk for early academic problems: The role of learning-related social skills. *Early Childhood Research Quarterly, 15*, 307–329.

Moshman, D., & Geil, M. (1998). Collaborative reasoning: Evidence for collective rationality. *Thinking & Reasoning, 4*, 231–248.

O'Donnell, A. M. (2006). The role of peers and group learning. In P. A. Alexander & P. H. Winne (Eds.), *Handbook of educational psychology* (pp. 781–802). Mahwah, NJ: Erlbaum.

Olweus, D. (1993). Bullies on the playground: The role of victimization. In C. H. Hart (Ed.), *Children on playgrounds: Research perspectives and applications* (pp. 85–127). Albany, NY: SUNY Press.

Parker J. G., & Asher, S. R. (1987). Peer relations and later personal adjustment: Are low-accepted children "at risk"? *Psychological Bulletin, 102*, 357–389.

Parker, J. G., & Asher, S. R. (1993). Friendship and friendship quality in middle childhood: Links with peer group acceptance and feelings of loneliness and social dissatisfaction. *Developmental Psychology, 29*, 611–621.

Parker, J. G., & Seal, J. (1996). Forming, losing, renewing, and replacing friendships: Applying temporal parameters to the assessment of children's friendship experiences. *Child Development, 67*, 2248–2268.

Perry, D. G., Kusel, S. J., & Perry, L. C. (1988). Victims of peer aggression. *Developmental Psychology, 24*, 807–814.

Perry, D. G., & Weinstein, R. S. (1998). The social context of early schooling and children's school adjustment. *Educational Psychologist, 33*, 177–125.

Peterson, P. L., Janicki, T. C., & Swing, S. R. (1981). Ability × treatment interaction effects on children's learning in large-group and small-group approaches. *American Educational Research Journal, 18*, 453–473.

Piaget, J. (1926). *The language and thought of the child.* New York, NY: Harcourt, Brace.

Piaget, J. (1965). *The moral judgment of the child.* New York, NY: Free Press.

Piaget, J. (1985). *The equilibrium of cognitive structures: The central problem of intellectual development.* Chicago, IL: University of Chicago Press.

Pianta, R. C., & Steinberg, M. (1992). Teacher-child relationships and the process of adjusting to school. In. R. C. Pianta (Ed.), *Beyond the parent: The role of other adults in children's lives. New directions for child development* (pp. 61–80). San Francisco, CA: Jossey-Bass.

Prague, S. V. (1989). Identifying social skills important to junior high school students working in cooperative groups. *Dissertation Abstracts International, 49*, 3255.

Puma, M. J., Jones, C. C., Rock, D., & Fernandez, R. (1993). *Prospects: The congressionally mandated study of educational growth and opportunity (Interim report).* Bethesda, MD: Abt Associates.

Putallaz, M. (1983). Predicting children's sociometric status from their behavior. *Child Development, 54*, 1417–1426.

Rubin, K. H., Bukowski, W., & Parker, J. G. (2006). Peer interactions, relationships, and groups. In W. Damon, R. M. Lerner, & N. Eisenberg (Eds.), *Handbook of child psychology: Vol. 3, Social, emotional and personality development* (6th ed., pp. 571–645). New York, NY: Wiley.

Rubin, K. H., Burgess, K. B., & Hastings, P. D. (2002). Stability and social-behavioral consequences of toddlers' inhibited temperament and parenting behaviors. *Child Development, 73*, 483–495.

Ryan, J. B., Reid, R., & Epstein, M. H. (2004). Peer-mediated intervention studies on academic achievement for students with EBD: A review. *Remedial and Special Education, 25*, 330–341.

Schwartz, D., Dodge, K. A., & Coie, J. D. (1993). The emergence of chronic peer victimization in boys' play groups. *Child Development, 64*, 1755–1772.

Schwartz, D., Gorman, A., Nakamoto, J. & Toblin, R. L. (2005). Victimization in the peer group and children's academic functioning. *Journal of Educational Psychology, 97*, 425–435.

Schwartz, D., Proctor, L. J., & Chien, H. (2001). The aggressive victim of bullying. In J. Juvonen & S. Graham (Eds.), *Peer harassment in school: The plight of the vulnerable and victimized* (pp. 147–174). NY: Guilford Press.

Sharan, S. (1980). Cooperative learning in small groups: Recent methods and effects on achievement, attitudes, and ethnic relations. *Review of Educational Research, 50,* 241–271.

Slavin, R. E. (1995). *Cooperative learning: Theory, research, and practice* (2nd Ed.). Boston, MA: Allyn & Bacon.

Smith, K. A., Johnson, D. W., & Johnson, R. T. (1981). Can conflict be constructive? Controversy versus concurrence seeking in learning groups. *Journal of Educational Psychology, 73,* 651–663.

Sullivan, H. S. (1953). *The interpersonal theory of psychiatry.* New York: Norton.

Troop-Gordon, W., & Quenette, A. (2010). Children's perceptions of their teacher's responses to students' peer harassment: Moderators of victimization-adjustment linkages. *Merrill-Palmer Quarterly, 56,* 333–360.

Tudge, J. R. (1992). Processes and consequences of peer collaboration: A Vygotskian analysis. *Child Development, 63,* 1364–1379.

Tudge, J., & Winterhoff, P. (1993). Can young children benefit from collaborative problem solving? Tracing the effects of partner competence and feedback. *Social Development, 2,* 242–259.

Vedder, P. H. (1985). *Cooperative learning: A study on processes and effects of cooperation between primary school children.* Gravenhage, The Netherlands: Stichting voor Onderzoek van het Onderwijs.

Vygotsky, L. S. (1978). *Mind in society: The development of higher psychological processes.* Edited by M. Cole, V. John-Steiner, S. Scribner, & E. Souberman. Cambridge, MA: Harvard University Press.

Vygotsky, L. S. (1986). *Thought and language.* Edited by Alex Kozulin. Cambridge, MA: MIT. (Original work published 1934)

Webb, N. (1985). Verbal interaction and learning in peer-directed groups. *Theory Into Practice, 24,* 32–39.

Webb, N. M., & Farivar, S. (1994). Promoting helping behavior in cooperative small groups in middle school mathematics. *American Educational Research Journal, 31,* 369–395.

Weinstein, C. S. (1991). The classroom as a social context for learning. *Annual Review of Psychology, 42,* 493–525.

Wentzel, K. R. (1998). Social relationships and motivation in middle school: The role of parents, teachers, and peers. *Journal of Educational Psychology, 90,* 202–209.

Wentzel, K. R., Barry, C. M., & Caldwell, K. A. (2004). Friendships in Middle School: Influences on Motivation and School Adjustment. *Journal of Educational Psychology. 96,* 195–203.

Wentzel, K. R., Filisetti, L., & Looney, L. (2007). Adolescent prosocial behavior: The role of self-processes and contextual cues. *Child Development, 78,* 895–910.

Wentzel, K. R., & Looney, L. (2007). Socialization in school settings. In J. Grusec & P. Hastings (Eds.), *Handbook of socialization: Theory and research,* (pp. 382–403). New York, NY: Guilford.

Wentzel, K. R., & McNamara, C. C. (1999). Interpersonal relationships, emotional distress, and prosocial behavior in middle school. *Journal of Early Adolescence, 19*, 114–125.

Wentzel, K R., & Watkins, D. E. (2002). Peer relationships and collaborative learning as contexts for academic enablers. *School Psychology Review. 31*, 366–377.

Youniss, J. (1980). *Parents and peers in social development.* Chicago, IL: University of Chicago Press.

CHAPTER 3

WILL THE REAL PEER GROUP PLEASE STAND UP?

A "Tensegrity" Approach to Examining the Synergistic Influences of Peer Groups and Friendship Networks on Academic Development

Thomas A. Kindermann and Ellen A. Skinner
Portland State University

Over the past decade, multiple strands of research have converged on the conclusion that peers play an important role in the academic success of children and youth. Two of the most prominent areas of research focus on different kinds of naturally occurring peer relationships: One examines *friendships* (e.g., Berndt & McCandless, 2009; see also Hartup 1995, 2009) and one examines children's *peer groups* (e.g., Cairns & Cairns, 1992; Kindermann, 2007). Both have demonstrated that peers have an effect on the development of students' academic motivation and achievement, but their target phenomena, methods, and theoretical traditions have remained largely distinct. The goal of this chapter is to begin bridging these areas in order to create a more complex and comprehensive map of the world of

Peer Relationships and Adjustment at School, pages 51–78
Copyright © 2012 by Information Age Publishing
All rights of reproduction in any form reserved.

peers that may be used to better guide the study of the effects of peers on the development of children and adolescents.

FRIENDS AND INTERACTION PARTNERS

The study of *friendships* focuses on intimate and enduring ties between students. These relationships are typically identified through children's self-nominations of agemates whom they consider friends. To be sure that nominations reflect actual relationships (and not just one-sided preferences), friendship studies typically rely on reciprocal nominations, in which both partners agree on the nature of the relationship. Although most studies highlight negative developmental influences from friends (e.g., Dishion, Andrews, & Crosby, 1995; Ennett & Bauman, 1994; Jaccard, Blanton, & Dodge, 2005; Popp, Laursen, Kerr, Stattin, & Burk, 2008; Urberg, Degirmencioglu, & Pilgrim, 1997), a growing number find that children's friendships in school can also exert positive effects on academic development (e.g., Altermatt & Pomeranz, 2003; Hallinan & Williams, 1990; Kandel, 1978; Ladd, 1990; Ladd, Kochenderfer, & Coleman, 1997; Ryan, 2001; Wentzel, McNamara-Barry, & Caldwell, 2004; for a review, see Bukowski, Motzoi, & Meyer, 2009). Especially noteworthy for our chapter is the research program of Tom Berndt and colleagues on the effects of friendship on students' school motivation and achievement (e.g., Berndt, 2004; Berndt & Keefe, 1995; Berndt, Hawkins, & Jiao, 1999; Berndt, Laychak, & Park, 1990).

The study of *peer groups* focuses on broader groups of frequent interaction partners (e.g., Cairns & Cairns, 1992; Furman, 1989; Kindermann & Gest, 2009). Unlike friendship research, most work in this area does not rely on self-reports of relationships. Instead, it employs a method called *socio-cognitive mapping* (SCM; developed by Robert Cairns and colleagues: Cairns, Perrin, & Cairns, 1985; Cairns, Gariépy, & Kindermann, 1990). Multiple students are interviewed as "expert" participant observers of everyday interactions in a setting, and report the groups of agemates who tend to "hang around" with one another. Students are asked to list all the groups they know, candidates can be in more than one group at the same time, and groups can be as small as dyads. The goal is to identify subgroups of frequent interaction partners. Like friendship studies, SCM studies also suggest that peers influence motivation and behavior in school (e.g., Cairns, Neckerman, & Cairns, 1989; Chen, Chang, & He, 2003; Estell, Farmer, Cairns, & Cairns, 2002; Gest, Rulison, Davidson, & Welsh, 2008; Kindermann, 1993, 2007; Kindermann, McCollam, & Gibson, 1996).

Although both friendship and peer group studies focus on peer relationships, they do so from different theoretical and methodological angles, focusing on different kinds of peers using different kinds of methods.

Prolonged study of peer influences has led to increased appreciation for the complexity of the peer worlds that students inhabit, and there have been calls for theoretical development and elaboration within these areas (e.g., Cairns et al., 1989; Furman, 1993; Rubin, Bukowski, & Parker, 2006). Nevertheless, research on different kinds of peer relationships has proceeded down largely unconnected avenues. Our primary goal is to instigate a debate about how to integrate areas of research relevant to the study of peer influences on children's and adolescents' academic development in school.

The Tensegrity Metaphor

If we want to capture the peer world of children in school, a larger perspective may be helpful that can accommodate multiple kinds of peer relationships and that can allow for the study of their similarities, differences, and potential overlap, both in composition and in their effects on development. The current paper was inspired by the potential of the idea of *tensegrity* to offer a guiding metaphor for integrating multiple perspectives on the world of peers. "Tensegrity" is a term coined by Buckminster Fuller as a composite of the constituting features of "tension" and "integrity" in structural designs. Tensegrity structures have been publicized by sculptor Kenneth Snelson (Whelan, 1981); the key ideas have been used by medical and biological researchers as well as architects (for a review, see Conelly & Back, 1998). Tensegrity follows the idea that in a given structure "muscles" can exist independently of a "skeleton" and that both components work together to give the structure flexibility while they hold it together at the same time. A simple form is a kite in which two bars are held together by wires across their ends. Figure 3.1 gives the example of a

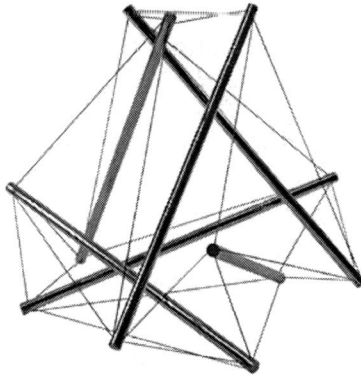

Figure 3.1　The Tetrahedon as an example of a tensegrity structure (www.kenneth snelson.net; reprinted with permission from the artist).

tetrahedon (taken from Snelson, www.kennethsnelson.net). Bars (or struts) and wires (or cables) work with each other to hold the structure together; they simultaneously push each other apart and pull each other together, maintaining a strong but flexible structure. If outside pressure is applied, the structures can adapt and change their form, but they regain their original form when pressure recedes. (More complex structures can be found at www.springie.com.)

Tensegrity may be taken as a theoretical analogy for peer group studies. One consequence of this analogy would be to ask whether, in social networks, there may be *different kinds of interconnections* among people that have different functions, but nevertheless all work together to form structures that are more complex (and flexible) than static grids. For example, close and intimate friendships may be interwoven with groups of peers who are not necessarily friends but regularly interact with one another at school— for example, in joint activities. Thus, it could be that friendships, because of their intimate nature, are more sturdy and stable, while peer group affiliations would be more flexible and fluid. In this case, both components would not be materially different but just differentially flexible. Alternatively, peers who are both friends and members of the same peer group may be important for holding a network together (struts or skeleton), whereas peers who are only friends or only members of a group (but not the other) may be more influential over time because they both may be able to exert more tension (wires or muscles). These two kinds of affiliations would not be redundant; instead they would be interconnected parts of the peer system and jointly influence people's development.

A second consequence may be to reexamine how we conceptualize social networks. Borgatti, Mehra, Brass, and Labianca (2009) identify several fundamental metaphors or models of how social networks are conceived in social network analysis (SNA): Most prominent are the *flow* model, the *interaction* model, and the *social relations* model. *Flow* conceptualizations regard a network as a system of "pipes" that transmit information from one person to another and constitute exchange relationships. *Interaction* and *relations* models regard networks as structures in which interpersonal connections create borders, distinctions, social roles (as defined by various network topologies), and social influences. The concept of tensegrity may be helpful for combining these metaphors (e.g., the skeleton of an organism or network serves different functions than its nervous system or its muscles; for a discussion see also Ingber, 2003). Or, to the functions of static connections among people in a network, tensegrity may add the notion of tension (e.g., exerted by wires that apply pressure to hold the structure together).

Application of Tensegrity to the Study of Peer Influences on Academic Development

The key insights from the tensegrity analogy are that there may be multiple kinds of connections between peers (i.e., bones and muscles, or friends and frequent interaction partners), and that these connections may have multiple features—some are architectural or topological features, as described by structural or compositional characteristics, and some would be flow or functional features, as described by the influence of the different kinds of peers on the academic development of children and youth.

Such an analogy is helpful in describing complex peer relationships under one condition—namely, as long as there is partial overlap between friends and frequent interaction partners. In other words, the sets of peers captured by reciprocal friendship nominations and those captured by SCM would be neither exactly the same nor completely different peers. If they are exactly the same sets of peers, then no distinctions between them are needed; if they are completely different, there is less need for models that integrate them. The few studies that have directly compared friends and peer groups in terms of membership suggest that, consistent with the tensegrity analogy, there is some overlap between peers who are friends and those who are frequent interaction partners, but they are not identical. Cairns, Leung, Buchanan, and Cairns (1995) found that at two time points during a school year, only about half of children's self-nominated friends were also members of their (SCM) peer group networks; nevertheless, overlap increased across the school year (there was 52% overlap halfway through the school year, and 82% overlap near the end of the year). Gest, Moody, and Rulison (2007) found fewer than 50% of the members of children's SCM groups to also be mutual friends; conversely, children who were friends did not necessarily affiliate in groups. Rodkin and Ahn (2009) report kappa agreement scores of .48 and .53 between SCM group networks and self-reported friendships.[1]

At the same time, research suggests that there are compositional similarities between friends and frequent interaction partners. Affiliates of both kinds are relatively homogeneous in terms of their academic characteristics. For example, friends are more similar than non-friends in their academic achievement and motivation (Berndt et al., 1999, 2009; Bukowski et al., 2009), and peer group members are also more similar than non-group members in how their academic motivation manifests itself in the classroom (i.e., in engagement; Kindermann, 1993, 2007). There also seem to be functional similarities. For example, the characteristics of students' friends and those of the members of their peer groups seem to have similar power in predicting changes in students' own school motivation over time (Berndt et al., 1999; Kindermann, 2007). However, the specific mechanisms of influence are assumed to be different (e.g., Kindermann & Gest, 2009; Wentzel, 2009). Friendship research builds on the assumption that important peer partners are those who share emotionally close, stable, and long-lasting *relationships* with a student. SCM network approaches focus on the *frequency of social interactions*, following the assumption that such interactions are the "engine" of development (Bronfenbrenner & Morris, 2006). According to this perspective, from frequent interactions, close relationships may or may not develop (e.g., Cairns et al., 1989).

The current chapter explores the idea that both kinds of affiliations show substantial but far from perfect membership overlap, that they may be genuinely different phenomena with their own attributes and compositional features, and that they nevertheless should work synergistically in influencing students' academic development. The goal is to compare students' reciprocal friendships with their observable peer groups in an existing data set that includes an entire cohort of sixth graders in a small town (Kindermann, 2007).

Focus on Classroom Engagement

The target feature of academic development in this chapter is students' engagement in the classroom (Fredricks, Blumenfeld, & Paris, 2004). In this context, *engagement* refers to students' active, enthusiastic, constructive emotionally positive participation in learning activities in the classroom. It can be contrasted with *disaffection*, which refers to passivity and withdrawal or to involvement in classroom activities that is half-hearted, anxious, or disruptive (Connell & Wellborn, 1991; Skinner, Kindermann, & Furrer, 2009). Engagement is a key marker of academic success, predicting students' learning, achievement, retention, and eventual school completion (e.g., Jimerson, Campos, & Greif, 2003; Skinner, Zimmer-Gembeck, & Connell, 1998). It also seems to be a protective factor against the risks of adolescence, including dropout, delinquency, substance abuse, and risky sexual behavior (O'Farrell & Morrison, 2003). Engagement and disaffection are critical to the dynamics of motivational and academic development (Skinner, Kindermann, Connell, & Wellborn, 2009; Skinner, Furrer, Marchand, & Kindermann, 2008). As a motivational construct, engagement captures the outward expression of a student's academic motivation, how it is enacted in the real world. As such, we see the construct as an indicator of the extent to which the (internal) motivational state of a student becomes visible to others and influences interactions. Although a great deal of work has focused on how teachers shape the development of student's engagement (Wentzel, 2009), much less research has examined the role of peers.

Structure and Nature of Friendships and Interaction Partners

The tensegrity analogy suggests that distinctions between several components of a network may be important, which focuses researchers on the structure, membership, and composition of the different kinds of peer relationships. A first expectation guiding this study was that there would be overlap between friends and peer group members, but overlap would be far from complete, indicating that networks of close friends are not necessarily identical to groups of frequent interaction partners. A second expectation was that the motivational composition of the two kinds of relationship partners would nevertheless be similar. Thus, following previous research on peer homogeneity, we expected that friends would be more similar than non-friends in their engagement, and that peer group members would also be more similar than non-peer group members.

However, the two kinds of relationships should also differ. An attribute likely to differentiate them is subjective relationship quality, with children likely to feel closer to peers they nominate as friends than to those with whom they interact but do not consider friends. This suggests the utility of examining different combinatorial subsets of peers, such as peers who are *both* friends and frequent interaction partners, compared to peers who are frequent interaction partners but *not* friends. In addition, there will be peers who are friends but are *not* known to engage in public interactions at school. For example, children may share friendships that are purposefully kept less visible to the general public (e.g., cross-gender friendships and romantic affiliations at an age when public interactions are largely gender segregated); some children may also be friends outside of school, even though in school, they would prefer to interact more with other agemates than these friends.

Functions of Peers

Finally, the tensegrity analogy suggests that the functional features of a system are also important, which focuses researchers on the effects of different kinds of peer relationships on academic development. It is important to note a required design feature for studies of peer influence: They need to examine the effects of peers on *changes* in target outcomes over time; social influences from peers need to lead to changes in individuals. Hence, the third expectation was that, despite their membership and compositional differences, each kind of peer context would nevertheless show similar contributions to changes in children's academic motivation across the school year. The fourth expectation was that a combination of *both* contexts would lead to better predictions of changes in engagement than either context independently, indicating synergistic effects. Such findings would be theoretically most interesting because they would highlight the benefits that can result from combining multiple approaches to studying peer affiliations.

METHOD

The study is a re-analysis of Kindermann's (2007) study on social network influences on school motivation in an entire cohort of sixth graders in a rural/suburban northeastern U.S. town. The school was the only public school in town for this age group; the next town was about 3.5 miles away. Out of the total of 366 students in the town (48% girls), nearly all participated (340, 93% had parental permission and consented themselves[2]). As in most U.S. school districts, sixth grade was the beginning of middle school, so students had just moved into a new building on the school grounds. Middle school was organized in homerooms, so that students had one class scheduled together each day; other classes varied in composition. All 13 homeroom teachers participated, and all stated that they were very familiar with the students' academic development.

Design and Measures

Student and teacher questionnaires were administered within the first two months during the first year of middle school (September–October), and within two months of its end (May–June).

Academic engagement was assessed using a 14-item scale that tapped teacher perceptions of students' behavioral and emotional engagement (Wellborn, 1991; e.g., "In my class, this student works as hard as he/she can"; "this student appears happy"). The two components are moderately intercorrelated, form an internally consistent and highly stable indicator of engagement, and are moderately correlated with grades and achievement (Skinner & Belmont, 1993; Skinner, Wellborn, & Connell, 1990; Skinner et al., 2009). In fall of sixth grade, teachers provided information on 318 students (87% of the population); in spring, reports on 322 students were obtained. Three hundred students had assessments at both time points.

Friendships

At the beginning of sixth grade, students were asked to nominate their three best friends in each of three contexts: in class, in school, and outside school. The goal was to capture all existing friendships of the children in the town, even those that were not based in school. A total of 314 children (86% of the cohort of 366 students) reported on their friendships, about half of them from each gender (48% girls). On average, students listed about 10 friends (one student nominated 17); 311 listed at least one friend, and 294 listed at least one friend who was identified in the school's grade rosters. A total of 3005 listed friends were identified using class and school rosters (ambiguous nominations were mostly settled by combining friend with SCM reports; e.g., in cases of misspellings or nicknames). Names of participants who were not reliably identified, names of nonparticipants, illegible nominations, and nominations denoting adults were dummy-coded (440 nominations, 13% of all nominations).

A total of 911 *reciprocal* friendships were identified, denoting that roughly every fourth nomination received reciprocation. Nominations for friends in class, in school, and outside of school were combined because agreement on the "location" of friendships was relatively low. This underestimates the actual amount of friendships in the town for two reasons: 13% of self-reported friends were students from other grades or were not identified (some are likely agemates who attended private schools in the vicinity or commuted to nearby towns), and those could not be reciprocated; 55 students (15% of the cohort) did not participate or did not report any friends, although about half of them received nominations from others; again, no reciprocity was possible.

Relationship Quality

Along with their friendship nominations, students were asked to indicate the quality of the friendship they felt with the respective nominee (on a scale from one to three, from "sort-of a friend" to "very good friend"). As a measure of the quality of reciprocal friendships, the average was taken of the ratings of each child in the dyad. This measure may be seen as an index of mutual closeness in the friendships.

Peer Group Networks

At the beginning of sixth grade, students were also asked to list those groups of agemates whom they observed to frequently "hang out" with one another. Students were asked to list as many groups and members as they knew (in and out of school), to include dyads, to include themselves, and to include the same children as members of different groups if that was appropriate (thus, a report could indicate that A, B, and C form one group, and that B and E form another). The questionnaires provided spaces to list up to 20 members of up to 20 groups (more detailed descriptions of SCM methods can be found in Cairns et al., 1990). None of the students exhausted the space, but several listed groups of 15 members.

Network Identification

280 students (76% of the cohort, 56% girls) provided information about peer group networks in sixth grade. Non-identified (e.g., illegible) candidates, teachers, and family members were dummy-coded (10%). Because reporters did not just report about their own groups but about groups they observed in their entire grade, network reports included participants as well as nonparticipants (as well as some children from different grades if

those were in groups with sixth graders, e.g., in sports teams or outdoor activities). A total of 3,047 group members were reported for a total of 694 peer groups, containing 2 to 15 members. A typical child nominated 2.67 groups with an average of 4.4 members.

The goal was to identify, for each student, those agemates who were known to be members of his or her peer group. The nominations were arranged in a co-occurrence matrix, denoting the numbers of times that pairs of students were reported to be in the same group (across 6th grade, see Kindermann, 2007). Binomial z-tests examined whether conditional probabilities of finding a specific student within the group of another student were higher than could be expected by chance. For example, out of 36 observations in which a student A was observed to be in a group, student B was found to be in the same group 28 times. The conditional probability of finding B, given that A had a group ($28/36 = .78$), was compared with the unconditional probability with which B was found in all 694 groups ($32/694 = .05$). The resulting z-score of 21.47 is highly significant and denotes that B was in A's peer group. The program NetJaws (Mehess & Kindermann, 2009: http://web.pdx.edu/~thomas/measures.html) was used to identify significant connections ($p < .01$; connections based on single co-nominations were not accepted; usually, these were just self-nominations). Because expected frequencies were often lower than recommended for the approximation to the normal distribution, Fisher's exact tests were used in addition (using Sterling's approximation; von Eye, 1990), and connections were only accepted when both tests were significant.

Based on the tests, a *composite social map* was formed of all network connections in sixth grade (the map can be viewed at http://web.pdx. edu/~thomas/). Overall, the individual informants' reports were highly consistent with the composite map (average *kappa* = .88) when only errors of commission were considered. (Errors of omission were not considered because it seems unrealistic to expect that every informant would know the same about every peer group in the school.) The high observer reliability indicates that the resulting composite map fits the data adequately.

Peer Group and Friendship Network Engagement Profiles

For each student, individual peer context profile scores were formed. Thus, a student's *peer group profile* was the average of the individual engagement scores of this student's peer group members; the students' *friendship network profile* was the average of the engagement scores of his or her reciprocal friends (the student's own score was not included). This was done separately for behavioral and emotional engagement. Basic analyses used engagement profiles of students' peer groups and friendship networks. More detailed analyses used combinatorial subsets (e.g., the engagement profiles of students' peer group members who were also reciprocal friends).

RESULTS

The results are presented in three parts. First, the proportions are present-ed of the different kinds of context agents (reciprocal friendship networks, peer groups, and the overlap of both contexts) that children had in sixth grade. Second, homogeneity of peer groups and friendship networks are calculated with regard to classroom engagement. Finally, analyses examine the extent to which both peer contexts have synergistic effects on change in students' motivation. Analyses were conducted using SEM (Amos 5; see Arbuckle, 2003), using its Full Information Maximum Likelihood (FIML) algorithm for missing value estimations.

Overall, description of the results will be general and pay relatively little attention to gender differences. Research shows that friendship networks and peer groups tend to differ for girls and boys, and gender differences in academic characteristics are ubiquitous in school. However, it is less clear whether, beyond gender segregation at this age range, gender differences in peer contexts mean much for academic development; boys and girls, de-spite their differences, do not seem to change differently over time (for a discussion, see Crosnoe, Riegle-Crumb, Field, Frank, & Muller, 2008). Thus, the main analyses do not focus on interindividual differences but on the general composition of peer group and friendship network contexts and on the differential contributions that both contexts can have for motivational development in school. Student gender will be controlled in most analyses.

Description of Peer Contexts

Reciprocal Friendship Networks

Two hundred ninety-four students (94% of participants; 80% of the en-tire cohort in the town) listed at least one friend in the town, and 289 had at least one reciprocal friend (79% and 87% of participants). Only 27 children had none. On average, a child had 2.7 reciprocal friends (ranging from 0 to 12); about half (53%) were from the same homeroom, and almost all were of the same sex (97%; note, though, that at least 20 children had cross-gender friendships and that there could have been more if 5th and 7th graders had been included).

Peer Groups

Students can have members in their peer groups who did not participate themselves as reporters, because SCM assesses public knowledge, over and above self-reports. A typical sixth grader had 4.9 agemates in his or her peer group (with a range from 0 to 17); 286 (78% of the cohort) had at least one agemate as a member of their peer group(s). Group members were almost entirely of the same sex (94%) and more than half (60%) were classmates from the same homeroom. Nearly all peer group members (98%) were from the same grade.

Peer Context Interrelations and Overlap

Students with many reciprocal friends also had larger peer groups ($r = .37$, $p < .001$), suggesting some similarity of the contexts. Nevertheless, both contexts did not consist of the same individuals. As Figure 3.2 shows, about half of a student's reciprocal friends were also members of his or her peer interaction network (52%), but only about a third of a students' peer network members were also his or her reciprocal friends (29%).

Thus, the two context measures are not just alternative assessments of the same underlying context construct, but represent different kinds of contexts. This can also be seen by looking at students who did not report that they had friends, were not chosen as friends, or had no network membership. Twenty students did not list a friend; however, they nevertheless received an average of 2.7 friendship nominations (ranging from 0–7) and were members of peer groups with an average of 2.1 members (range 0–8). Similarly, children who received no friendship nominations (N = 14) nevertheless nominated an average of 3.5 friends (range 0–9) and had peer groups with about 2.9 members (range 0–13). Children without reciprocal friends (N = 27) still had an average of 3.5 self-nominated friends (range

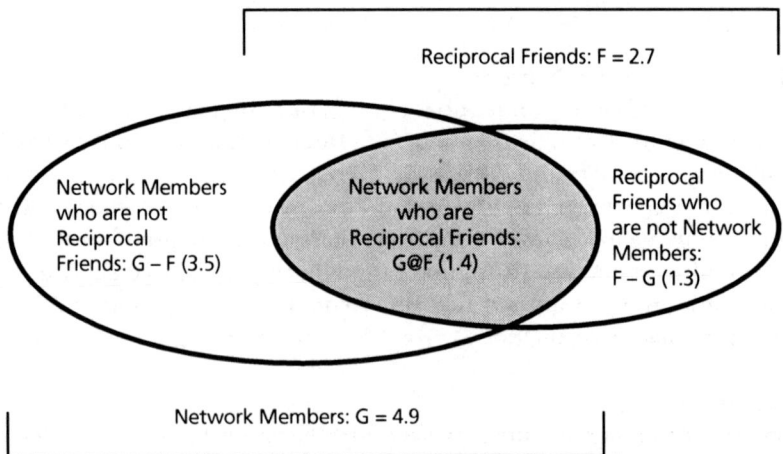

Figure 3.2 Overlap between the members of a 6th grader's peer group (G) and his or her group of reciprocal friends (F).

0–9), received 2.14 nominations (range 0–7), and had 3.14 members in their peer groups (range 0–13). Conversely, students without a peer group (N = 55), still nominated 4.3 friends (range 0–11), received 3.1 nominations (range 0–10), and had 1.3 reciprocal friends (range 0–6). Finally, even children without any kind of indication for a friendship (N = 6) were, on average, members of at least one peer group dyad (range 0–5).

Homogeneity of Peers' Motivational Profiles

Although friendship networks and peer groups consisted of largely different individuals, the contexts were nevertheless similarly homogeneous in terms of members' engagement levels. Individual students were as similar to the members of their peer groups ($r = .44$, $p < .001$) as they were to their friends ($r = .33$, $p < .001$). Thus, group member and friend selection processes seemed to follow similar criteria with regard to academic motivation. We do not assume that peer selection processes specifically targeted motivation levels of candidates, but rather that selection processes tend to follow a variety of interindividually different criteria (e.g., student interests, schedules). Some of the criteria are likely facilitative of academic motivation whereas others may not be.

Relationship Quality

Differences in relationship quality were expected between the two contexts (following Berndt, 2004). To examine this, a participant=s own rating of the quality of his or her reciprocal friendship with an agemate was averaged with the closeness rating that the participant received from the friend; then, the average was taken across all of that child's friends. Three relationship quality indices were formed for each student. For example, student A's closeness towards those of her *reciprocal friends who were also members of her peer group* was the average of her own ratings of "how good a friend" these friends were and of the ratings she received from each friend. Similarly, A's closeness towards her *friends who were not members of her peer group* was the average of her own closeness ratings towards these peers and of the closeness ratings she received from these peers. Finally, because peer group membership was determined from peer observations (and not from self-nominations), there were no closeness ratings for those *members of a student's peer group who were not reciprocal friends*. However, for a typical student, about half of these were (non-reciprocally) nominated as friends or had issued friendship nominations for that student, and their average was used.

As expected, relationships of highest quality existed among those peer group members of a student who were also his or her reciprocal friends (2.43 on the 3-point scale). Less close were relationships among friends who were not peer group members at the same time (2.20), and even less close were relationships with peer group members who were not friends (1.97; F

(208,1) = 36.34, $p < .001$; the differences were weaker when student gender was controlled but differences did not consistently favor girls or boys).

This was taken as suggesting that *three peer contexts* needed to be distinguished: friendships within peer groups of frequent interaction partners (G&F), friendships outside of peer groups (F–G), and peer groups that did not contain friendships (G–F). This matches with observations in a classroom of fourth and fifth graders (Kindermann & Sage, 1999) in which interactions during classroom lessons (and short breaks) were most frequent between a child and those members of that child's peer group who were also his or her friends. Thus, if there are two pathways of how peer influence can come about, namely, through *relationship* factors (e.g., emotional support, interpersonal attraction) and *interaction* factors (e.g., frequency of joint activities, instrumental support, learning from one another), friends who are also members of a child's group of frequent interaction partners combine both benefits and can be expected to be most influential.

To summarize, in terms of their *composition*, students' peer groups and friendship networks appeared to differ in several ways: They differed in size, consisted of fairly different individuals, and exhibited different levels of relationship quality. At the same time, however, a child was as motivationally similar to the members of his or her friendship network as to the members or his or her peer group.

Peer Influences on Classroom Engagement

The third part of analyses examined the *functions* that peer groups and friendship networks may have for motivational development over time. In a first set of analyses, peer and friendship networks were examined separately. SEM analyses used the engagement profiles of each kind of affiliation as predictors of changes in students' engagement across the school year. Because students' school motivation, gender, and size of their peer group or friendship networks were correlated, gender and number of respective affiliates were controlled.

By themselves, students' peer group profiles in the fall predicted individual change in motivation over time (*beta* = .12, $p < .05$, as reported in Kindermann, 2007). Profiles of students' friends were as predictive (*beta* = .11, $p < .05$). In each analysis, the respective peer context explained about 2% of the variance in changes in student motivation over the school year. This may appear small compared to the concurrent correlations (see Figure 3.3). However, it should not be considered small when one notes that engagement was highly stable over the school year and that influence effects were examined over and above stability and concurrent person-to-context peer correlations that can be assumed to denote selection effects.

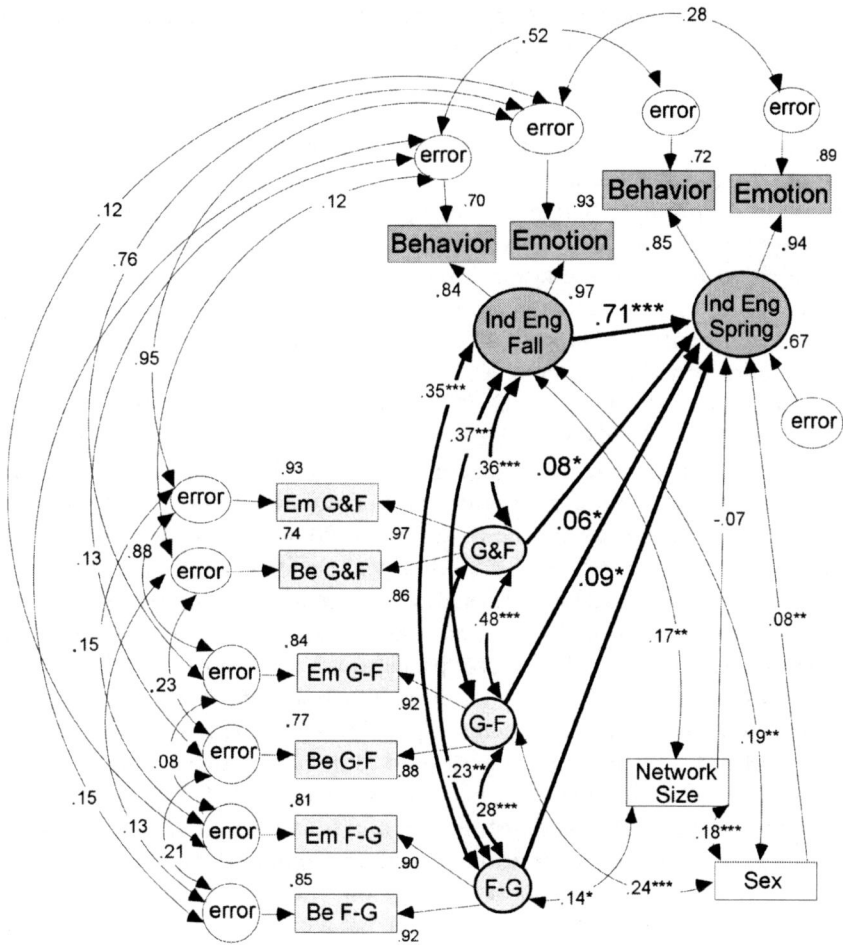

Figure 3.3 Peer group and friendship influences on individual students' change in motivation across the school year.

Notes: $X^2(24) = 40.220$, $p = .020$; CMIN/DF = 1.676; CFI = .992; RMSEA = .043. The three peer relationships paths were constrained to be equal, but there was no difference in fit to the unconstrained model, $X^2 = 0.882$, 2 DF.

Em, Be: Emotional, Behavioral Engagement; Ind Eng: Individual Engagement; G&F: Reciprocal friends who were also members of a child's peer group; G–F: Peer group members who were not a child's reciprocal friends; F–G: Reciprocal friends who were not members of a child's peer group.

In a second step, both peer context predictors were included simultaneously. Because the goal was to look at *combinations* of peer groups and friendship networks, three peer context indices were formed: engagement profiles (for behavior and emotion) of a students' peers who were peer group members *and* his or her reciprocal friend at the same time, engagement profiles of a student's group members who were *not* his or her friends, and engagement profiles of friends who were *not* members of the student's peer group.

The three peer contexts were correlated with one another (ranging from .23 to .48; see Figure 3.3), and contrary to our expectations, none was able to predict changes in engagement by itself over and above the contributions of the other two contexts. So, in a third step, the predictive coefficients for the three kinds of peer partners towards engagement were constrained to be equal, assuming that similar influence effects emerged from each context (Marsh, Balla, & McDonald, 1988). Figure 3.3 shows this model; it had an acceptable fit and there was no difference to the unconstrained model ($X^2 = 0.882$, 2 DF). Thus, it can be assumed that this model explains the data as well as the model without the constraints. We concluded that changes in engagement were predicted by the engagement levels of partners who were friends of a student and members of his or her peer network at the same time (G&F: *beta* = .08, $p < .05$), as well as by individuals who were members of his or her peer network but not friends (G–F: *beta* = .06, $p < .05$), and by individuals who were friends but not members of his or her peer network (F–G: *beta* = .09, $p < .05$). Again, this suggests that friendship networks and peer groups, although they consist of fairly different individuals, likely have similar developmental functions.

In a fourth step, the engagement profiles of a child's peer group members and of his or her friends were used as indicators of a higher-order latent variable that we called *peer group nexus;* see Figure 3.4. The rationale for this strategy was that if both peer groups and friendship networks serve similar functions with regard to motivational development, either one may be a good predictor of motivational change but their combination should be most powerful. Peer group nexus emerged as a particularly strong predictor (*beta* = .23, $p < .001$) of changes in engagement, and each peer context profile was a reasonable indicator of the latent nexus variable ($X^2(30) = 51.029$, p = .010; CMIN/DF = 1.701; CFI = .989; RMSEA = .044). In total, peer nexus explained 4% of the variance in students' changes in engagement over the school year. This was twice as much as peer groups or friendship networks were able to explain by themselves (as in Kindermann, 2007). This indicates that the different kinds of peer group affiliates can have *cumulative* and *synergistic effects* on children's developing school motivation.

DISCUSSION

The primary goal of this chapter was to direct attention towards how the complex world of peers can be conceptualized and measured when studying

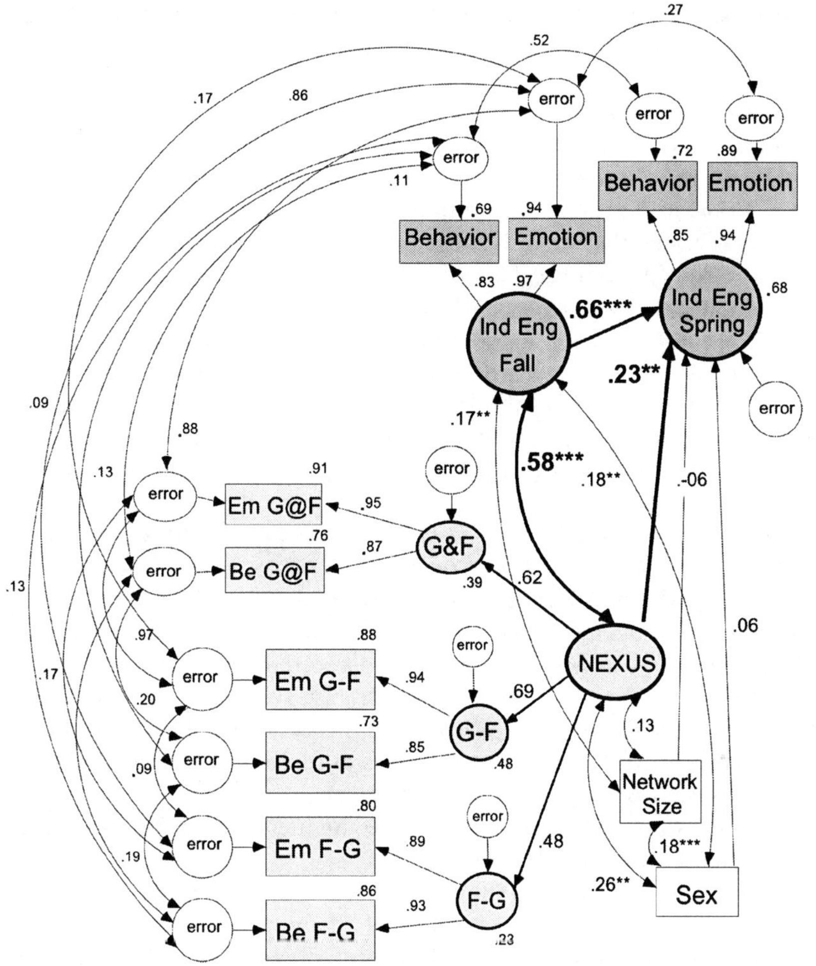

Figure 3.4 Hierarchical model of combined peer group and friendship influences on individual students' change in motivation across the school year.
Notes: $X^2(30) = 51.029$, $p = .010$; CMIN/DF = 1.701; CFI = .989; RMSEA = .044.
Em, Be: Emotional, Behavioral Engagement; Ind Eng: Individual Engagement; G&F: Reciprocal friends who were also members of a child's peer group; G–F: Peer group members who were not a child's reciprocal friends; F–G: Reciprocal friends who were not members of a child's peer group.

peer influences on children's and adolescents' development. For decades, researchers have been interested in how peers contribute to students' academic development in school, but their research has followed multiple largely unconnected paths, focusing on sociometric status (e.g., Bukowski & Cillessen, 1998; Moreno, 1934), friendships (e.g., Berndt & McCandless,

2009), peer crowds (e.g., Brown, 2004), or peer networks (e.g., Cairns et al., 1985; Kindermann & Gest, 2009). The metaphor of "tensegrity" suggests that these different peers are all members of a larger peer system that includes multiple kinds of connections and potentially different functions with regard to the academic development of children and youth.

The current findings are encouraging about the utility of such a metaphor. Consistent with its implications, analyses of an entire cohort of sixth graders revealed that there is substantial overlap between students' friends (as captured by reciprocal nominations) and their frequent interaction partners (as assessed through SCM). However, the members of these two groups are not the same. As would be expected, most of a student's friends are also part of their peer group of frequent interaction partners (52%), but some friends are not. Also in line with expectations, some of the members of a student's lager peer network are his or her friends (29%), but many of those peers with whom a student just "hangs out" are not his or her reciprocal friends.

Taken together, the findings suggest that the peer world contains at least three distinguishable subsets of peers: "friendship networks" consisting of friends with whom a student interacts frequently and publicly; "just friends" with whom a student is not known to interact much at school; and "just peer group members" consisting of peers who are frequent interaction partners but who do not share reciprocal ties of friendship. These three groups can be different on some characteristics and the same on others. For example, in the current study, these three groups differed in their relational closeness. As would be expected, students are closest to their friendship networks, then to their friends, and then to the members of their peer group whom they do not consider friends.

At the same time, groups of reciprocal friends and peer group members were also similar on some compositional attributes. Of interest in the present study were peer profiles of engagement, operationalized as the average engagement of a student's group of friends (friend engagement profile) and of their peer group members (peer group engagement profile). Correlations between students' own engagement and those of their peer profiles revealed that students are likely to have groups of friends and to belong to peer groups that are both similar to them in their levels of engagement. Children who are engaged tend to select friends and peer group members who are similarly engaged, whereas children who are disaffected tend to have friends and belong to peer groups who are similarly disaffected.

Functional analyses, in which these peer profiles were used to predict changes in individual engagement from fall to spring of the same school year suggested that each subset of peers has an impact on motivational development, and that their effects are not redundant; instead they are additive. We think that this represents a fairly accurate view of the effects of *peer influences* on individual children's development for three reasons: The model examines longitudinal change (individuals serve as their own controls), the model controls for person-to-nexus similarity at the beginning of the school year (i.e., substantial peer group and friendship selection effects), and the model controls for gender differences in motivation (making sure that the findings are not just that girls, who are with more engaged peer groups, change more favorably than boys). The idea of a "peer nexus," analogous to a tensegrity structure (Figure 3.1) which includes all three of the potential subsets, was used to organize analyses in a way that revealed their combined effects.

A more comprehensive picture of the nexus of peers also leads to reconsideration of the children and youth who are labeled as "socially isolated." Children who do not have any reciprocal friendships may still be regarded by others as friends or may still belong to peer groups. Likewise, children who are not observed to belong to a group of frequently interacting peers may still have reciprocal friendships. Other combinations are also possible: For example, students who receive no reciprocal friendship nominations and belong to no peer groups could still nominate friends and be nominated as friends. In the current set of 294 students, even the 5 students who did not nominate any friends and were never nominated did actually have (on average) one frequently interacting peer dyad. In studying "social isolation," it may be necessary to specify *which kind* of peer relationships students do not have and to rule out the entire range of relationships before concluding that a child is truly socially isolated. Of course, at some ages the absence of specific relationships, for example, reciprocal friendships, can be considered a risk factor for certain outcomes, if those relationships are really the only route toward the development of some important capacities.

Future Research on the Effects of Peers on Academic Development

Future studies may be able to benefit from the tensegrity metaphor and may wish to further develop some of the conceptual and methodological strategies suggested in this chapter. Conceptually, the metaphor suggests that the structural characteristics of different kinds of peer relationships can be examined separately from their functional effects. Structural analyses revealed overlap between friends and peer group members as well as distinctiveness. Compositional analyses examined the characteristics of these different sets of peers, showing that some differ across groups, such as relational closeness, whereas others are similar, such as motivational homogeneity.

Functional analyses focused on whether profiles of peer characteristics, such as engagement during academic activities in the classroom, can predict changes in individuals' academic development. Methodologically, the paper suggests a specific way to examine synergistic effects in children's or adolescents' world of peers: Apparently, there are similar kinds of influences that emerge from peer contexts that are overlapping and have similar developmental effects. To have the contexts compete against each other in analyses of their effects does not help because they are too similar and their effects cancel each other out. Multilevel approaches also do not help much because the contexts are overlapping and not distinct from one another. A *hierarchical solution* seems to work, in which the subsets of peer relations (e.g., friendship networks and groups of frequent interaction partners) are examined for their *combined influences* and synergistic effects. Both the engagement profiles of the members of students' interaction networks and the characteristics of their friends are seen as indicators of a higher-order latent variable, and thus do not compete with one another but are seen as complementary in predicting individual change in engagement over time.

Other Aspects of Academic Development

One direction for future studies would be to examine the effects of peer groups on other important aspects of students' academic development. Engagement is certainly a key predictor of school success, but other additional markers can be identified that would make good targets for study. Complementary candidates might include academic coping, an important process when ongoing engagement is disrupted by obstacles or problems (Skinner & Wellborn, 1997), as well as academic buoyancy or everyday resilience (Martin & Marsh, 2008). The engagement of a student's peers and friends may provide an energetic resource for dealing with difficulties and challenges in school. Especially interesting targets are academic resources that emerge during early adolescence, such as self-regulated learning, academic identity, or ownership of one's own academic progress.

Selection Processes

Although this paper focuses on the influence of peers, it is equally important to examine selection effects, or processes through which students join or leave peer groups and friendships. These processes *create* the peer contexts that turn out to be influential. If students who are disaffected from school tend to select other students who are disengaged as interaction partners or friends, then it is more likely that they will become even more disaffected over time. Following the tensegrity metaphor, it is possible that selection criteria and processes are different for friends compared to interaction partners, whether or not they end up producing homogeneous peer groups. It is also possible that selection processes for the two kinds of peers are closely connected. For example, friendships may emerge from frequent interactions with peers who were originally not friends. Or as friendships fade, students may still maintain their interactions with peers who were once friends.

Developmental Dynamics

Taken together, selection and socialization effects seem to produce cycles in which the "rich get richer" as engaged students join more engaged peer groups, which in turn promote their engagement over time (Kindermann, 1993, 2007). If engaged friends emerge from these peer groups and become more stable emotionally close social partners, then friends may act as "glue" that keeps children involved in supportive peer groups and academic tasks in school. In contrast, if more disaffected students join more disaffected peer groups where they make friends, then the combined effects of disengaged friends and peer group members may further undermine their constructive participation in school activities. Developmentally, it is likely that different kinds of peers may be differentially important to students in different grades; perhaps, this is part of the general trend in which peers seem to become more important to students as they become older and progress farther in school.

Building on the Tensegrity Metaphor

For different kinds of peer relationships to be successfully integrated into a more comprehensive model, researchers will be required to think more clearly and carefully about their target phenomena: who the peers are (membership), how children get into the target relationships (selection), the characteristics of the peers at the individual and group levels (composition), and, perhaps most importantly, the nature of the pathways though which peers exert their effects on individual development (socialization). In distinguishing and combining peer relationships, some of these features will be similar across relationships and some will be different.

In the movement from more static architectural models of peer relationships to models that are more dynamic and developmental, special attention will need to be devoted to the interrelations *among* these characteristics of peer relationships and what they imply for mechanisms of influence and methods for identifying the "real" peer group. According to the tensegrity metaphor, the "real" peer group includes the entire peer nexus—adolescents inhabit a complex multilevel network of agemates, some of whom they are close to and some of whom they spend time with, who are loosely configured in multiple overlapping groups that change in their membership, composition, and individual characteristics as rapidly as the adolescent himself or herself is developing. As we know from other strands of research, the "real" peer group is also likely weighted by the popularity of its members and sub-groups, as well as labeled and evaluated by the social categories used to describe its crowds and individuals.

Such a picture brings into stark relief the limitations of any specific method for capturing all of this complexity. For example, SCM approaches imply that social influence is a function of frequent interactions with peers. Hence the method focuses on observations of "who hangs around with whom" and peers are considered members of one's group if they interact frequently. However, what exactly is meant by "frequent" interactions depends on the distributions of interactions among all peers in school. It is likely that everybody interacts with almost everybody in the same grade in some form or another during a school day. The fact that students have reciprocal friends who are not part of their publically recognized groups of frequent interaction partners suggests that some low frequency interaction partners (i.e., kids who do *not* hang around together in school) can still represent "real" and important relationships.

In this chapter, we have emphasized the potential differences between kinds of relationship partners, but at the same time, tried to remain cautious about reifying the distinction between friendship and peer group affiliations. The tensegrity metaphor, whether using struts and wires or bones and muscles as components, can easily be interpreted to imply that the components are composed of qualitatively different materials, which is obviously not the case with peers. The same agemates can move in and out of peer groups and reciprocal friendship relationships, and can be both at the same time. If such caveats are kept in mind, the metaphor can be helpful for conceptualizing the multiple moving parts that make up peer networks and designing studies that examine their potential differences as well as their similarities.

These insights also apply to future research about the nature of social influence itself. The tensegrity model suggests that an important first step is to consider how selection, membership, and composition of different groups might shape the pathways through which they influence adolescent development. On the one hand, since both kinds of social partners are agemates, it is clear that all traditional mechanisms of social influence (e.g., persuasion, discussion, modeling, reinforcement, pressure) should be considered as candidate processes. On the other hand, friendships are characterized by close and intimate relationships, mutual understanding, respect, and support, whereas peer groups seem to be characterized more by shared preferences for activities, similarities in interests, and enjoyment in doing things together. As a result, friendship influences may occur more through emotional channels (e.g., emotional comfort and support), whereas peer group influences may occur more through social learning processes (e.g., reinforcement). It may even be that this balance shifts as children move through adolescence, or that youth may become more differentiated and thoughtful about which peers they rely on for which kinds of interactions and support (Zimmer-Gembeck & Skinner, in press).

At this point, we do not want to speculate too much about whether the social influences from friendship networks and peer groups occur through the same or different pathways. Perhaps the specific mechanisms will be similar and only differ in relative strength. Or, the pathways are similar but the targets differ. In the current paper, we looked at academic engagement, conceptualized as consisting of an emotional and a behavioral component. It would seem reasonable to expect that children's friendships would be most influential for the emotional features of children's motivated behavior in the classroom, whereas their public peer group affiliations may be more important for behavioral aspects. The tensegrity analogy suggests that different components of the peer world *can* differ. It does not stipulate that they always do. The metaphor suggests to researchers how to look at peer relationships, but it cannot tell them what they will see.

Overall, it is not surprising that the study of peers is currently segmented and resists integration. The complexity of the peer world can easily be overwhelming: It contains multiple members of differing closeness and frequency of interaction, consisting of many overlapping sets, which contain members with different characteristics and compositions, who are themselves developing, and whose membership is constantly changing. We hope that this chapter, in its use of a tensegrity metaphor, and the suggestions for conceptual and methodological strategies it inspired, can help contribute to building bridges across the many important areas that study the influences of peers on the academic development and success of children and youth.

NOTES

1. Some researchers have argued that differences in the specific peers captured by the two approaches are likely due to measurement error. If both assessment methods were more reliable, they would capture largely the same individuals. However, there is little empirical support for this assumption, since both kinds of approaches demonstrate high reliability (friendships based on reciprocity of nominations; SCM methods based on inter-observer consistency with kappa indices above .80; Kindermann, 1993, 2007). And logically, it seems clear that not all frequent interaction partners must be friends; there would be some friends with whom one would not spend a lot of time in school; for example, these may be cross-sex friendships or friendships based on non-school activities.

2. We estimate, from the numbers of non-identified lists of friends, that not more than 10% of children in this age group in town attended private schools and/or commuted to schools outside town. The numbers presented can thus be underestimations by about that amount.

AUTHORS' NOTE

We want to thank Cécile Kindelberger from the Université de Nantes, France, for discussions of critical issues in the overlap of peer groups and friendship networks. Justin Vollet, Shawn Mehess, and Price Johnson from Portland State University deserve our thanks for their help with the literature review, data analyses, and editing.

REFERENCES

Altermatt, E. R., & Pomerantz, E. M. (2003). The development of competence-related and motivational beliefs: An investigation of similarity and influence among friends. *Journal of Educational Psychology, 95,* 111–123.

Arbuckle, J. L. (2003). *Amos 5.* Chicago, IL: SmallWaters Corporation.

Berndt, T. J. (2004). Children's friendships: Shifts over a half-century in perspectives on their development and effects. *Merill-Palmer Quarterly, 50,* 206–223.

Berndt, T. J., Hawkins, J. A., & Jiao, Z. (1999). Influences of friends and friendships on adjustment to junior high school. *Merrill-Palmer Quarterly, 45,* 13–41.

Berndt, T. J., & Keefe, K. (1995). Friends' influences on adolescents' adjustment to school. *Child Development, 66,* 1312–1329.

Berndt, T. J., Laychak, A. E., & Park, K. (1990). Friends' influence on adolescents' academic achievement motivation: An experimental study. *Journal of Educational Psychology, 82,* 664–670.

Berndt, T. J., & McCandless, M. A. (2009). Methods for investigating children's relationships with friends. In K.H. Rubin, W.M. Bukowski, & B. Laursen (Eds.), *Handbook of peer interactions, relationships, and groups* (pp. 63–81). New York, NY: Guilford Press.

Borgatti, S. P., Mehra, A., Brass, D., & Labianca, G. (2009). Network analysis in the social sciences. *Science, 323,* 892–895.

Bronfenbrenner, U., & Morris, P. A. (2006). The bioecological model of human development. In W. Damon R. M. Lerner (Series Eds.) & R. M. Lerner (Vol. Ed.), *Handbook of child psychology: Vol. 1: Theoretical models of human development* (6th ed., pp. 793–828). New York, NY: Wiley.

Brown, B. B. (2004). Adolescents' relationships with peers. In R. M. Lerner & L. D. Steinberg (Eds.), *Handbook of adolescent psychology* (2nd ed., pp. 363–394). New York, NY: Wiley.

Bukowski, W. M. & Cillessen, A. H. (Eds.). (1998). *Sociometry then and now: Building on six decades of measuring children's experiences with the peer group.* (New Directions for Child Development, Vol. 80). San Francisco, CA: Jossey-Bass.

Bukowski, W. M., Motzoi, C., & Meyer, F. (2009). Friendship as process, function, and outcome. In K. H. Rubin, W. M. Bukowski, & B. Laursen (Eds.), *Handbook of peer interactions, relationships, and groups* (pp. 217–231). New York, NY: Guilford Press.

Cairns, R. B., & Cairns, B. D. (1992). *Lifelines and risk: Pathways of youth in our time.* New York, NY: Cambridge University Press.

Cairns, R. B., Gariépy, J.-L., & Kindermann, T. A. (1990). *Identifying social clusters in natural settings*. Unpublished manuscript, University of North Carolina at Chapel Hill, Social Development Laboratory.

Cairns, R. B., Leung, M.-C., Buchanan, L., & Cairns, B. D. (1995). Friendships and social networks in childhood and adolescence: Fluidity, reliability, and interrelations. *Child Development, 66,* 1330–1345.

Cairns, R. B., Neckerman, H. J., & Cairns, B. D. (1989). Social networks and the shadows of synchrony. In G. R. Adams, R. Montemayor, & T. P. Gullota (Eds.), *Biology of adolescent behavior and development* (pp. 275–305). Newbury Park, CA: Sage.

Cairns, R. B., Perrin, J. E., & Cairns, B. D. (1985). Social structure and social cognition in early adolescence: Affiliative patterns. *Journal of Early Adolescence, 5,* 339–355.

Chen, X., Chang, L., & He, Y. (2003). The peer group as a context: Mediating and moderating effects on relations between academic achievement and social functioning in Chinese children. *Child Development, 74.* 710–727.

Connell, J. P., & Wellborn, J. G. (1991). Competence, autonomy and relatedness: A motivational analysis of self-system processes. In M. Gunnar & L. A. Sroufe (Eds.), *Minnesota Symposium on Child Psychology: Vol. 23. Self processes in development* (pp. 43–77). Chicago, IL: University of Chicago Press.

Conelly, R., & Back, A. (1998). Mathematics and tensegrity. *American Scientist, 86,* 142–151.

Crosnoe, R., Riegle-Crumb, C., Field, S., Frank, K., & Muller, C. (2008). Peer contexts of girls' and boys' academic experiences. *Child Development, 79,* 139–155.

Dishion, T. J., Andrews, D. W., & Crosby, L. (1995). Antisocial boys and their friends in early adolescence. *Child Development, 66,* 139–151.

Ennett, S. T., & Bauman, K. E. (1994). The contribution of influence and selection to adolescent peer group homogeneity: The case of adolescent cigarette smoking. *Journal of Personality and Social Psychology, 67,* 653–663.

Estell, D. B., Farmer, T. W., Cairns, R. B., & Cairns, B. D. (2002). Social relations and academic achievement in inner-city early elementary classrooms. *International Journal of Behavioral Development, 26,* 518–528.

Fredricks, J. A., Blumenfeld, P. C., & Paris, A. H. (2004). School engagement: Potential of the concept, state of the evidence. *Review of Educational Research, 74,* 59–109.

Furman, W. (1989). Development of children's social networks. In D. Belle (Ed.), *Children's social networks and social supports* (pp. 151–172). New York, NY: Wiley.

Furman, W. (1993). Theory is not a four letter word: Needed directions in the study of adolescent friendships. In B. Laursen (Ed.), *New directions for child development: Close friendships in adolescence* (pp. 89–103). San Francisco, CA: Jossey-Bass.

Gest, S. D., Moody, J., & Rulison, K. L. (2007). Density or distinction? The roles of data structure and group detection methods in describing adolescent peer groups. *Journal of Social Structure, 4,* Retrieved from http://www.cmu.edu/joss/content/articles/volume8/GestMoody/

Gest, S. D., Rulison, K. L., Davidson, A. J., & Welsh, J. A. (2008) A reputation for success (or failure): The association of peer academic reputations with academic self-concept, effort, and performance across the upper elementary grades. *Developmental Psychology, 44,* 625–626.

Hallinan, M. T., & Williams, R. A. (1990). Students' characteristics and the peer-influence process. *Sociology of Education, 63,* 122–132.

Hartup, W.W (1995). The three faces of friendship. *Journal of Social and Personal Relationships, 12,* 569–574.

Hartup, W.W. (2009). Critical issues and theoretical viewpoints. In K. H. Rubin, W. M. Bukowski, & B. Laursen (Eds.), *Handbook of peer interactions, relationships, and groups* (pp. 3–19). New York, NY: Guilford Press.

Ingber, D. E. (2003). Tensegrity II: How structural networks influence cellular information processing networks. *Journal of Cell Science, 116,* 1397–1408.

Jaccard, J., Blanton, H., & Dodge, T. (2005). Peer influences on risk behavior: An analysis of the effects of a close friend. *Developmental Psychology, 41,* 135–147.

Jimerson, S. J., Campos, E., & Greif, J. L. (2003). Towards an understanding of definitions and measures of school engagement and related terms. *California School Psychologist, 8,* 7–27.

Kandel, D. B. (1978). Homophily, selection, and socialization in adolescent friendships. *American Journal of Sociology, 84,* 427–436.

Kindermann, T. A. (1993). Natural peer groups as contexts for individual development: The case of children's motivation in school. *Developmental Psychology, 29,* 970–977.

Kindermann, T. A. (2007). Effects of naturally-existing peer groups on changes in academic engagement in a cohort of sixth graders. *Child Development, 78,* 1186–1203.

Kindermann, T. A. & Gest, S. D. (2009). Assessment of the peer group: Identifying social networks in natural settings and measuring their influences. In K. H. Rubin, W. Bukowski, & B. Laursen (Eds), *Handbook of peer interactions, relationships, and groups* (pp. 100–117). New York, NY: Guilford.

Kindermann, T. A., McCollam, T. L., & Gibson, E. (1996). Peer group influences on children's developing school motivation. In K. Wentzel & J. Juvonen (Eds.), *Social motivation: Understanding children's school adjustment* (pp. 279–312). Newbury Park, CA: Sage.

Kindermann, T. A., & Sage, N. A. (1999, April). *Fifth graders' interaction frequencies with peer network members and the teacher during classroom lessons.* Poster at the Biennial Meetings of the Society for Research in Child Development, Albuquerque, NM.

Ladd, G. W. (1990). Having friends, keeping friends, making friends, and being liked by peers in the classroom: Predictors of children's early school adjustment? *Child Development, 61,* 1081-1100.

Ladd, G. W., Kochenderfer, B. J., & Coleman, C. C. (1997). Classroom peer acceptance, friendship, and victimization: Distinct relational systems that contribute uniquely to children's school adjustment? *Child Development, 68,* 1181–1197.

Marsh, H. W., Balla, J. R., & McDonald, R. P. (1988). Goodness-of-fit indexes in confirmatory factor analysis: The effect of sample size. *Psychological Bulletin, 103,* 391–410.

Martin, A., & Marsh, H. (2008). Academic buoyancy: Towards an understanding of students' everyday academic resilience. *Journal of School Psychology, 46,* 53–83.

Mehess, S., & Kindermann, T. A. (2009). *NETJAWS (version 7.7): A Java program to identify peer network members in Socio-cognitive mapping data* [Computer program]. Portland State University, Department of Psychology, Portland, OR.

Moreno, J. L. (1934). *Who shall survive? A new approach to the problem of human interrelations.* Washington, DC: Nervous and Mental Disease Publishing.

O'Farrell, S. L., & Morrison, G. M. (2003). A factor analysis exploring school bonding and related constructs among upper elementary students. *California School Psychologist, 8*, 53–72.

Popp, D., Laursen, B., Kerr, M., Stattin, H., & Burk, W. J. (2008). Modeling homophily over time with an actor-partner interdependence model. *Developmental Psychology, 44*, 1028–1039.

Rodkin, P. C., & Ahn, H-J. (2009). Social networks derived from affiliations and friendships, multi-informant and self-reports: Stability, concordance, placement of aggressive and unpopular children, and centrality. *Social Development, 18*, 556–576.

Rubin, K.H., Bukowski, W. & Parker, J.G. (2006). Peer interactions, relationships, and groups. In N. Eisenberg (Ed.), *Handbook of child psychology: Vol. 3. Social, emotional, and personality development* (6th ed., pp. 571–645). New York, NY: Wiley.

Ryan, A. M. (2001). The peer group as a context for the development of young adolescents' motivation and achievement. *Child Development, 72*, 1135–1150.

Skinner, E. A., & Belmont, M. J. (1993). Motivation in the classroom: Reciprocal effects of teacher behavior and student engagement across the school year. *Journal of Educational Psychology, 85*, 571–581.

Skinner, E. A., Furrer, C., Marchand, G., & Kindermann, T. (2008). Engagement and disaffection in the classroom: Part of a larger motivational dynamic? *Journal of Educational Psychology, 100*, 765–781

Skinner, E. A., Kindermann, T. A., Connell, J. P., & Wellborn, J. G (2009). Engagement as an organizational construct in the dynamics of motivational development. In K.R. Wentzel & A. Wigfield (Eds.), *Handbook of motivation in school* (pp. 223–245). Mahwah, NJ: Erlbaum.

Skinner, E. A., Kindermann, T. A., & Furrer, C. (2009). A motivational perspective on engagement and disaffection: Conceptualization and assessment of children's behavioral and emotional participation in academic activities in the classroom. *Educational and Psychological Measurement, 69*, 493–525.

Skinner, E. A., & Wellborn, J. G. (1997). Children's coping in the academic domain. In S. A. Wolchik & I. N. Sandler (Eds.), *Handbook of children's coping with common stressors: Linking theory and intervention* (pp. 387–422). New York, NY: Plenum Press.

Skinner, E. A., Wellborn, J. G., & Connell, J. P. (1990). What it takes to do well in school and whether I've got it: The role of perceived control in children's engagement and school achievement. *Journal of Educational Psychology, 82*, 22–32.

Skinner, E. A., Zimmer-Gembeck, M. J., & Connell, J. P. (1998). Individual differences and the development of perceived control. *Monographs of the Society for Research in Child Development, 6*(2/3), 1–220.

Urberg, K. A., Degirmencioglu, S. M., & Pilgrim, C. (1997). Close friend and group influence on adolescent cigarette smoking and alcohol use. *Developmental Psychology, 33,* 834–844.

von Eye, A. (1990). *Introduction to configural frequency analysis: The search for types and antitypes in cross-classifications.* New York, NY: Cambridge University Press.

Wellborn, J. G. (1991). *Engaged and disaffected action: The conceptualization and measurement of motivation in the academic domain.* Unpublished doctoral dissertation, University of Rochester.

Wentzel, K. R. (2009). Peers and academic functioning at school. In K. H. Rubin, W. Bukowski, & B. Laursen (Eds.), *Handbook of peer interactions, relationships, and groups* (pp. 531–547). New York, NY: Guilford.

Wentzel, K. R., McNamara-Barry, C., & Caldwell, K. A. (2004). Friendships in middle school: Influences on motivation and school adjustment. *Journal of Educational Psychology, 96,* 195–203.

Whelan, R. (1981, February). Kenneth Snelson: Straddling the abyss between art and science. *ARTnews, 80,* 68–74.

Zimmer-Gembeck, M. J., & Skinner, E. A. (2011). Review: The development of coping across childhood and adolescence: An integrative review and critique of research. *International Journal of Behavioral Development, 35,* 1–17.

CHAPTER 4

PEER RELATIONSHIPS AND SOCIAL MOTIVATIONAL PROCESSES

**Kathryn R. Wentzel, Alice Donlan,
and Danette Morrison**
University of Maryland at College Park

Being successful at school requires students to perform a range of social as well as academic tasks. In addition to mastering subject matter, developing effective learning strategies, and performing well on tests, adolescents also must work to maintain and establish interpersonal relationships, strive to develop social identities and a sense of belongingness, and observe and model standards for performance displayed by others. Although positive interactions with teachers and peers can motivate and support the development of these social and intellectual competencies, this chapter will focus on positive interactions with peers during adolescence. Adolescents who enjoy positive relationships with peers experience levels of emotional well-being, beliefs about the self, and values for prosocial forms of behavior and social interaction that are stronger and more adaptive than do those without positive peer relationships. Moreover, they also tend to be engaged in and even excel at academic tasks more than those who have peer relation-

Peer Relationships and Adjustment at School, pages 79–107
Copyright © 2012 by Information Age Publishing
79

ship problems (Wentzel, 2005). Therefore, finding ways to facilitate and support the development of adolescents' positive relationships with each other remains a central and important challenge for educators.

A central question that has yet to be answered, however, is how and why peer relationships might contribute to young adolescents' social and academic functioning at school. We address this question by focusing on ways in which peers support engagement and competence development at school. Toward this end, we first provide a definition of school engagement followed by a review of literature that links peer relationships to various types of engagement. We then consider potential mechanisms of influence that might explain these associations. The role of teacher–student relationships in facilitating and complementing peer influence also is discussed. Finally, we highlight remaining issues and provide future directions for the field.

DEFINING POSITIVE ENGAGEMENT AT SCHOOL

In the current chapter, engagement is defined as the motivational foundation of competence, where competence is a context-specific outcome reflecting the degree to which an individual meets the social demands of the environment, as well as achieve personal goals that result in positive developmental outcomes. In other words, competence reflects a balance between adherence to context-specific expectations for behavior and the achievement of positive outcomes for the self (see Wentzel, 2004, 2005). Engagement, therefore, is the pursuit of goals that result in social integration, as well as those resulting in positive outcomes for the individual. Socially integrative goals reflect outcomes that promote the smooth functioning of social groups, such as to behave appropriately or to gain social approval and social acceptance, whereas personal goals reflect the achievement of outcomes reflecting idiosyncratic interests, positive beliefs concerning competence and self-determination, and feelings of social and emotional well-being (Bronfenbrenner, 1989; Ford, 1992). With respect to classroom functioning, this approach suggests that students are engaged if they pursue goals that are valued by themselves as well as by teachers and peers (to include social and academic outcomes), and that set the stage for other positive outcomes for themselves, such as healthy self-concept or increased interest in academics.

Implicit in this perspective is that pursuit of socially integrative and self-assertive goals results in competent outcomes. Evidence supports this notion in that pursuit of socially integrative goals, such as to be prosocial and socially responsible, has been related consistently and positively to displays of prosocial and responsible behavior at school (A. Ryan & Shim, 2008; Salmivelli, Ojanen, Haanpaa, & Peets, 2005; Wentzel, 1991, 1994; Wentzel,

Filisetti, & Looney, 2007), and students who behave in a prosocial and responsible manner tend to gain social approval and acceptance from their peers (Wentzel, 1991, 1994) and teachers (Wentzel, 1994; Wentzel & Asher, 1995). In this work, prosocial behavior typically is defined as helping, sharing, and cooperating, and responsible behavior as following rules and keeping social commitments. Pursuit of these social goals also has been related to academic achievement (see Wentzel, 2002). By definition, self-assertive goals are unique to the individual. However, positive attributes that result from successful achievement of personal goals (e.g., positive self-concept, a sense of efficacy and self-determination, and emotional well-being) also have been related consistently and positively to various aspects of social and academic competence at school (see Wentzel & Wigfield, 2009, for reviews).

Our perspective also suggests that engagement is facilitated by contextual and relationship supports that afford opportunities for the achievement of personal as well as socially-valued goals (see Bronfenbrenner, 1989; Ford, 1992). Therefore, successful engagement and subsequent competence are dependent on contexts that provide support for personal growth and development and, support for learning and then accomplishing what is expected and valued by the social group. Members of the social group as well as the individual are responsible for positive adjustment within environmental constraints.

Given this perspective, what role might peer relationships play in supporting positive engagement and competence at school? In the following section, we review empirical literature that links peer interactions and relationships to adolescents' motivation to achieve positive social and academic outcomes and to actual behavioral and academic achievements. We then highlight ways in which peers can create positive contexts that promote these outcomes and discuss possible mechanisms by which peer influence might occur.

PEER RELATIONSHIPS, SCHOOL-RELATED ENGAGEMENT, AND COMPETENCE

Researchers typically have studied adolescents' interactions with peers at school in two ways, within the context of social relationships (e.g., degree of peer acceptance by the larger peer group, membership in specific peer groups, and dyadic friendships), and within structured academic activities (e.g., cooperative and collaborative learning). In the following section, we focus on evidence for the former, that is, how students' relationships with peers are associated with their engagement in the social and academic life of the classroom and with behavioral and academic outcomes. Evidence of associations between peer relationships and aspects of engagement and competence is presented first. Next, we describe peer contextual supports that can contribute to positive engagement and competence at school. Finally, we discuss mechanisms of influence that might account for relations between peer supports and school-related outcomes.

Correlates of Peer Relationships

Peer Acceptance

An extensive body of work supports the notion that peer acceptance is related to adolescents' motivational and academic functioning at school (see Wentzel, 2005, for a review). Students who are accepted or rejected by their peers are most often identified according to their sociometric status. Research indicates that sociometrically popular middle school students (i.e., those who are well-liked and not disliked by their peers) are academically proficient, whereas sociometrically rejected students (those who are highly disliked and not well-liked) experience academic difficulties; social preference scores on a continuum ranging from well-accepted to rejected yield highly similar findings. Results are most consistent with respect to classroom grades, although peer acceptance has been related positively to standardized test scores as well as to IQ, and longitudinal studies document the stability of relations between peer acceptance and academic accomplishments over time (e.g., Parker & Asher, 1987; Schwartz, Gorman, Nakamoto, & McKay, 2006; Wentzel & Caldwell, 1997). Sociometric status and peer acceptance also have been related to positive aspects of academic motivation, including satisfaction with school, pursuit of goals to learn, interest in school, and perceived academic competence (Wentzel, 2005).

In addition, researchers have documented associations between peer acceptance and social behavioral outcomes. In general, when compared to their average status peers, popular students tend to be more prosocial and sociable and less aggressive, and rejected students less compliant, less self-assured, less sociable and more aggressive and withdrawn (Newcomb, Bukowski, & Pattee, 1993; Wentzel, 1991; Wentzel & Asher, 1995). Peer status also has been related to prosocial and socially responsible goal pursuit during middle school (Wentzel, 1991). When compared with children of average sociometric status, popular children tend to report more frequent pursuit of prosocial goals (i.e., to help, cooperate and share). Students who are "neglected" (i.e., neither liked or disliked by their peers) also report more frequent pursuit of prosocial and social responsibility goals, whereas "controversial" students (i.e., either highly liked or disliked) report less frequent pursuit of responsibility goals (i.e., to follow classroom rules).

Peer Groups and Crowds

Adolescents' membership in specific peer groups also has been studied with regard to social and academic outcomes. Ethnographic studies have found typical adolescent crowds to include "populars," students who engage in positive forms of academic as well as social behavior but also in some delinquent activities; "jocks," students characterized by athletic accomplishments but also relatively frequent alcohol use; more alienated groups (e.g., "druggies") characterized by poor academic performance and engagement in delinquent and other illicit activities; and "normals," who tend to be fairly average students who do not engage in delinquent activities. (e.g., Brown, 1989). Researchers who identify friendship-based peer groups using statistical procedures also have reported significant relations between group membership and academic performance, with friendship-based groups in middle school being related to changes over the course of the school year in the degree to which students perform academically, and in their displays of prosocial and responsible behavior (A. Ryan, 2001; Wentzel & Caldwell, 1997). However, although most of these studies have followed students over time, few have documented long-term relations between group membership and competent outcomes (cf. Wentzel & Caldwell).

Friendships

Peer relationships also take the form of dyadic friendships. In this case, students are asked to nominate their best friends at school; nominations are then matched to determine reciprocity, or best friendships. The central distinction between friendships and involvement with the broader peer group is that friendships reflect relatively private, egalitarian relationships often formed on the basis of idiosyncratic criteria. Friendships also tend to be more enduring aspects of adolescents' peer relationships, whereas peer groups and crowds emerge primarily in the middle school years, peak at the beginning of high school, and then diminish in prevalence as well as influence by the end of high school (Brown, 1989).

Simply having a friend at school appears to be related to a range of positive outcomes at school. For example, having friends has been related positively to grades and test scores in middle school (Berndt & Keefe, 1995; Wentzel & Caldwell, 1997; Wentzel, Barry, & Caldwell, 2004), and to positive aspects of motivation and engagement in school-related activities (e.g., Berndt & Keefe, 1995; Epstein, 1983; Wentzel, Barry, & Caldwell, 2004; Wentzel & Caldwell, 1997). Students who do not make new friends over the middle school transition are more likely to avoid school than those who do (Tomada, Schneider, de Domini, Greenman, & Fonzi, 2005). Adolescents with friends also tend to be more sociable, cooperative, and self-confident when compared to their peers without friends (Newcomb & Bagwell, 1995; Wentzel et al., 2004). Children with reciprocated friendships also tend to be more independent, emotionally supportive, altruistic and prosocial, and less aggressive than those who do not have such friendships (Aboud & Mendelson, 1996; Wentzel et al., 2004). In addition, the quality of adolescent friendships has been related to school-based behavioral outcomes such as truancy and fighting (Crosnoe & Needham, 2004), and behavioral characteristics of friends have been related to students' prosocial behavior (Barry & Wentzel, 2006; Wentzel et al., 2004).

Summary

The literature on peer relationships provides strong and convincing evidence that various aspects of peer relationships are associated with a wide range of social and academic competencies at school. The picture that emerges from the literature on popular sociometric status and positive friendships is that these types of peer involvement are related to frequent displays of prosocial behavior (e.g., helping, sharing, caring), relatively infrequent displays of antisocial and disruptive behavior, and some modicum of academic success. Many of these characteristics also are endorsed by adolescent peer groups, although less predictably.

For the most part, however, this evidence is based on correlational studies lacking strong bases for drawing causal inferences; experimental studies that address these causal issues have not been conducted. Therefore, it is not clear whether positive social and academic outcomes are the result of having positive relationships with peers. Indeed, behavioral styles and levels of academic performance can lead to the formation of friendships and peer acceptance as well as the reverse. It also could be the case that these associations are part of more complex pathways of influence in which other variables mediate relations between peer relationships and these outcomes (e.g., Buhs & Ladd, 2001; Wentzel, 1991). Studies that examine these mediating and moderating pathways are rare. Finally, the fact that peer relationships can serve as stressors or detractors from positive engagement is also ignored in much of this literature.

Given these theoretical and methodological limitations, conclusions based on this work should be made with caution. However, it is reasonable to assume that for many adolescents, peers have the potential to influence the development and demonstrations of these competencies in a positive and direct fashion. Based on the assumption that some causal influence does occur, the following section will discuss perspectives on why and how such influence might take place.

Peer Relationships as Contextual Supports

Recall that our perspective on competence suggests that positive engagement in school is achieved to the extent that students accomplish goals that have personal as well as social value in a manner that supports continued psychological and emotional well-being. In addition, we proposed that a student's ability to be socially competent is contingent on opportunities and affordances of the school environment that allow students to pursue multiple goals that have personal relevance and that are socially valued. Applied specifically to peer activities as they occur in classroom and school settings, this perspective implies that students will engage in the pursuit of adaptive goals in part, when their peers create supportive contexts that afford their achievement.

A consideration of peer relationships as contextual affordances reflects the notion that at the core of positive peer relationships are the benefits they provide in the form of social supports (Bukowski & Hoza, 1989; Parker & Asher, 1993). At a general level, dimensions of support that promote allegiance to the broader peer group and to engagement in group-valued activities take the form of behavioral norms and standards that guide the pursuit of and achievement of specific outcomes. Supports also take the form of help to achieve these outcomes, providing safety from physical and psychological harm, and emotional nurturance (see Wentzel, 2004 for a review). These dimensions reflect essential components of social support that, if present, provide information concerning what is expected and valued by the group; help and instruction in response to attempts to achieve these valued outcomes; a safe, non-threatening environment; and an emotionally inclusive climate that makes individuals feel like a valued member of the group.

From a theoretical perspective, the aforementioned dimensions of support have been identified as essential characteristics of contexts that promote positive developmental outcomes (Bronfenbrenner, 1989; Ford, 1992; Wentzel, 2004) and engagement (Connell & Wellborn, 1991). For example, Ford has argued that evaluative beliefs about social relationships and settings can play an influential role in decisions to engage in the pursuit of personal goals. Specifically, individuals evaluate the correspondence between their personal goals and those of others, the degree to which others will provide access to information and resources necessary to achieve one's goals, and the extent to which social relationships will provide an emotionally supportive environment for goal pursuit. Extending this formulation to classroom settings, students should engage in the social and academic life of the classroom when they perceive their relationships with their classmates as providing opportunities to achieve personal as well as socially valued goals; as facilitating the achievement of these goals by providing help, advice, and instruction; as being safe and responsive to their goal strivings; and as being emotionally supportive and nurturing. In this manner, students' motivation to engage in multiple goals should serve to mediate relations between opportunities afforded by positive peer relationships and competent outcomes.

Following Ford's (1992) description of contexts that support social competence, we organize the following section around four dimensions of peer support that are highly relevant for promoting classroom engagement: communication of positive expectations and standards for achieving multiple goals; direct assistance and help in achieving goals; emotional support that facilitates positive engagement in socially valued classroom activities; and protection from physical threats and harm (see also Wentzel, 2004, 2005). Indeed, a growing body of research supports the notion that essential peer social supports at school reflect these four dimensions (see Wentzel, 1996; Wentzel, Battle, Russell, & Looney, 2010). Empirical evidence also suggests that these multiple supports contribute to students' school-related competencies in meaningful ways. Therefore, it is reasonable to speculate that these contextual supports provided by peers result in competent outcomes because they support the pursuit of multiple goals.

Communicating Goals and Expectations for Performance

A central question concerning peer supports and engagement is whether students express values and expectations concerning valued accomplishments to each other. Although not well documented, it is reasonable to assume that this takes place. For example, Wentzel et al. (2010) reported that young adolescents indicate that their classmates expect them to perform well academically at school; approximately 80% of students from three predominantly middle-class middle schools reported that their peers strongly valued academic learning. However, in samples of high school students, 40% of adolescents report similar levels of peer academic expectations (Wentzel, Monzo, Williams, & Tomback, 2007). These data suggest that as students advance through their middle school and high school years, the degree to which their goals and values support positive academic accomplishments might become fairly attenuated (see also, Eccles & Midgley, 1989).

Despite these developmental trends, it is reasonable to expect that at least in some schools, peers actively promote displays of positive social behaviors and the pursuit of academic accomplishments. Moreover, the extent to which young adolescents perceive their peers as expecting and wanting them to succeed academically also predicts their levels of engagement. For example, in samples of Caucasian middle-class students, findings indicate that perceived peer expectations for positive academic and social outcomes are significant positive predictors of goals to achieve academically (Wentzel, Filisetti, et al., 2007; Wentzel, Williams, & Tomback, 2006) and to display positive forms of behavior (Wentzel, Filisetti et al., 2007). In addition to general expectations concerning academic achievement, peers also provide proximal input concerning reasons for engaging in academic tasks. In support of this notion, students who perceive relatively high expectations for academic learning from their peers also report that they pursue goals to learn for internalized reasons (e.g., because it is important or fun) significantly more often than for more extrinsic reasons (e.g., because they believe they will get in trouble or lose social approval if they do not; Wentzel, 2004). In the social domain, research has been less frequent. However, perceived expectations from peers for behaving prosocially also are related significantly to internalized values for prosocial behavior (Wentzel, Filisetti et al., 2007).

Providing Help and Assistance

Perhaps the most explicit and obvious way in which peers can have a direct influence on students' engagement and competence development is by giving help (Newman, 2000). Although teachers play the central pedagogical function of transmitting knowledge and training students in academic subject areas, at least during adolescence, students report that their peers are as, or more, important sources of instrumental aid than are their teachers (Lempers & Clark-Lempers, 1992). Indeed, students who enjoy positive relationships with their peers are likely to have greater access to resources and information that can help them accomplish academic and social tasks than those who do not. These resources can take the form of information and advice, modeled behavior, or specific experiences that facilitate learning specific skills. In support of this notion are findings that students who believe that help is readily available from peers also tend to report positive levels of social and academic motivation (Wentzel et al., 2010). Moreover, research on middle school students making the transition into high school suggests that receiving academic help from familiar peers tends to increase over the course of the transition (Wentzel, Monzo, et al., 2007).

Providing Emotional Support

An extensive literature has documented associations between perceived emotional support from peers and positive social and academic motivation and outcomes. Adolescents who perceive that their peers support and care about them tend to be interested and engaged in positive aspects of classroom life, whereas students who do not perceive their relationships with peers as positive and supportive tend to be at risk for motivational, behavioral, and academic problems. Specifically, perceiving peers to be emotionally supportive and caring also has been related to the pursuit of goals to learn and to behave prosocially and responsibly, as well as displays of positive forms of classroom behavior and academic achievement (Wentzel, 1994, 1997, 2003).

Providing a Safe Environment

The importance of students' perceptions of classroom safety for understanding social and academic engagement is well-supported in the literature. Conflict with and threats from peers have been related negatively to middle school students' academic motivation, classroom behavior, and academic accomplishments (e.g., Juvonen, Nishina, & Graham, 2000; Wentzel et al., 2010). In contrast, researchers have documented the positive contributions that adolescents can make in problematic peer situations. For example, students who are accepted by their peers and who have established friendships with classmates are more likely to enjoy a relatively safe school environment and less likely to be the targets of peer-directed violence and harassment than their peers who do not have friends (Hodges, Boivin, Vitaro, & Bukowski, 1999; Pellegrini, Bartini, & Brooks, 1999; Schwartz et al., 2000). During early adolescence, having a friend is not only a protective factor against victimization, but students with aggressive tendencies who also have high-quality friendships are less likely to engage in bullying behavior (Bollmer, Milich, Harris, & Maras, 2005).

Mechanisms of Influence

How and why might these peer supports be related to positive engagement and school-related accomplishments? Several theoretical perspectives provide insights into possible mechanisms of influence. At the simplest level, social cognitive theory (Bandura, 1986) suggests that direct communication and instruction provides students with valuable information about what is expected and how to accomplish various tasks. Therefore, peers who convey expectations that academic engagement and positive social interactions are important and enjoyable are likely to lead others to form similar positive attitudes (Bandura, 1986). Although this type of support is probably provided most frequently within dyadic or small group interactions, the larger peer group also can be a source of behavioral standards, with group pressures providing a mechanism whereby adherence to group standards and expectations is monitored and enforced (see Brown, Bakken, Ameringer, & Mahon, 2008).

It should be noted, however, that peer monitoring of behavior will contribute to positive motivational orientations only insofar as peers have adopted adult standards for achievement and norms for conduct. For example, Clasen and Brown (1985) found that adolescent peer groups differ in the degree to which they pressure members to become involved in academic activities, with "jocks" and "popular" groups providing significantly more pressure for academic involvement than other groups. In addition, as children enter middle school, and establishing independence from adult influence becomes a developmental task, they are less likely to acknowledge the legitimacy of adult-imposed norms (Smetana & Bitz, 1996) or try to enforce classroom rules (Eccles & Midgley, 1989).

Modeling is a second social cognitive mechanism by which peers can influence students' adoption of goals (Bandura, 1986). Indeed, adolescents might develop specific behavioral styles or interests because they are desirable characteristics modeled by their peers. In support of a modeling hypothesis is evidence reported by Wentzel et al. (2004) that adolescents with initially low levels of prosocial behavior relative to those of their friends demonstrate increases in helpful and cooperative behavior over time when exposed to their more prosocial peers, and students with initially higher levels of prosocial behavior decrease their frequency of prosocial behavior when exposed to their less prosocial peers. In addition, results of this study supported Bandura's (1986) proposition that the most proximal influence of observational learning is on motivational processes, in this case, pursuit of goals to be prosocial: A friend's modeling of prosocial behavior in sixth grade was related to an adolescent's prosocial behavior over time by way of the adolescent's adoption of prosocial goals. Of further interest is that a sense of relatedness appears to bolster these modeling effects. In a second study (Barry & Wentzel, 2006), the long-term effects of a friend's prosocial behavior on an adolescent's motivation to be helpful and cooperative were most likely to be significant when the individual had a strong, positive bond with that friend.

Although research on adolescent modeling and academic achievement has not been frequent, as students work on academic tasks that require fairly specific skills and that are evaluated with respect to clearly defined standards, they use each other to monitor and evaluate their own abilities. These evaluations can influence students' beliefs about their academic efficacy, a powerful predictor of academic performance, especially when children observe similar peers who demonstrate successful ways to cope with failure (Schunk & Pajares, 2009). These modeling effects are especially likely to occur when students are friends (Crockett, Losoff, & Petersen, 1984).

A final mechanism involves the critical impact that peers can have on adolescents' emotional functioning. Few would argue that the need to belong and to experience a sense of relatedness with others is a powerful motivator of behavior (see Baumeister & Leary, 1995). Theoretical perspectives suggest that strong affective bonds and perceived support from others serve as buffers from stress and anxiety and contribute to a positive sense of emotional well-being (Sarason, Sarason, & Pierce, 1990). In turn, a sense of positive well-being is believed to promote efforts toward social integration and displays of socially desirable behavior (Connell & Wellborn, 1991). More specifically, feelings of emotional security and being socially connected are believed to facilitate the adoption of goals and interests valued by others, including goals to contribute in positive ways to the overall functioning of the social group (e.g., R. Ryan & Deci, 2000).

Evidence that supports this process suggests that exclusion from supportive peer relationships, and peer harassment and abuse, can result in adolescents feeling lonely, emotionally distressed, and depressed (Flook, Repetti & Ullman, 2005; Wentzel & Caldwell, 1997). In turn, these negative forms of affect are likely to result in less than positive social interactions and behavioral styles (Wentzel & McNamara, 1999). These findings are robust for perceived emotional support from classmates and acquaintances as well as from best friends. Researchers also have established significant positive relations between psychological distress and depression and a range of achievement-related outcomes including lack of interest in school, negative attitudes toward academic achievement, low levels of performance (Dubow & Tisak, 1989; Wentzel, Weinberger, Ford, & Feldman, 1990), and ineffective cognitive functioning (Jacobsen, Edelstein, & Hoffmann, 1994). Therefore, students' affective functioning is likely to be an important outcome that links peer-related activity to academic accomplishments.

Summary

In this chapter, social competence is defined as the achievement of context-specific goals that result in positive outcomes for the self but also for others. Therefore, a full appreciation of how and why students thrive or fail to thrive at school requires an understanding of a student's goals, including those that are personally valued as well as those that contribute to the stability and smooth functioning of interactions and relationships with others. In addition, our definition holds that contextual supports are crucial for the achievement of these multiple goals. In this regard, we have argued that peers can provide essential supports in the form of expectations and values, instrumental help, safety from physical threats and harm, and emotional support. In turn, these supports can facilitate the development of positive social and academic outcomes. Much correlational evidence supports these notions, especially with regard to the importance of peer supports for motivating positive engagement in social and academic activities.

Of additional interest, however, is that teachers and administrators are the primary architects of classroom and school contexts. In the following section, we describe the potential impact that teachers and the broader school context can have on students' abilities to provide these positive resources and to support each others' accomplishments.

EFFECTS OF TEACHERS ON PEER RELATIONSHIPS AND SUPPORTS

An important question that remains unanswered is whether peers exert a unique influence on students' engagement and actual accomplishments at school when supports from adults also are considered. Although the notion that peers can serve as potentially powerful motivators of academic engagement is generally supported in the empirical literature, few studies of peer interactions and relationships have taken into account the equally powerful influence of teachers and other adults in defining and promoting students' social as well as academic competencies. In recent years, however, researchers have begun to focus on the impact that teachers and their instructional practices can have on adolescents' peer-related experiences. In the following sections, literature on ways in which teachers might influence the formation and quality of adolescents' peer relationships and in which teacher–student relationships might counter or influence the effects of peers on each other is discussed.

Teachers' Influence on Peer Relationships

There is evidence that teachers' beliefs and behaviors; classroom organization; and school-wide structure, composition, and climate affects students' peer choices and general propensity to make friends, as well as levels of peer acceptance and friendship networks in classrooms (e.g., Crosnoe & Needham, 2004; Donohue, Perry, & Weinstein, 2003; Hughes, Cavell, Meehan, Zhang, & Collie, 2005; Stormshack, Bierman, Bruschi, Dodge, & Coie, 1999). For example, the instructional approach that a teacher adopts appears to have an impact on students' opportunities to make friends (Epstein, 1983). In this regard, researchers have examined the effects of learner-centered practices as opposed to teacher-centered practices on students' interactions and relationships with peers. In contrast to teacher-centered practices (e.g., instruction focused on rote learning, norm-referenced evaluation), learner-centered practices are those that involve students in decision making and emphasize the importance of building positive social relationships by encouraging students to talk to each other about class assignments, to work in small groups, and to move about while working on activities. Learner-centered practices have been related to lower rates of peer rejection, less student anger, and more student empathy than other types of instruction (Donohue et al., 2003; Gadeyne, Ghesquière, & Onghena, 2006). Middle and high school students in these classrooms also are less likely to be socially isolated or rejected by their classmates, enjoy greater numbers of friends, and experience more diversity and stability in their friendships (e.g., Epstein, 1983).

Standards for performance established by classroom teachers also can have a negative impact on ways in which students interact with each other and on subsequent academic motivation and achievement. This occurs most often when teachers promote competitive academic standards and use norm-referenced criteria for evaluating achievements. These practices heighten social comparison among students rather than an ethos of sharing and cooperation. Of relevance for understanding academic achievement is that high levels of social comparison tend to result in students adopting orientations toward learning that focus on performance rather than mastery of subject matter, and in lowered levels of academic efficacy and aspirations for achievement, especially among low ability students (Maehr & Midgley, 1991).

In addition, although the literature implies that peers might be the primary source of threats to students' physical safety and well-being, teachers and school administrators can play a central role in creating schools that are free of peer harassment and in alleviating the negative effects of harassment once it has occurred. For example, the Olweus Bullying Prevention Program focuses on improving peer relationships by creating and fostering a safe and positive school environment (Olweus, 1993). This is done by helping students interact with each other in more positive ways and by helping school staff identify strategies for preventing peer violence and harassment. Interventions designed to offset the often negative influence of peer groups and gangs are especially successful if students have access to adults who provide them with warmth and strong guidance (Heath & McLaughlin, 1993). There also is evidence that schools that stress intergenerational bonding (i.e., closeness between students and teachers) support the development of teacher–student relationships that can act as buffers against the potentially negative effects of aggressive peers on behavior (Crosnoe & Needham, 2004).

At a broader level, schools that employ universal school-wide policies and programs that accentuate the importance of students' prosocial development also can create environments where more positive relationships are likely to be formed. In this regard, proactive efforts to promote social skill development and positive social interactions among students have had some success, although mostly at the elementary-school level (for review, see Ang & Hughes, 2001). Other structured efforts to enhance prosocial behavior and corresponding peer interactions are exemplified by the Child Development Project (CDP). Highlights of the CDP intervention and curriculum include cooperative learning activities, classroom management practices designed to promote student self-regulation and social responsibility, and class meetings designed to communicate and reinforce positive behavioral and social norms of the classroom, foster cognitive and social problem-solving, and to build classroom unity and a sense of community. Formal evaluations have documented that CDP elementary schools out-perform comparison schools on a multitude of factors, including academic engagement and performance, feelings of connectedness to school, and displays of prosocial behavior; these positive effects have been found to carry over into the middle school years (Battistich, Schaps, & Wilson, 2004; Schaps, Battistich, & Solomon, 2004; see also Developmental Studies Center, n.d.).

From a developmental perspective, improving the quality of peer relationships has been of special concern for teachers and administrators who work with students during transitions to new schools. For example, many young adolescents enter new middle school structures that necessitate interacting with larger numbers of peers on a daily basis. In contrast to the greater predictability of self-contained classroom environments in elementary school, the relative uncertainty and ambiguity of multiple classroom environments, new instructional styles, and more complex class schedules often result in middle school students turning to each other for information, social support, and ways to cope. Students who have access to positive peer supports are likely to adapt to the demands of middle school transitions in more positive ways than those without such supports (Fenzel, 2000; Kingery & Erdley, 2007; Levitt et al., 2005).

Teacher–Student Relationships and Contextual Supports

As evidenced in previous sections, the notion that peers can serve as potentially powerful motivators of academic engagement is generally supported in the empirical literature. However, few of the studies on the quality of students' peer interactions and supports have also included assessments of the quality of teacher–student relationships. In support of a conclusion that adolescents' peer relationships have unique influence on school engagement and competence relative to teacher–student relationships, Wentzel, Filisetti, and Looney (2007) reported that perceived peer (but not teacher) expectations for positive social behavior predicted middle school students' prosocial behavior. In a study of young Hispanic adolescents, Wentzel, Russell, & Baker (2008) also found that perceived expectations from peers but not from teachers predicts positive forms of classroom behavior. Finally, behaviorally at-risk students' pursuit of goals to behave appropriately have been related to peer but not teacher expectations for positive behavior (Wentzel, Donlan, Morrison, Russell, & Baker, 2009).

Other studies have documented the differential effects of perceived emotional support from teachers and peers on student outcomes. For example, Wentzel et al. (2009) reported that perceived emotional support from peers but not from teachers predicts prosocial and responsible classroom behavior. Changes in perceived emotional support from teachers and peers as students transitioned from one year to the next also have been related to changes in aggressive behavior (Wentzel et al., 2006). In this latter case, students high in aggression at the first assessment remained so when their new peers were supportive regardless of teacher support; aggressive students became less aggressive in their new classrooms when new peers were not perceived as being emotionally supportive but teachers were. Therefore, peer relationships are likely to have a unique influence on students' academic goal pursuit by way of students' emotional well-being. However, these findings also remind us of the fact that some adolescents do not expect each other to comply with adult norms and values, and that positive emotional supports from these peers can promote negative forms of behavior not valued by adults.

Assigning a unique role to peers, however, assumes that all students value peer support and that peer rejection or lack of friends will automatically lead to emotional distress. In fact, some adolescents are likely to be more adult-oriented than others and thrive despite a lack of close friends. A study of middle school students without friends (Wentzel & Asher, 1995) supports this notion in that students who had few friends and were neither well-liked or disliked by their peers (sociometrically neglected adolescents), were the most well-liked by their teachers, the most highly motivated students, and were equally self-confident when compared to their average status peers. In a longitudinal study, Wentzel (2003) found that these adolescents remained academically and socially well-adjusted over the course of the middle school years. Whether these findings reflect a disinterest in the peer group and therefore a lack of emotional investment in peer relationships or a dependence on adults for emotional support remains a question for future research. However, it is likely that peers have little potential to influence some students and that peers and teachers might contribute to academic engagement by way of different pathways.

Finally, although the unique contributions of teachers and peers to adolescents' social and academic engagement is of interest to researchers as well as practitioners, it is important to note that teacher–student and peer relationships likely function as interrelated systems (e.g., Hinde, 1979). In fact, when teachers and students hold similar values toward social behavior and academic achievement, they are likely to bolster each others' impact and influence on engagement in ways that they could not on their own.

Reciprocal influences also are likely to be in play. Just as teachers' behaviors are likely to influence peer relationships, students' relationships and interactions with each other are likely to influence teachers' instructional decisions, especially whether they condone or impose strict limits on peer interactions in their classrooms. Research that examines these more complex interactions in secondary classrooms is rare. However, studies that address these issues are necessary to understand ways in which teacher practices might hinder or facilitate students' ability to motivate each other in positive ways at school.

REMAINING ISSUES AND FUTURE DIRECTIONS

The underlying premise of this chapter is that being accepted by classmates, having friends, and establishing memberships in larger peer groups has the potential to support and facilitate engagement in and the achievement of social and academic competencies at school. Although interactions with peers have been viewed most often as having a potentially negative impact on the pursuit and achievement of educational goals and accomplishments, the positive and supportive role that students play in each others' lives must be acknowledged. It is clear that enjoying positive and healthy relationships with peers is of central importance to children throughout adolescence.

Despite progress in understanding the positive contribution of peers to school-related outcomes, there are many unanswered questions concerning how peers exert their influence. In this section, we focus on three issues of interest to educators that we believe are especially important to address as researchers continue to work in this area: models of causal influence, differential effects of various types of peer interactions on school-related outcomes, and the generalizability of findings to diverse samples of adolescents.

Models of Influence

In this chapter, we have focused on causal models and mechanisms in which peer supports influence positive school-related outcomes. However, few experimental studies have been conducted to support conclusions about causality (see Ladd, Herald-Brown, & Kochel, 2009). Therefore, the possibility of alternative models of influence need to be considered. For example, it is reasonable to assume that aspects of peer relationships are simply correlated to social and academic outcomes without any direction of effects. Indeed, positive correlations could reflect reputational biases rather than causal influence (Wentzel, 1991; Wentzel & Asher, 1995). In studies in which peer ratings are used to assess student outcomes, positive correlations between peer acceptance and academic accomplishments might simply reflect a halo effect that leads students to evaluate well-liked classmates positively in the academic as well as social domain. Alternatively, significant associations between various aspects of peer relationships and other outcomes might simply reflect the fact that students who demonstrate competence in one domain of functioning (i.e., making friends) often do so in other domains.

It also is possible that a third set of factors contributes to competence in both domains. These could reflect specific types of social behavior as well as psychological or emotional processes that support positive peer relationships as well as school success. A large body of evidence supports the notion that certain types of social behavior related to peer acceptance also are related to academic accomplishments. In particular, prosocial displays of behavior such as helping, cooperating, and sharing have been linked to peer acceptance and popularity as well as to academic achievement, whereas aggression and antisocial displays of behavior have been related to peer rejection and academic problems (Wentzel, 2005). Work on peer collaborative learning also has documented the important role of social competencies in facilitating the positive effects of peer interactions on cognitive gains (see Wentzel & Watkins, 2002, 2011). In addition, self-regulatory processes such as goal-setting, emotion regulation, self-monitoring, and means–end thinking have been proposed as factors that contribute to the ability to implement strategic and planful behavior; in turn, these skills are believed to promote positive peer relationships, acceptable forms of social behavior, and academic performance (e.g., Crick & Dodge, 1994; Ford, 1992).

In short, alternative models and pathways of influence need to be explored further to understand fully the role of peers in motivating school-related engagement and competence. Examining the extent that behavioral styles and underlying psychological processes account for positive associations between peer relationships, collaborative interactions, and academic outcomes is a critical next step in understanding the role of peers in facilitating intellectual growth and academic accomplishments. Along these lines, other individual characteristics such as attachment security, family functioning, cultural identity, and the extent to which adolescents are oriented towards gaining social approval from peers also are likely to influence the degree to which adolescents value peer relationships and therefore benefit from interactions with classmates.

Finally, questions concern the timing, stability, and quality of peer relationships need to be acknowledged. For example, are there sensitive periods during which peer relationships have more powerful effects on certain developmental outcomes? Can a student be friendless in middle school, establish a friendship in high school, and still experience the protective and positive effects that friendships are proposed to offer? In this regard, some researchers have suggested that it is the cumulative experience of friendships and other types of peer relationships that is important to development rather than any one particular friendship in one place or time (Hartup & Stevens, 1997). Others suggest that in times of school transitions, when peer relationships tend to be disrupted, students who are unsuccessful in making friends and in forming new peer connections are especially at risk for negative forms of adjustment. For instance, adolescents who transition without friends experience increased loneliness (Kingery & Erdley, 2007; Levitt et. al, 2005; Paul & Brier, 2001), and stress (Fenzel, 2000), which in turn, are associated with negative academic outcomes (Newman, Lohman, Newman, Myers, & Smith, 2000).

In summary, although few would dispute the notion that peers have influence on each others' school-related functioning, empirical evidence that addresses issues of causality is limited. Alternative pathways of influence need to be explored further to understand the causal role of peers in motivating school-related engagement and competence. Longitudinal studies that assess the characteristics of peer relationships and supports at multiple points in time are necessary to determine the nature and magnitude of change in adolescents over time. There is also an evident gap in the literature addressing peer relationships outside of the classroom or school. The role of these non-school relationships in promoting school-based competencies warrants further study.

Differential Roles of Peer Relationships

An additional set of issues to be addressed concerns the varied nature of peer interactions and relationships that adolescents experience at school. Just as few researchers have explored the unique contributions of peers and teachers to student outcomes, few have examined the relative or unique contribution of various types of peer relationships. For instance, friends are believed to be unique in providing contexts for self-expression, validation, and affirmation, and to play a relatively minor role in socializing each other with respect to larger group norms and expectations (Hartup & Stevens, 1997). If so, the role of individual friendships in defining and supporting classroom engagement and competence should be minimal (Wentzel & Caldwell, 1997).

In contrast, adolescent peer groups and crowds are believed to facilitate the formation of identity and self-concept (Brown, Mory, & Kinney, 1994) and to structure the nature of ongoing social interactions within and across groups (Cairns, Xie, & Leung, 1998). In both of these roles, peer groups and crowds are likely to provide students with values, norms, and interaction styles that are sanctioned and commonly valued. Within groups and crowds, competent behavior also is modeled frequently so that it can be easily learned and adopted by group members (Brown et al., 1994). Therefore, the influence of the broader peer group and peer acceptance should play a relatively strong role in defining standards for classroom behavior and norms for academic accomplishments. Despite these differences between friendships and group membership, the influence of engagement on different types of peer supports as a function of the source of supports remains a relatively unexplored area of research.

Of additional importance is that most studies of peer interactions and relationships in relation to school-based competencies have not considered the role of various qualities and characteristics of peer involvement. For instance, friendships as well as group membership differ with respect to stability, status, and roles of the individual members of the relationship or group, the degree to which friendships and group membership overlap with other friendships or groups, or quality of experience as a function of involvement in the group or friendship. In addition, ways in which friendships and groups are assessed often do not take into account reciprocity (see Kindermann, McCollam, & Gibson, 1996; Newcomb & Bagwell, 1995). Moreover, although adolescents are quick to identify school-related groups, they are loath to admit membership in any one group themselves (Matyanowski, 2001). In short, much work is still needed to resolve issues concerning how to define and assess various aspects of peer relationships before we can truly understand the influence of peers on adolescents' school-related competencies.

Issues of Diversity

A third area for additional focus concerns the degree to which findings from predominantly White, middle-class samples can be generalized to more diverse samples. In this regard, conceptual models that take into account the diversity of student backgrounds need to be developed. The importance of this undertaking is evident in research on peer values and norms, peer emotional support, and classroom composition. With regard to peer values and norms, little is understood about peer cultures and what students themselves value and expect of each other in order to gain approval. However, there is evidence to suggest that personal attributes and behavior valued by students tend to differ as a function of race as well as gender (see Graham, Taylor, & Ho, 2009). Of relevance for the current discussion is that African American and Latino adolescent males tend to devalue achievement as a characteristic of admired peers when compared to Caucasian males and females (e.g., Graham, Taylor, & Hudley, 1998; Taylor & Graham, 2007). These findings suggest that the ability to coordinate and achieve a balance between multiple and conflicting socially valued goals might be especially relevant for understanding levels of school adjustment for these students. Indeed, understanding the potentially demanding and stressful effects of competing, incongruent goals promoted by peers, teachers, and broader classroom contexts often experienced by minority students (Phelan, Davidson, & Cao, 1991; Spera, Wentzel, & Motto, 2009) is likely a critical first step in developing programs that support school success for these students.

Similarly, the role of peer supports in motivating engagement and competence might differ for ethnic minority students. On the one hand, similar to findings in Caucasian middle-class samples, research has shown that receiving instrumental help and emotional support relates positively to African American students' persistence at academic tasks and motivation for learning (Faircloth & Hamm, 2005; Hamm & Faircloth, 2005). However, lack of peer supports related to emotional caring and safety are likely to be more detrimental for minority students than for White students. Although research on nationally representative samples indicates that Caucasian adolescents are more likely to be involved in bullying activities than are African-

American or Hispanic adolescents (Nansel, Overpeck, Pilla, Ruan, Simons-Morton, & Scheidt, 2001), peer harassment in the form of discrimination is of unique relevance to ethnic minority students. In this case, discriminatory behaviors on the part of majority (e.g., White) students can communicate to ethnic minority students that they are not a member of the "in group" (Crocker, Major, & Steele, 1998), conveying that these students have characteristics that make them inferior to their peers. These messages often are targeted at intellectual abilities, suggesting that minority students' abilities are deficient (Steele & Aronson, 1995).

The negative consequences of these forms of discrimination are well documented. Perceived discrimination from peers has been related negatively to African American adolescents' sense of academic efficacy (Chavous, Rivas-Drake, Smalls, Griffin, & Cogburn, 2008; Wong, Eccles, & Sameroff, 2003), positive values for academic achievements (Chavous et al.), and academic persistence and curiosity (Smalls, White, Chavous, & Sellers, 2007), and positively to disruptive behavior and depressive affect (Smalls et al., 2007; Wong et al., 2003). Studies of stereotype threat also have linked discriminatory practices negatively to academic accomplishments; interventions to alleviate the negative effects of stereotyping have resulted in gains in academic achievement (see Good, Aronson, & Inzlicht, 2003).

Finally, variations in the ethnic composition of middle school and high school classrooms also are known to influence friendship dynamics. Specifically, African American students in classrooms that are ethnically diverse tend to report having more high quality friendships than those in less diverse classrooms where they are clearly in the minority (Jackson, Barth, Powell, & Lochman, 2006). The degree to which middle schools and high schools are ethnically diverse, as opposed to having clear majority and minority groupings, also can influence the nature and stability of students' friendships, with greater diversity resulting in more positive outcomes (Urberg, Degirmencioglu, Tolson, & Halliday-Scher, 1995). Of additional interest is that ethnic minority students attending schools with higher concentrations of other minority students are more likely to graduate than those who are a distinct minority in their school (Goza & Ryabor, 2009; Kirkpatrick-Johnson, Crosnoe, & Elder, 2001). Composition of peer groups also has been related to achievement, with African American adolescents earning higher grades when members of mixed-race peer groups; the reverse tends to be true for Asian, Latino, and non-Hispanic White students (Goza & Ryabov, 2009).

CONCLUSION

In this chapter, we have argued that positive engagement in the social and academic life of the classroom reflects the degree to which students try to meet the social demands of the classroom as well as pursue their own personal goals; the achievement of these dual sets of goals is reflected in the psychological and emotional growth of the student as well as the smooth functioning of the classroom. By definition, positive engagement is always defined in context-specific terms and, therefore, is dictated by the social demands of others. A perspective on classroom competence that describes ways in which contextual supports promote students' engagement in positive goal pursuits also was presented. Specifically, clear expectations for goal pursuit, peer provisions of instrumental help, safety and responsivity, and emotional support represent social motivational processes that support engagement. Research provides support for this model in that peers appear to have the capacity not only to provide guidelines and boundaries for defining competence, but also to provide help, create safe environments for each other, and to provide emotional nurturance and support.

Much work, however, remains to be done. At the most general level, expanded models must focus on the multiple sources of influence that contribute to student engagement. For instance, we need to address the possible ways in which adolescents and the various social systems in which they develop, including home, peer groups, and schools, interact over time to create definitions of school-related competence (see Bronfenbrenner, 1989). In this regard, researchers need to identify ways in which students learn to coordinate their own social and academic goals with those prompted by others. Issues concerning cause and effect also necessitate continued focus on underlying psychological processes and skills that promote the development and display of competent outcomes. Finally, investigations of socially valued goals and expectations also must be conducted within developmental and ecological frameworks, taking into account the age-related interests and capabilities of the child and cultural constraints. Within these frameworks, identification of student characteristics that facilitate their attention to and acceptance of peer communications and influence will be of critical importance for moving this field of research forward.

REFERENCES

Aboud, F. E., & Mendelson, M. J. (1996). Determinants of friendship selection and quality: Developmental perspectives. In W. M. Bukowski, A. F. Newcomb, & W. W. Hartup (Eds.), *The company they keep: Friendship during childhood and adolescence* (pp. 87–112). New York, NY: Cambridge University Press.

Ang, R., & Hughes, J. (2001). Differential benefits of skills training with antisocial youth based on group composition: A meta-analytic review. *School Psychology Review, 31,* 164–185.

Bandura, A. (1986). *Social foundations of thought and action: A social cognitive theory.* Englewood Cliffs, NJ: Prentice-Hall.

Barry, C., & Wentzel, K. R. (2006). The influence of middle school friendships on prosocial behavior: A longitudinal study. *Developmental Psychology, 42*, 153–163.

Battistich, V., Schaps, E., & Wilson, N. (2004). Effects of an elementary school intervention on students' "connectedness" to school and social adjustment during middle school. *The Journal of Primary Prevention, 24*, 243–262.

Baumeister, R. F., & Leary, M. R. (1995). The need to belong: Desire for interpersonal attachments as a fundamental human motivation. *Psychological Bulletin, 117*, 497–529.

Berndt, T. J., & Keefe, K. (1995). Friends' influence on adolescents' adjustment to school. *Child Development, 66*, 1312–1329.

Bollmer, J. M., Milich, R., Harris, M. J., & Maras, M. A. (2005). A friend in need: The role of friendship quality as a protective factor in peer victimization and bullying. *Journal of Interpersonal Violence, 20*, 701–712.

Bronfenbrenner, U. (1989). Ecological systems theory. In R. Vasta (Ed.), *Annals of child development* (Vol. 6, pp. 187–250). Greenwich, CT: JAI.

Brown, B. B. (1989). The role of peer groups in adolescents' adjustment to secondary school. In T. J. Berndt & G. W. Ladd (Eds.), *Peer relationships in child development* (pp. 188–215). New York, NY: Wiley.

Brown, B. B., Bakken, J. P., Ameringer, S. W., & Mahon, S. D. (2008). A comprehensive conceptualization of the peer influence process in adolescence. In M. Prinstein & K. Dodge (Eds.), *Understanding peer influence in children and adolescents* (pp. 17–44). New York, NY: Guilford Press.

Brown, B. B., Mory, M. S., & Kinney, D. (1994). Casting adolescent crowds in a relational perspective: Caricature, channel, and context. In R. Montemayor, G. R. Adams, & T. P. Gullotta, T. P. (Eds.), *Personal relationships during adolescence* (pp. 123–167). Newbury Park, CA: Sage.

Buhs, E. S., & Ladd, G. W. (2001). Peer rejection as an antecedent of young children's school adjustment: An examination of mediating processes. *Developmental Psychology, 37*, 550–560.

Bukowski, W. M., & Hoza, B. (1989). Popularity and friendship: Issues in theory, measurement, and outcome. In T. J. Berndt & G. W. Ladd (Eds.), *Peer relationships in child development* (pp. 15–45). New York, NY: Wiley & Sons.

Cairns, R., Xie, H., & Leung, M. (1998). The popularity of friendship and the neglect of social networks: Toward a new balance. *New Directions for Child Development, 80*, 25–53.

Chavous, T. M., Rivas-Drake, D., Smalls, C., Griffin, T., & Cogburn, C. (2008). Gender matters, too: The influence of school racial discrimination and racial identity on academic engagement outcomes among African American adolescents. *Developmental Psychology, 44*, 637–654.

Clasen, D. R., & Brown, B. B. (1985). The multidimensionality of peer pressure in adolescence. *Journal of Youth and Adolescence, 14*, 451–468.

Connell, J., & Wellborn, J. (1991). Competence, autonomy, and relatedness: A motivational analysis of self-system processes. In M. R. Grunnar & L. A. Sroufe (Eds.), *Self processes and development* (pp. 43–77). Hillsdale, NJ: Lawrence Erlbaum.

Crick, N., & Dodge, K. A. (1994). A review and reformulation of social information-processing mechanisms in children's social adjustment. *Psychological Bulletin, 115*, 74–101.

Crocker, J., Major, B., & Steele, C. (1998). Social stigma. In D. M. Gilbert, S. T. Fiske, & G. Lindzey (Eds.), *The handbook of social psychology* (pp. 504–553). New York, NY: McGraw Hill.

Crockett, L., Losoff, M., & Petersen, A. C. (1984). Perceptions of the peer group and friendship in early adolescence. *Journal of Early Adolescence, 4,* 155–181.

Crosnoe, R., & Needham, B. (2004). Holism, contextual variability, and the study of friendships in adolescent development. *Child Development, 75,* 264–279.

Developmental Studies Center. (n.d.). Home page. Retrieved from www.devstu.org/

Donohue, K., Perry, K., & Weinstein, R. (2003). Teachers' classroom practices and children's rejection by their peers. *Journal of Applied Developmental Psychology, 24,* 91–118.

Dubow, E. F., & Tisak, J. (1989). The relation between stressful life events and adjustment in elementary school children: The role of social support and social problem-solving skills. *Child Development, 60,* 1412–1423.

Eccles, J. S., & Midgley, C. (1989). Stage-environment fit: Developmentally appropriate classrooms for young adolescents. In C. Ames & R. Ames (Eds.), *Research on motivation in education: Vol. 3* (pp. 139–186). New York, NY: Academic Press.

Epstein, J. L. (1983). The influence of friends on achievement and affective outcomes. In J.L. Epstein & N. Karweit (Eds.), *Friends in school* (pp. 177–200). New York, NY: Academic Press.

Faircloth, B. S. & Hamm, J. V. (2005). Sense of belonging among high school students representing four ethnic groups. *Journal of Youth and Adolescence, 34,* 293–309.

Fenzel, L. M. (2000). Prospective study of changes in global self-worth and strain during the transition to middle school. *Journal of Early Adolescence, 20,* 93–116.

Flook, L., Repetti, R. L., & Ullman, J. B. (2005). Classroom social experiences as predictors of academic performance. *Developmental Psychology, 41,* 319–327.

Ford, M. E. (1992). *Motivating humans: Goals, emotions, and personal agency beliefs.* Newbury Park, CA: Sage.

Gadeyne, E., Ghesquière, P., & Onghena, P. (2006). Psychosocial educational effectiveness criteria and their relation to teaching in primary education. *School Effectiveness and School Improvement, 17*(1), 63–85.

Good, C., Aronson, J., & Inzlicht, M. (2003). Improving adolescents' standardized test performance: An intervention to reduce the effects of stereotype threat. *Journal of Applied Developmental Psychology, 24,* 645–662.

Goza, F., & Ryabov, I. (2009). Adolescents' educational outcomes: Racial and ethnic variations in peer network importance. *Journal of Youth Adolescence, 38,* 1264–1279.

Graham, S., Taylor, A. Z., & Ho, A. Y. (2009). Race and ethnicity in peer relations research. In K Rubin, W. Bukowski, & B. Laursen (Eds.), *Handbook on peer relationships* (pp. 394–413). New York, NY: Guilford.

Graham, S., Taylor, A. Z., & Hudley, C. (1998). Exploring achievement values among ethnic minority early adolescents. *Journal of Educational Psychology, 90,* 606–620.

Hamm, J. V., & Faircloth, B. S (2005). Peer context of mathematics classroom belonging in early adolescence. *Journal of Early Adolescence, 25,* 345–366

Hartup, W. W., & Stevens, N. (1997). Friendships and adaptation in the life course. *Psychological Bulletin, 121,* 355–370.

Heath, S. B., & McLaughlin, M. W. (1993). *Identity and inner-city youth.* New York, NY: Teachers College Press.

Hinde, R. A. (1979). *Towards understanding relationships.* London, UK: Academic Press.

Hodges, E. V., Boivin, M., Vitaro, F., & Bukowski, W. M. (1999). The power of friendship: Protection against an escalating cycle of peer victimization. *Developmental Psychology, 35,* 94–101.

Hughes, J., Cavell, T., Meehan, B., Zhang, D., & Collie, C. (2005). Adverse school context moderates the outcomes of selective interventions for aggressive children. *Journal of Consulting and Clinical Psychology, 73,* 731–736.

Jackson, M., Barth, J., Powell, N., & Lochman, J. (2006). Classroom contextual effects of race on children's peer nominations. *Child Development, 77,* 1325–1337.

Jacobsen, T., Edelstein, W., & Hofmann, V. (1994). A longitudinal study of the relation between representations of attachment in childhood and cognitive functioning in childhood and adolescence. *Developmental Psychology, 30,* 112–124.

Juvonen, J., Nishina, A., & Graham, S. (2000). Peer harassment, psychological adjustment, and school functioning in early adolescence. *Journal of Educational Psychology, 92,* 349–359.

Kindermann, T. A., McCollam, & Gibson, E. (1996). Peer networks and students' classroom engagement during childhood and adolescence. In J. Juvonen & K. R. Wentzel (Eds.), *Social motivation: Understanding children's school adjustment* (pp. 279–312). New York, NY: Cambridge University Press.

Kingery, J. N., & Erdley, C. A. (2007). Peer experiences as predictors of adjustment across the middle school transition. *Education and Treatment of Children, 30*(2), 73–88.

Kirkpatrick-Johnson, M., Crosnoe, R., & Elder, G. H. (2001). Students' attachment and academic engagement: The role of race and ethnicity. *Sociology of Education, 74,* 318–340.

Ladd, G. W., Herald-Brown, S. L., & Kochel, K. P. (2009). Peers and motivation. In K. R. Wentzel & A. Wigfield (Eds.), *Handbook of motivation at school* (pp. 323–348). New York, NY: Taylor & Francis.

Lempers, J. D., & Clark-Lempers, D. S. (1992). Young, middle, and late adolescents' comparisons of the functional importance of five significant relationships. *Journal of Youth and Adolescence, 21,* 53–96.

Levitt, M. J., Levitt, J., Bustos, G. L., Crooks, N. A., Santos, J. D., Telan, P., Hodgetts, J., & Milevsky, A. (2005). Patterns of social support in the middle childhood to early adolescent transition: Implications for adjustment. *Social Development, 14,* 398–420.

Maehr, M. L., & Midgley, C. (1991). Enhancing motivation: A schoolwide approach. *Educational Psychologist, 26,* 399–427.

Matyanowski, M. L. (2001). Adolescent peer group memberships, peer group characteristics, and self-concept. *Dissertation Abstracts International, 62*(1-B), 577.

Nansel, T. R., Overpeck, M., Pilla, R. S., Ruan, J., Simons-Morton, B., & Scheidt, P. (2001). Bullying behaviors among U.S. youth: Prevalence and association with psychosocial adjustment. *Journal of the American Medical Association*, 2094–2100.

Newcomb, A. F., & Bagwell, C. L. (1995). Children's friendship relations: A meta-analytic review. *Psychological Bulletin, 117*, 306–347.

Newcomb, A. F., Bukowski, W. M., & Pattee, L. (1993). Children's peer relations: A metaanalytic review of popular, rejected, neglected, and controversial socio-metric status. *Psychological Bulletin, 113*, 99–128.

Newman, R. S. (2000). Social influences on the development of children's adaptive hold seeking: The role of parents, teachers, and peers. *Developmental Review, 20*, 350–404.

Newman, B. M., Lohman, B. J., Newman, P. R., Myers, M. C., & Smith, V. L. (2000). Experiences of Urban Youth Navigating the Transition to Ninth Grade. *Youth & Society, 31*, 387–416.

Olweus, D. (1993). Victimization by peers: Antecedents and long-term outcomes. In K. Rubin & J. B. Asendorf (Eds.), *Social withdrawal, inhibition, and shyness in childhood* (pp. 315–341). Chicago, IL: University of Chicago Press.

Parker, J. G., & Asher, S. R. (1987). Peer relations and later personal adjustment: Are low-accepted children at risk? *Psychological Bulletin, 102*, 357–389.

Parker, J. G., & Asher, S. R. (1993). Friendship and friendship quality in middle childhood: Links with peer group acceptance and feelings of loneliness and social dissatisfaction. *Developmental Psychology, 29*, 611–621.

Paul, E. L., & Brier, S. (2001). Friendsickness in the transition to college: Precollege predictors and college adjustment correlates. *Journal of Counseling & Development, 79*, 77–89.

Pellegrini, A. D., Bartini, M., & Brooks, F. (1999). School bullies, victims, and aggressive victims: Factors relating to group affiliation and victimization in early adolescence. *Journal of Educational Psychology, 91*, 216–224.

Phelan, P., Davidson, A. L., & Cao, H. T. (1991). Students' multiple worlds: Negotiating the boundaries of family, peer, and school cultures. *Anthropology and Education Quarterly, 22*, 224–250.

Ryan, A. (2001). The peer group as a context for the development of young adolescent motivation and achievement. *Child Development, 72*, 1135–1150.

Ryan, A., & Shim, S. (2008). An exploration of young adolescents' social achievement goals and social adjustment in middle school. *Journal of Educational Psychology, 100*, 672–687.

Ryan, R. M., & Deci, E. L. (2000). Self-determination theory and the facilitation of intrinsic motivation, social development, and well-being. *American Psychologist, 55*, 68–78.

Salmivalli, C., Ojanen, T., Haanpaa, J., & Peets, K. (2005). "I'm ok but you're not" and other peer-relational schemas: Explaining individual differences in social goals. *Developmental Psychology, 41*, 363–375.

Sarason, B. R., Sarason, I. G., & Pierce, G. R. (1990). Traditional views of social support and their impact on assessment. In B. R. Sarason, I. G. Sarason, & G. R. Sarason (Eds.), *Social support: An interactional view* (pp. 9–25). New York, NY: Wiley.

Schaps, E., Battistich, V., & Solomon, D. (2004). Community in school as key to student growth: Findings from the Child Development Project. In J. Zins, R.

Weissberg, M. Wang, & H. Walberg (Eds.), *Building academic success on social and emotional learning: What does the research say?* (pp. 189–205). New York, NY: Teachers College Press.

Schunk, D., & Pajares, F. (2009). Self-efficacy theory. In K. R.Wentzel & A. Wigfield (Eds.), *Handbook of motivation at school* (pp. 35–54). New York, NY: Taylor & Francis.

Schwartz, D., Dodge, K. A., Pettit, G. S., Bates, J. E., & The Conduct Problems Prevention Research Group. (2000). Friendship as a moderating factor in the pathway between early harsh home environment and later victimization in the peer group. *Developmental Psychology, 36,* 646–662.

Schwartz, D., Gorman, A.H., Nakamoto, J., & McKay, T. (2006). Popularity, social acceptance, and aggression in adolescent peer groups: Links with academic performance and school attendance. *Developmental Psychology, 42,* 1116–1127.

Smalls, C., White, R., Chavous, T., & Sellers, R. (2007). Racial ideological beliefs and racial discrimination experiences as predictors of academic engagement among African American adolescents. *Journal of Black Psychology, 33,* 299–330.

Smetana, J., & Bitz, B. (1996). Adolescents' conceptions of teachers' authority and their relations to rule violations in school. *Child Development, 67,* 1153–1172.

Spera, C., Wentzel, K. R., & Motto, H. (2009). Parental educational aspirations for their children: Relations to ethnicity, parent education, child GPA, and school climate. *Journal of Youth and Adolescence, 38,* 1140–1152.

Steele, C. & Aronson, J. (1995). Stereotype threat and the intellectual performance of African Americans. *Journal of Personality and Social Psychology, 69,* 797–811.

Stormshack, E., Bierman, K., Bruschi, C., Dodge, K., & Coie, J. (1999). The relation between behavior problems and peer preference in different classroom contexts. *Child Development, 70,* 169–182.

Taylor, A. Z., & Graham S. (2007). An examination of the relationship between achievement values and perceptions of barriers among low-SES African American and Latino students. *Journal of Educational Psychology, 99,* 52–64.

Tomada, G., Schneider, B. H., de Domini, P., Greenman, P. S., & Fonzi, A. (2005). Friendship as a predictor of adjustment following a transition to formal academic instruction and evaluation. *International Journal of Behavioral Development, 29,* 314–322.

Urberg, K., Degirmencioglu, S., Tolson, J., & Halliday-Scher, K. (1995). The structure of adolescent peer networks. *Developmental Psychology, 31,* 540–547.

Wentzel, K. R. (1991). Relations between social competence and academic achievement in early adolescence. *Child Development, 62,* 1066–1078.

Wentzel, K. R. (1994). Relations of social goal pursuit to social acceptance, classroom behavior, and perceived social support. *Journal of Educational Psychology, 86,* 173–182.

Wentzel, K. R. (1996). Social goals and social relationships as motivators of school adjustment. In J. Juvonen & K. R. Wentzel (Eds.), *Social motivation: Understanding children's school adjustment* (pp. 226–247). New York, NY: Cambridge University Press.

Wentzel, K. R. (1997). Student motivation in middle school: The role of perceived pedagogical caring. *Journal of Educational Psychology, 89,* 411–419.

Wentzel, K. R. (2002). The contribution of social goal setting to children's school adjustment . In A. Wigfield & J. Eccles (Eds.), *Development of achievement motivation* (pp. 221–246). New York, NY: Academic Press.

Wentzel, K. R. (2003). Sociometric status and academic adjustment in middle school: A longitudinal study. *Journal of Early Adolescence, 23,* 5–28.

Wentzel, K. R. (2004). Understanding classroom competence: The role of social-motivational and self-processes. In R. Kail (Ed.), *Advances in child development and behavior* (Vol. 32, pp. 213–241). New York, NY: Elsevier.

Wentzel, K. R. (2005). Peer relationships, motivation, and academic performance at school. In A. Elliot & C. Dweck (Eds.), *Handbook of competence and motivation* (pp. 279–296). New York, NY: Guilford.

Wentzel, K. R., & Asher, S. R. (1995). Academic lives of neglected, rejected, popular, and controversial children. *Child Development, 66,* 754–763.

Wentzel, K. R., Barry, C., & Caldwell, K. (2004). Friendships in middle school: Influences on motivation and school adjustment. *Journal of Educational Psychology, 96,* 195–203.

Wentzel, K. R., Battle, A., Russell, S., & Looney, L. (in press). Teacher and peer contributions to classroom climate in middle school. *Contemporary Educational Psychology, 35,* 193–202.

Wentzel, K. R., & Caldwell, K. (1997). Friendships, peer acceptance, and group membership: Relations to academic achievement in middle school. *Child Development, 68,* 1198–1209.

Wentzel, K. R., Donlan, A., Morrison, D., Russell, S., & Baker, S. (2009, April). *Adolescent non-compliance: A social ecological perspective.* Poster presented at the Society for Research on Child Development, Denver, CO.

Wentzel, K. R., Filisetti, L., & Looney, L. (2007). Adolescent prosocial behavior: The role of self-processes and contextual cues. *Child Development, 78,* 895–910.

Wentzel, K. R., & McNamara, C. (1999). Interpersonal relationships, emotional distress, and prosocial behavior in middle school. *Journal of Early Adolescence, 19,* 114–125.

Wentzel, K. R., Monzo, J., Williams, A. Y., & Tomback, R. M. (2007, April). *Teacher and peer influence on academic motivation in adolescence: A cross-sectional study.* Paper presented at the biennial meeting of the Society for Research in Child Development, Boston, MA.

Wentzel, K. R., Russell, S., & Baker, S. (2008, April). *Social supports, social goal pursuit, and behavioral engagement of Hispanic adolescents.* Poster presented at the annual meeting of the American Educational Research Association, New York, NY.

Wentzel, K. R., & Watkins, D. E. (2002). Peer relationships and collaborative learning as contexts for academic enablers. *School Psychology Review, 31,* 366–377.

Wentzel, K. R., & Watkins, D. E. (2011). Peer relationships and learning: Implications for instruction. In R. Mayer and P. Alexander (Eds.), *Handbook of research on learning and instruction* (pp. 322–343). New York, NY: Routledge.

Wentzel, K. R., Weinberger, D. A., Ford, M. E., & Feldman, S. S. (1990). Academic achievement in preadolescence: The role of motivational, affective, and self-regulatory processes. *Journal of Applied Developmental Psychology, 11,* 179–193.

Wentzel, K. R., & Wigfield, A. (2009). *Handbook of motivation at school.* New York, NY: Taylor & Francis.

Wentzel. K. R., Williams, A., & Tomback, R. (2006, April). *Teacher and peer support as predictors of academic performance and classroom behavior: A longitudinal study.* Poster presented at the annual meeting of the American Educational Research Association, San Francisco, CA.

Wong, C. A., Eccles, J. S., & Sameroff, A. (2003). The influence of ethnic discrimination and ethnic identification on African American adolescents' school and socioemotional adjustment. *Journal of Personality, 71,* 1197–1232.

CHAPTER 5

CHILDREN'S ACHIEVEMENT-RELATED DISCOURSE WITH PEERS

Uncovering the Processes of Peer Influence

Ellen Rydell Altermatt
Hanover College

There is substantial evidence that peers play an important role in children's school adjustment. Positive school adjustment has been linked to being well accepted by one's peers (e.g., Ladd, 1990; Ladd, Herald-Brown, & Reiser, 2008; Ladd, Kochenderfer, & Coleman, 1997; Vandell & Hembree, 1994), having one or more close friends (e.g., Diehl, Lemerise, Caverly, Ramsay, & Roberts, 1998; Ladd, 1990; Ladd et al., 1997; Wentzel, Barry, & Caldwell, 2004; Wentzel & Caldwell, 1997), having friendships marked by high levels of positive qualities (e.g., validation, aid) and relatively low levels of negative qualities (e.g., conflict) (e.g., Berndt, Hawkins, & Jiao, 1999; Berndt & Keefe, 1995; Ladd, Kochenderfer, & Coleman, 1996), and belonging to

Peer Relationships and Adjustment at School, pages 109–134
Copyright © 2012 by Information Age Publishing
All rights of reproduction in any form reserved.

109

peer groups or participating in friendships with children who are, themselves, academically well-adjusted (e.g., Altermatt & Pomerantz, 2003; Berndt & Keefe, 1995; Kindermann, 2007; Ryan, 2001; but see Altermatt & Pomerantz, 2005).

Together, these studies provide ample evidence that peers *do* influence children's school adjustment, but *how* they do so is less well understood (Brown, Bakken, Ameringer, & Mahon, 2008; Guryan, Jacob, Klopfer, & Groff, 2008). Various mechanisms have been proposed in the extant literature, including modeling, reinforcement, information exchange, expectancy socialization, and the provision of informational and emotional support (see Altermatt & Kenney-Benson, 2006; Berndt, 1999; Berndt & Murphy, 2002; Rubin, Bukowski, & Parker, 2006; Ryan, 2000; Wentzel, 1999, 2005, 2009, for reviews). For example, it has been suggested that children with academically well-adjusted friends become more academically well-adjusted themselves over time because they model the behaviors of friends, and friends provide reinforcement for positive school attitudes and behaviors (e.g., Altermatt & Pomerantz, 2003; Ryan, 2001). Likewise, it has been suggested that children who have friends or who are well-liked by their classmates exhibit more positive school adjustment than children who do not have friends or who are less well-liked because they are less likely to have social and/or academic reputations that cause them to be excluded, ignored, or ridiculed, and, in turn, have more opportunities to receive advice and support from peers when faced with academic challenges (e.g., Ladd, 1990; Ladd et al., 1997). Surprisingly, however, very little research has examined these processes directly. Much work remains to be done to document the everyday interactions children have with peers in achievement contexts and to empirically link these interactions to changes in children's school adjustment over time.

The current chapter reviews research that has begun to uncover the processes of peer influence on children's school adjustment, focusing on research that has examined children's achievement-related discourse with peers. I argue that careful attention to this discourse can provide critical insights into many of the proposed mechanisms by which peers influence children's school adjustment—in ways that complement and extend other methods for examining peer influence processes. Methodological problems that have contributed to the dearth of research on children's achievement-related discourse with peers as a window onto the mechanisms by which peers may influence children's school adjustment are described, and directions for future inquiry are suggested.

The term *school adjustment* has been used quite broadly in the extent literature (see Berndt & Keefe, 1996; Birch & Ladd, 1996; Wentzel, 2003). The current chapter focuses on peers' influence on three aspects of school adjustment: achievement-related beliefs (e.g., school liking, perceptions of academic competence), classroom behaviors (e.g., persistence on school-work; disruptiveness), and the performance outcomes that these often predict (e.g., academic achievement as assessed by report card cards). Indicators of children's relationships with peers (e.g., sociometric status, friendship quality) are viewed as correlates of school adjustment rather than as markers of school adjustment.

APPROACHES TO STUDYING PROCESSES OF PEER INFLUENCE

Despite calls for investigators to supplement research examining *whether* peers are influential with research examining *how* peers exert their influence, empirical studies examining the processes of peer influence on children's school adjustment remain scarce (see Guryan et al., 2008). However, a number of different approaches have begun to emerge in the extant literature.

One approach to studying the processes of peer influence involves examining proposed mechanisms of influence (e.g., reinforcement or the provision of emotional support) *at a macro level* and empirically linking these processes to children's school adjustment. Studies on children's general perceptions of peer pressure often fall within this tradition. For example, drawing on work by Berndt (1979) and Clasen and Brown (1985) and supporting the notion that reinforcement of peer group norms and values is an important mechanism of peer influence, Sim and Koh (2003) found that children who believe that their peers are supportive of positive school involvement report a greater desire to earn good grades in school. Research on children's general perceptions of social support from peers also falls within this tradition. For example, based on her finding that students who believe that their peers care about their feelings and their learning report greater engagement in prosocial activities in the classroom context (e.g., helping a peer who is experiencing academic difficulty) than students who view their peers as less supportive, Wentzel (1998) suggests that emotional support is an important mechanism of influence (see also Dubow & Tisak, 1989; Hirsch & DuBois, 1992; Ladd et al., 1996; Wentzel, 1998).

Several recent studies have begun to unpack these associations by examining more specific aspects of children's experiences with peers. Often, these studies have tested models that include peer variables (e.g., children's levels of peer acceptance), school adjustment variables (e.g., children's school engagement), and variables that are proposed to mediate the relationship between peer and school adjustment variables. A recent study by Buhs, Ladd, and Herald (2006) provides a particularly compelling example of this type of research. Here, the authors sought to better understand why children who are rejected by their peers experience declines in academic achievement over time. In a six-year longitudinal study, these authors found support for a model wherein peer rejection in kindergarten predicted chronic peer exclusion (e.g., consistently being ignored or avoided by peers). Chronic peer exclusion, in turn, predicted reductions in classroom participation and, ultimately, declines in achievement as children approached the transition to middle school (see also Ladd et al., 2008). These findings are consistent with the notion that children may develop social and academic reputations among their peers that influence the types of interactions in which they engage (e.g., rejected children may begin to avoid classroom activities in which they are likely to be excluded) and, ultimately, their ability to succeed academically.

Both of these approaches are important in beginning the work of uncovering the processes of peer influence. At the same time, these approaches often leave unanswered questions about the precise nature of children's everyday interactions with peers in achievement contexts and their consequences for children's school adjustment. For example: How (and how often) do children express a desire to be involved in the classroom? How (and how often) do children express care and concern for classmates? How (and how often) do children express a desire to exclude peers in classroom settings? What evidence do we have that children model and support these expressed attitudes and behaviors (e.g., by repeating them or expressing agreement) or reject them (e.g., by teasing or expressing disagreement)? How do children respond to specific instances of peer support or peer exclusion, and do responses change over time? Can these specific interactions predict immediate or day-to-day changes in children's school attitudes, behaviors, or outcomes?

These types of questions suggest the need for another, complementary approach to the study of the processes of peer influence. Specifically, more research is needed to closely examine the *micro-interactions* that children engage in with peers in achievement-related settings and, more importantly, to link these micro-interactions to changes in children's school adjustment over time (Berndt & Murphy, 2002; Ladd, 2009). This type of research is difficult insofar as it often necessitates direct observations of children's interactions with peers—either in naturalistic or laboratory settings—but is critical to the extent that it can help to uncover the mechanisms by which everyday interactions may contribute to short-term changes in children's achievement-related beliefs and behaviors, which, presumably, accumulate to produce stable, long-term changes in school adjustment (Pomerantz, Ruble, & Bolger, 2004).[1] Studies that take a micro-analytic approach to the study of peer influence processes—including our own and others' work on children's achievement-related discourse—are the focus of the remainder of this chapter.

Given that this research is still in its infancy, I begin by briefly describing research that demonstrates that careful examination of children's discourse with peers has been important in understanding mechanisms of peer influence in other domains. Specifically, I describe research that has examined children's discourse with peers to better understand the processes by which peers influence children's experiences with externalizing and internalizing symptoms (see Bukowski, Brendgen, & Vitaro, 2007, for a review). I then discuss research that has examined children's discourse with peers in achievement contexts, focusing on how these studies can provide important insights into several of the proposed mechanisms of influence including modeling, expectancy socialization, and the provision of informational and emotional support.

PEER DISCOURSE AND EXTERNALIZING SYMPTOMS

One focus of peer influence research has been to examine whether and how peers might contribute to the development of externalizing behaviors in children and adolescents. *That* peers are influential is clear. For example, there is ample evidence that children who associate with peers who engage in externalizing behaviors—including substance use and violence—engage in more of these same behaviors themselves over time (Engels, Knibbe, DeVries, Drop, & van Breukelen, 1999; Hawkins, Catalano, & Miller, 1992; Snyder et al., 2005). Although modeling and reinforcement have been suggested as key mechanisms by which peer affiliation and these problem behaviors are linked, rarely have these processes been examined in actual interactions among peers (Bukowksi et al., 2007; Dishion & Dodge, 2006).

Dishion and his colleagues have begun to fill this gap in the literature by carefully observing the specific social interactions in which delinquent youth and their peers engage. Results suggest that delinquent friendship dyads engage in more deviant talk (e.g., conversations about engaging in illegal acts) than non-delinquent dyads, that delinquent dyads respond more positively to one another in response to deviant talk (e.g., by laughing), and that the duration of deviant talk (together with other indicators of deviant friendship processes, including time spent with deviant friends) predicts adjustment problems including substance abuse and violent behavior (Piehler & Dishion, 2007; see Dishion, McCord, & Poulin, 1999, and Granic & Dishion, 2003, for reviews). Subsequent work employing a dynamic systems framework indicates that children who exhibit high levels of problem behaviors often become "stuck" in patterns of deviant talk (i.e., they find themselves engaged in deviant talk for increasingly longer durations) and that children who are increasingly drawn to deviant talk may be particularly vulnerable to long-term behavioral problems (Dishion, Piehler, & Myers, 2009; Granic & Dishion, 2003).

Together, these results confirm that peers can be powerful socializers of problem behaviors in children and adolescents. Moreover, they suggest that careful attention to the ways in which the conversations of deviant youths differ from those of their normative counterparts can provide insights into the processes of peer influence and, ultimately, into the development of effective interventions. For example, interventions designed to assist deviant youth in regulating negative emotions (e.g., anger) may also be beneficial in helping these youths avoid becoming "absorbed" in deviant talk.

PEER DISCOURSE AND INTERNALIZING SYMPTOMS

Another focus of peer influence research has been to examine whether and how peers might contribute to children's psychological well-being, particularly to internalizing symptoms such as loneliness, depression, or anxiety. Again, there is clear evidence *that* peers are influential. For example, a wealth of research indicates that children who have at least one stable friendship (with a well-adjusted peer) are less likely to report feelings of depression and loneliness than children who are friendless (Bagwell, Newcomb, & Bukowski, 1998: Bukowski et al., 2007; Pedersen, Vitaro, Barker, & Borge, 2007).

Several mechanisms have been suggested to explain these linkages. First, friendships may offer children a "stable base" from which they can explore and develop self-confidence in new domains (Birch & Ladd, 1996). Second, close friends may help children better cope with stressors by providing a forum for self-disclosure and both emotional and instrumental support (Bukowski et al., 2007; Klima & Repetti, 2008). Third, children with friends may be more likely than children without friends to enjoy protection from the negative consequences of peer harassment (Hodges, Boivin, Vitaro, & Bukowski, 1999).

Again, however, the specific social interactions that contribute to better adjustment among "friended" children have received very little attention (see Vitaro, Boivin, & Bukowski, 2009, for a review). This lack of attention is especially problematic given that one of the hypothesized mechanisms of influence (i.e., the provision of emotional support) has received, at best, mixed support in the extant literature. In particular, the hypothesis that interactions between friends will be more supportive than interactions between non-friends has not always been supported, especially in studies employing observational (rather than survey-based) methodologies (Berndt, Perry, & Miller, 1988; Newcomb & Brady, 1982; see Newcomb & Bagwell, 1995, for a review).[2] Similarly, there is increasing evidence that seeking and receiving emotional support is not always associated with positive outcomes and, at high levels, may actually be associated with negative outcomes (e.g., Altermatt, 2007; Causey & Dubow, 1992; Harlow & Cantor, 1994: Rose, 2002).

The lack of clear associations between emotional support and adjustment has led several researchers to call for research examining how *specific* interpersonal exchanges in *specific* contexts may contribute to *specific* indices of adjustment (see Coyne & DeLongis, 1986; Heller, Swindle, & Dusenbury, 1986; Rook, 1987). Research in this area is still relatively new, but it has yielded interesting findings about the nature and consequences of friendship support. For example, Denton and Zarbatany (1996) examined the conversations of pre-adolescent, adolescent, and adult friends after one friend disclosed a negative event (e.g., conflict with a friend or relative). Results indicated that pre-adolescents' friends frequently used distraction during the conversations and that distraction led pre-adolescents to feel better about the negative event post-discussion. Interestingly, distraction was not effective in reducing the negative affect of adolescents or adults. The authors hypothesize that distraction may be effective among pre-adolescents because it is a technique that is easily understood and implemented by pre-adolescents. It gives disclosers a chance to regain composure, and friends—who may be just learning effective social support skills—a chance to generate alternative, more sophisticated support strategies. By adulthood, distraction may communicate a lack of concern or effort and, therefore, be insufficient to reduce negative affect. Instead, adults may rely on friends to help them co-construct a reality in which they are not responsible for the negative event. Indeed, the only support strategy that reduced negative affect among adults was excuse-validation (excuse-validation was not effective among adolescents, perhaps because they frequently missed opportunities to validate excuses). Interestingly, responses that included the provision of emotional support (e.g., "I know how you feel") occurred relatively infrequently and were not predictive of changes in negative affect in any of the age groups.

The importance of examining these processes in the actual conversations of friends should not be underestimated. Although distraction and excuse-validation have rarely been identified in self-report studies of social support (in which children and adults are asked to report on their memories or expectations of friends' social support strategies), the results of this study suggest that they are both prevalent in the everyday conversations of friends and predictive of individuals' ability to reduce the negative affect associated with negative events.

PEER DISCOURSE AND SCHOOL ADJUSTMENT

Despite its potential to provide a window onto the processes by which peers contribute to changes in children's school attitudes and behaviors, research on children's conversations with peers in achievement contexts is quite scarce. Here, I review the limited research that has examined children's discourse with peers to better understand modeling, expectancy socialization, and informational and emotional support as potentially important mechanisms of influence. Next, I discuss reasons for the dearth of studies in this area and suggest directions for future inquiry.

Modeling

Modeling has been identified as a potentially important mechanism of peer influence in the achievement context in a number of prior reviews of the literature (see Brown et al., 2008; Hartup, 2009; Ryan, 2001). In the current review, modeling is broadly defined to include the processes by which children adopt, via observation of peer models, both specific (e.g., How long must I persist on this problem?) and more general (e.g., How important is it to do well in school?) achievement-related attitudes and behaviors. Although there is considerable evidence to suggest that children and adolescents can improve their academic performance by engaging in peer tutoring and cooperative learning (e.g., Azmitia, 1988; Bargh & Schul, 1980; Shachar & Sharan, 1994), the processes by which modeling might contribute to children's acquisition of specific academic skills (e.g., the ability to solve fractions) is beyond the scope of this chapter.

Early support for the importance of modeling as a mechanism of peer influence derives from a set of experimental studies assessing the degree to which children self-reward on an experimental task after observing the self-reinforcing behavior of a peer. These studies generally indicate that children who observe a peer model imposing strict standards for reward subsequently apply stringent criteria for reinforcing their own performance (e.g., Bandura, 1971; Masters & Mokros, 1974). Consistent with this trend, Lepper, Sagotsky, and Mailer (1975) found that when children observed a peer model verbalize high standards for reward (e.g., "That's an OK score, but it's not good enough to deserve a penny"), they adopted these same high standards for themselves. Sagotsky and Lepper (1982) extended this work to peer model influences on children's choice of difficult versus easy tasks and, furthermore, demonstrated that these effects are both relatively persistent and generalizable. Children who were exposed to a peer model who demonstrated a preference for challenge on physical tasks also oriented toward more difficult physical tasks. These same children showed a preference for difficult academic tasks in the classroom setting three weeks later.

Though this literature provides clear evidence that children's task-specific behaviors (e.g., criteria for self-reward) are influenced via peer modeling, much additional work is needed to determine the degree to which children and adolescents rely on peer models to form more general orientations toward school (e.g., attitudes about the extent to which education should be valued). A handful of studies examining children's discourse with peers have yielded promising findings. In one study, Berndt, Laychak, and Park (1990) presented eighth-grade students with achievement dilemmas in which they had to make a decision that reflected either a high level of achievement motivation or a low level of achievement motivation. High-achievement alternatives were designed to characterize students who placed a high priority on school-related activities and who were interested in their schoolwork (e.g., studying for an examination rather than going to a rock concert). Low-achievement alternatives reflected a devaluing of school and a desire to avoid challenge. Students made a decision alone and, then, after discussing the dilemma with a close friend. As predicted, adolescents came to make decisions that reflected high levels of achievement motivation when friends supported these decisions in their conversations.

Similar evidence for modeling as an important mechanism of evidence comes from our own work. In a laboratory-based study, we examined the types of conversations fourth through sixth grade focal children had with friends after focal children experienced difficulty completing a series of geometric puzzles (Altermatt & Broady, 2009). Our results indicated that when friends made negative task statements ("Those puzzles were stupid"), focal children responded to the failure in more learned helpless ways (e.g., they were less interested in attempting the puzzles a second time). Sequential analyses were used to better understand this phenomenon by examining what happened *after* friends made these statements. Results indicated that focal children responded by modeling (i.e., repeating) these statements more often than expected by chance.

Together, these results suggest that modeling may, indeed, play an important role in explaining why children and their friends come to adopt similar achievement-related beliefs and behaviors over time. Additional research is needed, however. For example, although our own work suggests that children demonstrate increasingly negative responses to failure when children's friends make disparaging comments about the task at hand *because* children model friends' statements, a more compelling case for the importance of modeling requires additional evidence. Specifically, research is needed to demonstrate that children who model task-negative statements are more likely than children who do not model these statements (and, instead, ignore them or evaluate the task positively) to develop learned helpless responses to failure.

Expectancy Socialization

Expectancy socialization may also be an important mechanism of peer influence. In the current review, expectancy socialization is defined to include the processes by which others' perceptions (e.g., regarding the child's likely academic success) shape the child's own expectations and, ultimately, their behavior. Most often, expectancy socialization has been demonstrated by showing predictive relationships between the perceptions of a given socializing agent (usually parents and teachers) and the child's own perceptions. This literature provides clear evidence that others' perceptions can have a powerful impact on children's achievement-related beliefs and behaviors. For example, Frome and Eccles (1998) found that parents' perceptions of children's academic competence predicted children's own perceptions of competence and had a stronger effect on children's competence perceptions than children's grades (see Pomerantz, Grolnick, & Price, 2005, for a review). Less attention has been paid to the ways in which expectancy messages are communicated. One possibility is that socializing agents communicate their expectations directly. Alternatively, communication may be primarily indirect, perhaps included quite subtly as part of the way in which praise, criticism, and help are administered (e.g., Eccles Parsons, Adler, & Kaczala, 1982; Graham & Barker, 1990; Hokoda & Fincham, 1995; Jodl, Michael, Malanchuk, Eccles, & Sameroff, 2001; Jussim, 1986).

Although most work on expectancy socialization has focused on parents and teachers as the key agents of socialization, a growing literature on peer reputations suggests that similar processes may be at work in peer groups. Most of this work has focused on children's *social* reputations with peers and suggests that these reputations can be important predictors of long-term outcomes. For example, Gest, Sesma, Masten, and Tellegen (2006) found that children who had a reputation for popularity/leadership experienced greater social successes and reported greater romantic competence ten years later than children who did not have this reputation. Questions regarding whether children develop *academic* reputations among their peers and the extent to which these reputations are predictive of changes in achievement-related outcomes have received less attention, but recent work by Gest and his colleagues (Gest, Domitrovich, & Welsh, 2005; Gest, Rulison, Davidson, & Welsh, 2008) has yielded promising results. For example, Gest et al. (2008) found that children's positive and negative academic peer reputations (e.g., for being a good or poor reader) predicted changes in children's academic self-concept, teacher-rated effort, and report card grades over time, even after controlling for teacher ratings of children's academic skills.

The specific social interactions that lead to the formation of peer reputations in academic contexts have yet to be uncovered. One possibility is that children pick up on the expectancy cues used by parents and teachers (e.g., verbal comparisons, differential praise) and use these to form their own beliefs and modify their behaviors toward their peers accordingly (e.g., Ames & Ames, 1984; Schwartz, 1981). These behaviors, in turn, may lead the targeted child to respond in ways that perpetuate the perceptions of their peers. Another possibility is that students are more directly attuned to the achievement-related behaviors of their classmates. Indeed, there is reason to believe that peers may have some *unique* insights into peers' achievement-related behaviors because of their close vantage point for observing peer behaviors and that these insights might influence children's day-to-day interactions with peers (Gest et al., 2008). Consistent with this viewpoint, research by Weiner (1980) suggests that college students feel less sympathy toward and report being less willing to lend their notes to a classmate who is perceived to be responsible for missing class than to a peer who is deemed to have missed class due to reasons beyond his or her control. Juvonen and Nishina (1997) suggest that similar processes may be at work in junior high school classrooms. Requests for help from students who are perceived by their peers as academically motivated may be met by elaborated information regarding the method by which a correct solution can be reached. Students who are perceived as lazy and unmotivated may, in contrast, be provided only with the correct answer.

Very little attention has been paid to children's actual classroom interactions to determine how (and how often) expectancy messages are communicated and whether these messages contribute to long-term academic peer reputations. However, some of our own findings suggest that this may be a fruitful area of inquiry. For example, in Altermatt, Pomerantz, Ruble, Frey, and Greulich (2002), we report the results of an observational study in which we attempted to predict changes over time in elementary school children's perceptions of academic competence from the types of verbal interactions in which they and their peers engaged in the naturalistic setting of the classroom. Based on some preliminary analyses, we anticipated that children who made statements in which they evaluated themselves positively (e.g., "My picture is the best!") would report more positive competence perceptions over time, but *only* if peers responded in a way that communicated (implicitly or explicitly) that they agreed with children's positive self-assessments. Consistent with this prediction, we found that children who were permitted opportunities to follow one positive self-evaluation with another or who had a classmate respond with a statement in which the classmate evaluated himself or herself negatively and the focal child positively (e.g., "Yeah. Yours is good. I can't draw") reported significantly higher self-perceptions of competence, controlling for earlier competence perceptions, than children whose positive self-evaluations were not affirmed.

Although these findings suggest that peers may communicate their expectations via the types of praise they give (and the types of self-praise they allow children to engage in), much additional work is needed. A promising area of inquiry will be to link children's academic peer reputations to particular social interactions (see Gest et al., 2008). Do children with positive peer reputations differ from those with negative peer reputations in the types of praise they are given or in the types of help they receive? Are these children more likely to be sought out for academic assistance? Research that can empirically demonstrate that these everyday interactions predict changes in children's academic peer reputations over time will be especially valuable.

Informational and Emotional Support

A final way in which peers have been theorized to influence children's achievement-related behaviors and beliefs is by providing social support. Two types of support are generally discussed. First, peers may offer informational support, serving as a resource that children can tap when they experience academic difficulties and find themselves in need of assistance. Second, peers may offer emotional support, bolstering students' self-esteem and reducing feelings of emotional distress that come with academic challenges (see Berndt, 1999; Ladd, 1990; Ladd et al., 1997; Wentzel, 1998; Wentzel & Caldwell, 1997; Wentzel et al., 2004). Both types of support have generally been viewed as a positive function of children's friendships. However, as noted earlier, there is increasing evidence—including evidence derived from our own research examining children's achievement-related discourse with peers—that the consequences of seeking (and receiving) social support can sometimes be negative.

One reason why seeking social support from peers may lead to negative outcomes is simply that children do not always receive the social support they need or desire. Our observations of children's everyday interactions in classroom settings support this notion. For example, in Altermatt et al. (2002), we reported sex differences in the consequences of seeking and receiving help from peers. Girls who frequently sought help from classmates experienced gains in their academic competence perceptions over time. In contrast, seeking help did not significantly predict changes in boys' perceptions of competence. To explore this finding further, we used sequential analyses to examine what happened after children asked for assistance. The results suggested that help-seeking was more efficacious for girls than for boys. For example, girls were significantly more likely than boys to receive help when they requested it. In contrast, boys were significantly more likely than girls to have classmates respond to requests for help by evaluating themselves negatively (e.g., "I don't know what I'm doing"). Future work will be important in examining why girls are more likely than boys to secure effective assistance from classmates. On the one hand, boys may be asking for help from other boys who, as a group, are typically more competitive and less cooperative in their communication styles than are girls (see Leaper, 1991; Leaper, Tenenbaum, & Shaffer, 1999; Maccoby, 1990). On the other hand, it is possible that boys are equally likely to select male and female classmates as potential helpers, but are either less successful at or less concerned about selecting a classmate who can provide reasonable assistance. Boys may, for example, make their choices based on factors other than achievement level, including the proximity of the classmate, whether the classmate is a friend, or how well-liked the classmate is in general. Alternatively, boys may actually purposely choose to ask for help from classmates whom they deem to be academically inferior to themselves. Such choices would be consistent with the suggestion made by Maccoby (1995) that boys are motivated to conceal their shortcomings, particularly from other boys.

A second reason why social support may not predict positive outcomes is that it may lead children to focus excessively on the source of their distress (or simply be a marker that they *are* focused excessively on the source of their distress). This hypothesis has found some support in research on college students' responses to academic difficulties. For example, Harlow and Cantor (1994) found that college women who frequently sought reassurance from friends when they encountered academic problems reported lower social satisfaction than those who sought reassurance relatively infrequently. Results from our own research (Altermatt, 2007) suggest that a similar phenomenon may occur among school-aged children and adolescents. Here, we asked children to report on the nature of their interactions with friends following everyday academic challenges. Children also reported on their levels of academic worry at two time points, six months apart. On the surface, girls' interactions appeared more positive than those of boys. Specifically, girls were more likely than boys to report sharing academic failure experiences with friends, doing so for the purposes of receiving emotional support, and receiving the emotional support they desired. However, girls also reported significantly higher levels of academic worry than boys at both time points. One reason for these apparently inconsistent findings is that the types of interactions that girls are engaged in are not as positive as they might appear. Indeed, we found that children—regardless of gender— who frequently shared failures for the purposes of gaining emotional support reported higher—not lower—levels of worry over time. One reason is that high levels of sharing reflect a continued preoccupation with the failure experience and concern with how one's friends might evaluate oneself in light of the failure. These findings are consistent with those reported by Rose and her colleagues in their research on co-rumination. Rose (2002) defined co-rumination as an extreme form of self-disclosure in which personal problems are discussed excessively. Co-rumination is associated with some positive outcomes. Specifically, children who engage in high levels of co-rumination also report that their friendships are characterized by high friendship quality and closeness. However, co-rumination also has its costs: Co-ruminators report higher levels of anxiety and depression over time.

Together, these results suggest that simple, straightforward relationships between informational and emotional support seeking and school adjustment are unlikely to be found. Instead, the consequences of these interactions are likely to depend on a number of factors—including the gender of the participants, their relative levels of achievement, the goals children have for seeking social support, the responses of friends, and children's willingness to incorporate information gleaned from help-seeking into their problem-solving (see Kempler & Linnenbrink, 2006, for a review). To examine these factors, a combination of methods must be used—including studies that carefully observe the actual conversations that children have with peers, especially in naturalistic settings. To date, this research is quite limited.

CHALLENGES AND DIRECTIONS FOR FUTURE INQUIRY

One of the challenges faced by researchers interested in examining children's discourse with peers to better understand the processes of peer influence is that the types of conversations that are most likely to contribute to changes in children's school adjustment over time (e.g., instances in which peers express disapproval for off-task behavior or instances in which peers praise or criticize the competence of a target child) may occur relatively infrequently, especially in naturalistic settings.

Two recent studies demonstrate this problem. In the first, Sage and Kindermann (1999) recorded over 12,000 behaviors in a fifth-grade classroom, including instances of on-task and off-task behavior (as exhibited by focal children) and instances of approval and disapproval for these behaviors (as exhibited by peers). Supporting the notion that everyday behavioral contingencies may be an important mechanism of influence, these authors found that highly- motivated students were more likely than less highly-motivated students to receive approval for on-task behaviors from members of their peer group (who were also, typically, highly motivated). Somewhat surprisingly, however, the authors did not find evidence that less highly motivated children were more likely than more highly motivated children to receive approval for off-task behaviors. On the one hand, these null results may indicate that off-task behaviors were enjoyed by classmates, regardless of peer group affiliations. On the other hand, they may reflect the difficulty of using naturalistic observations to examine behaviors with low base rates: both off-task behaviors (defined as behaviors that represented a clear disruption of ongoing classroom activities) and peer disapproval made up only a small proportion of children's observed interactions with peers. We have noted similar challenges in our own research. For example, in Altermatt et al. (2002), we recorded over 6,000 statements made by children and their classmates, anticipating, among other things, that children who were frequently criticized by classmates would experience declines in their competence perceptions over time. Surprisingly, we found no evidence to support this hypothesis. On the one hand, these null results may indicate that even very young children have begun to master what appears to be a broader human tendency to eschew information that reflects unfavorably on the self and interpret negative feedback in a manner that is less damaging to one's self-image (see Taylor & Brown, 1988; Wood, 1989).[3] On the other hand, the null findings may simply be the result of the relatively low frequency of these types of statements.

Importantly, the challenges that researchers face in capturing particular types of discourse among peers in naturalistic settings do not render this discourse unimportant. Typically, researchers capture only a very small sample of children's experiences. Even a single instance of praise or criticism received during a thirty-minute or one-hour time frame implies that a student may receive considerable amounts of praise or criticism during the course of an average week. Moreover, the very distinctiveness of certain types of achievement-related discourse may encourage children to pay particularly close attention to it (e.g., being told you are stupid by an admired peer may have a significant impact on perceptions of competence, even if it occurs only once; see Eccles Parsons et al., 1982). Still, the relative infrequency of certain types of discourse in classroom contexts has implications for the analyses we can do and the interpretations we can draw from these analyses. For example, in our own work (Altermatt et al., 2002), we have had to pool data across multiple children, ignoring a number of potentially important individual differences (e.g., in academic performance or sociometric status) that may moderate the effects of achievement-related discourse on school adjustment and allowing for the generalization of the results only to the subset of students and their interaction partners who actually engaged in the types of discourse examined (see also Bakeman & Gottman, 1997).

One solution to this conundrum is to supplement classroom-based work with research conducted in semi-naturalistic or laboratory-based settings where heightened levels of achievement-related discourse (or other behaviors of interest) can be promoted (see, for example, Altermatt & Broady, 2009; Altermatt & Ivers, 2011). Of course, this type of research presents its own problems and questions. Most importantly, to what extent do interactions observed in a laboratory really reflect children's interactions in class-room settings? To the degree that findings from classroom-based studies and lab-based studies overlap, we can feel more confident.

A second challenge faced by researchers interested in examining chil-dren's discourse with peers to better understand the processes of peer in-fluence is that peer influence is a bidirectional process involving two (and often more) interaction partners (Ladd, 2009). Few methods have been designed to address this bidirectionality (Brown et al., 2008) and, as a re-sult, researchers have often focused on the behaviors of a single interaction partner (e.g., a randomly selected focal child *or* his or her friend). This approach is problematic at many levels, especially insofar as it ignores the reality that peers' responses to children's discourse play a critical role in the effects of this discourse on children's school adjustment. The importance of the responses of interaction partners has been demonstrated in research on parent–child interactions (e.g., Hokoda & Fincham, 1995) as well as in research on peer interactions, including our own. For example, in Alter-matt & Broady (2009), we observed conversations between children and their same-sex friends after children performed poorly on a puzzle task. We found that boys who frequently commented on their poor performance (e.g., "I didn't get *any*") reported more learned helpless responses to fail-ure than boys who commented on their poor performance less frequently. These types of negative performance statements did not predict maladap-tive responses to failure among girls. We then used sequential analyses to examine whether boys' and girls' friends differed in their responses to neg-ative performance statements. They did—and in ways that provided some insight into why negative performance statements predicted maladaptive responses to failure for boys, but not girls. Specifically, boys' friends were more likely than girls' friends to respond to negative performance state-ments by checking on the focal child's performance, in effect asking them to repeat the negative performance statements (e.g., "*How* many did you miss?). Boys' friends were also more likely to respond by making positive statements about their own performance (e.g., "Really? I got them all"). These types of responses likely highlighted boys' poor performance in ways that made them less than anxious to tackle additional puzzles. In contrast, girls were significantly more likely than boys to have friends respond by mir-roring the negative performance statements (e.g., "Yeah. Me too"). Thus, the social comparison information that girls received was far less damaging than that received by boys. We found similar evidence for the importance of friends' responses to children's requests for help. Here, children who frequently asked for help from friends reported more adaptive responses to failure, but only when their friends also failed. Sequential analyses again provided some insights into this phenomenon. Specifically, children were less likely to receive help immediately after asking for it when friends succeeded than when friends failed. The reason may be that successful friends realized the potentially negative self-evaluative consequences of needing to ask for help (see Ryan, Pintrich, & Midgley, 2001) and held off providing it to help the focal "save face." This approach may, however, have forced children to ask for help a second time, leading children to feel less competent than if their friend had offered immediate assistance. Together, these findings confirm the importance of examining the behaviors of both interaction partners in future studies of peer influence processes.

A third challenge faced by researchers interested in examining children's discourse with peers to better understand the processes of peer influence is that it can be difficult for observers to appreciate the meaning of exchanges between children without substantial knowledge about the characteristics of the children involved (e.g., what are their relative levels of achievement? what are their academic goals?), their relationship status and history (e.g., is help-seeking a typical or atypical feature of this particular relationship?; what types of interactions did these students have earlier in the day?), and the classroom context in which discourse occurs (e.g., is this a classroom in which help-seeking is encouraged? is this a classroom in which relative performance is made salient?). This problem is not completely surmountable in any given study, but reinforces the point that researchers interested in studying the mechanisms of peer influence (via observational methods or any other method) must recognize that peer influence is not a monolithic process that works similarly in all peer interactions and in all contexts (see Brown et al., 2008). Uncovering some of the factors that influence the nature and consequences of children's interactions with peers will be critical in future research.

One source of debate in the extant literature concerns which types of peer relationships are most likely to be influential. One possibility is that peer influence will be strongest in the context of stable, close friendships. This assumption seems reasonable given (some) evidence that friends are more likely than non-friends to engage in frequent conversation and to interact in ways that are characterized by high levels of sharing, cooperation, and advice-giving (see Newcomb & Bagwell, 1995, and Rubin, Bukowksi, & Parker, 1998, for reviews; but see Berndt et al., 1988). However, some have argued that the attention afforded to stable, close friendships may be misguided. For example, Brown and his colleagues (2008) suggest that peer influence effects may be most powerful in the very early stages of friendship formation (when children are most concerned about gaining the approval of others) or even when children are not yet friends, but have opportunities to observe and interact with highly admired peers. Both hypotheses have received some empirical support. For example, Barry and Wentzel (2006) found that friends' prosocial behavior predicted positive changes in children's prosocial goal pursuit, but only when children and friends interacted frequently. In contrast, in a study in which children reported on the relative influence of friends and acquaintances, Burton, Ray, and Mehta (2003) found that children expected acquaintances to have more influence than best friends on their decision to cheat (or not to cheat) in school.

There are a number of potential reasons for these discrepant findings. One possibility is that children's self-reports on the processes of influence (as reported in Burton et al., 2003) are unreliable simply because children are unaware of which peers are most influential or are underestimating the role that close friends play in a culture that emphasizes the importance of independent thinking (see Brown et al., 2008; Berndt & Murphy, 2002; Ladd, 2009, for reviews). A second possibility is that the relative influence of close friends, frequent interaction partners, highly-respected peers, acquaintances, and the larger peer group will depend on the outcome variable of interest. This possibility has met with some support. For example, Molloy, Gest, and Rulison (2011) found that changes in seventh graders' *self-concept* were predicted most strongly by the self-concept scores of peers with whom these students interacted most frequently. However, changes in seventh graders' *school engagement* were predicted most strongly by the engagement scores of close friends. A third possibility is that the relative influence of various types of peer relationships will depend on the larger contexts in which peer interactions occur. For example, critical statements from classmates may be both more frequent and more likely to influence students' school adjustment in classrooms in which relative performance is made salient and competition is highlighted over cooperation.

Direct observations of children's interactions with peers will be helpful in gaining insights into the processes of influence as they occur in different peer and classroom contexts and into the veracity of children's self-reports of these processes: Are children more likely to attend to the achievement-related behaviors of friends than non-friends? Do high-status or highly respected peers (who may not be friends) garner special attention? How do children respond when they are confronted with conflicting messages from friends and non-friends? To what degree does the tone set by teachers in classrooms (e.g., the degree to which performance goals are highlighted over mastery goals or the degree to which students are nurtured and supported) change the tenor of students' achievement-related discourse with peers or the implications of this discourse for students' school adjustment?

CONCLUSIONS

To date, most research on peer influence in academic (and other) contexts has either ignored or made assumptions about the specific mechanisms by which peers exert their influence (Brown et al., 2008; Ryan, 2001). One reason for this lack of attention lies in the difficulties inherent in capturing processes of peer influence at work and linking these processes to changes in children's school adjustment over time: Children's school adjustment is influenced—often simultaneously and sometimes in inconsistent ways—by the interactions they have with acquaintances, close friends, cliques, and the larger peer group; peer influence sometimes results in immediate behavioral or attitudinal change, and sometimes the effects of peer interactions aren't seen for quite some time; children are influenced not only by the actual behaviors of peers, but by their perceptions of these behaviors. Despite these challenges, I have, in this chapter, echoed calls made by others for researchers to begin to carefully examine mechanisms of peer influence in their work (see also Berndt & Murphy, 2002; Brown, 2008; Ladd, 2009; Ryan, 2001) and have suggested that observational work examining children's achievement-related discourse with peers may offer some important insights. This work will be most effective to the degree that it is conducted in conjunction with research employing other methods, including survey assessments of children's daily interactions with peers (see Altermatt, 2007, 2011) and phenomena thought to be linked to these everyday interactions (e.g., peer academic reputations or chronic peer rejection; see Gest et al., 2005, 2008; Ladd et al., 2008). Together, this work will help us to better understand the ways in which peers contribute to (or undermine) the types of positive academic attitudes and behaviors that are, in turn, predictive of school success.

NOTES

1. Research that employs daily diary measures of children's everyday interactions with peers may complement observational work. This methodology has been used infrequently to date, but may yield promising insights into peer influence processes. For example, Sandstrom and Cillessen (2003) noted that children who were not well liked by peers reported greater levels of daily mistreatment from peers than children who were well liked. Children's social reputations did not predict differences in daily positive interactions.

2. One interpretation of these findings is that children may overestimate the supportiveness of their friendships. Consistent with this view, Ray and Cohen (1996) provide evidence that although children hold high expectations for social support for best friends in general (e.g., for an ideal best friend), they are much less likely to hold these expectations for their actual friendships. Children seem to expect that their actual relationships will be characterized by competition and conflict (see Berndt & Murphy, 2002).

3. This hypothesis is consistent with results from follow-up sequential analyses in which children responded to classmate criticism by evaluating themselves positively (e.g., "I know what I'm doing") significantly more often than would be expected by chance (see Altermatt et al., 2002).

REFERENCES

Altermatt, E. R. (2007). Coping with academic failure: Gender differences in students' self-reported interactions with family members and friends. *The Journal of Early Adolescence, 27,* 479–508.

Altermatt, E. R. (2011). Capitalizing on academic success: Students' interactions with friends as predictors of school adjustment. *The Journal of Early Adolescence, 31,* 174–203.

Altermatt, E. R., & Broady, E. F. (2009). Coping with achievement-related failure: An examination of conversations between friends. *Merrill-Palmer Quarterly, 55*(4), 454–487.

Altermatt, E. R., & Ivers, I. E. (2011). Friends' responses to children's disclosure of an achievement-related success: An observational study. *Merrill-Palmer Quarterly, 57*(4), 429–454.

Altermatt, E. R., & Kenney-Benson, G. A. (2006). Friends' influence on school adjustment: A review of three perspectives. In A. V. Mitel (Ed.), *Trends in educational psychology* (pp. 137–153). New York, NY: Nova Science Publishers.

Altermatt, E. R., & Pomerantz, E. M. (2003). The development of competence-related and motivational beliefs: An investigation of similarity and influence among friends. *Journal of Educational Psychology, 95,* 111–123.

Altermatt, E. R., & Pomerantz, E. M. (2005). The implications of having high-achieving versus low-achieving friends: A longitudinal analysis. *Social Development, 14,* 61–81.

Altermatt, E. R., Pomerantz, E. M., Ruble, D. N., Frey, K. S., & Greulich, F. K. (2002). Predicting changes in children's self-perceptions of academic competence: A naturalistic examination of evaluative discourse among classmates. *Developmental Psychology, 38,* 903–917.

Ames, C., & Ames, R. (1984). Systems of student and teacher motivation: Toward a qualitative definition. *Journal of Educational Psychology, 76,* 535–556.

Azmitia, M. (1988). Peer interaction and problem solving: When are two heads better than one? *Child Development, 64,* 430–444.

Bagwell, C. L., Newcomb, A. F., & Bukowski, W. M. (1998). Preadolescent friendship and peer rejection as predictors of adult adjustment. *Child Development, 69,* 140–153.

Bakeman, R., & Gottman, J. (1997). *Observing interaction: An introduction to sequential analysis* (2nd ed.). New York, NY: Cambridge University Press.

Bandura, A. (1971). Vicarious and self-reinforcement processes. In R. Glaser (Ed.), *The nature of reinforcement.* New York, NY: Academic Press.

Bargh, J. A., & Schul, Y. (1980). On the cognitive benefits of peer teaching. *Journal of Educational Psychology, 72,* 593–604.

Barry, C. H., & Wentzel, K. R. (2006). Friend influence on prosocial behavior: The role of motivational factors and friendship characteristics. *Developmental Psychology, 42*(1), 153–163.

Berndt, T. J. (1979). Developmental changes in conformity to peers and parents. *Developmental Psychology, 15,* 606–616.

Berndt, T. J. (1999). Friends' influence on students' adjustment to school. *Educational Psychologist, 34,* 15–28.

Berndt, T. J., & Keefe, K. (1995). Friends' influence on adolescents' adjustment to school. *Child Development, 66,* 1312–1329.

Berndt, T. J., & Murphy, L. M. (2002). Influences of friends and friendships: Myths, truths, and research recommendations. *Advances in Child Development and Behavior, 30,* 275–310.

Berndt, T. J., Hawkins, J. A., & Jiao, Z. (1999). Influences of friends and friendships on adjustment to junior high school. *Merrill-Palmer Quarterly, 45,* 13–41.

Berndt, T. J., Laychak, A. E., & Park, K. (1990). Friends' influence on adolescents' academic achievement motivation: An experimental study. *Journal of Educational Psychology, 82,* 664–670.

Berndt, T. J., Perry, B. T., & Miller, K. E. (1988). Friends' and classmates' interactions on academic tasks. *Journal of Educational Psychology, 80,* 506–513.

Birch, S. H., & Ladd, G. W. (1996). Interpersonal relationships in the school environment and children's early school adjustment: The role of teachers and peers. In J. Juvonen, & K. R. Wentzel (Eds.), *Social motivation: Understanding children's school adjustment* (pp. 199–225). New York, NY: Cambridge University Press.

Brown, B. B., Bakken, J. P., Ameringer, S. W., & Mahon, S. D. (2008). A comprehensive conceptualization of the peer influence process in adolescence. In M. J. Prinstein & K.A. Dodge (Eds.), *Understanding peer influence in children and adolescents* (pp. 17–44). New York, NY: Guilford Press.

Buhs, E. S., Ladd, G. W., & Herald, S. L. (2006). Peer exclusion and victimization: Processes that mediate the relation between peer group rejection and children's classroom engagement and achievement. *Journal of Educational Psychology, 98,* 1–13.

Bukowski, W. M., Brendgen, M., & Vitaro, F. (2007). Peers and socialization: Effects on externalizing and internalizing problems. In J. E. Grusec, & P. D. Hastings (Eds.), *Handbook of socialization: Theory and research* (pp. 355–381). New York, NY: Guilford.

Burton, B., Ray, G., & Mehta, S. (2003). Children's evaluations of peer influence: The role of relationship type and social situation. *Child Study Journal, 33*(4), 235–255.

Causey, D. L., & Dubow, E. F. (1992). Development of a self-report coping measure for elementary school children. *Journal of Clinical Child Psychology, 21,* 47–59.

Clasen, D. R., & Brown, B. B. (1985). The multidimensionality of peer pressure in adolescence. *Journal of Youth and Adolescence, 14,* 451–468.

Coyne, J. C., & DeLongis, A. (1986). Going beyond social support: The role of social relationships in adaptation. *Journal of Consulting and Clinical Psychology, 54,* 454–460.

Denton, K., & Zarbatany, L. (1996). Age differences in support processes in conversations between friends. *Child Development, 67,* 1360–1373.

Diehl, D. S., Lemerise, E. A., Caverly, S. L., Ramsay, S., & Roberts, J. (1998). Peer relations and school adjustment in ungraded primary children. *Journal of Educational Psychology, 90,* 506–515.

Dishion, T. J., & Dodge, K. A. (2006). Deviant peer contagion in interventions and programs: An ecological framework for understanding influence mechanisms. In K. A. Dodge, T. J. Dishion, & J. E. Lansford (Eds.), *Deviant peer influences in programs for youth: Problems and solutions* (pp. 14–43). New York, NY: Guilford Press.

Dishion, T. J., McCord, J., & Poulin, F. (1999). When interventions harm: Peer groups and problem behavior. *American Psychologist, 54*(9), 755–764.

Dishion, T. J., Piehler, T. F., & Myers, M. W. (2009). Dynamics and ecology of adolescent peer influence. In M. J. Prinstein, & K. A. Dodge (Eds.), *Understanding peer influence in children and adolescents* (pp. 72–93). New York, NY: Guilford.

Dubow, E. R., & Tisak, J. (1989). The relation between stressful life events and adjustment in elementary school children: The role of social support and social problem-solving skill. *Child Development, 60,* 1412–1423.

Eccles Parsons, J., Adler, T., & Kaczala, C. (1982). Socialization of achievement attitudes and perceptions: Parental influences. *Child Development, 53,* 310–321.

Engels, R. C. M. E., Knibbe, R. A., De Vries, H., Drop, M. J., & van Breukelen, G. J. P. (1999). Influences of parental and friends' smoking and drinking on adolescent use: A longitudinal study. *Journal of Applied Social Psychology, 29,* 337–361.

Frome, P., & Eccles, J. (1998). Parents' influence on children's achievement-related perceptions. *Journal of Personality and Social Psychology, 74*(2), 435–452.

Gest, S. D., Domitrovich, C. E., & Welsh, J. A. (2005). Peer academic reputation in elementary school: Associations with changes in self-concept and academic skills. *Journal of Educational Psychology, 97,* 337–346.

Gest, S. D., Rulison, K. L., Davidson, A. J., & Welsh, J. A. (2008). A reputation for success (or failure): The association of peer academic reputations with academic self-concept, effort, and performance across the upper elementary grades. *Developmental Psychology, 44,* 625–636.

Gest, S. D., Sesma, A., Masten, A. S., & Tellegen, A. (2006). Childhood peer reputation as a predictor of competence and symptoms 10 years later. *Journal of Abnormal Child Psychology, 34,* 509–526.

Graham, S., & Barker, G. P. (1990). The downside of help: An attributional–developmental analysis of helping behavior as a low-ability cue. *Journal of Educational Psychology, 82,* 7–14.

Granic, I., & Dishion, T. (2003). Deviant talk in adolescent friendships: A step toward measuring a pathogenic attractor process. *Social Development, 12,* 314–334.

Guryan, J., Jacob, B., Klopfer, E., & Groff, J. (2008). Using technology to explore social networks and mechanisms Underlying peer effects in classrooms. *Developmental Psychology, 44,* 355–364.

Harlow, R. E., & Cantor, N. (1994). Social pursuit of academics: Side effects and spillover of strategic reassurance seeking. *Journal of Personality and Social Psychology, 66,* 386–397.

Hartup, W. (2009). Critical issues and theoretical viewpoints. In K. H. Rubin, W. M. Bukowski, & B. Laursen (Eds.), *Handbook of peer interactions, relationships, and groups* (pp. 3–19). New York, NY: Guilford Press.

Hawkins, J. D., Catalano, R. F., & Miller, J. Y. (1992). Risk and protective factors for alcohol and other drug problems in adolescence and early adulthood: Implications for substance abuse prevention. *Psychological Bulletin, 112,* 64–105.

Heller, K., Swindle, R. W., & Dusenbury, L. (1986). Component social support processes: Comments and integration. *Journal of Consulting and Clinical Psychology, 54,* 466–470.

Hirsch, B. J., & DuBois, D. L. (1992). The relation of peer social support and psychological symptomatology during the transition to junior high school: A two-year longitudinal analysis. *American Journal of Community Psychology, 20,* 333–347.

Hodges, E. V., Boivin, M., Vitaro, F., & Bukowski, W. M. (1999). The power of friendship: Protection against an escalating cycle of peer victimization. *Developmental Psychology, 35,* 94–101.

Hokoda, A., & Fincham, F. D. (1995). Origins of children's helpless and mastery achievement patterns in the family. *Journal of Educational Psychology, 87,* 375–385.

Jodl, K. M., Michael, A., Malanchuk, O., Eccles, J. S., & Sameroff, A. (2001). Parents' roles in shaping early adolescents' occupational aspirations. *Child Development, 72,* 1247–1265.

Jussim, L. (1986). Self-fulfilling prophecies: A theoretical and integrative review. *Psychological Review, 93*(4), 429–445.

Juvonen, J., & Nishina, A. (1997). Social motivation in the classroom: Attributional accounts and developmental analysis. In P. R. Pintrich, & M. L. Maeher (Eds.), *Advances in motivation and achievement* (Vol. 10, pp. 181–211). Greenwich, CT: JAI.

Kempler, T. M., & Linnenbrink, E. A. (2006). Helping behaviors in collaborative groups in math: A descriptive analysis. In S. Karabenick & R. Newman (Eds.), *Help seeking in academic settings: Goals, groups, and contexts* (pp. 89–115). Mahwah, NJ: Lawrence Erlbaum Associates.

Kindermann, T. A. (2007). Effects of naturally existing peer groups on changes in academic engagement in a cohort of sixth graders. *Child Development, 78,* 1186–1203.

Klima, T., & Repetti, R. L. (2008). Children's peer relations and their psychological adjustment: Differences between close friendships and the larger peer group. *Merrill-Palmer Quarterly, 54*(2), 151–178.

Ladd, G. W. (1990). Having friends, keeping friends, making friends, and being liked by peers in the classroom: Predictors of children's early school adjustment? *Child Development, 61,* 1081–1100.

Ladd, G. W. (2009). Trends, travails, and turning points in early research on children's peer relationships: Legacies and lessons for our time? In K. H. Rubin, W. M. Bukowski, & B. Laursen (Eds.), *Handbook of peer interactions, relationships, and groups* (pp. 20–41). New York, NY: Guilford Press.

Ladd, G. W., Herald-Brown, S. L., & Reiser, M. (2008). Does chronic classroom peer rejection predict the development of children's classroom participation during the grade-school years? *Child Development, 79,* 1001–1015.

Ladd, G. W., Kochenderfer, B. J., & Coleman, C. C. (1996). Friendship quality as a predictor of young children's early school adjustment. *Child Development, 67,* 1103–1118.

Ladd, G. W., Kochenderfer, B. J., & Coleman, C. C. (1997). Classroom peer acceptance, friendship, and victimization: Distinct relational systems that contribute uniquely to children's school adjustment. *Child Development, 68,* 1181–1197.

Leaper, C. (1991). Influence and involvement in children's discourse: Age, gender, and partner effects. *Child Development, 62,* 797–811.

Leaper, C., Tenenbaum, H. R., & Shaffer, T. G. (1999). Communication patterns of African American girls and boys from low-income, urban background. *Child Development, 70,* 1489–1503.

Lepper, M. R., Sagotsky, G., & Mailer, J. (1975). Generalization and persistence of effects of exposure to self-reinforcement models. *Child Development, 46,* 618–630.

Maccoby, E. E. (1990). Gender and relationships: A developmental account. *American Psychologist, 45,* 513–520.

Maccoby, E. E. (1995). The two sexes and their social systems. In P. Moen, G. H. Elder, & K. Luscher (Eds.), *Examining lives in context: Perspectives on the ecology of human development* (pp. 347–364). Washington, DC: American Psychological Association.

Masters, J. C., & Mokros, J. (1974). Self-reinforcement processes in children. In H. W. Reese (Ed.), *Advances in child development and behavior.* New York, NY: Academic Press.

Molloy, L. E., Gest, S. D., & Rulison, K. L. (2011). Peer influences on academic motivation: Exploring multiple methods of assessing youths' most "influential" peer relationships. *The Journal of Early Adolescence, 31,* 13–40.

Newcomb, A. F., & Bagwell, C. L. (1995). Children's friendship relations: A meta-analytic review. *Psychological Bulletin, 117,* 306–347.

Newcomb, A. F., & Brady, J. E. (1982). Mutuality in boys' friendship relations. *Child Development, 53,* 392–395.

Pedersen, S., Vitaro, F., Barker, E. D., & Borge, A. I. H. (2007). The timing of middle-childhood peer rejection and friendship: Linking early behavior to early-adolescent adjustment. *Child Development, 78,* 1037–1051.

Piehler, T. F., & Dishion, T. J. (2007). Interpersonal dynamics within adolescent friendships: Dyadic mutuality, deviant talk, and patterns of antisocial behavior. *Child Development, 78*(5), 1611–1624.

Pomerantz, E. M., Grolnick, W. S., & Price, C. E. (2005). The role of parents in how children approach achievement. In A. J. Elliot, & C. S. Dweck (Eds.), *Handbook of competence and motivation* (pp. 259–278). New York, NY: Guilford.

Pomerantz, E. M., Ruble, D. N., & Bolger, N. (2004). Supplementing the snapshots with video footage: Taking a developmental approach to understanding social psychological phenomena. In C. Sansone, C. C. Morf, & A. T. Panter (Eds.), *The Sage handbook of methods in social psychology* (pp. 405–425). Thousand Oaks, CA: Sage.

Ray, G. E., & Cohen, R. (1996). Children's friendships: Expectations for prototypical versus actual best friends. *Child Study Journal, 26,* 209–227.

Rook, K. S. (1987). Social support versus companionship: Effects on life stress, loneliness, and evaluations by others. *Journal of Personality and Social Psychology, 52,* 1132–1147.

Rose, A. J. (2002). Co-rumination in the friendships of girls and boys. *Child Development, 73,* 1830–1843.

Rubin, K. H., Bukowski, W., & Parker, J. (2006). Peer interactions, relationships, and groups. In N. Eisenberg (Ed.), *The handbook of child psychology* (6th ed., pp. 571–645). New York, NY: Wiley.

Ryan, A. M. (2000). Peer groups as a context for the socialization of adolescents' motivation, engagement, and achievement in school. *Educational Psychologist, 35,* 101–111.

Ryan, A. M. (2001). The peer group as a context for the development of young adolescent motivation and achievement. *Child Development, 72,* 1135–1150.

Ryan, A. M., Pintrich, P. R., & Midgley, C. (2001). Avoiding seeking help in the classroom: Who and why? *Educational Psychology Review, 13,* 93–114.

Sage, N. A., & Kindermann, T. A. (1999). Peer networks, behavior contingencies, and children's engagement in the classroom. *Merrill-Palmer Quarterly, 45,* 143–171.

Sagotsky, G., & Lepper, M. R. (1982). Generalization of changes in children's preferences for easy or difficult goals induced through peer modeling. *Child Development, 53,* 372–375.

Sandstrom, M. J., & Cillessen, A. H. N. (2003). Sociometric status and children's peer experiences: Use of the daily diary method. *Merrill-Palmer Quarterly, 49*(4), 427–452.

Schwartz, F. (1981). Supporting or subverting learning: Peer group patterns in four tracked schools. *Anthropology and Education Quarterly, 12,* 99–121.

Shachar, H., & Sharan, S. (1994). Talking, relating, and achieving: Effects of cooperative learning and whole-class instruction. *Cognition and Instruction, 12*(4), 313–353.

Sim, T. N., & Koh, S. F. (2003). Domain conceptualization of adolescent susceptibility to peer pressure. *Journal of Research on Adolescence, 13*(1), 58–80.

Snyder, J., Schrepferman, L., Oeser, J., Patterson, G., Stoolmiller, M., Johnson, K., & Snyder, A. (2005). Deviancy training and association with deviant peers in young children: Occurrence and contribution to early-onset conduct problems. *Development and Psychopathology, 17*(2), 397–413.

Taylor, S. E., & Brown, J. (1988). Illusion and well-being: A social psychological perspective on mental health. *Psychological Bulletin, 103,* 193–210.

Vandell, D. L., & Hembree, S. E. (1994). Peer social status and friendship: Independent contributors to children's social and academic adjustment. *Merrill-Palmer Quarterly, 40,* 461–470.

Vitaro, F., Boivin, M., & Bukowksi, W. M. (2009). The role of friendship in child and adolescent psychosocial development. In K. H. Rubin, W. M. Bukowksi, & B. Laursen (Eds.), *Handbook of peer interactions, relationships, and groups* (pp. 568–585). New York, NY: Guilford.

Weiner, B. (1980). May I borrow your class notes? An attributional analysis of help-giving in an achievement related context. *Journal of Educational Psychology, 72,* 676–681.

Wentzel, K. R. (1998). Social relationships and motivation in middle school: The role of parents, teachers, and peers. *Journal of Educational Psychology, 90,* 202–209.

Wentzel, K. R. (1999). Social influences on school adjustment: Commentary. *Educational Psychologist, 34,* 59–69.

Wentzel, K. R. (2003). School adjustment. In G. E. Miller & W. M. Reynolds (Eds.), *Handbook of psychology: Educational psychology* (Vol. 7, pp. 235–258). New York, NY: Wiley.

Wentzel, K. R. (2005). Peer relationship, motivation and academic performance at school. In A. J. Elliot, & C. S. Dweck (Eds.), *Handbook of competence and motivation* (pp. 279–296). New York, NY: Guilford.

Wentzel, K. R. (2009). Peers and academic functioning at school. In K. H. Rubin, W. M. Bukowksi, & B. Laursen (Eds.), *Handbook of peer interactions, relationships, and groups* (pp. 531–547). New York, NY: Guilford.

Wentzel, K. R., & Caldwell, K. (1997). Friendships, peer acceptance, and group membership: Relations to academic achievement in middle school. *Child Development, 68,* 195–203.

Wentzel, K. R., Barry, C. M., & Caldwell, K. A. (2004). Friendships in middle school: Influences on motivation and school adjustment. *Journal of Educational Psychology, 96,* 195–203.

Wood, J. V. (1989). Theory and research concerning social comparisons of personal attributes. *Psychological Bulletin, 106,* 231–248.

CHAPTER 6

POPULARITY AND SCHOOL ADJUSTMENT

Antonius H. N. Cillessen and Yvonne H. M. van den Berg
Radboud University, Nijmegen, The Netherlands

INTRODUCTION

Popularity in the peer group is a topic that catches the attention and imagination of many—educators, parents, the "popular" media, and of course the students themselves in schools across the world. Popular students are often well-liked, attractive, seen as "cool," and doing well in school and in extracurricular activities. However, the story about popularity in schools is more complex than this picture suggests and not always uniformly positive. While they may still be seen as attractive and cool, not all popular students are well-liked or doing well in school. Some popular students are bullies who do not excel academically. Others may engage in risky behaviors that jeopardize their health and school achievement. They may also influence others who look up to them to do the same. Thus, while the popular student in the classroom or school may catch our attention and imagination, this student may also be a source of concern. The goal of this chapter is to examine the complex association between popularity in the peer group and social and academic adjustment in school.

Peer Relationships and Adjustment at School, pages 135–164
Copyright © 2012 by Information Age Publishing
135

Four specific topics will be addressed. First, we examine how popularity is defined and measured. In this context, it is important to make a distinction between popularity and peer acceptance. Second, we review research on the associations of popularity and acceptance with four types of school adjustment: academic achievement; truancy, absenteeism, and dropping out of school; school attitudes and motivation; and classroom behavior. Third, in order to better understand the school adjustment outcomes of popular and accepted students, we discuss popularity and peer acceptance as indicators of two different ways to be socially successful or competent in the peer group, each with their own developmental trajectories. Fourth and finally, we discuss implications for educational practice and for interventions aimed at preventing academic problems among youth. As part of this discussion, we present results from an intervention study that focused on improving peer relationships in the classroom.

CONCEPTUALIZING AND MEASURING POPULARITY

Background

In the beginning years of intensive research on peer relationships during the 1980s and 1990s, the primary focus of this research was on children or adolescents who were rejected by their peers, or had problems in their peer relationships or the peer group more generally (e.g., because they were aggressive or withdrawn). Thus, the focus was on the low end of a continuum of social status in the peer group. This focus was important and necessary, because children or adolescents who are rejected, aggressive, or withdrawn often have various problems at school.

During the 1980s and 1990s, there was not much interest in the other end of the continuum of social status in the peer group, that is, students who are well-accepted or popular in the peer group. Those students were seen as role models of social competence or social skills, but they were not the focus of much research interest. In research studies, data for accepted or popular students were often presented as a contrast to those of rejected or neglected students.

This situation changed at the end of the 1990s, due to several influences. One influence was a study by Parkhurst and Hopmeyer (1998), who proposed a distinction between two dimensions of popularity that they labeled sociometric popularity and perceived popularity. They showed that these two dimensions are not identical, and have different correlations with concurrent measures of social behavior. A second influence was an experimental study by LaFontana and Cillessen (1998), who asked early adolescents to make attributions about peers who were described to them as popular.

They found, somewhat surprisingly, that the attributions that early adolescents made of popular peers were not uniformly positive, and sometimes
as negative as the attributions they made of an unpopular peer. A third
influence was a study by Rodkin, Farmer, Pearl, and Van Acker (2000), who
asked teachers to identify popular boys in the classroom and subsequently
identified two subgroups of popular peers within this larger group, one subgroup ("model" boys) who were examples of social and academic competence, and another subgroup ("tough" boys) who were also popular in the
peer group according to their teachers but also scored high on measures of
aggression. De Bruyn and Cillessen (2006) later found a similar distinction
among popular girls. A fourth influence was another study by LaFontana
and Cillessen (2002) who analyzed early adolescents' open-ended descriptions of popular peers, and also found that teens described popular peers
in both positive and negative terms.

These studies demonstrated two important facts that have now been
replicated in other research. First, they showed that peer popularity is a
heterogeneous construct. Apparently, in the perceptions of both peers
and teachers, there are two ways to think about high status in the peer
group, reflected in differing dimensions or subgroups of popularity. Second, and consistent with the evidence for the heterogeneity of popularity,
not everything about popularity is positive. Popularity is associated with
both positive and negative correlates and outcomes. This finding, and
especially the fact that popularity is sometimes associated with social and
academic adjustment problems, inspired much new research on the nature of popularity.

Measurement of Popularity and Social Status

Popularity, and peer group status more generally, are typically measured
with sociometric methods. Sociometry has a long history, dating back to
Moreno (1934; for reviews of the history of sociometry, see Cillessen & Bukowski, 2000; Cillessen, 2009). A sociometric test is a method to measure
relationships in groups and group structure by asking all group members to
evaluate each other on one or more sociometric criteria using peer nominations, peer ratings, or a similar method (see Cillessen, 2009, for a description of all elements of a sociometric procedure). Coie, Dodge, and
Coppotelli (1982) created a modern version of Moreno's (1934) original
procedures that has since been used extensively in research in developmental and educational psychology.

In this version, students are asked to nominate peers in their classroom
or grade (the "reference group") who they like the most and who they like
the least. The number of choices received is then counted for each group

member. This leads to scores on four sociometric dimensions: acceptance, rejection, (social) preference, and (social) impact. *Acceptance* is the number of "liked most" nominations received. *Rejection* is the number of "liked least" nominations received. *Preference* is the number of liked most nominations received minus the number of liked least nominations received. *Impact* is the sum of liked most and liked least votes received. As part of the calculation of these scores, there is usually a correction for the number of students in the reference group, so that the resulting scores can be compared between classrooms and grades, even when they differ in the number of students in them.

On the basis of the continuous sociometric scores, each student is then assigned to one of five sociometric status types: "*popular*" (high preference; liked by many, disliked by few), *rejected* (low preference; disliked by many, liked by few), *neglected* (low impact; neither liked nor disliked), *controversial* (high impact; liked by some and disliked by others), and *average* (average on all four dimensions). These groups are known as the "traditional sociometric status categories." In this classification system, the label "popular" is placed in quotes. Although this group has traditionally been called "popular," we believe today that it would be better to call this group "accepted" because it is based on judgments of likeability (liked by many, disliked by few; see Cillessen & Marks, 2011). Calling this group "accepted" also makes it easier to distinguish it from children or adolescents who are popular according to "most popular" peer judgments (see below).

The traditional sociometric classification system was the basis for much research on child and adolescent peer relationships in the 1980s and 1990s. The main concern of this research was with children or adolescents with problematic peer relations, in particular those who were classified as rejected. This research yielded much information about the correlates, precursors, and consequences of peer rejection. There was not much interest in popularity during this period; the major focus was on peer rejection and aggression. Researchers focused on adolescents with behavior and relationship problems, and on creating successful interventions to help them. There was some awareness that the "accepted" classification was not the same as adolescents' experiences with popularity in high school, but this was not the focus of much research.

This changed in the late 1990s, when researchers began to include "most popular" and "least popular" nominations in sociometric data collections, in addition to the "liked most" and "liked least" questions that they had always used. By doing this, peer relationships researchers added *popularity* as a fifth sociometric dimension to the previous four (acceptance, rejection, preference, impact). Popularity is determined by counting the number of "most popular" and "least popular" nominations each adolescent receives from their peers. Popularity is then either the total number of most popular nominations received, or the difference between most popular and least popular nominations (again correcting for differences in classroom or grade size).

As is clear from the operational definitions of these constructs, popularity is not the same as acceptance or preference. Acceptance and preference measure likeability, derived from peer nominations of who is most and least liked. Popularity, in contrast, is a dimension of power, prestige, or visibility, derived from peers' perceptions of who is most and least popular in their group. Therefore, popularity is closer to the traditional sociometric dimension of social impact that is defined as the sum of liked most and liked least nominations received. Social impact is also an indicator of how socially visible an adolescent is in the group, independent of whether they are liked or disliked—they are just highly noticed.

Because popularity and acceptance are independently interesting and complementary dimensions of the adolescent peer group, studies have begun to measure both. In a sociometric study with peer nominations, this means that four sociometric questions are used: "whom do you like most?", "whom do you like least?", "who is most popular?", and "who is least popular?" The inclusion of all four peer nomination questions is ideal for a sociometric study on adolescents, because it allows researchers to examine the unique characteristics of both dimensions of high status in the peer group, as well as their overlap. It then also becomes possible to identify adolescents who score high on one dimension but not on the other, such as popular adolescents who are not well liked by the majority of their peers. This turns out to be a fascinating and important group for the study of adolescent peer relationships and social development.

Some studies have used peer nominations that measure an aspect of social visibility of power, such as admiration, attractiveness, coolness, dominance, network centrality, or perceived peer affiliation. Examples are nominations of students who are "cool," "the center of attention," "people everyone wants to spend time with," or "people everyone wants to be friends with." Such constructs have a clear theoretical connection to popularity, but are not direct measures of popularity themselves. Only peer nominations that directly assess popularity should be called "popularity." Measures of other constructs should be carefully labeled to represent the constructs that they measure. Doing otherwise would obfuscate the popularity construct.

In addition to nominations, researchers have used peer ratings to determine popularity and status. In a rating procedure, adolescents are asked to rate all peers in their classroom or grade on several scales, such as likeability and popularity. Ratings and nominations each have advantages and disadvantages. Ratings have the advantage that every member of a classroom or grade directly evaluates each other member. However, this is time consuming and difficult to conduct when the reference group (classroom or grade) is large. Nominations have the advantage that they are relatively easy to collect. But peer nominations are partial rank orderings in which adolescents only identify their top choices for a question, and leave all other peers unranked.

Not many studies have used nominations and ratings of popularity in the same data collection. As an exception, van den Berg (2009) collected peer nominations and ratings of popularity and likeability in grades 7 and 8 of elementary school at three times during the school year. Nominations and ratings received for popularity (and also for likeability) were significantly and positively correlated at each time during the school year, indicating significant consistency between both methods for the study of the peer group.

Two Definitions of Popularity

The previous section indicates that there are two ways to think about popularity. On the one hand, when students evaluate how much they like or dislike their classmates or grade members, a group of students is identified that is liked by many and disliked by few. In the traditional sociometric system, this group was labeled "popular." According to this definition, popularity is equated with being likeable, accepted, or preferred in the peer group, and a popular child or adolescent is someone who is well liked by others. On the other hand, when peer nominations of popularity rather than likeability are used, a group of students is identified that is seen as popular. Children and especially adolescents may be seen as popular because they are dominant, cool, or have influence over others (LaFontana & Cillessen, 2002). However, they are not necessarily liked by the other students in their classroom or grade, as research has shown.

Rodkin and colleagues (2000) identified two subgroups of popular boys. They described the first subgroup of popular boys as "toughs" (popular and aggressive) and the other as "models" (popular and prosocial). Similarly, de Bruyn and Cillessen (2006) identified two subgroups of popular girls. They described one subgroup of popular girls as studious (like the "models") and the other subgroup of popular girls as getting in trouble (like the "toughs"). In both cases, researchers identified two groups of popular adolescents: those who are popular and well liked by their peers at the same time, and others who are popular but not well liked, for example because they are dominant or aggressive. These studies show that some popular students are disliked by parts of the peer group. The reasons may be the behaviors of the popular peers themselves or jealousy on the part of the peers who judge them.

Popularity and Acceptance

The studies on subgroups of popularity clearly have shown that popularity and likeability are not the same, but different dimensions of the peer group. Different names have been used for these two dimensions in the literature. Popularity has often been called "perceived popularity," because it refers to popularity as a reputation assessed by who is seen as popular in the peer group. Likeability has sometimes been called "sociometric popularity" because the popular group in the traditional sociometric system was based on likeability judgments (specifically, acceptance or preference scores). The terms "sociometric popularity" and "perceived popularity" were proposed by Parkhurst and Hopmeyer (1998), and have served a useful purpose in the literature to make clear that there are two forms of popularity. However, these terms also have disadvantages. They are somewhat awkward to use, and because "perceived popularity" is also assessed with sociometric methods (peer nominations of who is most and least popular), the distinction becomes confusing. Therefore, more recently researchers (see Cillessen & Marks, 2011) recommend that *sociometric popularity* should simply be called *acceptance* or *preference* (depending on how it is measured), and could be referred to as *likeability*. Similarly, *perceived popularity* should simply be called *popularity*, measured by either "most popular" nominations, "most popular" minus "least popular" nominations, or popularity ratings.

In this chapter, we do not use the terms sociometric and perceived popularity. We use *acceptance* to refer to students who are highly accepted by their peers, as indicated by peer nominations or ratings of likeability. These students have often been identified as sociometrically "popular" but we use "accepted" instead. We use *popularity* for students who are seen as popular by their peers, as indicated by peer nominations or ratings using popularity as the criterion.

There are several other sources of evidence for the distinction between popularity and acceptance. First, popularity and acceptance are moderately correlated. Although the correlation varies across studies and age groups, they indicate discriminant validity (Cillessen & Mayeux, 2007). Second, popularity and acceptance differ in stability. Popularity is more stable than acceptance, even across school transitions when peer groups change. Children and adolescents vary in who they like over the course of a school year and from year to year. They vary less in who they see as popular in their peer groups. Third, acceptance and popularity have different profiles of social behavior and other related characteristics, to which we turn in the next sections. The profile of likeability is primarily prosocial; the profile of popularity is a mixture of prosocial and not so prosocial behaviors. Fourth, popularity and acceptance play different roles in processes of peer influence (Prinstein & Dodge, 2008). The locus of peer influence resides more with popular peers than with likeable peers. Fifth, popularity and acceptance have different associations with adjustment outcomes. Likeability is associated with prosocial outcomes such as academic achievement; popularity is also associated with antisocial outcomes such as health risk behaviors.

In the next two sections, we discuss the associations of acceptance and popularity with school adjustment. School adjustment is a broad term that can include a number of specific aspects. First, school adjustment obviously should include students' actual academic achievement in school. Second, school adjustment should also include the degree to which students come to school and stay in school—a more fundamental problem that heavily influences actual achievement. Therefore, we also consider drop-out, truancy, and absenteeism, variables that previously have been associated with rejection and aggression (Asher & Coie, 1990; Newcomb, Bukowski, & Pattee, 1993). Fourth, even when school attendance is not a problem, attitudes toward school and school motivation may largely vary. Therefore, they are also included as important aspects of school adjustment. Fourth, classroom behaviors should be considered. These include both task-related behaviors such as effort, engagement, and cooperation, and social behaviors that are not directly related to school tasks but significantly influence school task performance as well, such as disruptive behavior and aggression in the classroom. Research findings in each of these four aspects of school adjustment are presented.

ACCEPTANCE AND SCHOOL ADJUSTMENT

Academic Achievement

A number of studies have addressed the associations between peer acceptance and measures of academic achievement. From the perspective of their classmates, accepted children have been described by their peers as academically inclined, prosocial, and generally helpful to their peers (Lease, Musgrove, & Axelrod, 2002). Other studies have shown that this perspective was shared by both teachers and peers. In a study by Wentzel and Asher (1995), accepted children were perceived by teachers to be more helpful to others and they were more often nominated by their classmates as being good students, whereas rejected students were preferred less by teachers and perceived by their classmates as not being good students (Wentzel & Asher, 1995). Objective test scores confirm these differences. Comparisons of group means indicated that accepted and neglected children earned higher grades and rejected children earned lower grades than average children (Wentzel, 1991). Finally, these findings hold across various sociocultural contexts. Students who are well liked by their peers tend to be characterized by relatively high achievement, although there is some variability across sociocultural contexts this finding is robust across context (Guay, Boivin, & Hodges, 1999). In summary, an association between peer acceptance and positive school achievement (and by implication between low acceptance or peer rejection and poor school achievement) was found according to peers, teachers, and objective test scores, and across various contexts.

This general conclusion about the association between peer acceptance and school competence was also achieved in a meta-analytic review by Newcomb and colleagues (1993). They conducted an extensive meta-analysis of the differences in measures of school competence between the traditional sociometric status groups accepted, rejected, controversial, neglected, and average. They concluded that accepted children evidenced stronger cognitive abilities than children in de other four sociometric groups, whereas rejected children's cognitive abilities were significantly lower than the other four groups (Newcomb et al., 1993).

The general conclusion about the association between acceptance and academic achievement was also supported Wentzel (2005). Wentzel (2005) concluded that the literature shows consistent associations of peer acceptance with successful academic performance and of peer rejection and low levels of acceptance with academic difficulties. According to Wentzel (2005), these general conclusions apply equally to elementary school-age children as well as adolescents, and have been found when using classroom grades, standardized test scores, and measures of IQ as dependent variables. Results from longitudinal studies also show that the positive associations between peer acceptance and academic accomplishments are stable over time when students are followed across multiple years in school (Wentzel, 2005). This latter conclusion was confirmed by a recent study by Schwartz and colleagues, who also found stable associations between social acceptance and grade point average across the high school years (Schwartz, Gorman, Nakamoto, & McKay, 2006).

Research has also been conducted to shed light on the causal direction of the association between peer acceptance and academic achievement. Several studies suggest that peer acceptance has a causal effect on school achievement. Peer acceptance was a significant predictor of students' grades, both concurrently and over time (Wentzel & Caldwell, 1997). In contrast, early peer rejection predicted underachievement during the first year of school (Ladd, 2005). O'Neil and colleagues (O'Neil, Welsh, Parke, Wang, & Strand, 1997) found that lower levels of social acceptance in kindergarten predicted deficits in classroom social skills and work habits and lower academic performance as assessed by grades and standardized achievement test scores in first and second grade. They concluded that rejected children appear to begin their school careers with both classroom behavior problems and academic performance deficits.

Results from other studies also suggest that the association between peer acceptance and academic achievement may be due to underlying cognitive skills. Underlying deficits in academic skills may then be responsible for peer rejection. Estell (2008) found that students with learning disabilities scored lower than their typically achieving peers in best friend nominations, had marginally lower peer-nominated popularity, and were rated much lower in social preference. The academic performance and intelligence level of rejected boys and girls were short of the standards of children from the other status groups, while the scores of accepted boys and girls were of superior standard (Zettergren, 2003). Meijs, Cillessen, Scholte, Segers, and Spijkerman (2009) found effects of both social intelligence and academic functioning on measures of peer status. Their results suggested that the effects of cognitive intelligence on positive peer relationships may be due to its correlation with social intelligence, and that more positive peer relationships emerge for students with higher levels of social intelligence and related social skills.

Together, these studies evidencing the link between peer acceptance and academic achievement suggest a bidirectional association. On the one hand, good peer relationships as reflected in acceptance in the peer group seem to be a precondition for adequate academic functioning in school. On the other hand, students with low academic abilities also seem to pay a price in terms of their social relationships at school. Both of these findings point to the relevance of the school context for understanding social competence with peers (Wentzel, 2005).

Drop-Out, Truancy, and Absenteeism

There is clear evidence that low peer acceptance is correlated with measures of drop-out, truancy, and absenteeism. In their meta-analysis of risks associated with peer rejection, Parker and Asher (1987) concluded that children who were poorly accepted by their peers are more likely to drop out of school than children who were better accepted. Later studies have further confirmed this conclusion. Kupersmidt and Coie (1990) found that rejected students were more likely to drop out of school, to be retained in grade, to become truant, and to be suspended from school. DeRosier, Kupersmidt, and Patterson (1994) found that the chronicity and proximity of peer rejection was associated with greater absenteeism from school. Zettergren (2003) also found that the school dropout rate of rejected boys was much higher than that of other boys. Schwartz et al. (2006) found that changes in social acceptance were not predictive of changes in unexplained absences across the high school years, suggesting that the correlation between low peer acceptance and unexplained absences was identical across these years.

As for the association between peer acceptance and academic achievement, the question of causality can also be asked for the association of peer acceptance with measures of drop-out, truancy, and absenteeism. However, there are fewer studies available that directly tested this issue. Strongly indicative of a causal effect of low peer acceptance on such school problems later on are the results of longitudinal studies across multiple school years in which low peer acceptance was a significant antecedent of later school adjustment problems, particularly dropping out of high school (Parker & Asher, 1987; see also Ladd, 2005), although in these analyses it was not always possible to control for earlier levels of the same school problems.

There are no studies that have directly tested the causal effects of truancy, absenteeism, or dropping out of school on peer relationships. It can easily be envisioned that students who start to miss a lot of school time due to truancy and absenteeism and the corresponding corrections and perceptions they received from school administrators and staff will develop different relationships with the peer group at school, especially with those who continue to do well, and will become estranged from the mainstream peer group. Interestingly, they may become part of a smaller subsection of the school population, especially in high school, that form a counter culture against regular school values and in which they might become quite popular (see Brown, 2011). Future research on peer cliques, and on the perceptions and status positions within and between peer cliques with different values, could illustrate these processes. Things become even more complicated for students who go further than staying away from school regularly and drop out completely. In that case, collecting peer relationships data within the context of the school becomes impossible, as they will no longer be regular members of the school population. Their peer group changes entirely, depending on what they do after having dropped out of school. It is simply not known what the effect of dropping out of school is on subsequent peer relationships. This is an interesting area for future research.

Attitudes and Motivation

Sociometric status and peer acceptance also have been related to motivation, including satisfaction with school, pursuit of goals to learn, interest in school, and perceived academic competence (Wentzel, 2008). There are some indications that rejected girls (but not rejected boys) had negative attitudes towards school and schoolwork, and that accepted girls had positive school attitudes (Zettergren, 2003). Interestingly, neglected children have quite positive academic profiles. They reported higher levels of school motivation, were perceived by teachers to be more independent, less impulsive, more appropriate with respect to classroom behavior, and were preferred more by teachers (Wentzel & Asher, 1995). Early peer rejection was found to predict negative school attitudes during the first year of school. Later in the elementary year, low peer acceptance was linked with loneliness and emotional distress (Ladd, 2005). There is also evidence that social acceptance enhances an adolescent's motivation and interest in school environment (Wentzel, 1991). Together with the previous results for academic achievement and school problems, these findings indicate that good relationships with peers as indicated by peer acceptance have positive effects on students' attitudes and motivation related to school.

Classroom Behavior

One important factor in understanding the association between peer acceptance and academic adjustment, whether measured by school grades, truancy and absenteeism, or school interest and motivation, is the role that actual behaviors in the classroom play in this association. In fact, analyses by Wentzel (1991) of the association between peer acceptance and academic achievement indicated that socially responsible behavior in the classroom mediated entirely the link between peer status and academic grades (Wentzel, 1991). Thus, the consideration of classroom behavior is important. A number of studies have found links between peer acceptance or sociometric status more generally and classroom social behaviors.

Importantly, highly accepted children were perceived by teachers to be more helpful to others, and they were more often nominated by their classmates as being good students (Wentzel & Asher, 1995). In addition to being academically inclined, well-accepted children have also been described as prosocial, likeable, and generally helpful to others (Lease et al., 2002).

In contrast, low peer acceptance or rejection predicted (negatively) children's academic adjustment as measured by classroom social behavior (Vandell & Hembree, 1994). Other studies focuses on detailed behaviors showed that rejected boys, especially low achievers, spent proportionately less time on task and more time off task, were more often disruptive, initiated more aversive interactions, and initiated more interactions during structured time than non-classroom time (Asher & Coie, 1990). There is also evidence that the effect of peer group rejection on low scholastic achievement is mediated by low classroom participation (Ladd, 2005). Rejected children were perceived by teachers to be less self-assured and to start fights more often than average status students. Rejected students were also preferred less by teachers and perceived by their classmates as not being good students (Wentzel & Asher, 1995). O'Neil and colleagues (1997) concluded that rejected children appear to begin their school careers with both classroom behavior problems and academic performance deficits.

In addition to examining accepted and rejected students, researchers have also addressed the classroom behaviors or neglected and controversial students. Neglected children seem to have quite positive academic profiles. They reported higher levels of school motivation; were perceived by teachers to be more independent, less impulsive, more appropriate with respect to classroom behavior; and were preferred more by teachers (Wentzel & Asher, 1995). Neglected children seem to show few early problems in the area of classroom behaviors, but some early academic performance difficulties (O'Neil et al., 1997). Controversial status children were perceived by teachers to be less independent, less likely to follow rules, and more likely to start fights than average children. They were also preferred less by teachers than were average students (Wentzel & Asher, 1995). Controversial children, particularly boys, appear to evidence early classroom behavior difficulties and fewer early academic difficulties (O'Neil et al., 1997).

The findings on the classroom behaviors associated with peer status are important, as they suggest mechanisms through which peer acceptance may be related to academic grades, school problems, and attitudes and motivation. These mechanisms may not be the same for every subgroup of students, but here we focus on main differences along the acceptance–rejection continuum, the basis for what was previously called sociometric popularity. Students who score high in this dimension appear to be cooperative and helpful in interactions with their classmates. They feel comfortable in the classroom environment, and may not worry too much about what others think of them. They have friends who support them. Because they are well connected and cooperative in the peer group, they can ask others for help or information when needed easily, and others will not have trouble sharing information with them. Since interactions with these students are positive and prosocial, they will be rewarding to interaction partners. Others will like to work with these students, fostering a good basis for reciprocal relationships characterized by peer learning and collaboration. For these students, coming to school is rewarding in both social and academic ways. They can focus on tasks at hand and not be distracted by social processes, aggressive incidents, and competition, or worried about isolation or rejection.

In contrast, the academic lives of students at the opposite end of this continuum of peer acceptance will look entirely different. Children who are not accepted by their peers in the classroom face numerous distractions that will keep them from staying on task and focusing on their school work. First, because they are often aggressive, they may be focused on conflicts with peers rather than their school work. Second, when others dislike and reject them, they may worry about social isolation and engage in activities to attract others' attention. Furthermore, children who are rejected seem less prepared generally for academic work when they come to school, as indicated by some of the studies reviewed above. In that case, in addition to the above distractions, they have to overcome the additional disadvantage of being less prepared for school work to begin with. Finally, students who are rejected are either isolated or others find interacting with them not rewarding when they are aggressive or prone to conflict. In either of these two cases, they have a harder time finding classmates for peer learning and collaboration, and they will also simply face more difficulties obtaining information from peers about substantive issues and school work when needed. For all these reasons, students who are not well accepted in the peer group face a number of challenges that are not faced by students who are well accepted. These differences can explain the clearly documented association between peer acceptance and measures of academic achievement, school problems (truancy, absenteeism, drop-out), and academic attitudes and motivation towards school and school work.

POPULARITY AND SCHOOL ADJUSTMENT

The same four categories of school adjustment can be distinguished for the association between popularity and social and academic functioning in school. However, because research on the correlates and consequences of popularity has a shorter history than research on the correlates and consequences of peer acceptance, less is known about popular students' school adjustment in each of these four categories. Further, some additional findings are known about risk factors associated with peer popularity that do not fall directly in our four main categories but are relevant indirectly for academic adjustment and functioning at school. These additional outcomes will be discussed as well.

Academic Achievement

There are fewer studies on the associations of popularity with measures of academic achievement than of peer acceptance with academic achievement. Two studies have examined how students see popular peers in terms of academic abilities. Boyatzis, Baloff, and Durieux (1998) asked ninth-graders to rate the popularity of hypothetical peers when they provided information about academic achievement. In this study, academic achievement did not predict ratings of popularity. LaFontana and Cillessen (2002) followed the reverse procedure by asking fourth through ninth graders to provide open-ended descriptions of hypothetical popular and unpopular peers. In this study, hypothetical popular peers were spontaneously described as more academically able and intelligent than hypothetical unpopular peers. Thus, the information about the association between academic ability and popularity is mixed.

Research by Schwartz and colleagues (2006) shed light on the reason for this mixed association. Schwartz and colleagues (2006) asked students to rate their peers on popularity using a continuous rating score and determined average popularity ratings received for every student. In general, this measure of popularity correlated negatively with GPA. In addition, in this study, increases in popularity were associated with increases in unexplained absences and decreases in grade point average for adolescents who were also highly aggressive (Schwartz et al., 2006). Thus, the combination of popularity and aggression was particularly predictive of low academic achievement. This research suggests that the association between popularity and academic achievement is moderated by aggression. Adolescents who were both popular and aggressive scored high on academic difficulties. For adolescents who are popular but not aggressive, there was no association between popularity and academic difficulties. The open-ended descriptions of popular peers provided by LaFontana and Cillessen (2002) could be reanalyzed to examine if indeed popular students who were described as academic achievers were not described as aggressive.

These findings are consistent with studies identifying subgroups of popular peers. As indicated above, Rodkin and colleagues (2000) identified two subgroups of popular boys, called "toughs" and "models." The "models" score low on aggression but high on measures of academic achievement. The "toughs" score high on aggression but low on measures of academic achievement. Similarly, de Bruyn and Cillessen (2006) identified two subgroups of popular girls, who displayed similar behavioral profiles as the groups identified by Rodkin and colleagues: a subgroup of "troubled" popular girls who scored high on aggression and low on school achievement, and a subgroup of "studious" popular girls who scored the reverse.

These findings are also consistent with what has been found for controversial students in the traditional sociometric classification system. It has been noted that controversial students often look like popular students (see Parkhurst & Hopmeyer, 1998), in that they are also liked by some but disliked by others in the classroom and clearly score high on aggression (Newcomb et al., 1993). In one study, controversial status in sixth grade negatively predicted GPA in eighth grade (Wentzel, 2003). In another study, controversial students, especially boys, demonstrated early classroom behavior difficulties (O'Neil et al., 1997).

These studies converge in showing that the association between popularity and academic difficulties only occurs for popular students who are also aggressive and manipulative in the peer group. As for students who score low on peer acceptance, these students may be preoccupied with social processes in the classroom, the establishment of dominance relationships, or conflicts with peers. Such preoccupations may then interfere with their focus on academic work.

Schwartz and Gorman (2011) suggested that the association between popularity and academic difficulties is also influenced by existing norms of the social context of these students. In a school where academic achievement is not the norm, but misconduct or academic disengagement is the norm, students who want to be popular should not focus on academic achievement. In a school where academic achievement is the norm, students can be popular with their peers and academically engaged at the same time. The first explanation for the association between popularity and academic difficulties focuses on a behavioral process (distraction by other issues); the second focuses on the influence of the social context. Both explanations may be valid and occur at the same time. Further research that addresses these issues to further understand the association between popularity and low academic achievement when it occurs, and the mechanisms that is reinforce or maintain this association, is important.

Drop-out, Truancy, and Absenteeism

Relatively little is known about the association between popularity and truancy, absenteeism, and dropping out of school. The evidence comes from one study. Schwartz and colleagues (2006) found a positive correlation between popularity and unexplained absences in high school. Further, for adolescents who were highly aggressive, increases in popularity were associated with increases in unexplained absences.

As for low academic achievement, popularity may be associated with truancy and absenteeism in schools where academic achievement is not the norm. The association may be particularly strong for adolescents who are part of cliques with anti-academic values. Such students may believe that they gain in status in the eyes of their peers by not following the rules of school and engaging in academic misconduct.

The association with dropping out of school is more complex, because students who drop out of school are not longer part of the peer system that they may value. If adolescents who desire to be popular engage in academic misconduct to gain status in the eyes of their peers, and they subsequently drop out of school, they no longer enjoy the audience that they desired to be popular amongst in the first place. Although we do not know of available data on this association, we hypothesize that the association between popularity and dropping out of school is negative, even for adolescents who are also aggressive, manipulative, or antisocial as part of their attempts to be cool and win status in the peer group. While they may temporarily engage in such anti-academic behaviors to win status, their focus on peer group status would also motivate them to stay part of the peer group at school. Examining the association between popularity and drop-out, and how it varies between schools with different behavioral norms, is an interesting topic for further research.

Attitudes and Motivation

Relatively little is known directly about the associations of popularity with academic attitudes and school motivation. Based on the earlier findings discussed above, indicating mixed associations of popularity with academic achievement and school problems, similar results can be expected. As before, it can be expected that there are two groups of popular youth: those with high levels of motivation to succeed academically, and those for whom these levels are expected to be low. The latter group might be more concerned with their image and status in the peer group and their lack of academic interest is expected to be more exacerbated if they are part of a school context when high academic achievement is not the norm.

Indirect evidence for an association between popularity and academic motivation comes from a recent study by LaFontana and Cillessen (2010). In this study, the authors examined the degree to which children and adolescents over a wide age range prioritize popularity in the peer group over other domains of their social and academic lives. Participants were children and adolescents from first grade through senior year of college, representing all ages from 6 to 22 years, who were presented with a series of social dilemmas in which achieving popularity was opposed to five other priorities: friendship, academic and athletic accomplishments, following rules, being prosocial, and romantic interests. A curvilinear trend was found for the priority of popularity that peaked in early adolescence. At this age especially, participants prioritized status enhancement over the other domains. Across the age range of this study, boys and majority students were more preoccupied with reputational status than girls and minority students. The fact that these findings are stronger for majority students suggests that when students prioritize popularity they are focusing on a group norm carried by the peer group at large.

There is a challenge that results from these findings, especially for relatively low-functioning schools or schools in neighborhoods where striving towards academic excellence may not be an a priori giving. In those cases, teachers and school administrators face the additional challenge of peer group norms towards low achievement (or at least avoidance of achievements), especially in the essential middle and early high school years when concern about popularity is high. Because adolescents' concerns about popularity and their status in the peer group and their peer relationships are a normative aspect of adolescent development, peer group pressures against achievement are difficult to overcome.

Classroom Behavior

Classroom behaviors include both "on task" behaviors such as effort, engagement, and cooperation, and "off task" behaviors that impact task performance, such as classroom disruptiveness and aggression. Much is known about the classroom behaviors that are associated with acceptance and popularity. Studies have focused on the unique behavioral correlates of acceptance and popularity. Measures of social behavior have been derived from other peer nominations, teacher reports, or self-reports, and can be divided into behaviors that are generally prosocial (e.g., cooperation, sharing) or generally antisocial (e.g., aggression, bullying, starting fights). These studies show that acceptance is consistently correlated with prosocial behaviors; popularity, in contrast, is consistently correlated with a mixture of prosocial and antisocial behaviors (e.g., Cillessen & Mayeux, 2004; Rose, Swenson, & Waller, 2004; see, for reviews, Cillessen & Rose, 2005; Mayeux, Houser, & Dyches, 2011).

One important finding that stands out in this research is the opposite association of aggression with acceptance and popularity. Aggression is consistently negatively correlated with acceptance, but positively with popularity. This finding holds true for both overt aggression and relational aggression. Overt aggression is open and clearly visible and consists of obvious aggressive acts such as calling someone names, starting a physical fight, or kicking or pushing someone. Relational aggression is less clearly visible and direct and consists of attempts to hurt someone else in the relational domain. Examples are excluding someone from a group, spreading a rumor about someone, or setting one person up against another.

Interestingly, the opposite associations of aggression with acceptance and popularity apply to both types of aggression. Cillessen and Mayeux (2004) found that overt and relational aggression both were positively correlated with popularity in grades 5 through 9. Using open-ended descriptions as well as sociometric methods in grades 4 through 8, LaFontana and Cillessen (2002) also found that both forms of aggression predicted lower acceptance, but higher popularity. Thus, popularity is clearly associated with a mixture of prosocial and antisocial behaviors. The antisocial behaviors involved may be disruptive in the school context, for the students themselves, or for their social environment at school. This is especially seen in the association with bullying.

The antisocial behaviors associated with popularity that are disruptive in the school context in particular include bullying. In a study with early adolescents, de Bruyn, Cillessen, and Wissink (2010) examined the role of acceptance and popularity in bullying and victimization in the peer group. They hypothesized that acceptance negatively predicts bullying, whereas popularity positively predicts bullying, and that both acceptance and popularity negatively predict victimization. Interactions between acceptance and popularity were predicted as well. Participants were 13–14 year-old adolescents who completed sociometric assessments in their classrooms. Both bullying and victimization were predicted by an interaction between acceptance and popularity. Bullying increased when popularity increased, and this effect was further exacerbated when acceptance decreased. Victimization increased when popularity decreased, and this effect was also stronger when acceptance was lower.

The positive association between popularity and bullying behavior implies that some students with a position of high status in the peer group engage in aggressive or manipulative behaviors to maintain their own position of prominence. At the level of the individual, bullying can be expected to correlate negatively with school achievement. In addition, bullying behavior has a negative effect on classroom and school climate and also impairs school functioning indirectly in that way. Those, to the degree that popularity leads to aggressive and/or bullying behaviors aimed at status maintenance and control, these classroom behaviors play a role in causing a negative association between bullying and school achievement. They further reinforce the necessity to reduce bullying in schools, but also point to a mechanisms in which bullying behavior may be maintained or reinforced in peer groups—through the rewards they have in terms of high status, dominance, and control in the peer group. In the same way that negative school attitudes may be maintained by peer-related processes, the same applies to bullying. The challenge for intervention in both cases is high, when these outcomes are reinforced and maintained by popularity or high status in the peer group.

Other Outcomes Relevant for School Functioning

Several studies have evidenced other risk factors associated with popularity that may indirectly impact school functioning. Mayeux, Sandstrom, and Cillessen (2008) examined the associations of peer acceptance and popularity with substance use and abuse and early sexual behavior in high school students. Popularity in 10th grade predicted the increased use of alcohol and more risky sexual behavior in 12th grade for both boys and girls. Smoking in 10th grade also predicted increased 12th grade popularity for boys, suggesting that the associations between popularity and its correlates are bidirectional. Peer acceptance was not associated with any of the risk behaviors measured.

Sandstrom and Cillessen (2006) examined the predictions of internalizing and externalizing problems over time. Fifth grade students completed peer nominations assessing peer acceptance and popularity. Measures of behavior problems were assessed through a composite of peer, teacher, and self-reports at the end of the eighth grade. Examination of the unique concurrent associations of each popularity type with peer-nominated social characteristics in fifth grade demonstrated that peer acceptance was positively associated with prosocial behavior and inclusive behavior, while popularity was positively associated with overt and relational aggression. Acceptance and popularity also had unique associations with adjustment over time. Acceptance in the fifth grade was associated with lower levels of externalizing behavior problems three years later, while popularity was associated with higher levels of these problems over time.

Sandstrom and Cillessen (2010) combined the approaches from these previous studies to examine the effects of high school popularity on social and academic adjustment after high school. This study examines the adjustment consequences of popularity beyond high school and the role of relational aggression in this process. Yearly sociometric measures of popularity and relational aggression were gathered across grades 9–12 in high school. Data on post-high school adjustment were collected from three yearly self-report assessments of depression, psychopathology, workplace victimization, and risk behavior. The results indicated a positive association between popularity in high school and risk behaviors in emerging adulthood, after controlling for prior levels of risk behaviors.

The results from these studies show across various age groups that popularity is associated with risks that may impair school functioning. Moreover, some of these risks may carry over from the immediate school context of middle or high school to later functioning even after high school. Similar risks were not associated with peer acceptance. This leads us to further speculate about the unique meanings of peer acceptance and popularity in the peer group.

TWO FORMS OF SOCIAL COMPETENCE

One way to achieve this is to think of peer acceptance and popularity as indicators of two different form of being socially competent or socially skilled in interactions with others and in the peer group in general. The nature and definition of social competence is a much-debated issue in the social development literature. General definitions of social competence have referred to adequacy, effectiveness, or success in interactions with peers. Beyond such abstract definitions, a common operational definition of social competence has been in terms of peer acceptance (Rose-Krasnor, 1997). Indeed, and as indicated, peer acceptance correlates with many prosocial behaviors and skills. However, the distinction between acceptance and popularity suggests that a one-dimensional view of social competence as represented by peer acceptance only is incomplete. The distinction suggests that there is not one way to be socially competent with peers, but two. Cillessen and Bellmore (2010) theorized that acceptance and popularity reflect two different ways of being competent or successful in the peer group.

The first form of social competence refers to youths' abilities to be prosocial and cooperative, to perceive others accurately, take their perspective, and properly read and understand their emotions. Prosocial behavior, interpersonal perception accuracy, perspective taking, and emotion understanding enable the child or adolescent to be empathic, understanding, and supportive, and to respond to the needs of peers. Children and adolescents who possess these skills behave in ways that make them well liked. They do not need force to express or assert themselves; hence, aggression or dominant behaviors are not part of their behavioral repertoire.

The second form of social competence refers to youths' abilities to be interpersonally effective, achieve goals in social situations, either for themselves or the group, in principle through playing by the rules, but if needed through convincing argumentation, coercion and forcefulness, strong self-assertions, or intelligent manipulation. A child or adolescent who excels in this domain may not be the most interpersonally sensitive, but is a well-connected leader who can achieve goals in effective ways that may be seen as domineering, aggressive, or manipulative by some, but as assertive, socially savvy, and effective by others. Those who possess these skills behave in ways that make them visible, prestigious, and central in the peer group; hence they are seen as popular, but not necessarily well-liked. They may use force to assert themselves; therefore, certain forms of aggression or dominant behaviors are in their behavioral repertoire.

The view that dominance and aggression may be associated with social competence is not without controversy. On the one hand are researchers who, from various theoretical perspectives, point to the benefits associated with certain forms of aggression and to the fact that highly successful individuals (e.g., those who control resources) often use aggression or a combination of prosocial and aggressive tactics. This is perfectly consistent with the behavioral correlates profile of popularity. On the other hand are researchers who argue that any form of aggression is in the end always maladaptive and dysfunctional and a sign of underlying psychopathology, even when there are short-term gains associated with it. This is not an either/or issue, but there seems some truth to both perspectives. The data on the concurrent behavioral correlates of likeability and popularity reviewed above clearly and consistently show positive correlations of aggression, especially relational aggression, with popularity, and indicate that relational aggression can be used to win prestige in the peer group. However, the long-term consequences of popularity indicate that there are also costs associated with it.

These two forms of social competence may have different developmental origins. Almost nothing is known about the roots of popularity, its developmental precursors, and childhood antecedents. Almost no prospective longitudinal research has been conducted on the development of popular status. As a result, little is known about the early predictors of popularity, such as early childhood behaviors or strengths. However, there are some exceptions.

Rodkin and Roisman (2010) analyzed data from the National Institute of Child Health and Human Development (NICHD) Study of Early Child Care and Youth Development (SECCYD) to examine childhood precursors of popularity and found significant predictors in children's experiences at daycare. Based on teacher ratings aggregated over grades 3–6, participants were classified as popular–aggressive, popular–nonaggressive, aggressive–nonpopular, or nonpopular–nonaggressive. Children who were both popular and aggressive in elementary school spent more hours per week in nonmaternal childcare before they went to grade school. This indicates that certain roots of popularity in elementary school are present in children's early socialization experiences with peers before elementary school.

In another study, Peters, Cillessen, Riksen-Walraven, and Haselager (2010) examined the childhood precursors of acceptance and popularity in early adolescence. The study used data collected at 15 months of age, 5 years, and 9–10 years. At 15 months, two dimensions of parent–child interaction were observed. *Effective guidance* is marked by effective structure and limit setting, high quality of instructions, and supportive presence by parents, as well as compliance and low avoidance by the child. *Negative interaction* is marked by hostility and lack of respect and support from parents, and child negativity and the absence of positive affect. At 5 years, preschool teachers evaluated children's ego-resilience and ego-control with the California Child Q-Sort. *Ego-resilience* is the child's capacity to respond flexibly but persistently to challenging social situations. *Ego-control* is the child's capacity to regulate emotions, without being excessively inhibited (overcontrol) or impulsive (undercontrol). At 9–10 years, popularity and acceptance were assessed with peer nominations in the participants' classrooms.

Analyses indicated that from 15 months to 5 years, effective guidance predicted ego-resilience for girls, and negative interactions predicted ego-undercontrol for boys. From 5 years to 9–10 years, ego-resilience predicted peer acceptance for both genders. The prediction of popularity varied by gender: It was predicted by earlier ego-resilience for girls, but by earlier ego-undercontrol for boys. This suggests that popularity depends on a dominant or forceful presence for boys, but on more subtle aspects of social interaction for girls.

These studies suggest that popularity in school is rooted in earlier relationships with parents and peers. The unique antecedents of acceptance and popularity validate that they are separate dimensions of peer group functioning in the school context. Popularity has a developmental history that differs from peer acceptance, for example in ego-undercontrol for boys that typically predicts low peer acceptance. This further supports the idea that popularity also has unique consequences for school adjustment. As indicated in the previous sections, there are risks associated with low peer acceptance and risks associated with high popularity. In the next section we discuss implications for the practice of education.

IMPLICATIONS FOR EDUCATION AND INTERVENTION

Role of Peer Influence

Because popular students are often seen as cool and have influence over others (complex association with peer influence), if popular students do engage in behaviors that are undesirable, their behavior may spread across the classroom or the grade at large (in middle or high school grades) and as a result have a larger impact on others beyond the adjustment of the individual student. It could influence the classroom climate with further negative consequences for all involved. In such cases, it may be difficult to change the allure that the individual popular and influential student has on the classroom or peer group at large. Intervention in that case may take a more systemic approach.

Popularity has a complex connection to peer influence. Given the key elements of popularity as impact and an interaction between dominant behaviors and desirable characteristics, it is not surprising that popular peers have influence. The *popularity effect* is the influence that popular peers have over others. Sandstrom (2011) described what is known about this effect. The popularity effect leads to the *popularity risk hypothesis*. This is the idea that certain risks are associated with being popular. Schwartz and Gorman (2011) described what is known about the concurrent and later risks of popularity.

The popularity effect and the popularity risk hypothesis are two sides of the same coin. Popular peers can influence others because of their position of high status and their skills (Sandstrom, 2011). However, being in a position of high status often comes with the desire to maintain it (e.g., Eder, 1985; Merten, 1997). As a result, popular peers not only influence others but are also susceptible to influence from others (Lansu, Cillessen, & Karremans, 2009). In order to maintain their position of prominence, they adopt behaviors that carry high status in the peer group; some of these behaviors are deviant from the mainstream but highly status-enhancing, such as alcohol or drug use (e.g., Mayeux et al., 2008).

Further, maintaining a position of prominence and influence is hard work and may fail. That may be why stress and depression are also among the risks of popularity (Sandstrom & Cillessen, 2010). Finally, those who engage in status-maintaining aggression and manipulation are at risk of reciprocation, as aggression is a highly reciprocal behavior. This places popular students at risk for victimization, especially when the power balance in the peer group tips into a direction that is unfavorable for them (see Eder, 1985; Merten, 1997). In summary, while popularity means impact and influence, the nature of popularity also implies various risks.

These processes, specified by the popularity effect and the popularity risk hypotheses, can also be applied to the school adjustment variables that have been considered in this chapter. On the one hand, if a popular student decides to set a trend of poor achievement and school attendance, a negative attitude towards school and teachers, and disruptive off-task behaviors in the classroom, other students will be motivated to emulate this student's behavior. On the other hand, if a popular student perceives that such a pattern of behaviors is a norm for admiration, coolness, or high status among a substantial segment of the school population, she or he may adopt these behaviors to maintain her or his status or to further enhance it. It is clear, then, that there is a reciprocal relationship between the behavior or popular students and certain norms among the student population, and that it is possible that a negative vicious circle can emerge between the two that may be hard to break and turn into a positive direction. This further strengthens the importance of paying attention to the dynamics of the peer group in general, and of popular students in particular, when examining school adjustment problems.

Example Intervention Study

In an example of an intervention, van den Berg, Segers, and Cillessen (2010) tested whether an experimental manipulation of distance between classmates can change how they see each other and can also change overall classroom climate. In this intervention, seating arrangements in classrooms were changed on the basis of peer nominations and likeability ratings. Students who had negative perceptions of each other, as determined by negative peer nominations and low likeability ratings, were seated closer together. This was expected to have two effects. First, it was examined if decreasing the seating distance between students who did not get along would make them see each other more positively. Second, it was examined if this might generalize to a positive effect on overall classroom climate, as indicated by a reduction in aggression and bullying and an increase in overall peer acceptance, cooperation, and friendship.

The experiment included 817 fifth- and sixth-grade students in randomly assigned intervention and control classrooms with a pretest and posttest. The pretest took place in the first four weeks of school after the summer. Peer affiliations were measured with a standard sociometric procedure; interpersonal distance data were derived from a map of the classroom seating arrangement. Based on these data, a new seating arrangement was made for the intervention classrooms based on the criterion that the distance between target pairs of students with negative relationships should be reduced by at least 50% on average. The arrangements were approved by the teacher, and then implemented. The children were not told that the new seating arrangements were based on their pretest sociometric data. The new arrangements were implemented in the intervention classrooms 10 to 12 weeks after the pretest and lasted 12 to 14 weeks, after which the posttest took place. Children again completed the sociometric measures from the pretest.

The results indicated that the intervention indeed had large effects on the likeability ratings of children who were perceived the most negatively. The decrease in distance led to higher peer acceptance ratings for students who were perceived the most negatively in the beginning of the school year. In addition, the intervention classrooms looked significantly less hostile than the control classrooms at the posttest. The intervention led to an overall reduction in victimization and withdrawn behavior nominations, suggesting that bringing negative peer pairs closer together can generalize to an overall effect on classroom climate that includes less bullying and less social isolation.

Several processes may explain why children became more positive towards peers they initially did not like when their distance from them in the classroom was reduced. One possibility is that the reduced distance created opportunities for positive peer interactions such as sharing or working together on a classroom assignment that they simply never had before. It is also possible that the peer they disliked was more similar to themselves than they had thought. It is also possible that by having more frequent interactions they became more involved in each other's circle of friends on the playground or outside of school, which might have fostered further positive interactions. Future research should determine the exact mechanisms through which a reduced interpersonal distance among antagonistic peers led to more positive peer relationships and a more positive overall classroom climate. The findings support the focus on peer group dynamics and strategies to reduce peer rejection and victimization at school.

This study did not examine the status of the peers involved, only their mutual relationships. It would be possible to further refine this study by examining whether the effects would change if one of the members of an antagonistic dyad was popular, for example. On the one hand, given the popularity effect discussed above, improved perceptions of a rejected peer might spread faster in the peer group if the agent of change is a high-status popular student rather than a less prominent student. On the other hand, given the popularity risk hypothesis, the popular student might also become a ringleader bully of further bullying against the rejected student, if the popular student would find the rejected student an easy victim in-strumental in improving his own status. The effects of reduced distance between antagonistic peers are not the same as the effects of popularity, but the effects of popularity may interact with the effects of distance reduction in ways that may either increase or reduce their beneficial effects. Future studies should examine these interactions to determine which combinations of interpersonal distance manipulations with peer status of the actors involved are most likely to benefit classroom climate.

CONCLUSION

Popularity and acceptance are unique dimensions of peer groups in classrooms and schools and reflect two different ways of being successful with peers. Clearly, more is known about the associations of acceptance with school adjustment than of popularity. This is not surprising given the longer tradition of studying peer acceptance than of studying popularity.

For the associations between acceptance and school adjustment, the picture is generally positive. Accepted and well-liked students generally do well in school on each of the measures of school adjustment that were considered in this chapter. They do well in terms of actual achievement and have positive attitudes and motivation towards school. They score low on measures of absenteeism and truancy, and low on disruptive school behaviors.

For the associations between popularity and school adjustment, the picture is clearly mixed. Some studies found positive associations of popularity with school adjustment, while others find negative associations. A factor that clearly plays a role in these different results is the degree to which the popular student is involved in bullying or other aggressive or manipulative behaviors in school. Popular students who score high on these variables might be considered "popular bullies" and clearly are the ones scoring lower on school engagement and adjustment. Popular students who do not engage in bullying aggression score high on school adjustment outcomes. This seems to be true for both boys and girls. These findings strengthen the idea that there are two subgroups of popular students, as indicated by several studies.

Future research on popularity and school adjustment should examine the exact nature of the school adjustment differences between both sub-groups of popular youth. On which of the measures of school adjustment that were considered do they actually differ? Are the differences located more in the domain of abilities or in the domain of motivation and attitudes? And what can be said about the causes of such differences? Longitudinal data over several subsequent school years would be needed to address this last question. Not only should we look at the causes and developmental histories of such differences among popular youth, but also on their consequences and unique effects on other students. Popular youth with negative attitudes towards school can have a substantial negative impact on their peers' school engagement. In contrast, popular youth with positive school engagement can play a substantial role as agents of positive change. Research should examine what role they can play in interventions to improve classroom climate, and thereby the school adjustment of all other students in a classroom or grade. The role of popular peers in school adjustment, both at the level of the individual student and at a systemic level, continues to be an important issue on our research agenda.

REFERENCES

Asher, S. R., & Coie, J. D. (1990). *Peer rejection in childhood.* New York, NY: Cambridge University Press.

Boyatzis, C. J., Baloff, P., & Durieux, C. (1998). Effects of perceived attractiveness and academic success on early adolescent peer popularity. *Journal of Genetic Psychology, 159,* 337–344.

Brown, B. B. (2011). Popularity in peer group perspective: The role of status in adolescent peer systems. In A. H. N. Cillessen, D. Schwartz, & L. Mayeux (Eds.), *Popularity in the peer system* (pp. 165–192). New York, NY: Guilford Press.

Cillessen, A. H. N. (2009). Sociometric methods. In K. H. Rubin, W. M. Bukowski, & B. Laursen (Eds.), *Handbook of peer interactions, relationships, and groups* (pp. 82–99). New York, NY: Guilford Press.

Cillessen, A. H. N., & Bellmore, A. D. (2011). Social skills and social competence in interactions with peers. In P. K. Smith & C. H. Hart (Eds.), *Wiley-Blackwell handbook of childhood social development* (2nd ed., pp. 393–412). Malden, MA: Blackwell.

Cillessen, A. H. N., & Bukowski, W. M. (Eds.), (2000). *Recent advances in the measurement of acceptance and rejection in the peer system: New Directions for Child and Adolescent Development (No. 88).* San Francisco, CA: Jossey-Bass.

Cillessen, A. H. N., & Marks, P. E. L. (2011). Conceptualizing and measuring popularity. In A. H. N. Cillessen, D. Schwartz, & L. Mayeux (Eds.), *Popularity in the peer system* (pp. 25–56). New York, NY: Guilford Press.

Cillessen, A. H. N., & Mayeux, L. (2004). From censure to reinforcement: Developmental changes in the association between aggression and social status. *Child Development, 75,* 147–163.

Cillessen, A. H. N., & Mayeux, L. (2007). Expectations and perceptions at school transitions: The role of peer status and aggression. *Journal of School Psychology, 45,* 567–586.

Cillessen, A. H. N., & Rose, A. J. (2005). Understanding popularity in the peer system. *Current Directions in Psychological Science, 14,* 102–105.

Coie, J. D., & Dodge, K. A., & Coppotelli, H. (1982). Dimensions and types of social status: A cross-age perspective. *Developmental Psychology, 18,* 557–569.

de Bruyn, E. H., & Cillessen, A. H. N. (2006). Heterogeneity of girls' consensual popularity: Academic and interpersonal behavioral profiles. *Journal of Youth and Adolescence, 35,* 435–445.

de Bruyn, E. H., Cillessen, A. H. N., & Wissink, I. B. (2010). Associations of peer acceptance and perceived popularity with bullying and victimization in early adolescence. *Journal of Early Adolescence, 30,* 543–566.

DeRosier, M. E., Kupersmidt, J. B., & Patterson C. J. (1994). Children's academic and behavioral adjustment as a function of the chronicity and proximity of peer rejection. *Child Development, 65,* 1799–1813.

Eder, D. (1985). The cycle of popularity: Interpersonal relations among female adolescents. *Sociology of Education, 58,* 154–165.

Estell, D. B. (2008). Peer groups, popularity, and social preference: Trajectories of social functioning among students with and without learning disabilities. *Journal of Learning Disabilities, 41,* 5–14.

Guay, F., Boivin, M., & Hodges, E. V. E. (1999). Predicting change in academic achievement: A model of peer experiences and self-system processes. *Journal of Educational Psychology, 91,* 105–115.

Kupersmidt, J. B., & Coie, J. D. (1990). Preadolescent peer status, aggression, and school adjustment as predictors of externalizing problems in adolescence. *Child Development, 61,* 1350–1362.

Ladd, G. W. (2005). *Children's peer relations and social competence. A century of progress.* New Haven, CT: Yale University.

LaFontana, K. M., & Cillessen, A. H. N. (1998). The nature of children's stereotypes of popularity. *Social Development, 7,* 301–320.

LaFontana, K. M., & Cillessen, A. H. N. (2002). Children's perceptions of popular and unpopular peers: A multi-method assessment. *Developmental Psychology, 38,* 635–647.

LaFontana, K. M., & Cillessen, A. H. N. (2010). Developmental changes in the priority of perceived status in childhood and adolescence. *Social Development, 19,* 130–147.

Lansu, T. A. M., Cillessen, A. H. N., & Karremans, J. C. (2009). *Effects of actor and target status on implicit measures of peer influence.* Society for Research in Child Development, Denver, CO.

Lease, A., Musgrove, K. T., & Axelrod, J. L. (2002). Dimensions of social status in preadolescent peer groups: Likeability, perceived popularity, and social dominance. *Social Development, 11,* 508–533.

Mayeux, L., Houser, J. J., & Dyches, K. D. (2011). Social acceptance and popularity: Two distinct forms of peer status. In A. H. N. Cillessen, D. Schwartz, & L. Mayeux (Eds.), *Popularity in the peer system* (pp. 79–102). New York, NY: Guilford Press.

Mayeux, L., Sandstrom, M. J., & Cillessen, A. H. N. (2008). Is being popular a risky proposition? *Journal of Research on Adolescence, 18*, 49–74.

Meijs, N., Cillessen, A. H. N., Scholte, R. H. J., Segers, E., & Spijkerman, R. (2010). Social intelligence and academic achievement as predictors of adolescent popularity. *Journal of Youth and Adolescence, 39*, 62–72.

Merten, D. E. (1997). The meaning of meanness: Popularity, competition, and conflict among junior high school girls. *Sociology of Education, 70*, 175–191.

Moreno, J. L. (1934). *Who shall survive?* Washington, DC: Nervous and Mental Disease Publishing Company.

Newcomb, A. F., Bukowski, W. M., & Pattee, L. (1993). Children's peer relations: A meta-analytic review of popular, rejected, neglected, controversial, and average sociometric status. *Psychological Bulletin, 113*, 99–128.

O'Neil, R., Welsh, M., Parke, R.D., Wang, S., & Strand, C. (1997). A longitudinal assessment of the academic correlates of early peer acceptance and rejection. *Journal of Clinical Child Psychology, 26*, 290–303.

Parker, J. G., & Asher, S. R. (1987). Peer relations and later personal adjustment: Are low accepted children at risk? *Psychological Bulletin, 102*, 357–389.

Parkhurst, J. T., & Hopmeyer, A. (1998). Sociometric popularity and peer-perceived popularity: Two distinct dimensions of peer status. *Journal of Early Adolescence, 18*, 135–144.

Peters, E., Cillessen, A. H. N., Riksen-Walraven, J. M., & Haselager, G. T. J. (2010, March). *Developmental precursors of sociometric and perceived popularity in early adolescence.* Paper presented at the biennial meeting of the Society for Research on Adolescence, Philadelphia, PA.

Prinstein, M. J., & Dodge, K. A. (2008). *Understanding peer influence in children and adolescents.* New York, NY: Guilford Press.

Rodkin, P. C., & Roisman, G. I. (2010). Antecedents and correlates of the popular-aggressive phenomenon in elementary school. *Child Development, 81*, 838–852.

Rodkin, P. C., Farmer, T. W., Pearl, R., & Van Acker, R. (2000). Heterogeneity of popular boys: Antisocial and prosocial configurations. *Developmental Psychology, 36*, 14–24.

Rose, A. J., Swenson, L. P., & Waller, E. M. (2004). Overt and relational aggression and perceived popularity: Developmental differences in concurrent and prospective relations. *Developmental Psychology, 40*, 378–387.

Rose-Krasnor, L. (1997). The nature of social competence: A theoretical review. *Social Development, 6*, 111–135.

Sandstrom, M. J. (2011). The power of popularity: Influence processes in childhood and adolescence. In A. H. N. Cillessen, D. Schwartz, & L. Mayeux (Eds.), *Popularity in the peer system* (pp. 219–244). New York, NY: Guilford Press.

Sandstrom, M. J., & Cillessen, A. H. N. (2006). Likable versus popular: Distinct implications for adolescent adjustment. *International Journal of Behavioral Development, 30*, 305–314.

Sandstrom, M. J., & Cillessen, A. H. N. (2010). Life after high school: Adjustment of popular teens in emerging adulthood. *Merrill-Palmer Quarterly, 56,* 474–499.

Schwartz, D., & Gorman, A. H. (2011). The high price of high status: Popularity as a mechanism of risk. In A. H. N. Cillessen, D. Schwartz, & L. Mayeux (Eds.), *Popularity in the peer system* (pp. 245–270). New York, NY: Guilford Press.

Schwartz, D., Gorman, A. H., Nakamoto, J., & McKay, T. (2006). Popularity, social acceptance, and aggression in adolescent peer groups: Links with academic performance and school attendance. *Developmental Psychology, 42,* 1116–1127.

Vandell, D. L., & Hembree, S. E. (1994). Peer social status and friendship: Independent contributors to children's social and academic adjustment. *Merrill-Palmer Quarterly, 40,* 461–477.

van den Berg, Y. H. M. (2009). *Interpersonal distance and peer relations: A longitudinal field experiment.* Unpublished master's thesis, Behavioural Science Institute, Radboud University, Heijendaal, The Netherlands,

van den Berg, Y. H. M., Segers, E., & Cillessen, A. H. N. (2011). Changing peer perceptions and victimization through classroom arrangements: A field experiment. *Journal of Abnormal Child Psychology.*

Wentzel, K. R. (1991). Relations between social competence and academic achievement in early adolescence. *Child Development, 62,* 1066–1078.

Wentzel, K. R. (2005). Peer relationships, motivation, and academic performance at school. In A. J. Elliot & C. S. Dweck (Eds.), *Handbook of competence and motivation* (pp. 279–296). New York, NY: Guilford Press.

Wentzel, K. R. (2008). Peers and academic functioning at school. In K. H. Rubin, W. M. Bukowski, & B. Laursen (2009). *Handbook of peer interactions, relationships, and groups* (pp. 531–547). New York, NY: Guilford press.

Wentzel, K. R., & Asher, S. R. (1995). The academic lives of neglected, rejected, popular, and controversial children. *Child Development, 66,* 754–763.

Wentzel, K. R., & Caldwell, K. (1997). Friendships, peer acceptance, and group membership: Relations to academic achievement in middle school. *Child Development, 68,* 1198–1209.

Zettergren, P. (2003). School adjustment in adolescence for previously rejected, average and popular children. *British Journal of Educational Psychology, 73,* 207–221.

CHAPTER 7

SOCIAL ACHIEVEMENT GOALS AND ADJUSTMENT AT SCHOOL DURING EARLY ADOLESCENCE

Allison M. Ryan, Rhonda S. Jamison, Huiyoung Shin, and Geneene N. Thompson

There is a long tradition of considering students' motivation to understand their academic engagement and achievement (Wigfield, Eccles, Schiefele, Roeser, & Davis-Kean, 2006). Such work has illustrated that motivation is distinct from other factors like ability and prior knowledge and is important to understanding engagement and achievement. Scholars concerned with peer relations have also drawn attention to motivation and distinguished its unique role in social functioning from social skills and self-regulatory capacities such as perceiving social cues and selecting appropriate strategies (Rose-Krasnor & Denham, 2009). In models of social information processing, social motivation plays a role in children's choice of strategies and evaluation of outcomes (Crick & Dodge, 1994). Social cognition and motivation are important to understanding students' success in forging friendships, gaining peer acceptance, and achieving status among peers at school.

Peer Relationships and Adjustment at School, pages 165–186
Copyright © 2012 by Information Age Publishing
165

Goals are a central aspect of motivation (see Wentzel, Donlan & Morrison, this volume). Goals are cognitive representations of things individuals want to accomplish and provide direction and energy for behavior (Pintrich, 2000). In our work we have used an achievement goal approach to social motivation that has provided new insights into adolescents' adjustment at school (e.g., Ryan & Shim, 2008).

In this chapter, we review our research on social achievement goals and adjustment at school during adolescence. Given the focus of the book on peer relationships and adjustment at school, we focus on our work with young adolescents. First, we discuss the nature of social achievement goals and how they differ from other conceptualizations of social goals. Second, we provide an overview of our conceptualization of social achievement goals and social adjustment. Third, we consider evidence for the relevance of achievement goals in the social domain. Next, we present our measure of social achievement goals, and then we discuss our research showing linkages between social achievement goals and adjustment at school for young adolescents. We consider both social and academic adjustment at school. We conclude with a discussion of future directions for research and educational implications.

SOCIAL GOALS

Many scholars have drawn attention to the importance of children's social goals in their peer relations (e.g., Crick & Dodge, 1994; Renshaw & Asher, 1983; Wentzel, 2005). Most work on social goals has identified categories of goals that represent outcomes or end-states that children and adolescents focus on when with their peers (Wentzel, 2000). With this approach scholars have highlighted that students often have goals for affiliation, approval, cooperation, responsibility, nurturance, intimacy, companionship, fun, revenge, domination, or control over others (e.g., Anderman, 1999; Chung & Asher, 1996; Ford, 1992; Jarvinan & Nicholls, 1996; McAdams, 1987; Rose & Asher, 1999; Wentzel, 2001). In general, goals that concern a prosocial orientation promote adaptive behaviors that lead to harmonious peer relationships and overall social adjustment, whereas goals that concern an antisocial orientation predict aggression, helplessness, or solitary behavior that lead to peer difficulties and social maladjustment (Chung & Asher; 1996; Erdley & Asher, 1996; Ojanen, Grönroos, & Salmivalli, 2005; Rose & Asher, 1999).

In the past several decades, scholars have highlighted more than a dozen different types of social goals that children and adolescents might pursue with their peers (e.g., Anderman, 1999; Chung & Asher, 1996; Jarvinan & Nicholls, 1996; Rose & Asher, 1999; Wentzel, 2001). In response to such numerous categories, researchers have recently called for a broader view on social goals, one that explicates an overarching framework that provides parsimony and key distinctions (see Ojanen et al., 2005; Ryan & Shim, 2006). Ojanen and her colleagues (2005) made the distinction between agency and communion goals and showed that such goals were correlated with peer nominations of social behaviors and status.

Social Achievement Goals

In our research, we have investigated adolescents' social achievement goals, which concern different orientations toward social competence that motivate behavior in social settings. Consistent with theory and research in other domains, our research has examined three different goal orientations in the social domain. A *social development goal* concerns a focus on developing social competence. With a social development goal, intrapersonal standards are used for evaluating one's competence. The focus is on whether one is learning new things, growing, and expanding. Success is judged by whether one is improving social skills, deepening the quality of relationships, or developing their social life in general.

In contrast, social demonstration goals concern a focus on demonstrating social competence. A *social demonstration-approach goal* concerns a focus on gaining from others positive judgments that one is socially skilled and desirable. A *social demonstration-avoid goal* concerns a focus on avoiding doing something that would incur negative judgments from others and indicate social undesirability. With both social demonstration goals, interpersonal standards, which concern social comparisons with others, are used for judging one's competence. With both social demonstration goals, attention is focused on the appearance of the self, and the reason for effort is to demonstrate self-worth. For a social demonstration-approach goal, success is garnering positive feedback from others, social prestige, and having a good reputation (e.g., being "popular" or seen as important), and for a social demonstration-avoid goal, success is avoiding negative judgments from others and lack of a reputation as socially awkward or ineffective (e.g., not being seen as a "loser" or "geek").

An achievement goal approach is different than a social-information processing or content approach to goals, which have been the predominant approaches to social goals. A social-information processing perspective concerns the specific outcome goals that children or adolescents formulate in response to a particular situation (e.g., Crick & Dodge, 1994; Erdley & Asher, 1996). A content approach concerns documenting the different outcomes that adolescents pursue and identifies categories of goals that characterize what adolescents want. Achievement goals differ from these approaches in their specificity and nature. Achievement goals are broader than the specific outcome goals identified in social-information processing research. Achievement goals embody an integrated system of beliefs focused on key distinctions in *why* individuals engage in behavior rather than identifying categories of goals that characterize what individuals want (Dweck, 1986; Pintrich, 2000). Thus, achievement goals transcend various content or outcome goals that are salient to adolescents in social settings (Dweck, 1996; Wentzel, 2005). Regardless of whether someone wants intimacy or fun or both in a social situation, it is likely they also want to feel socially competent (or at least not feel incompetent). Whether they strive to develop their social competence, demonstrate their social competence, or possibly both, has implications for their beliefs, behavior, and overall functioning. Thus, an achievement goal approach provides a new angle on social goals complementing and expanding current understanding of adolescents' social motivation.

SOCIAL ACHIEVEMENT GOALS AND SOCIAL ADJUSTMENT: A CONCEPTUAL FRAMEWORK

Based on extensive theory and research in other domains we proposed a conceptual framework articulating achievement goals and their relation to adjustment in the social domain (Ryan, Kiefer, & Hopkins, 2004). A social development goal is analogous to a mastery goal orientation in the academic realm, where success is defined in terms of internal standards of learning and growth more than external standards of display and social comparison. A social demonstration goal is analogous to a performance-approach goal orientation in the academic realm, where the goal is get higher grades or be seen as smarter than other students, not necessarily to increase knowledge and mastery. A social demonstration-avoid goal is analogous to a performance-avoid goal orientation in the academic realm, where the goal is to avoid getting the lowest grades or being seen as one of the worst students in the class.

Similar to other domains, we posit that achievement goals predict different patterns of cognition, affect, and behavior (Duda, 2005; Elliot, 2005; Kanfer & Ackerman, 2005). Achievement goals are a function of both personality and cues in the environment (see Dweck & Leggett, 1988; Elliot & Church, 1997). Achievement goals are viewed as the proximal influence on competence-relevant processes and outcomes (Elliot & Church, 1997). Achievement goals are conceptualized as a precursor to behaviors (i.e., why students do something precedes whether, if, and how they actually do it). Achievement goals set in motion different processes and lead to different outcomes (Dweck, 1999; Urdan, 1997). Thus, it is hypothesized that different social achievement goals will have different implications for social behavior, coping, and adjustment. Next, we provide an overview of our conceptual framework.

A Social Development Goal

With its focus on improving social competence, a social development goal is expected to be related to adaptive beliefs and behaviors. The nature of peer relationships evolves markedly during early adolescence, and it is likely that a social development goal would be adaptive in successfully navigating the changing terrain of peer relationships during early adolescence. As an approach goal, a social development goal is undergirded by positive views of one's social competence and enhanced efficacy to achieve desired social outcomes. Many social situations are likely to offer opportunities for developing social skills and friendships and thus social development goals are likely to lead to initiating interactions, foster prosocial behavior and diminish aggressive behavior with peers. Congruent with the focus on positive possibilities, a social development goal will be negatively associated with anxiety in social situations. Inherent in a social development goal is the belief that one can improve and grow in positive ways and thus mistakes are not threatening, which diminishes anxiety around peers. Novel and challenging situations are likely to be viewed as offering opportunity for development and thus be embraced. The quality of peer relationships is also likely to be enhanced because to achieve the goal of developing positive relationships, adolescents are more likely to attend to cues regarding the compatibility with others, to be thoughtful and reflect deeply regarding what is best for the relationship, and to be interested and remember information about their peers. Thus, a social development goal will foster the development of reciprocated friendships as well as positive features within those close friendships (e.g., intimacy, mutual support) and peer acceptance in students' larger peer networks. In sum, it is theorized that a social development goal leads to adaptive cognitive, affective, and behavioral processes and thus enhances social adjustment.

Social Demonstration Goals

During adolescence, peer relationships also change regarding social comparison behavior and self-conscious emotions, which is relevant for social demonstration goals. In the context of school, students spend an incredible amount of time in the presence of their peers and have much opportunity to observe and evaluate characteristics of their peers in a variety of situations. During early adolescence there is an increased focus on peer acceptance and the emerging social phenomenon of "popularity" (high prestige and visibility among students at school; Kinney, 1993; Rodkin & Ryan, 2012). Peer acceptance and popularity become salient concerns during early adolescence. Students can readily describe their position in the social hierarchy and identify who the most popular kids are at their school (Adler & Adler, 1998; Eder, 1985; LaFontana & Cillesen, 2002). Thus, given the increasing attention to comparisons of social attributes, it is likely that social demonstration goals are salient to many young adolescents.

A Social Demonstration-Avoid Goal

With its focus on avoiding negative judgments, a social demonstration-avoid goal is expected to lead to maladaptive beliefs and behaviors. As an avoidance goal, it is undergirded by negative views of one's social competence and fear of failure and thus associated with diminished efficacy to achieve desired social outcomes. Avoidance or withdrawal from social situations is likely to be preferred to engaging in social interactions, as it is safer and satisfies the goal of avoiding possible negative outcomes. Congruent with the focus on negative possibilities, a social demonstration-avoid goal will be associated with social anxiety. Inherent in a social demonstration-avoid goal is the belief that others' judgments determine their success and failure, and others' judgments are not completely under their control, which heightens anxiety. Mistakes or misunderstandings may incur negative evaluations and are therefore threatening. Thus, difficult situations would lead to disengagement rather than persistence. The quality of peer relationships would also suffer, because a focus on negative outcomes and being overly self-conscious and afraid of failure are likely to undermine positive interactions with peers by increasing anxious or avoidant strategies and behaviors. Thus, it is expected that a social demonstration-avoid goal will undermine the development of reciprocated friendships and positive features in those close friendships (e.g., intimacy, mutual support) as well as peer acceptance and social status in students' larger peer networks. In sum, it is expected that a social demonstration-avoid goal would lead to maladaptive cognitive, affective, and behavioral processes, and thus hinder social adjustment.

A Social Demonstration-Approach Goal

A social demonstration-approach goal is expected to have the potential to bring about both adaptive and maladaptive beliefs and behaviors. It is conceptualized to be a more complex goal, serving both approach tendencies (striving to achieve success, undergirded by high perceived social competence) and avoidance tendencies (concern with others' judgments and thus also undergirded by fear of failure; see Elliot & Church, 1997 for evidence in academic domain). Given the inherent approach nature of a social demonstration-approach goal, it will be positively associated with approaching and engaging in social situations with peers. Students who strive to achieve socially because they desire social status or recognition are likely to feel efficacious and interact with peers to achieve their goal. A social demonstration-approach goal may lead to prosocial behavior, but it is likely to be strategically targeted to individuals they want to impress. Further, with the goal being to achieve status as opposed to developing positive relationships, behavioral tactics may include manipulation and even overt aggression (see LaFontana & Cillesen, 2002; Rodkin, Farmer, Pearl, & vanAcker, 2000 for discussion of behaviors associated with social status in early adolescence). The strategies associated with a social demonstration-approach goal are likely to be focused on social appearance and concern impression-making rather than relationship-building. In this way a social demonstration-approach goal will facilitate social status among peers (i.e., being "popular" or "cool") but carry no benefits (i.e., be unrelated) for developing positive qualities in close friendships (e.g., intimacy, mutual support) or general peer acceptance (i.e., likeability).

EVIDENCE FOR THE RELEVANCE OF ACHIEVEMENT GOALS IN THE SOCIAL DOMAIN

Prior research provides support for extension to the social domain (Dweck, 1996). In an experimental design, Erdley, Loomis, Cain, and Dumas-Hines (1997) manipulated children's goal orientations on a social task—trying out for a pen pal. One group was given instructions emphasizing the evaluation of their social skills (the "demonstration" condition, called "performance" in their study), whereas another group was given instructions that emphasized the improvement of their social skills (the "development" condition, called "mastery" in their study). When rejected by their potential pen pal, children in the demonstration goal condition reacted in a more helpless manner compared to children in the development goal condition. In a second study, Erdley at al. (1997) found that children were consistent in development versus demonstration choices when presented with six hypothetical social dilemmas (e.g., decision regarding who to invite to a party—invite children you would like to get to know better or invite the most popular children in the class).

The Erdley et al. (1997) research established that children can be manipulated to pursue development or demonstration goals on a social activity and, when presented with hypothetical vignettes, consistently endorse development or demonstration goals. Further, social goals relate to social beliefs and behavior in a manner consistent with how academic goal orientations relate to academic beliefs and behavior.

In our research we have extended this work beyond the lab and hypothetical vignettes. We created several open-ended questions about social goals for young adolescent students who had just made the transition to middle school (Ryan & Shim, 2008, study 1; see also Ryan & Shim, 2006 for a similar study with college-age students). We examined students' social goals in their own words and in relation to what they were trying to achieve socially in their first year in middle school. This allowed us to see if different orientations to social competence could be seen when students wrote a few sentences about their social motivation their first year in middle school.

Students responded to one of three different versions of open-ended questions designed to elicit descriptions of their social goals. The questions were:

1. "What are your social goals for this year in school? Please elaborate *why* these goals are important to you."
2. Part A: "If you were a social success this year in sixth grade, what would this look like? Please elaborate *why* you would feel like a success."
   Part B: "If you were a social failure this year in sixth grade what would this look like? Please elaborate *why* you would feel like a failure."
3. "Sometimes kids feel good about how they get along with other kids at school. Other times kids do *not* feel good about how they get along with other kids at school. Think about how you are with other kids at school. Now think about the rest of the school year. What are your goals for getting along with other kids at school? Please elaborate *why* these goals are important to you."

For all three questions, students were told that by "social," we meant how you get along with other kids at school, friendships, and social life in general at school.

Each student's response was coded as evidence of a social development goal, a social demonstration goal, or neither. A response was coded as social development if it concerned a focus on developing social competence. To be coded as evidence of a social development goal, comments needed to go beyond achieving a certain outcome and make explicit reference to improvement. Thus, comments such as "develop *better* friendships," "be *more* friendly," and "be *less* selfish," were considered evidence for a social development goal, whereas comments such as "make friends," "be nice," or "have fun" were not (and thus, were coded as "neither achievement goal"). A small number of responses were double coded as they contained evidence of both development and demonstration goals.

A response was coded as evidence for a social demonstration goal if it concerned a focus on others' judgments of social competence and how one looked in front of others. Thus, comments such as "I would be seen as having lots of friends" and "Many people would like me" were considered evidence of a social demonstration goal because they explicitly refer to others' impressions, whereas comments such as "I would have lots of friends" were not. Further, comments such as "I would be popular," "I would be cool," "I would have popular friends," or "I would have cool friends" were coded as a social demonstration goal because the use of the term "popular" or "cool" connotes a focus on social recognition from others and a concern with high social status or a social standing that is "better" than others (i.e., the unpopular or uncool people). We also coded for approach-avoid valence in the responses. For example, "be more generous" would be coded approach, "be less selfish" would be coded avoid and "stay the same" would be coded neutral. We only examined this in responses to questions one and three (since question two explicitly asked about success and failure).

Across all three questions, 46% made reference to social development goals, 35% made reference to social demonstration goals, and 26% had responses that did not contain strong evidence for either social development or social demonstration goals. For the responses that had been coded as having evidence of a social development goal, 65% were approach and 15% were avoid; 13% contained both, and 7% were neutral. For the responses that were coded as having evidence of a social demonstration goal, 48% were approach, 24% were avoid, 29% contained both, and none were neutral.

In summary, the different orientations towards developing or demonstrating social competence can be seen in young adolescents' descriptions of their social goals and evaluations of social competence. The majority of students had comments that could be coded as evidence of a social development or social demonstration goal orientation. A distinction between approach and avoid orientations could be seen, particularly in relation to demonstration goals. Thus, a social achievement goal approach seems relevant to young adolescents' social motivation in middle school.

CREATING A MEASURE OF SOCIAL GOALS

In the next phase of our research we created a measure of social achievement goals for young adolescents (see Table 7.1). This was informed by our work on social achievement goals in college students (Ryan & Shim, 2006), the open-ended data from young adolescents, and pilot testing of survey items with young adolescents (see also Ryan, Kiefer, & Hopkins, 2004 for an earlier version of the measure). Our survey measure of social goals allowed us to examine the extent to which students endorsed different social goals in relation to their social lives at school and further understand the nature and structure of social achievement goals.

TABLE 7.1 Measure of Social Achievement Goals

Social Development Goal

I like it when I learn better ways to get along with friends.
I feel successful when I learn something new about how to get along with other kids.
I try to figure out what makes a good friend.
One of my goals is that my friendships become even better over time.
It is important to me to learn more about other kids and what they are like.
In general, I try to develop my social skills.

Social Demonstration-Approach Goal

It is important to me that other kids think I am popular.
It is important to me to have "cool" friends.
I want to be friends with the "popular" kids.
It is important to me to be seen as having a lot of friends.
I try to do things that make me look good to other kids.
My goal is to show other kids how much everyone likes me.

Social Demonstration-Avoid Goal

I try not to do anything that might make other kids tease me.
It is important to me that I don't embarrass myself around my friends.
I try to avoid doing things that make me look foolish to other kids.
When I am around other kids, I don't want to be made fun of.
When I am around other kids, I mostly just try not to goof up.
One of my main goals is to make sure other kids don't say anything bad about me.

Note: From Ryan & Shim (2008). All items are rated on a scale that ranged from 1 (*not at all true of me*) to 5 (*very true of me*).

In line with our conceptualization, exploratory factor analyses indicated a three factor model (social development, social demonstration-approach and social development-avoid goals; Ryan & Shim, 2008, study 2). Further, reliability analyses indicated that the social achievement goal measures had good internal consistency. Students differentiate among the various dimensions of social goal orientations in a manner consistent with what has been found in the academic and sports domains. This structure seems to span ages, as similar results have been found in college-age students (Horst, Finney, & Barron, 2007; Ryan & Shim, 2006) and elementary-age students (Ryan, Rodkin, Jamison, & Wilson, 2009).

SOCIAL ACHIEVEMENT GOALS
AND ADJUSTMENT AT SCHOOL

To examine if social goals relate to adjustment at school, we administered several different measures of adjustment to our young adolescent sample (many of whom had participated in our study concerning the open-ended responses about social goals in the early fall and all of whom had taken our measure of social achievement goals in the late fall). Consistent with our conceptual framework, students' social achievement goals were associated with their school adjustment. Social achievement goals were linked to students' social adjustment, coping with peer problems, as well as academic help-seeking. We describe each of these three studies in the next three sections.

Social Adjustment

In the first report from this dataset, we examined the implications of students' social achievement goals in the fall of the school year with their social adjustment at the end of the year (see Ryan & Shim, 2008, study 2). We examined a wide array of indicators of students' social adjustment at school, including three social behaviors that capture key distinctions in how children interact with peers and have been the source of much social development research: *prosocial, aggressive,* and *anxious-solitary* behavior (Ladd, 2005; Rubin, Bukowski, & Parker, 2006). We asked students and teachers to report on these behaviors. We also supplemented our measure of anxious-solitary behavior with a student-reported measure of *worry* in social situations. In addition, we considered social adjustment at both the friendship level and the wider peer network at school. For friendships, we examined student reports of the *positive qualities of a best friendship* (e.g., intimacy and mutual support; see Parker & Asher, 1993). For the wider peer network, we examined student reports of *popularity.*

A social development goal promoted social adjustment during the first year in middle school. Specifically, a social development goal was positively associated with prosocial behavior and best friendship quality and negatively associated with aggressive behavior. A focus on developing social competence seems to be a positive orientation towards the social world that sets in motion adaptive beliefs and behaviors. Interestingly, a social development goal was not associated with teacher ratings of social behavior.

A social demonstration-avoid goal hindered social adjustment during the first year in middle school. Specifically, a social demonstration-avoid goal was positively associated with subsequent anxious-solitary behavior. This was true for both self and teacher reports of anxious-solitary behavior. A social demonstration-avoid goal was also positively associated with subsequent student reports of social worry. Further, endorsement of a social demonstration-avoid goal was also negatively associated with subsequent self-ratings of popularity. A social demonstration-avoid goal had a null relation with positive features in close friendships, indicating that in familiar, private friend relations, an avoid orientation did not undermine the development of qualities such as intimacy and support. Overall, a focus on avoiding negative judgments of others sets in motion maladaptive beliefs and behaviors.

A social demonstration-approach goal had benefits and drawbacks for social adjustment during the first year in middle school. Specifically, a social demonstration-approach goal was positively associated with aggressive behavior and negatively associated with prosocial behavior. This pattern was found for both self and teacher reports of behavior. As expected, a social demonstration-approach goal was positively related to perceived popularity. Collectively, these results suggest that the pursuit of high social status may lead to aggressive or manipulative behavior to manage others' perceptions. This may explain why a social demonstration-approach goal was positively associated with social worry. Interestingly, for self-reports, a social development goal ameliorated the positive relation between a social demonstration-approach goal and aggressive behavior. This suggests that an additional benefit of a social development goal is that it can minimize the aggressive behavior that is associated with a social demonstration-approach goal.

There were several significant interactions among the social goals that indicated that it is important to appreciate that students pursue multiple goals that need to be considered jointly to understand their implications. For example, a social development goal was also related to subsequent perceived popularity but only when a social demonstration-avoid goal was low, indicating that when a student is focused on both goals, the drawbacks of a social demonstration-avoid goal neutralize the benefits of a social development goal. An interaction involving a social demonstration-avoid goal, perceived social competence, and gender indicated that for socially confident girls, a social demonstration-avoid goal was positively associated with aggressive behavior, whereas for socially unconfident girls and all boys, a social demonstration-avoid goal was negatively associated with aggressive behavior.

Coping with Peer Problems

In another report from this dataset, we examined the implications of social achievement goals for coping with peer problems at school (Shin & Ryan, 2011). As articulated in our conceptual framework, we posit that social achievement goals have important ramifications for how young adolescents cope when they experience a social failure or distressing social event in school. In the academic domain, failure situations have elucidated the divergent patterns of cognition, affect, and behavior stemming from achievement goals (Dweck & Leggett, 1988).

In the late fall, when we administered our measure of social achievement goals, we also administered a measure of coping with peer problems. We asked students to "think about a time when they had a problem with another kid at school (not a friend). For example: someone was mean to you or spreading a rumor about you. You didn't like it and wanted it to stop." Students were asked how they typically cope with such a problem.

Our coping with peer problem measure (created for this study) had three dimensions: mastery, avoidant, and nonchalance, which corresponded with the three social achievement goals (development, demonstration-avoid, and demonstration-approach). *Mastery coping with friends* refers to discussion with friends to gain advice on how to improve the situation. It is viewed as an adaptive response to stress because it involves efforts to change the situation and thus is more likely to diminish the problem and foster adjustment. *Avoidance coping with friends* refers to avoiding the topic with friends. It is viewed as a maladaptive response to stress because it involves disengagement and efforts to escape the problem. Such avoidance coping is unlikely to remedy problems and thus, over time it will undermine adjustment. *Nonchalance coping with friends* refers to nonchalant posturing or actively portraying oneself as not bothered by the problem. Nonchalance coping is distinct from mastery coping in that it discounts the problem to friends rather than trying to solve it; it is distinct from avoidance coping in that the problem is not hidden but reframed as not a real threat. It is viewed as maladaptive because portraying oneself as not bothered by a problem denies attention to potential solutions.

Individual differences in social achievement goals were related to different coping behavior, which in turn was associated with subsequent social behavior. A social development goal was associated with mastery coping with friends, which in turn was associated with subsequent best friendship quality. However, when controlling for all other variables, mastery coping with friends was also associated with subsequent anxious solitude. This is reminiscent of work on co-rumination that shows excessive discussion of problems between friends has trade-offs: heightened intimacy with friends over time but also heightened depression (Rose, 2002). Future work could investigate when mastery coping with friends turns into co-rumination (or vice versa) to better understand coping with friends.

A social demonstration-avoid goal was associated with avoidance coping with friends, which in turn was associated with subsequent anxious solitude. When students are concerned with avoiding embarrassment, they retreat when they experience a social problem at school. This is consistent with other research linking social demonstration-avoid goals to avoidant behavior but extends it to the realm of friends. Young adolescents with a social demonstration avoid goal are concerned about how they look even when they are with friends. This is interesting given that we had found that a social demonstration-avoid goal did not undermine best friend quality (Ryan & Shim, 2008, study 2).

In contrast, a social demonstration-approach goal was associated with nonchalance coping with friends, which in turn was associated with subsequent overt aggression. When it is important to students to have high social status, they are more likely to downplay the problem and portray that they are not bothered, and ultimately this can lead to an aggressive response, perhaps because the problem never gets addressed in a constructive manner with friends. These results provide some insight into why a social demonstration-approach goal leads to aggressive behavior.

Help Seeking with Academic Difficulties

Recently, we have been examining the implications of social achievement goals for academic adjustment (Ryan & Shin, 2011). Students learn in the presence of peers. Social achievement goals may have implications for students' academic adjustment as well social adjustment. This idea is line with findings that other facets of social motivation and types of social goals are related to academic motivation and engagement (Anderman, 1999; Dowson & McInerney, 2001; Ryan & Pintrich, 1997; Wentzel, 2005). In our study of young adolescents, teachers reported on students' help seeking at the same time that students reported on their social achievement goals.

Help seeking is an important self-regulatory strategy that contributes to student learning (Karabenick & Newman, 2006). Inevitably, students will encounter ambiguity or difficulty in their schoolwork and need assistance. In such a situation, it is adaptive for students to use others as a resource to secure the necessary help and continue the learning process (Nelson-Le Gall, 1985). When students do ask for help, the nature of their help seeking varies and may or may not be adaptive for their learning (see Newman, 2006 for a review). We examined help-seeking behavior because it is both a learning strategy and a social interaction. Thus, it is at the intersection of the academic and social domains and particularly relevant to social achievement goals. Further, we examined students' grades to see if changes in help seeking would predict changes in achievement during the first year in middle school.

We examined social demonstration goals in relation to teacher-reported help seeking. Specifically, teachers were asked to report on students' avoidant help-seeking behavior (the tendency to avoid asking for help altogether when they need it) and appropriate help-seeking behavior (the tendency to ask for help when they truly need it but are not overly dependent; do not ask for help the minute they encounter difficulty). These types of help-seeking behaviors have been found to capture meaningful distinctions in students' help-seeking behavior in the classroom (Ryan, Patrick, & Shim, 2005). We had two different teachers both rate students' help-seeking behavior. This was done because students have different teachers for different subjects throughout the day. By asking two different teachers, we could better assess students' general help-seeking tendencies in middle school.

A social demonstration-approach goal was negatively related to adaptive help-seeking tendencies. Thus, students who reported that they were concerned with looking cool and being popular were less likely to be rated by their teacher as engaging in adaptive help seeking. Interestingly, the hypothesized relation between a social demonstration-avoid goal and avoidant help-seeking behavior was not found. Help-seeking behavior predicted changes in achievement across students' first year in middle school. Specifically, adaptive help-seeking tendencies were positively associated with third quarter grades, controlling for first quarter grades. Avoidant help-seeking tendencies were negatively associated with third quarter grades, controlling for first quarter grades.

Social Achievement Goals in International and College Samples

Our recent research supports our contention that social achievement goals provide new insights into social motivation and school adjustment. The results of our investigations with young adolescents in middle schools are consistent with others' work. In a study of Greek elementary school students, Mouratidis and Sideridis (2009) found that a social development goal was positively related to belonging and negatively related to loneliness at school. In contrast, a social demonstration-avoid goal was positively related to loneliness. A social demonstration-approach goal was negatively related to the number of friendship nominations students received from classmates. In a study of Japanese early adolescent students, Kuroda and Sakurai (2011) found that a social development goal reduced the effects of interpersonal stress and protected against depression, whereas a social development-avoid goal exacerbated the effects of interpersonal stress and heightened depression. A social demonstration-approach goal had no relation to interpersonal stress.

Studies with college students have investigated some different variables than the investigations with young adolescents, but in general, the patterns are similar across these two age groups. Ryan and Shim (2006) found that a social development goal was positively associated, and a social demonstration-avoid goals was negatively associated, with self-reports of several facets of well-being (positive relations, self-acceptance, personal growth, autonomy). A social demonstration-approach goal was mostly unrelated to these facets of well-being. For the most part, these relations held in a second study when social achievement goals were measured in the beginning of the semester and well-being was measured at the end of the semester. In addition, a social development goal was positively associated with instructor ratings of social competence in the classroom (both social demonstration goals were not related to instructor-rated social competence).

Shim and Ryan (2012) wanted to investigate further if social achievement goals have implications for behaviors observed by others in a more social setting where students would be seen interacting with a wider range of peers and more social behaviors would be evident than the classroom setting. They investigated if the social achievement goals that students endorsed at the beginning of their freshman year were associated with resident advisor ratings of social adjustment in the dormitory six months later. A social development goal promoted adjustment, indicated by a positive association with ratings of overall of social competence and prosocial behavior (although the latter finding was only marginally significant). A social demonstration-avoid goal hindered adjustment, indicated by negative associations with ratings of overall social competence, popularity, and prosocial behavior, and positive associations with anxious and internalizing behavior. A social demonstration-approach goal had benefits, as shown by positive associations with ratings of overall social competence and popularity, and negative associations with anxious behavior, but also drawbacks for adjustment, as shown by a positive association with aggression.

Horst et al. (2007) found that a social development goal was positively correlated with positive relations with others, whereas both social demonstration-approach and social demonstration-avoid goals were positively related to fear of negative evaluation by others. Elliot, Gable, and Mapes (2006) investigated social achievement goals specific to friends and found that friendship approach goals (similar to social development goals) were positively related to relationship satisfaction, the frequency of positive events with friends, and the impact of those positive events with friends. In contrast, friendship-avoid goals (similar to social demonstration-avoid goals) were positively related to frequency of negative events with friends and the impact of those negative events with friends.

In sum, evidence is accruing that social achievement goals are important for many aspects of adjustment for younger and older students. While the consequences of social achievement goals have been addressed, less attention has been directed to understanding the antecedents of social achievement goals. In the next section we turn our attention to implicit theories as an important antecedent.

FUTURE DIRECTIONS: IMPLICIT THEORIES OF SOCIAL COMPETENCE AND SOCIAL ACHIEVEMENT GOALS

Implicit theories about the nature of academic competence are an antecedent of academic achievement goals and have been found to be amenable to intervention. Thus, an important direction for future work is to investigate implicit theories of social competence and social achievement goals in young adolescent students (Dweck, 2006, 2008; Dweck & Leggett, 1988). Dweck argues that implicit theories about the nature of competence are core beliefs that shape people's goals (Dweck, 2008). Implicit theories concern people's beliefs about the fixedness or malleability of their personal qualities. Relevant to the social domain is individual views of whether their social competence is something that is a fixed trait (entity view) or a malleable characteristic (incremental view). In line with Dweck's theorizing and research, an incremental view should be related to the pursuit of a social development goal because believing that social competence grows and develops with effort goes hand in hand with a focus on improving and developing one's social competence. An entity view should be related to the pursuit of social demonstration goals (both approach and avoid) because believing that social competence is a fixed attribute goes hand in hand with a focus on external validation of one's social ability. Several studies in the social domain have found evidence for Dweck's view and have linked implicit theories to various social goals for adults (e.g., see Beer, 2003 for an investigation of shyness and Kammrath & Dweck, 2006 for an investigation of dealing with interpersonal conflict; but see also Horst et al., 2007 where they found no correlation between implicit theories and social achievement goals).

Research indicates that even brief interventions can change implicit theories (Aronson, Fried, & Good, 2002; Blackwell, Trzesniewski, & Dweck, 2007). In a study of young adolescents who had just made the transition to middle school (Blackwell et al., 2007), students who were given an intervention that exposed them to the malleable nature of intelligence increased in mastery goals (i.e., a focus on developing academic competence) and improved their grades more than those who did not get the "malleable intelligence" intervention. In a study with college students (Aronson et al., 2002), an experimental group was shown a film highlighting how the brain forges new connections between neurons throughout life, especially in response to learning and challenge. Students wrote letters to struggling younger students emphasizing that the brain and intelligence are malleable and change greatly in response to effort and hard work. The experimental group, compared to two control groups (who did not learn that the brain and intelligence were malleable) reported higher value and enjoyment of their academic work and had higher achievement. Given that implicit theories are relevant across all aspects of competence (Dweck, 2006), such work suggests that targeting implicit theories of social competence would increase social development goals and promote adjustment at school. It might also be interesting to investigate interventions that target multiple types of implicit theories and multiple aspects of adjustment. For example, given that peer relations and academics are so central and intertwined in the school setting, would it be possible to promote a "growth mindset" for social and academic competence in one intervention and see positive social and academic adjustment?

CONCLUSION

The classroom and school peer ecology is not a singular experience for students. Children perceive and engage differently in the peer ecology at school. While children and adolescents have shared knowledge and understanding about the groups, norms, and status hierarchies among their peers at school, the personal meaning of these social entities varies for students. Psychological processes occur in tandem to the visible social dynamics present in the classroom. Individual differences in psychological processes contribute to varied social behavior and adjustment of children and adolescents in school. Our chapter highlights social achievement goals as an important individual difference variable relevant to psychological processes and school adjustment.

An achievement goal approach has proven to be powerful in explaining processes and outcomes for adolescents in the academic and athletic domains (Elliot, 2005). By building on this well-articulated theoretical framework of achievement goals and situating it in the social domain during early adolescence, our work provides insights into general motivational processes that promote or hinder adjustment. Our findings provide new insights into adolescents' school adjustment which is a critical concern in our society. In general, a social development goal promotes adjustment, a social development-avoid goal undermines adjustment, and a social demonstration-approach goal has benefits and drawbacks for adjustment. As achievement goals and their antecedents (e.g., implicit theories) are influenced by context, this approach has implications for interventions to promote adjustment in middle school students.

REFERENCES

Adler, P. A., & Adler, P. (1998). *Peer power: Preadolescent culture and identity*. Piscataway, NJ: Rutgers University Press.

Anderman, L. H. (1999). Classroom goal orientation, school belonging and social goals as predictors of students' positive and negative affect following the transition to middle school. *Journal of Research & Development in Education, 32*(2), 89–103.

Aronson, J., Fried, C., & Good, C. (2002). Reducing the effects of stereotype threat on African American college students by shaping theories of intelligence. *Journal of Experimental Social Psychology, 38*, 113–125.

Beer, J. S. (2002). Implicit self-theories of shyness. *Journal of Personality and Social Psychology, 83,* 1009–1024.

Blackwell, L., Trzesniewski, K., & Dweck, C.S. (2007). Implicit theories of intelligence predict achievement across an adolescent transition: A longitudinal study and an intervention. *Child Development, 78,* 246–263.

Chung, T., & Asher, S. R. (1996). Children's goals and strategies in peer conflict situations. *Merrill-Palmer Quarterly: Journal of Developmental Psychology. Special Issue: Conflicts in Families and between Children: Advances in Theory and Research, 42*(1), 125–147.

Crick, N. R., & Dodge, K. A. (1994). A review and reformulation of social information-processing mechanisms in children's social adjustment. *Psychological Bulletin, 115*(1), 74–101.

Dowson, M., & McInerney, D. M. (2001). Psychological parameters of students' social and work avoidance goals: A qualitative investigation. *Journal of Educational Psychology, 93*(1), 35–42.

Duda, J. L. (2005). Motivation in sport: The relevance of competence and achievement goals. In A. J. Elliot & C. Dweck (Eds.) *Handbook of competence and motivation* (pp. 318–335). New York, NY: Guilford Press.

Dweck, C. S. (1986). Motivational processes affecting learning. *American Psychologist, 41*(10), 1040–1048.

Dweck, C. S. (1996). Social motivation: Goals and social-cognitive processes. A comment. In J. Juvonen & K. R. Wentzel (Eds.), *Social motivation: Understanding children's school adjustment* (pp. 181–195). New York, NY: Cambridge University Press.

Dweck, C. S. (1999). *Self-theories: Their role in motivation, personality, and development.* New York, NY: Psychology Press.

Dweck, C.S. (2006). *Mindset.* New York, NY: Random House

Dweck, C.S. (2008). Can personality be changed? The role of beliefs in personality and change. *Current Directions in Psychological Science, 17*(6), 391–394.

Dweck, C. S., & Leggett, E. L. (1988). A social-cognitive approach to motivation and personality. *Psychological Review, 95*(2), 256–273.

Eder, D. (1985). The cycle of popularity: Interpersonal relations among female adolescents. *Sociology of Education, 58*(3), 154–165.

Elliot, A. J. (2005). A conceptual history of the achievement goal construct. In A. Elliot & C. Dweck (Eds.), *Handbook of competence and motivation* (pp. 52–72). New York, NY: Guilford Press.

Elliot, A. J., & Church, M. A. (1997). A hierarchical model of approach and avoidance achievement motivation. *Journal of Personality and Social Psychology, 72*(1), 218–232.

Elliot, A. J., Gable, S. L., & Mapes, R. R. (2006). Approach and avoidance motivation in the social domain. *Personality and Social Psychology Bulletin, 32,* 378–391.

Erdley, C. A., & Asher, S. A. (1996). Children's social goals and self-efficacy perceptions as influences on their responses to ambiguous provocation. *Child Development, 67*(4), 1329–1344.

Erdley, C. A., Loomis, C. C., Cain, K. M., & Dumas-Hines, F. (1997). Relations among children's social goals, implicit personality theories, and responses to social failure. *Developmental Psychology, 33*(2), 263–272.

Ford, M. E. (1992). *Motivating humans: Goals, emotions, and personal agency beliefs.* Thousand Oaks, CA: Sage.

Horst, S. J., Finney, S. J., & Barron, K. E. (2007). Moving beyond academic achievement goal measures: A study of social achievement goals. *Contemporary Educational Psychology, 32*(4), 667–698.

Jarvinen, D. W., & Nicholls, J. G. (1996). Adolescents' social goals, beliefs about the causes of social success, and satisfaction in peer relations. *Developmental Psychology, 32*(3), 435–441.

Kammrath, L., & Dweck, C.S. (2006). Voicing conflict: Preferred conflict strategies among incremental and entity theorists. *Personality and Social Psychology Bulletin, 32,* 1497–1508.

Kanfer, R., & Ackerman, P. L. (2005). Work competence: A person-oriented perspective. In A. J. Elliot & C. S. Dweck (Eds.). *Handbook of competence and motivation* (pp. 336–353). New York, NY: Guilford Press.

Karabenick, S. A. & Newman, R. S. (Eds.). (2006). *Help seeking in academic setting: Goals, groups, and contexts.* Mahwah, NJ: Lawrence Erlbaum.

Kinney, D. A. (1993). From nerds to normals: The recovery of identity among adolescents from middle school to high school. *Sociology of Education, 66*(1), 21–40.

Kuroda Y., & Sakurai, S. (2011). Social goal orientations, interpersonal stress, and depressive symptoms among early adolescents in Japan: A test of Diathesis-Stress model using the Trichotomous framework of social achievement goal orientations. *The Journal of Early Adolescence, 31,* 300–322.

Ladd, G. W. (2005). *Children's peer relations and social competence: A century of progress.* New Haven, CT: Yale University Press.

LaFontana, K. M., & Cillessen, A. H. N. (2002). Children's perceptions of popular and unpopular peers: A multimethod assessment. *Developmental Psychology, 38*(5), 635–647.

McAdams, D. P. (1987). Motivation and friendship. In S. Duck & D. Perlman (Eds.), *Understanding personal relationships: An interdisciplinary approach* (pp. 85–105). Thousand Oaks, CA: Sage Publications.

Mouratidis, A., & Sideridis, G. (2009). On social achievement goals: Their relations with peer acceptance, classroom belongingness, and perceptions of loneliness. *The Journal of Experimental Education, 77*(3), 285–307.

Nelson-Le Gall, S. (1985). Help-seeking behavior in learning. In E. W. Gordon (Ed.), *Review of research in education, vol. 12* (pp. 55–90). Washington, DC: American Educational Research Association.

Newman, R. S. (2006). Students' adaptive and nonadaptive help seeking in the classroom: Implications for the context of peer harassment. In S. A. Karabenick & R. S. Newman (Eds.), *Help seeking in academic setting: Goals, groups, and contexts* (pp. 225–258). Mahwah, NJ: Lawrence Erlbaum.

Ojanen, T., Grönroos, M., & Salmivalli, C. (2005). An interpersonal circumplex model of children's social goals: Links with peer-reported behavior and sociometric status. *Developmental Psychology, 41*(5), 699–710.

Parker, J. G., & Asher, S. R. (1993). Friendship and friendship quality in middle childhood: Links with peer group acceptance and feelings of loneliness and social dissatisfaction. *Developmental Psychology, 29*(4), 611–621.

Pintrich, P. R. (2000). An achievement goal theory perspective on issues in motivation terminology, theory, and research. *Contemporary Educational Psychology. Special Issue: Motivation and the Educational Process, 25*(1), 92–104.

Renshaw, P. D., & Asher, S. R. (1983). Children's goals and strategies for social interaction. *Merrill-Palmer Quarterly: Journal of Developmental Psychology, 29*(3), 353–374.

Rodkin, P. C., Farmer, T. W., Pearl, R., & Van Acker, R. (2000). Heterogeneity of popular boys: Antisocial and prosocial configurations. *Developmental Psychology, 36*(1), 14–24.

Rodkin, P., & Ryan, A. M. (2012). Child and adolescent peer relations in an educational context. In K. Harris, S. Graham, & T. Urdan (Eds.) *Educational psychology handbook* (pp. 363–389). Washington DC: APA Publications.

Rose, A. J. (2002). Co-rumination in the friendships of girls and boys. *Child Development, 73*(6), 1830–1843.

Rose, A. J., & Asher, S. R. (1999). Children's goals and strategies in response to conflicts within a friendship. *Developmental Psychology, 35*(1), 69–79.

Rose-Krasnor, L., & Denham, S. (2009). Social-emotional competence in early childhood. In K. H. Rubin, W. M Bukowski, & B. Laursen (Eds.), *Handbook of peer interactions, relationships and groups* (pp. 531–547). New York, NY: Guilford.

Rubin, K. H., Bukowski, W., & Parker, J. G. (2006). Peers, interactions, relationships, and interactions. In W. Damon & R. Lerner (Series Eds.) & N. Eisenberg (Vol. Ed.), *Handbook of child psychology: Vol. 3. Social, emotional, and personality development* (6th ed., pp. 571–645). New York, NY: Wiley.

Ryan, A. M., Kiefer, S. M., & Hopkins, N. B. (2004). Young adolescents' social motivation: An achievement goal perspective. In M. L. Maehr & P. R. Pintrich (Eds.), *Advances in motivation and achievement, Volume 13* (pp. 30–330). New York, NY: Elsevier Ltd.

Ryan, A. M., Patrick, H., & Shim, S. (2005). Differential profiles of students identified by their teacher as having avoidant, appropriate, or dependent help-seeking tendencies in the classroom. *Journal of Educational Psychology, 97*(2), 275–285.

Ryan, A. M., & Pintrich, P. R. (1997). "Should I ask for help?" The role of motivation and attitudes in adolescents' help seeking in math class. *Journal of Educational Psychology, 89*(2), 329–341.

Ryan, A.M., Rodkin, P., Jamison, J., & Wilson, T. (2009, April). *Social goals in middle childhood: Relations to social behavior and social status.* Paper presented at the biennial meeting of the Society for Research on Child Development, Denver, CO.

Ryan, A. M., & Shim, S. S. (2008). An exploration of young adolescents' social achievement goals and social adjustment in middle school. *Journal of Educational Psychology, 100*(3), 672–687.

Ryan, A. M., & Shim, S. S. (2006). Social achievement goals: The nature and consequences of different orientations toward social competence. *Personality and Social Psychology Bulletin, 32*(9), 1246–1263.

Ryan, A. M., & Shin, H. (2011). Help-seeking tendencies: An examination of motivational correlates and consequences for achievement during the first year of middle school. *Learning and Instruction, 21*, 247–256.

Shim, S. S., & Ryan, A.M. (2012, January 20). What do students want socially when they arrive at college? Implications of social achievement goals for social behaviors and adjustment during the first semester of college. Advance online publication. doi: 10.1007/s11031-011-9272-3.

Shin, H., & Ryan, A. M. (2011, December 13). Coping with social stress the first year in middle school: An examination of social goals, coping with friends and social adjustment. *Journal of Early Adolescence.* Advance online publication. doi: 10.1177/0272431611429944.

Urdan, T. C. (1997). Examining the relations among early adolescent students' goals and friends' orientation toward effort and achievement in school. *Contemporary Educational Psychology, 22*(2), 165–191.

Wentzel, K. R. (2000). What is it that I'm trying to achieve? Classroom goals from a content perspective. *Contemporary Educational Psychology, 25*(1), 105–115.

Wentzel, K. R. (2001). The contribution of social goal setting to children's school adjustment. In A. Wigfield, & J. S. Eccles (Eds.), *Development of achievement motivation* (pp. 221–246). San Diego, CA: Academic Press.

Wentzel, K. R. (2005). Peer relationships, motivation, and academic performance at school. In A. Elliot & C. Dweck (Eds.), *Handbook of competence and motivation* (pp. 279–296). New York, NY: Guilford.

Wigfield, A., Eccles, J. S., Schiefele, U., Roeser, R. W., & Davis-Kean, P. (2006). Development of achievement motivation. In N. Eisenberg, W. Damon & R. M. Lerner (Eds.), *Handbook of child psychology: Vol. 3. Social, emotional, and personality development* (pp. 933–1002). Hoboken, NJ: John Wiley & Sons.

PART II

PRACTICES AND INTERVENTIONS THAT SUPPORT POSITIVE PEER RELATIONSHIPS AT SCHOOL

CHAPTER 8

TEACHERS AS MANAGERS OF STUDENTS' PEER CONTEXT

Jan N. Hughes
Texas A&M University

CHAPTER OVERVIEW

Children spend more time interacting with peers in school than in any other setting. At school, children forge friendships with others, form cliques, relate to diverse individuals, accept or resist group norms and expectations for behavior, manage their emotions, coordinate their actions with those of others, and function as members of a community on a daily basis. Through classroom interactions, students accrue peer reputations as bully or victim, popular or rejected, class clown or teacher's pet, academically capable or not, leader or follower. Recent research on social processes in classrooms demonstrates that these naturally occurring interactions affect children's social, emotional, and academic learning, for good or for ill.

As the chief architects and managers of classroom contexts, teachers exert considerable influence on students' peer contexts and peer relationships. This influence is exerted via multiple processes operating at both the individual and classroom levels. At an individual level, the affective quality of the teacher–student relationship may exert influences on students' peer relationships via multiple processes, including the nature and

Peer Relationships and Adjustment at School, pages 189–218
Copyright © 2012 by Information Age Publishing
All rights of reproduction in any form reserved.

quality of students' classroom participation (Hughes, Luo, Kwok, & Loyd, 2008; Ladd, Birch, & Buhs, 1999). Classmates may also rely on their observations of teacher–student instructional and social interactions in making judgments about classmates' social and academic traits (Hughes, Cavell, & Willson, 2001). On a classroom level, through their instructional and social-emotional practices, teachers establish the context in which learning takes place, peers relate to each other, and students develop views of self as capable or not, and as cared for or not. Stated somewhat differently, the teacher is the primary architect of the classroom context, a context that surrounds and regulates interactions within it (Pianta & Walsh, 1996). A teacher's instructional practices, such as grouping students for instruction by ability level, may make relative ability differences in the classroom more or less salient to students and communicate which student characteristics are most highly valued. These practices have implications not only for students' motivation and engagement in learning, but also for their peer reputation on a number of social and academic dimensions (Urdan & Schoenfelder, 2006; Wigfield, Eccles, Schiefele, Roeser, & Davis-Kean, 2006). Teacher practices also establish the social-emotional climate of the classroom, creating norms and shared expectations for how students relate to each other (Battistich & Horn, 1997; Wentzel, 1999).

The metaphor of the invisible hand refers to the impact of teachers' everyday interactions in the classroom, including instructional and non-instructional interactions, on the classroom social structure (Farmer, Lines, & Hamm, 2011). Many of these activities operate without teacher awareness of their impact on students' behaviors, motivations, or peer relationships. As educators and psychologists have turned their attention to how classroom and school contexts impact students, the mechanisms by which the "invisible hand" operates are being elucidated. The purpose of this chapter is to review the research on those teacher interactions and strategies that impact students' social lives in classrooms. A more complete understanding of these mechanisms requires a developmental systems perspective (Lerner, 1998). Such a perspective acknowledges that the impact of teacher–student interactions and instructional and social-emotional practices on students' peer experiences may differ at different developmental periods (Hughes et al., 2008; Weinstein, Marshall, Sharp, & Botkin, 1987). Furthermore, the impact of these practices on development is expected to vary based on characteristics of the student and characteristics of the broader cultural and organizational contexts in which they are embedded (Chang, 2004). An understanding of the different processes by which teachers influence peer relationships at different ages, for different students, in different contexts would permit more targeted teacher preparation and professional development efforts to utilize the teacher–student relationship to promote students' social and academic success.

AFFECTIVE QUALITY OF TEACHER–STUDENT
RELATIONSHIP AND PEER RELATIONSHIPS

Research spanning the past three decades supports the proposition that students who experience a relationship with their teachers characterized by high levels of positive, supportive interactions, and low levels of rejection and conflict have better school outcomes, including more positive peer relationships (for review, see Hamre & Pianta, 2006). Evidence that such a relationship with a teacher influences a student's peer relationships is provided by classroom-based experimental studies demonstrating that when teachers are instructed to increase their praise to low-accepted primary grade children, these children increase in their level of peer acceptance (Flanders & Havumaki, 1960; Retish, 1973). Analogue experimental studies document that positive and negative teacher interactions with a child influence students' liking for and perceptions of the child's prosocialness and academic behaviors (White & Kistner, 1992; White, Sherman, & Jones, 1996). Prospective studies find that teacher-reported liking for and support to individual students predicts cross-year improvements in peer acceptance (Hughes & Kwok, 2006; Taylor & Trickett, 1989).

Drawing from diverse theoretical conceptualizations, researchers have posited a number of different mechanisms that may account for the association between an affectively positive teacher–student relationship and students' peer experiences in the classroom. Furthermore, different theoretical conceptualizations are applied at different ages. Researchers studying teacher–student relationship quality in the preschool and early elementary grades have often drawn from attachment theory (Bowlby, 1980). Researchers studying preadolescents and adolescents have typically relied on social motivation theory (Deci & Ryan, 1985) and social cognitive theory (Bandura, Barbaranelli, Caprara, & Pastorelli, 1996; Schunk & Zimmerman, 2006; Weiner, 1974) in understanding the effect of teacher–student relationship on school adjustment. Next I describe how each conceptualization has led to an increased understanding of the processes by which teacher–student relationship quality directly and indirectly influence students' peer experiences at school.

Attachment Theory Conceptualizations

According to Bowlby (1980), individuals are born with an innate psychobiological system, the attachment behavioral system, that motivates them to seek proximity to significant others (attachment figures) when faced with a threat to their security. Children who experience responsive and sensitive interactions with their early care givers develop a sense of felt security in the presence of attachment figures (Bretherton & Munholland, 1999). These children learn that that they are worthy of being cared for and that others are available to support them when they experience distress. Several researchers have posited that the teacher–child relationship serves attachment functions (Birch & Ladd, 1997; Pianta & Steinberg, 1992). According to this view, a close and warm relationship with one's teacher promotes a child's sense of felt security, enabling the child to freely explore the classroom environment, take risks, ask for help appropriately, and recover quickly from distress without falling to pieces (Little & Kobak, 2003; Pianta, Hamre, & Stuhlman, 2003). In other words, a supportive relationship with the teacher may serve as an external source of motivation and regulation.

Empirical studies support the proposition that a secure relationship with one's teacher facilitates a student's self-regulation. For example, preschool and kindergarten children with secure teacher relationships (high in closeness and warmth, low in conflict) more actively explore their environment and cope more effectively with novel academic and social demands than do children with insecure relationships with their teachers (Howes, Hamilton, & Matheson, 1994; Pianta & Steinberg, 1992). Among elementary children, felt emotional security with one's teacher attenuates children's stress reactivity to negative teacher and peer events in the classroom (Little & Koback, 2003). It is important to note that child characteristics may account for some of the observed association between teacher–student relationship and child self-regulation. Indeed, children with better self-regulation tend to form more positive relationships with teachers (Birch & Ladd, 1998; Vondra, Shaw, Swearingen, Cohen, & Owens, 2001). However, longitudinal studies that control for prior levels of child self-regulation still find associations between teacher–student relationship quality and self-regulation (Silver, Measelle, Armstrong, & Essex, 2005). It is likely that teacher support and child self-regulatory skills affect each other in a reciprocal manner (Doumen, Verschueren, Buyse, Germeijs, Luyckx, & Soenens, 2008; Hughes et al., 2008).

In turn, students who are able to regulate their emotions and behaviors are better accepted by peers and rated by teachers as more socially competent. For example, preschoolers who have difficulty managing negative emotions of anger and sadness are more likely to be peer rejected in kindergarten (Denham, Blair, DeMulder, Levitas, Sawyer, & Auerbach-Major, 2003). Young children who have difficulty with inhibitory control (i.e., inhibiting a dominant response such as running to recess and instead responding with a subdominant response such as lining up) are likely to be rejected by peers (Trentacosta & Shaw, 2009). Conversely, good behavioral regulation is associated with greater social competence and peer acceptance (Fabes et al., 1999). For example, first to fourth graders who expressed more positive than negative emotions at school were rated by teachers as more liked by peers (Jones, Eisenberg, Fabes, & MacKinnon, 2002). The relationship between behavioral and emotional self-regulation and peer competence is found from preschool through adolescence (Martel et al., 2007). Poor self-regulation is also associated with poor academic performance, presumably due to the negative impact of difficulty in attending, persisting, and inhibiting behaviors that interfere with learning on achievement (Blair & Razza, 2007; Valiente, Lemery-Chalfant, Swanson, & Reiser, 2008).

A supportive relationship with one's teacher might be especially important to the social and academic performance of students with poor self-regulatory skills. Relative to children with good self-regulation, children with poor self-regulatory skills might be more dependent on the sense of felt security that an available and supportive adult provides in order to persist in the face of failure, pay attention to instruction, and cope with negative emotions. In the elementary grades, a supportive teacher–student relationship buffers students with poor behavior regulation from escalating externalizing behaviors (Meehan, Hughes, & Cavell, 2003; Silver et al., 2005). In a recent study, Liew, Chen, and Hughes (2010) expected that a supportive relationship with a teacher would serve as an external source of motivation and regulation that facilitates learning and achievement among first grade students who exhibited poor temperament-based self-regulation. As expected, children with good self-regulation made good progress in reading and math achievement regardless of the quality of their relationship with teachers. However, for students with poor regulation, growth in reading depended on the level of teacher support. Indeed, children with poor regulatory control who received support from teachers improved at the same rate as did children with good regulatory control. Based on longitudinal research demonstrating that increases in achievement contribute to higher levels of peer acceptance (Gleason, Kwok, & Hughes, 2007), it is reasonable to expect that teacher–student relationship quality may indirectly affect peer status via its direct effect on student achievement.

Self-Determination Theory Conceptualizations

According to self-determination theory (SDT; Connell & Wellborn, 1991; Deci & Ryan, 1985) the need for relatedness is one of three basic psychological needs, along with the need for autonomy and competence. The need for relatedness is defined as "the need to feel securely connected to the social surround and the need to experience oneself as worthy and capable of love and respect" (Connell & Wellborn, 1991, pp. 51–52). These three psychological needs are met through interactions between people and within contexts that provide structure, autonomy, support, and involvement. Self-system processes related to these basic needs are translated into patterns of engaged or disaffected action within particular contexts that, in turn, affect one's development of competence (defined as skills, abilities, and adjustment). Thus, the SDT model posits that engagement mediates the relationship between self-appraisals related to autonomy, competence, and relatedness and academic achievement. Early research within this model was conducted primarily with preadolescent and adolescent populations. In a sample of fourth- to sixth-grade students, Connell and Wellborn (1991) found that students' perceptions of the degree to which their needs for competence, autonomy, and relatedness were met predicted their engagement in school, which in turn predicted grades and achievement scores. Ryan, Stiller, and Lynch (1994) reported that adolescents reporting supportive relationships with parents and teachers showed better school adaptation and academic motivation. Midgley, Feldlauffer, and Eccles (1989) found that when middle school students moved from classrooms where they experience high teacher support to settings where they perceive lower support, they show lowered academic motivation.

Studies with younger students also find an effect of teacher support on students' classroom engagement (Decker, Dona, & Christenson, 2007; Ladd et al., 1999). Among a sample of academically at-risk first-grade students, Hughes and Kwok (2006) directly tested for an indirect effect of provision of teacher support on peer acceptance via its direct effect on student engagement. Consistent with their hypothesized model, teacher support in first grade predicted students' peer acceptance the following year, above students' prior peer acceptance and level of externalizing problems (a strong correlate of peer acceptance). Furthermore, this effect was mediated by changes in students' effortful and cooperative engagement in the classroom. In a three-year longitudinal study in which measures of teacher support, student engagement, and academic achievement were assessed each year, Hughes and colleagues (2008) found that the effect of teacher support on achievement is mediated by its direct effect on students' engagement. Taken together, these studies strongly suggest that the provision of a supportive teacher relationship contributes to students' cooperative and effortful engagement in the classroom (either due to enhanced regulation or motivation), which promotes both their academic achievement and peer acceptance. Furthermore, this effect is evident from kindergarten through adolescence.

Social Cognitive Conceptualizations

Considerable research documents that adults play a central role in shaping children's social cognitions, including their perceptions of peers (Graham & Barker, 1990). According to attribution theory (Weiner, 1974), students use information about teacher–student interactions to make inferences concerning one's own and others' ability and effort. For example, teacher responses to students' academic efforts indirectly communicate information about students' abilities. Such seemingly positive teacher behaviors as expressing sympathy to students who are struggling, praising students who do well on easy tasks, offering help to students, and waiting a short period of time for the student to respond to a question may be interpreted by recipients of this feedback as well as to classmates as evidence of low ability.

Students as young as first grade are aware of differences in teacher-student interactions with high- and low-achieving students and draw inferences about children's abilities based on teacher feedback (see Stipek & Tannatt, 1984; Babad, 1993). White and Kistner (1992) report that the emotional tone of teacher feedback (not solely the content of feedback) influences children's peer preferences. Using an experimental design, Retish (1973) found that teacher reinforcement patterns to low-accepted children influenced second graders' liking for them. As early as second grade, students' perceptions of the quality of classmates' relationships with the teacher are highly consistent with teachers' reports of relationship quality (Yi, Hughes, Hsu, & Kwok, 2011). Importantly, both peer and teacher reports of a child's relationship with the teacher are associated with higher peer acceptance and school adjustment (Yi et al., 2009).Whereas a student's opportunities to interact with each student in the classroom may be limited, students typically have many opportunities to observe teacher–student interactions with a given student. Furthermore, opportunities to observe teacher–student interactions are shared by students in the same classroom. The quality of that teacher–student interaction thus becomes part of the shared information classmates have about that child, thereby promoting a group consensus about the child's attributes. The group consensus may operate as an affective filter that influences how classmates view the child on multiple dimensions (Hymel, 1986). Consistent with this reasoning, in a sample of third and fourth grade children, classmates' perceptions of the affective quality of the teacher–student relationship predicted students' peer acceptance, above classmates' and teachers' evaluations of children's aggression (a strong predictor of peer acceptance) (Hughes et al., 2001).

The impact of teacher–student relationships on peer experiences in the classroom may reach beyond peer acceptance. Classroom peer relationships are multidimensional, including dyadic friendships, experiences of loneliness, peer acceptance, peer reputation on various academic and behavioral traits, and peer exclusion. Furthermore, different dimensions of classroom peer relatedness predict changes on different indices of school adjustment (Ladd, Kochenderfer, & Coleman, 1997). Recent research has investigated the developmental significance of a student's academic reputation within the classroom. Peer academic reputation refers to the collective judgment of one's classmates regarding one's academic competence and is assessed by asking students to nominate classmates who meet one or more descriptors of an academically competent student (Gest, Domitrovich, & Welsh, 2005). Elementary students' peer academic reputation predicts both within grade and across-grade improvements in academic self-efficacy, behavioral engagement, and achievement (Gest, Rulison, Davidson, & Welsh, 2008; Hughes, Dyer, Luo, & Kwok, 2009). Such a finding is consistent with empirical studies demonstrating that students' perceptions of their own academic abilities are influenced by the reflected appraisals of their classmates (Cole, Maxwell, & Martin, 1997; Harter, 1998). Of particular interest to the current discussion is the finding that among elementary students, higher levels of teacher–student support predicted improved peer acceptance and peer academic reputation. In turn, improved peer academic reputation mediated the effect of teacher support on increases in children's academic self efficacy (Hughes & Chen, in press).

Consistent with the developmental systems theory of development (Lerner, 1998), students' academic and social functioning in school is likely the result of the dynamic and reciprocal relationships among students' academic self-efficacy, academic performance, teacher–student interactions, and peer interactions. Thus, changes in one system (e.g., teacher–student relationship) are expected to exert both direct and indirect effects on other systems (e.g., the child's self-views and peer relationships). Few researchers have investigated the reciprocal nature of teacher–student relationships and peer relationships. Using a cross-lag model across grades 2 to 4, Hughes and Chen (2011) found bidirectional effects between students' peer acceptance and teacher–student support Thus, social ties in one domain may have implications for social ties in the other. Furthermore, these social ties may directly and indirectly affect children's academic achievement (Hughes et al., 2008; Chen, Hughes, Kwok, & Liew, 2010).

CLASSROOM CONTEXT AND PEER RELATIONSHIPS

Classrooms vary on many dimensions that have implications for how students relate with one another. Classrooms are systems that are embedded within larger systems, such as schools and communities and that contain subsystems, such as teacher–student interactions and peer interactions. According to developmental system theory, the classroom is a context that surrounds and regulates interactions in these subsystems (Pianta & Walsh, 1996), and development is a result of the dynamic interplay of factors at the level of the individual child, the subsystems within the classroom, and the broader classroom levels of analysis. In this view, dyadic interactions within a classroom gain meaning and developmental significance in part from properties of the classroom setting. Classroom instructional practices such as grouping children for instruction based on ability, rewarding correct answers versus effort and improvements, and responding differently to students for whom the teacher holds high or low expectations for achievement are part of the shared classroom context. As discussed below, these and other instructional practices (e.g., classroom management and child-directed practices) influence students' perceptions of their own and others' abilities, the quality of students' engagement in the classroom, and patterns of peer interaction in the classroom. Classrooms also vary on dimensions of the social-emotional climate, including the typical level of teacher warmth and responsiveness to students, teacher respect for students (including student choice), and the normative level of prosocialness in students' interactions with each other (e.g., sharing, helping and supporting each other, respecting each other, resolving conflicts non-aggressively). As discussed below, these differences also have implications for peer interactions and relationships.

One might expect that elementary classrooms in public schools would be fairly similar to each other in terms of instructional and social-emotional practices, since most elementary teachers graduate from teacher education programs that meet similar state and professional accreditation standards for the preparation of educators and practice in educational settings where teachers work with and learn from other teachers. However, recent large-scale national studies find that preschool and elementary classrooms vary tremendously on almost every dimension of instructional and social-emotional climate (Rimm-Kaufmann, La Paro, Downer, & Pianta, 2005). In a study with 5,147 first- and second-grade students in 179 classrooms in three school districts in Texas (Hughes, Zhang, & Hill, 2006), researchers asked students in individual interviews to name as few or as many classmates as they wanted who met the following description of teacher support: "These children get along well with their teacher. They like to talk to their teachers, and their teachers enjoy spending time with them." Of note is the finding that the average percentage of students nominated for this description in a given classroom ranged from 0% to 40% of the students available to be nominated. That is, in some classes none of the students named a single student who got along with the teacher and with whom the teacher enjoyed spending time, whereas in other classrooms students, on average, nominated nearly half of their classmates. Furthermore, in classrooms in which students perceived that the teacher enjoyed interacting with more students, academically at-risk students experienced higher levels of peer acceptance and were more engaged in the classroom. The level of classroom support contributed to student outcomes above the level of individual support students received from the teacher as well as relevant background variables.

Large-scale national studies have consistently identified instructional and social-emotional dimensions of classroom climate as distinct factors that contribute differentially to child outcomes (Hamre & Pianta, 2005). However, it is important to note that the two dimensions are moderately correlated (Mashburn et al., 2008; Matsumura, Slater, & Crosson, 2008). This finding is good news, because it means teachers do not need to choose between focusing on providing high-quality instructional support or high-quality emotional support. Noddings (1992) coined the term "pedagogical caring" to underscore that teachers communicate caring by preparing high-quality lessons, carefully listening to students in order to construct a response that builds their conceptual understanding, giving students choices, and adjusting instruction to individual differences. Teachers who engage in these behaviors also tend to establish a positive social-emotional climate and maintain a well-managed classroom.

Teachers, like other individuals, value certain behaviors and traits more than others. Teachers, however, have the social power to establish norms in the classroom for interpersonal relationships, by rewarding the values and behaviors they believe are appropriate. Furthermore, teachers' enacted values have implications for peer relationships. In a sample of middle school classes in China, Chang (2003) found that teachers' beliefs about aggressive and withdrawn behaviors in the classrooms influenced the relations between these classroom behaviors and peer acceptance and self-perceived social competence. Aggressive youth were more likely to be rejected in classrooms in which teachers were less tolerant of aggression than in classrooms in which teachers were more tolerant of aggression. Teacher tolerance for withdrawn behavior also moderated the association between withdrawal and peer rejection.

Instructional Dimensions of Classrooms and Peer Relationships

Salience of Cues Regarding Relative Ability

Considerable research conducted over three decades has documented the impact of teacher practices that highlight differences in children's relative abilities on children's achievement, motivation, and self-views. This body of evidence has drawn from research on teacher expectancy effects (for review see Jussim & Harber, 2005), classroom goal structure (for review see Urdan & Midgley, 2003), classroom task structures (Simpson & Rosenholtz, 1986), and teacher frame of reference (Marsh & Craven, 2002). These diverse theoretical and empirical literatures share a focus on the degree to which the classroom context provides cues that permit students to draw inferences about their own and others' relative abilities. Social comparison theory posits that individuals use cues in their environment to make inferences about their own and others' relative abilities.

Classrooms provide multiple cues about children's relative abilities. Drawing from the teacher expectancy literature, researchers document that the well known "self-fulfilling prophesy effect" (Rosenthal & Jacobson, 1968) is a result of teachers responding differently to students for whom they hold biased high or low achievement expectations (for review, see Jussim & Harber, 2005). Biased expectations are defined as achievement expectations that are high or low relative to predicted expectations (see Boer, Bosker, & van der Werf, 2010). Teachers provide more emotional support, choice, praise, response opportunities, and special privileges to high-expectation students and more criticism and direction to low-expectation students. Furthermore, children as young as first grade use these cues in making inferences about their own and peers' abilities (Stipek & Tannatt, 1984). However, not all students are equally susceptible to expectancy bias effects. More vulnerable students, defined in terms of low SES, minority status, or low achievement, appear to be more effected by positively or negatively biased expectations (Madon, Jussim, & Eccles, 1997; McKown, & Weinstein, 2002).

According to achievement goal theory (Ames, 1992), classrooms differ in the importance placed on mastery versus performance achievement goals. Achievement goals represent students' reasons or purposes for engaging in academic tasks (Lau & Nie, 2008). Teachers create a performance goal structure by emphasizing student performance relative to normative standards rather than to the student's prior performance; providing more public contrast, a mastery goal structure, also referred to as a task structure, as characterized by versus private performance feedback; and valuing correct answers versus effort and learning in instructional practices that emphasize effort and improvement over correct answers, development of competencies, and intrinsic motivation (Ames, 1992; Urdan & Midgley, 2003).

Researchers theorize that instructional practices that are performance goal-oriented, especially social comparison feedback and competition between students, make ability differences salient in the classroom and undermine motivation, especially for low-achieving students (Wigfield et al., 2006). In performance goal classrooms, students view achievement situations as means of demonstrating one's ability and self-worth (Dweck, 1986). As a result, students adopt either a *performance approach* goal orientation (i.e., demonstrating high academic competence to others) or a *performance avoidance* goal orientation (i.e., avoiding the demonstration of incompetence and negative evaluation from others—Skaalvik, 1997). Consistent with such reasoning, an extensive body of research documents an association between classroom goal or task structures and students' personal learning goal orientations, emotional well-being, cognitive engagement, feeling of school belonging, persistence in the face of failure, and achievement (for reviews, see Wigfield et al., 2006).

Of special interest to this chapter is the influence of dimensions of classroom instructional practices on students' peer relationships. Given the effects of goal structure on students' individual functioning in the classroom, one would expect the goal structure to affect social relationships in the classroom. Surprisingly, the literature investigating the effect of teacher instructional practices on children's peer relationships is sparse. In a large national sample of fifth-grade students, observed classroom instructional quality (e.g., quality of evaluative feedback, child-centered practices, quality of literacy instruction) predicted observed peer social competence and cooperation, above students' teacher-rated social competence the prior year (Luckner & Pianta, 2009).

Some researchers have suggested that teacher practices that highlight relative differences in ability have implications for peer relationships. In classrooms in which social comparison cues are more salient, students demonstrate a higher degree of consensus in their perceptions of classmates' abilities, and students' ability perceptions tend to focus on relatively few children, rather than being dispersed across students (Filby & Barnett, 1982; Rosenholtz & Simpson, 1984). Because peers' perceptions of classmates' abilities are associated with their liking for classmates (Ladd et al., 1999), lower ability students may experience lower levels of peer acceptance in classrooms in which students' perceptions of ability are more hierarchical and less dispersed. In support of this reasoning, Schuncke (1978) found that in fifth and sixth grade classrooms that employed ability grouping, a practice that makes relative ability highly salient, low-ability students were less accepted by their classmates than were those in classrooms that did not use ability grouping. Schuncke described how ability grouping might impact peer status:

> The academic status of boys...was daily brought to the attention of the total class as the teacher worked with different ability groups. Because it was reinforced, this hierarchy was much more available for pupils of ability-grouped classes to use as a basis for allocating status in the other dimensions (academic ability and social influence) of the classroom social structure. (p. 307)

Few studies have investigated the effect of classroom or individual achievement goal structures on students' social behaviors or peer relationships. In a study with ninth grade students, disruptive behavior was higher in classrooms with a performance goal structure relative to a mastery goal structures (Kaplan, Gheen, & Midgley, 2002). A study of middle school youth found that a relative emphasis on individual mastery goals was positively associated with more prosocial and close peer relationships and less mistrust and tension (Levy-Tossman, Kaplan, & Assor, 2007). The authors reasoned that students who are focused on mastery goals rather than on outperforming other students will be more likely to share resources, offer help to others, and trust each other. Conversely, "when schooling and school work are constructed as a continual competitive struggle in which self-worth depends on performance relative to others, students may be less able or willing to develop high quality friendships" (p. 246).

Of interest is whether achievement goal structures influence peer social preferences or friendship choices. One might expect that in classrooms with a performance goal structure, students who make the best grades would enjoy the highest peer status, whereas in classrooms in which mastery goals predominate, student social preferences would be based on more diverse criteria. Although no research has investigated whether classroom goal structure moderates the relationship between students' achievement and peer acceptance, support for such a conclusion is provided by a study with second graders. Using peer sociometric ratings of liking and of academic ability, Hughes and Zhang (2007) found that the degree to which students' perceptions of ability demonstrated high consensus and focused on relatively few students, the positive relationship between students' measured reading achievement and their sociometric peer acceptance was stronger. Specifically, children with lower reading ability in classrooms with centralized (i.e., shared) perceptions of academic abilities were less accepted and less engaged in school, relative to children with similarly low reading ability in classrooms with less centralized perceptions of academic abilities. Stated differently, lower achieving students were less well accepted in classrooms in which the demarcation between the smart children and the not-so-smart children was more obvious.

Cooperative Goal Structures

Research emanating from social interdependence theory (Roseth, Johnson, & Johnson, 2008) has investigated how cooperative versus competitive classroom goal structures may affect peer relationships. Negative interdependence exists when students perceive that they can obtain their goals only if other students who whom they are competitively linked fail to obtain their goals. Positive interdependence exists when students perceive that they can reach their goals only if the other students with whom they are cooperatively linked also reach their goals. When students perceive that achieving their goals is not affected by whether others achieve their goals or not, there is no social interdependence. "The basic premise of social interdependence theory is that the way in which interdependence is structured determines how individuals interact" (Roseth et al., 2008, p. 225). Positive interdependence promotes sharing, mutual help and assistance, and trust, whereas negative interdependence promotes negative interactions such as hindering others and withholding help and resources. Considerable research supports the proposition that cooperative goal structures are associated with more positive peer interactions and higher achievement than competitive or independent goals structures (Johnson & Johnson, 2005; Roseth et al., 2008). In situations characterized by cooperative goal structures, students are more likely to engage in those prosocial behaviors (e.g., sharing resources, helping, encouraging others' efforts) that promote peer acceptance. Furthermore, in cooperative goal structures, the relationship between students' positive peer interactions and their achievement is stronger than is the case in competitive or independent goal structures (Roseth et al., 2008). In cooperative goal structures, students do not have to choose between being accepted by one's peers and achieving; rather, by working cooperatively on academic assignments, students gain in terms of positive social relationships and achievement.

Classroom Social Emotional Climate and Peer Relationships

In some classrooms, students help each other and share, laugh a lot, negotiate conflicts effectively, and treat each other with respect and kindness. In these classrooms students feel that they are valued members of the class and are more willing to actively participate in the classroom and to take risks. In other classrooms, the social emotional climate is very different, and students feel neither safe nor cared for. Several studies have demonstrated that classrooms characterized by caring and supportive interpersonal relationships between students and teachers and among students and opportunities for autonomy and challenge are associated with greater student academic motivation and engagement, prosocial behaviors, higher achievement, and low levels of problem behaviors (for reviews see Brophy, 2004).

Researchers have identified specific teacher practices that contribute to either a positive or negative social and emotional climate. These practices include the establishment of clear classroom rules and routines, non-punitive discipline practices, child-centered practices (i.e., granting students choice, following the student's lead), instruction that is responsive to individual differences, and high levels of positive emotional expressions and low levels of negative emotional expressions (Hamre & Pianta, 2005; La Paro, Pianta, & Stuhlman, 2004; Masbburn et al., 2008). Factor analytic studies find that these practices are indicators of a supportive classroom emotional climate, a factor that is distinct from but moderately related to a supportive instructional climate (La Paro et al., 2004). A supportive emotional climate is thought to promote students' self-determined motivation by meeting students' needs for relatedness, competence, and autonomy (Baker, Dilly, Aupperlee, & Patil, 2003). For younger students, these same practices contribute to the regulation of emotions and behavior in social interactions (Howes, Whitebrook, & Phillips, 1992; Liew et al., 2010).

A growing body of research documents an effect of a supportive emotional climate on children's social competencies. Using a longitudinal sample of children identified in kindergarten as being at risk for school failure, Hamre and Pianta (2005) found that the quality of the emotional supports available in their first grade classrooms predicted lower levels of individual teacher–student conflict, above kindergarten levels of conflict, for students with poor regulatory control. Wilson, Pianta, and Stuhlman (2007) used cluster analysis to identify four classroom types based on instructional and emotional climate. Children in classrooms with high quality on both dimensions were rated by teachers as more socially competent and self-regulated and were observed to engage in more positive peer interactions and exhibit lower negative behavior than students in mediocre or overall low-quality classrooms. Mashburn et al. (2008) found a unique effect of both observed instructional support and emotional support in pre-K classrooms on teacher-rated social competence and problem behaviors.

Effect of Interventions Targeting Teacher Social-Emotional Practices on Peer Relationships

Intervention studies that target teacher social-emotional practices report improvement in children's social adjustment and peer relationships. Some programs help improve teachers' behavior management practices (Lyon, Gershenson, Farahmand, Thaxter, Behling, & Budd, 2009; Raver, Jones, Li-Grining, Metzger, Champion, & Sardin, 2008). When teachers establish clear rules, intervene proactively to prevent behavior problems, and reinforce compliant behavior, children exhibit lower levels aggressive behaviors and increased levels of prosocial behavior (for reviews of classroom management strategies and their effects on classroom social behaviors see Bear, 2007).

An increasingly common approach to helping teachers establish positive classroom climates involves supporting teachers in implementing classroom-based social-emotional curricula. Hughes and Barrois (2010) identified three such programs that have strong evidence of efficacy for increasing students' social competencies: Promoting Alternative Thinking Strategies (PATHS; Kusché & Greenberg, 1995); the Seattle Social Development Program (SSDP, Abbott, O'Donnell, Hawkins, Hill, Kosterman, & Catalano, 1998), and Second Step (Frey, Nolen, Edstrom, & Hirschstein, 2005). These programs demonstrate that well-implemented teacher professional efforts directed to teachers' roles in promoting children's social and emotional skills improve those social competencies that are critical to children's successful friendships and peer interactions. Each one of these evidence-based programs is briefly described.

The PATHS curriculum is designed for grades K–5 and attempts to increase students' social and emotional competence. In this teacher-led curriculum, students receive instruction in emotion knowledge and awareness of emotions in one's self and others, emotional and behavioral self-regulation, and social problem-solving skills. Teachers present lessons using a variety of methods including didactic instruction, class discussion, modeling, role play, social and self reinforcement, and worksheets. In addition to teaching lessons, teachers are encouraged to generalize their use of PATHS concepts across the school day. In an early efficacy trial (Conduct Problems Prevention Research Group, 1999), the PATHS program delivered in first-grade classrooms had a positive effect on classroom climate (i.e., following rules, ability to express feelings appropriately, level of interest and enthusiasm, and ability to stay focused and on-task) and on disruptive student behaviors. Greenberg, Kusché, Cook, and Quamma (1995) found that third graders exposed to the PATHS program for one to two years were able to generate more words to describe positive and negative feelings, and they were better able to describe negative feelings, provide examples of their own feelings and understand that emotions can be hidden or changed. Domitrovich, Cortes, and Greenberg (2007) evaluated a modified PATHS program for preschool students and found that, compared to control students, intervention students were rated by teachers as more socially competent and as less socially withdrawn and demonstrated better emotion knowledge skills.

The SSDP (Hawkins, Kosterman, Catalano, Hill, & Abbott, 2005) aims to promote positive social development by utilizing classroom management and instructional practices, implementing a cognitive behavioral instructional program addressing self-control and social competencies, and providing parent workshops. Teachers are taught to establish classroom routines at the beginning of the year, to develop clear and explicit expectations for behavior, to praise positive behavior, and to provide frequent assessments of student learning and feedback. In a series of quasi-experimental studies conducted over varying intervals post-intervention (Hawkins et al., 2005), the program had a beneficial effect on classroom aggressive behavior, alcohol use, and delinquency. Among low-income students, the program reduced the number of antisocial friendships and increased students' commitment to school and achievement.

The Second Step Program (Committee for Children, 2002) seeks to increase elementary and middle school students' social competence by improving students' skills in the areas of social problem solving, perspective taking, impulse control, and anger management. In addition to weekly teacher-delivered lessons, teachers are given instruction in ways to generalize taught skills to everyday classroom activities. The program has beneficial effects on students' classroom aggression and prosocial attitudes and behaviors (Grossman et al., 1997; Frey et al., 2005).

Developmental Issues

Very little research has examined developmental changes in the influence of teacher–student relationships or classroom context on students' peer relationships. However, several studies document a decreased reliance on teachers and increased reliance on peers for social support as children transition from the early elementary grades to middle school (Cole, Martin, & Powers, 1997). In a cross-sectional study, the greatest decline in perceptions of support in relationships with seven different significant others (e.g., parents, best friend, teacher, sibling, grandmother) from grade 4 to grade 7 occurred for relationships with teachers (Furman & Buhrmester, 1992). Based on these findings, one might expect that as students enter adolescence, teachers would exert less influence on students' values and behaviors. However, the developmental research necessary to test this expectation is not yet available.

Research on developmental differences in the effect of teacher instructional practices on students' social adjustment is also lacking. However, developmental theory and empirical findings related to students' self-appraisals and friendship networks suggest that peer perceptions of their own and classmates' academic abilities would play a larger role in peer social networks at the transition to middle school than in the elementary grades. Adolescence is a time of heightened sensitivity to peers' perceptions of one's competencies (Furman & Buhrmester, 1992; Juvonen & Cardigan, 2002). The transition from elementary grades to middle school is also a time of increased availability of social comparison cues (Anderman, 2003; Roeser, Midgley, & Urdan, 1996; Urdan & Schoenfelder, 2006). Relative to elementary schools, middle schools involve greater use of ability grouping and grading based on absolute standards versus effort or improvement, and use of grades as extrinsic rewards. Thus the increase in the importance of peers as sources of social support occurs at the same developmental period when information about students' relative abilities is more readily available. These two developmental changes may account for the increased correspondence in middle and high school between one's own academic achievement and the achievement levels of one's friends. That is, peer social networks demonstrate greater within group similarity on achievement values and achievement in middle grades relative to elementary school, a tendency that is due both to selection effects and to socialization effects (Kindermann, 2008). Based on these findings, one would expect that in settings in which information about relative ability is more available to students, social networks would show greater similarity in terms of achievement. Empirical research testing this reasoning, however, does not yet exist.

Broader Contextual Influences on Classroom Peer Relationships

The influence of the teacher on peer relationships may vary based on the broader school context. For example, a central feature of efforts to redesign middle schools was the creation of smaller personalized learning communities within larger schools, greater opportunities for cooperative learning, and closer relationships between adults and students. The smaller learning communities are accomplished by assigning students to learning teams of 60–100 students who attend core classes together that are taught by a team of teachers who plan together to meet students' needs. Students within a team are assigned to a homeroom in which the role of the teacher has been redefined so that the homeroom period, or another designated time period, becomes part of a teacher-based advisory program. A number of experimental and quasi-experimental studies document an effect of these changes on student academic motivation and achievement and dropout rates (for review see Felner, Favazza, Shim, Brand, Gu, & Noonan, 2001). Although the effect of these structural and role definition changes on peer relationships has not been investigated, these changes are associated with an increased sense of school belonging and decreases in social and behavioral problems (Felner et al., 2001). These reform efforts underscore that both teacher practices and peer relationships are constrained by school structural characteristics, such as the number of classmates and teachers with whom students interact and the stability of the peer group.

The standards-based reform movement may also affect classroom practices and peer relationships. Since the mid 1990s, schools have experienced increased pressure for their students to perform well on state-level accountability tests. Teachers and schools report intense pressure to report a high "passing rate" on state accountability tests (Booher-Jennings, 2005; Watanabe, 2007). In response to these pressures, teachers may increase their emphasis on performance goals, at the expense of mastery goals, with a corresponding increase in teacher control and decrease in student choice over what and how they learn and cooperative learning tasks. These practices, in turn, are expected to negatively affect peers' pursuit of prosocial goals and positive peer interactions

Being preferred by the teacher may have different effects on a student's peer acceptance in different classroom contexts. Babad (1993) found that when "teacher pets" (based on peer report of teacher preference) were considered as classroom leaders, the classroom climate has positive, whereas when teacher pets were not considered as leaders by classmates, the classroom climate was negative. Babad suggested that student resentment at a teacher showing a preference for unpopular students who did not deserve this attention led to a negative climate. This finding suggests that teacher liking for a student may have different implications for students' social acceptance based on whether the preferred student is viewed positively by peers.

EDUCATIONAL IMPLICATIONS OF TEACHERS AS MANAGERS OF STUDENTS' PEER CONTEXTS

In a time of heightened press for schools to be accountable for student outcomes, teachers and schools are increasingly evaluated and rewarded or sanctioned based on student performance on standardized tests of academic skills. The narrow focus of such evaluations is inconsistent with a body of research demonstrating the importance of social and emotional learning to students' success both within and outside of school (Zins, Bloodworth, Weissberg, & Walberg, 2007). Incorporating reliable and valid measures of the social and emotional context of classrooms and schools and of the social and emotional health of students into education accountability practices would give greater visibility to this undervalued dimension of teacher quality.

The No Child Left Behind Act (U.S. Department of Education, 2002) requires that each classroom be taught by a "qualified" teacher. A qualified teacher is defined by college degrees and certification. The past decade has witnessed a sharp increase in research on classroom quality (for reviews see Atkins-Burnett, 2007). Several observational measures predict children's growth in social-emotional and academic competencies. This research supports the conclusion that classroom quality is defined more by what teachers do than by teacher training, certification, or other traditional measures of teacher quality (Mashburn et al., 2008). La Paro et al. (2004) argued that "interactions between children and teachers are a primary mechanism through which classroom experiences affect development" (p. 412). Thus, a comprehensive assessment of classroom quality would measure teacher-student interactions. The Classroom Assessment Scoring System (CLASS; Pianta, La Paro, & Hamre, 2008), an observational measure with strong evidence of inter-rater reliability and validity, consists of seven scales assessing teacher–student interactions that load on two factors: emotional support and instructional support. Both scales are predictive of student growth in learning behaviors and achievement.

These findings have several implications. Decisions regarding teacher retention and promotion should be made, in part, on the basis of their interactions in the classroom, including their ability to connect with students, establish an affectively positive climate, and offer a secure and organized learning environment. Teacher training programs should intentionally focus on those practices shown empirically to predict student learning and should evaluate teachers-in-training on the basis of these practices. Mentorship programs for new teachers should include the opportunity to receive coaching and feedback on those practices that define instructional and emotional quality teaching (Murray, 2005).

A new generation of teacher professional development interventions shows promise in improving teachers' ability to promote student learning (Landry, Anthony, Swank, & Monseque-Bailey, 2009; Pianta, Mashburn, Downer, Hamre, & Justice, 2008; Raver et al., 2008). These new professional development programs occur over months rather than days, target specific teacher practices known to promote student learning, provide classroom-based feedback in the application of taught concepts and practices, respect teacher autonomy and professionalism, and include opportunities for teachers to reflect on their practices in real-world contexts with a supportive consultant. Thus these new approaches to teacher professional development provide teachers with opportunity to develop the autonomous motivation and self-efficacy necessary to incorporate the taught practices into their classroom interactions.

It is also important for educators to embrace the teacher's role as manager of the social and emotional climate of the classroom. Findings from a study of middle school homeroom teachers (Davis & Lease, 2007) suggest that many teachers have not embraced this message. Over one-third of the teachers were uncertain as to whether developing relationships with students was their responsibility, and a sizeable number of teachers expressed the belief that they were not obligated to meet students' relational needs, or that doing so would not improve or might hamper students' academic motivation and achievement. Elementary teachers are more likely to accept this responsibility but feel ill-prepared for this role (Murray, 2005). Thus, interventions must address teachers' beliefs about their role and perceived efficacy for effectively building positive social-emotional climates that promote academic and social competences.

DIRECTIONS FOR FUTURE RESEARCH ON TEACHERS' ROLES IN PEER RELATIONSHIPS

A substantial body of research supports the importance of teacher practices to students' social, behavioral, and academic adjustment at school. This review has focused on two broad dimensions of teachers' practices—affective and instructional practices. Through their affective responses to children, provision of social support, and classroom management practices, teachers create a social-emotional climate that facilitates or hinders proso-cial peer interactions and cooperative engagement in learning and buffers low-achieving and poorly regulated children from peer rejection. Affective interactions with students also influence students' peer reputation and ac-ceptance in the classroom. Through their instructional practices, including their relative emphasis on mastery versus performance learning goals, use of cooperative goal structures, and differential behaviors to students for whom they hold high or low achievement expectations, teachers influence students' individual learning goals and achievement as well as peer class-room interactions.

Despite the progress that has been made understanding the role of teachers in peer relationships, research in this area is still in its infancy, and many questions remain. Four topics show particular promise for advancing this area of research. First, research that addresses the affective and instruc-tional dimensions of teacher practices simultaneously is needed. Research in these two broad topics has largely progressed along separate lines. Yet classrooms are multidimensional contexts, and different dimensions are likely to exert both separate and interactive effects on peer relationships. For example, a mastery goal orientation may have different effects on class-room peer relationships depending on the level of teacher provision of warmth and respect. Specifically, a mastery goal orientation may lead to a positive association between students' academic effort and peer acceptance only in classrooms in which the teacher is supportive and respects students' autonomy. In these classrooms, students may adopt the teachers' valuing of academic effort; consequently, they may prefer peers who are invested in learning. If a teacher emphasizes mastery goals and effort over correct answers, but students do not experience the teacher as caring about them, they may be less likely to value effort.

Second, research is needed that addresses developmental aspects of the role of teachers in influencing peer relationships. It is likely that the con struct of teacher support differs at different developmental periods. Mea-sures of teacher–student support at preschool and early elementary grades are based on attachment perspectives of the relationship, whereas mea-sures of teacher–student support at later elementary and secondary levels are based on social-motivational and social-cognitive theories. It is likely that these measures assess somewhat different aspects of the teacher–stu-dent relationship. Similarly, it is likely that the mechanisms that account for the effect of teacher–student relationship quality on students' behav-ioral, social, and academic adjustment differ at different developmental pe-riods. In early childhood, an affectively positive relationship may promote a child's sense of felt security, permitting the child to cope with stressors and to more freely explore and participate in the classroom. These behav-iors may mediate the effect of the relationship on students' peer relationships. During the elementary grades, the affective quality teacher–student interactions may serve as a referent for peers' affectively laden perceptions of the child. During middle and high school, the affective quality of the relationship may indirectly affect peer relationships via its direct effect on students' academic engagement and achievement.

Third, research on the role of teacher instructional practices and peer relationships is needed. Very little research examines how instructional practices influence peer relationships. Of particular interest is how teachers influence which student characteristics are associated with higher levels of peer acceptance. Are lower-achieving students at greater risk of being rejected in classrooms characterized by a teacher performance goal orientation? Are rebellious or resistive children less likely to be rejected in classrooms characterized by low teacher support? Fourth, research on aspects of the broader context that influence those aspects of teacher–student interactions that affect students' peer relationships is needed. Consistent with social ecological theory (Bronfenbrenner, 1979), just as the classroom context influences students' motivation and behavior, the school context influences teachers' motivation, professional identity, and teaching strategies—aspects of the school context that may influence teacher practices as well as moderate the effect of teacher practices on peer relationships. For example, do policies that hold teachers accountable for student performance on state accountability tests affect the social and emotional climate of classrooms? Do campus-provided opportunities to work collaboratively with other teachers influence peer relationships via teachers' affective and instructional practices in the classroom? A more integrative and systems-oriented approach to understanding the classroom contexts holds considerable promise for identifying strategies to assist teachers in carrying out their role as managers of students' peer contexts.

REFERENCES

Abbott, R.D., O'Donnell, J., Hawkins, J.D., Hill, K.G., Kosterman, R. & Catalano, R.F. (1998). Changing teaching practices to promote achievement and bonding to school. *American Journal of Orthopsychiatry, 68*, 542–552.

Ames, C. (1992). Classrooms: Goals, structures, and student motivation. *Journal of Educational Psychology, 84*, 251–271.

Anderman, L. H. (2003). Academic and social perceptions as predictors of change in middle school students' sense of school belonging. *Journal of Experimental Education, 72*, 5–22.

Atkins-Burnett, S. (2007). *Measuring children's progress from preschool through third grade.* Mathematica Policy Research, Inc: Washington, DC. Retrieved from http://www.mathematica-mpr.com/publications/PDFs/measchildprogress.pdf

Babad, E. (1993). Teachers' differential behavior. *Educational Psychology Review, 5,* 347–376.

Baker, J. A., Dilly, L. J., Aupperlee, J. L., & Patil, S. A. (2003). The developmental context of school satisfaction: Schools as psychologically healthy environments. *School Psychology Quarterly, 18,* 206–221.

Bandura, A., Barbaranelli, C., Caprara, G. V., & Pastorelli, C. (1996). Multifaceted impact of self-efficacy beliefs on academic functioning. *Child Development, 67,* 1206–1222.

Battistich, V., & Horn, A. (1997). The relationship between students' sense of their school as a community and their involvement in problem behaviors. *American Journal of Public Health, 87,* 1997–2001.

Bear, G. G. (2007). *Developing self-discipline and preventing and correcting misbehavior.* Boston, MA: Pearson.

Birch, S. H., & Ladd, G.W. (1997). The teacher-child relationship and children's early school adjustment. *Journal of School Psychology, 35,* 61–80.

Blair, C., & Razza, R. P. (2007). Relating effortful control, executive function, and false belief understanding to emerging math and literacy ability in kindergarten. *Child Development, 78,* 647–663.

Booher-Jennings, J. (2005). Below the bubble:"Educational triage" and the texas accountability system. *American Educational Research Journal, 42,* 231–231.

Bowlby, J. (1980). *Attachment and loss: Vol. III. Loss, sadness, and depression.* New York, NY: Basic Books.

Bretherton, I., & Munholland, K. A. (1999). Internal working models in attachment relationships: A construct revisited. In J. Cassidy and P. R. Shaver (Eds), *Handbook of attachment: Theory, research, and clinical applications* (pp. 89–111). New York, NY: Guilford.

Bronfenbrenner, U. (1979). *The ecology of human development.* Cambridge, MA: Harvard University Press.

Brophy, J. (2004). *Motivating students to learn* (2nd ed). Mahwah, NJ: Lawrence Erlbaum.

Chang, L. (2003). Variable effects of children's aggression, social withdrawal, and prosocial leadership as functions of teacher beliefs and behaviors. *Child Development, 74,* 535–548.

Chang, L. (2004). The role of classroom norms in contextualizing the relations of children's social behaviors to peer acceptance. *Developmental Psychology, 40,* 691–702.

Chen, Q., Hughes, J. N., Kwok, O., & Liew, J. (2010). Joint contributions of peer acceptance and peer academic reputation to achievement in academically at risk children: Mediating processes. *Journal of Applied Developmental Psychology, 31,* 448–459.

Cole, D. A., Martin, J. M., & Powers, B. (1997). A competency-based model of child depression: A longitudinal study of peer, parent, teacher, and self-evaluations. *Journal of Child Psychology and Psychiatry, 38,* 505–514.

Cole, D. A., Maxwell, S. E., & Martin, J. M. (1997). Reflected self-appraisals: Strength and structure of the relation of teacher, peer, and parent ratings to children's self-perceived competencies. *Journal of Educational Psychology, 89,* 55–70.

Committe for Children. (2002). *Second step: A violence prevention curriculum*. Seattle, WA: Committee for Children.

Conduct Problems Prevention Research Group. (1999). Initial impact of the Fast Track prevention trial for conduct problems: II: Classroom effects. *Journal of Consulting and Clinical Psychology, 67,* 648–657.

Connell, J. P., & Wellborn, J. G. (1991). Competence, autonomy, and relatedness: A motivational analysis of self-system processes. In M. Gunnar & L. A. Sroufe (Eds.), *Minnesota symposium on child psychology* (Vol. 22, pp 43–77). Hillsdale, NJ: Erlbaum.

Davis, H. A., & Lease, A. M. (2007). Perceived organizational structure for teacher liking: The role of peers' perceptions of teacher liking in teacher–student relationship quality, motivation, and achievement. *Social Psychology of Education, 10,* 403–427.

Deci, E. L., & Ryan, R. M. (1985). *Intrinsic motivation and self-determination in human behavior.* New York, NY: Plenum.

Decker, D. M., Dona, D. P., & Christenson, S. L. (2007). Behaviorally at-risk african american students: The importance of student-teacher relationships for student outcomes. *Journal of School Psychology, 45*(1), 83–109.

Denham, S. A., Blair, K. A., DeMulder, E., Levitas, J., Sawyer, K., & Auerbach-Major, S. (2003). Preschool emotional competence: Pathway to social competence. *Child Development, 74,* 238–256.

Domitrovich, C.E., Cortes, R.C., & Greenberg, M.T. (2007). Improving young children's social and emotional competence: A randomized trial of the preschool "PATHS" curriculum. *Journal of Primary Prevention, 28*(2), 67–91.

Doumen, S., Verschueren, K., Buyse, E., Germeijs, V., Luyckx, K., & Soenens, B. (2008). Reciprocal relations between teacher–child conflict and aggressive behavior in kindergarten: A three-wave longitudinal study. *Journal of Clinical Child and Adolescent Psychology, 37,* 588–588.

Dweck, C. S. (1986). Motivational processes affecting learning. *American Psychologist, 41,* 1040–1048.

Fabes, R. A., Eisenberg, N., Jones, S., Smith, M., Guthrie, I., Poulin, R., Shepard, S., & Friedman, J. (1999). Regulation, emotionality, and preschoolers' socially competent peer interactions. *Child Development, 70,* 432–442.

Farmer, T. W., Lines, M. M., & Hamm, J. V. (2011). Revealing the invisible hand: The role of teachers in children's peer experiences. *Journal of Applied Developmental Psychology, 32.5,* 247–256.

Felner, R. D., Favazza, A., Shim, M., Brand, S., Gu, K., & Noonan, N. (2001). Whole school improvement and restructuring as prevention and promotion: Lessons from STEP and the project on high performance learning communities. *Journal of School Psychology, Special Schooling and Mental Health Issues, 39,* 177–202.

Filby, N. N., & Barnett, B. G. (1982). Student perceptions of "Better Readers" in elementary classrooms. *The Elementary School Journal, 82,* 435–449.

Flanders, N., & Havumaki, S. (1960). The effect of teacher–pupil contacts involving praise on the sociometric choices of students. *Journal of Educational Psychology, 51*(2), 65–68.

Frey, K.S., Nolen, S.B., Edstrom, L.V., & Hirschstein, M.K. (2005). Effects of a school-based social–emotional competence program: Linking children's goals, attributions, and behavior. *Applied Developmental Psychology, 26,* 171–200.

Furman, W., & Buhrmester, D. (1992). Age and sex differences in perceptions of networks of personal relationships. *Child Development, 63,* 103–115.

Gest, S. D., Domitrovich, C. E., & Welsh, J. A. (2005). Peer academic reputation in elementary school: Associations with changes in self-concept and academic skills. *Journal of Educational Psychology, 97,* 337–346.

Gest, S. D., Rulison, K. L., Davidson, A. J., & Welsh, J. A. (2008). A reputation for success (or failure): The association of peer academic reputations with academic self-concept, effort, and performance across the upper elementary grades. *Developmental Psychology, 44*(3), 625–636.

Gleason, K. A., Kwok, O-M, & Hughes, J. N. (2007). The short-term effect of grade retention on peer relations and academic performance of at-risk first graders. *The Elementary School Journal, 107,* 327–340.

Graham, S., & Barker, G. P. (1990). The down side of help: An attributional–developmental analysis of helping behavior as a low-ability cue. *Journal of Educational Psychology, 82,* 7–14.

Greenberg, M. T., Kusche, C. A., Cook, E. T., & Quamma, J. P. (1995). Promoting emotional competence in school-aged children: The effects of the PATHS curriculum. *Development and Psychopathology, 7,* 117–136.

Grossman, D.C., Neckerman, H.J., Koepsell, T.D., Liu, P., Asher, K.N., Beland, K., Frey, K. & Rivara, F.P. (1997). Effectiveness of a violence prevention curriculum among children in elementary school. *Journal of the American Medical Association, 277,* 1605–1611.

Hamre, B. K., & Pianta, R. C. (2005). Can instructional and emotional support in the first-grade classroom make a difference for children at risk of school failure? *Child Development, 76,* 949–967.

Hamre, B. K., & Pianta, R. C. (2006). Student–teacher relationships. In G. C. Bear & K. M. Minke (Eds.), *Children's needs III: Development, prevention, and intervention* (pp. 59–71). Washington, DC: National Association of School Psychologists.

Harter, S. (1998). The development of self-representations. In W. Damon (Series Ed.) & N. Eisenberg (Vol. Ed.), *Handbook of child psychology: Volume 3. Social, emotional, and personality development* (5th ed., pp. 553–617). New York, NY: John Wiley & Sons, Inc.

Hawkins, J.D., Kosterman, R., Catalano, R.F., Hill, K.G., & Abbott, R.D. (2005). Promoting positive adult functioning through social development intervention in childhood: Long-term effects from the Seattle Social Development Project. *Archives of Pediatrics and Adolescent Medicine, 159,* 25–31.

Howes, C., Hamilton, C. E., & Matheson, C. C. (1994). Children's relationships with peers: Differential associations with aspects of the teacher-child relationship. *Child Development, 65,* 253–263.

Howes, C., Whitebrook, M., & Phillips, D. (1992). Teacher characteristics and effective teaching in child care: Findings from the National child Care Staffing Study. *Child & Youth Care, 21,* 399–414.

Hughes, J. N., & Barrois, L. (2010). The developmental implications of classroom social relationships and strategies for improving them. In B. Doll, W. Pfohl,

& J. Yoon (Eds.), *Handbook of youth prevention science* (pp. 194–217). New York, NY: Routledge.

Hughes, J. N., Cavell, T. A., & Willson, V. (2001). Further support for the developmental significance of the quality of the teacher-student relationship. *Journal of School Psychology, 39*(4), 289–301.

Hughes, J. N., & Chen, Q. (2011). Reciprocal effects of student-teacher and student-peer relatedness: Effects on academic self efficacy. *Journal of Applied Developmental Psychology, 32*, 278–287.

Hughes, J. N., Dyer, N., Luo, W., & Kwok, O. (2009). Effects of peer academic reputation on achievement in academically at-risk elementary students. *Journal of Applied Developmental Psychology, 30*,182–194.

Hughes, J. N., & Kwok, O. (2006). Classroom engagement mediates the effect of teacher-student support on elementary students' peer acceptance: A prospective analysis. *Journal of School Psychology, 43*, 465–480.

Hughes, J. N., Luo, W., Kwok, O., & Loyd, L. (2008). Teacher–student support, effortful engagement, and achievement: A three year longitudinal study. *Journal of Educational Psychology, 100*, 1–14.

Hughes, J. N., & Zhang, D. (2007). Effects of the structure of classmates' perceptions of peers' academic abilities on children's academic self-concept, peer acceptance, and classroom engagement. *Journal of Contemporary Educational Psychology, 32*, 400–419.

Hughes, J. N., Zhang, D., & Hill, C. R. (2006). Peer assessments of normative and individual teacher–student support predict social acceptance and engagement among low-achieving children. *Journal of School Psychology, 43*, 447–463.

Hymel, S. (1986). Interpretations of peer behavior: Affective bias in childhood and adolescence. *Child Development, 57*(2), 431–445.

Johnson, D. W., & Johnson, R. T. (2005). New developments in social interdependence theory. *Genetic, Social, and General Psychology Monographs, 131*, 285–358.

Jones, S., Eisenberg, N., Fabes, R. A., & MacKinnon, D. P. (2002). Parents' reactions to elementary school children's negative emotions: Relations to social and emotional functioning at school. *Merrill-Palmer Quarterly, 48*, 133–159.

Jussim, L., & Harber, K. D. (2005). Teacher expectations and self-fulfilling prophecies: Knowns and unknowns, resolved and unresolved controversies. *Personality and Social Psychology Review, 9*, 131–155.

Juvonen, J. & Cardigan, R. J. (2002). Social determinants of public behavior of midddle school yuth. In F. Pajares & T. Urdan (Eds), *Adolescents and education. Academic motivation* of adolescents (vol. 2, pp. 277–298). Greenwich, CT: Information Age Publishing.

Kaplan, A., Gheen, M., & Midgley, C. (2002). Classroom goal structure and student disruptive behaviour. *British Journal of Educational Psychology, 72*, 191–212.

Kindermann, T. A. (2008). Can we make causal inferences about the influence of children's naturally existing social networks on their school motivation? In N. A. Card, J. P. Selig & T. D. Little (Eds.), Modeling dyadic and interdependent data in the developmental and behavioral sciences. (pp. 335–368). New York, NY: Routledge/Taylor & Francis.

Kusché, C. A., & Greenberg, M. T. (1995). *The PATHS curriculum.* Seattle, WA: Developmental Research & Programs.

La Paro, K. M., Pianta, R. C., & Stuhlman, M. (2004). The classroom assessment scoring system: Findings from the prekindergarten year. *The Elementary School Journal, 104*(5), 409-426. doi:10.1086/499760

Ladd, G. W., Birch, S. H., & Buhs, E. S. (1999). Chidlren's social and scholastic lives in kindergarten: Related spheres of influence? *Child Development, 70,* 1373–1400.

Ladd, G. W., Kochenderfer, B. J., & Coleman, C. C. (1997). Classroom peer acceptance, friendship, and victimization: Distinct relational systems that contribute uniquely to children's school adjustment? *Child Development, 68,* 1181–1197.

Landry, S. H., Anthony, J. L., Swank, P. R., & Monseque-Bailey, P. (2009). Effectiveness of comprehensive professional development for teachers of at-risk preschoolers. *Journal of Educational Psychology, 101,* 448–465.

Lau, S., & Nie, Y. (2008). Interplay between personal goals and classroom goal structures in predicting student outcomes: A multilevel analysis of person-context interactions. *Journal of Educational Psychology, 100,* 15–29.

Lerner, R. (1998). Theories of human development: Contemporary perspectives. In W. Damon & R. M. Lerner (Eds.), *Handbook of child psychology, 5th ed.* (pp. 1–24). New York, NY: Wiley.

Levy-Tossman, I., Kaplan, A., & Assor, A. (2007). Academic goal orientations, multiple goal profiles, and friendship intimacy among early adolescents. *Contemporary Educational Psychology, 32,* 231–252.

Li, Y, Hughes, J. N., Kwok, O, & Hsu, H. (2011). Evidence of convergent and divergent validity of child, teacher, and peer reports of teacher–student support. *Psychological Assessment,* July 18, 2011. Electronic copy available at http://lib-ezproxy.tamu.edu:2048/login?url=http://search.proquest.com/docview/877850313?accountid=7082.

Liew, J., Chen, Q., & Hughes, J. N. (2010). Child effortful control, teacher–student relationships, and achievement in academically at-risk children: Additive and interactive effects. *Early Childhood Research Quarterly, 25,* 51–64

Little, M., & Kobak, R. (2003). Emotional security with teachers and children's stress reactivity: A comparison of special-education and regular-education classrooms. *Journal of Clinical Child & Adolescent Psychology, 32,* 127–138.

Luckner, A. E., & Pianta, R.C. (2009, April). *The importance of classroom quality for children's peer experiences in fifth grade.* Paper presented at biennial meeting of the Society for Research in Child Development, Denver, CO.

Lyon, A. R., Gershenson, R. A., Farahmand, F. K., Thaxter, P. J., Behling, S., & Budd, K. S. (2009). Effectiveness of teacher–child interaction training (TCIT) in a preschool setting. *Behavior Modification, 33,* 855–884

Madon, S., Jussim, L., & Eccles, J. (1997). In search of the powerful self-fulfilling prophecy. *Journal of Personality & Social Psychology, 72,* 791–809.

Marsh, H. W., & Craven, R. (2002). The pivotal role of frames of reference in academic self-concept formation: The big fish little pond effect. In F. Pajares & T. Urdan (Eds.), *Adolescence and education* (Vol. II, pp. 83–123). Greenwich, CT: Information Age.

Martel, M. M., Nigg, J. T., Wong, M. M., Fitzgerald, H. E., Jester, J. M., Puttler, L. I., Glass, J. M., Adams, K. M., & Zucker, R. A. (2007). Childhood and adolescent resiliency, regulation, and executive functioning in relation to adolescent problems and competence in a high-risk sample. *Development and Psychopa-thology, 19,* 541–563.

Mashburn, A. J., Pianta, R. C., Hamre, B. K., Downer, J. T., Barbarin, O. A., Bryant, D., . . . Howes, C. (2008). Measures of classroom quality in prekindergarten and children's development of academic, language, and social skills. *Child Development, 79,* 732–749.

Matsumura, L. C., Slater, S. C., & Crosson, A. (2008). Classroom climate, rigorous instruction and curriculum, and students' interactions in urban middle schools. *The Elementary School Journal, 108,* 293–312.

McKown, C., & Weinstein, R. S. (2002). Modeling the role of child ethnicity and gender in children's differential response to teacher expectations. *Journal of Applied Social Psychology, 32,* 159–184.

Meehan, B. T., Hughes, J. N., & Cavell, T. A. (2003). Teacher–student relationships as compensatory resources for aggressive children. *Child Development, 74,* 1145–1157.

Midgley, C., Feldlaufer, H., & Eccles, J. S. (1989). Change in teacher efficacy and student self- and task-related beliefs in mathematics during the transition to junior high school. *Journal of Educational Psychology, 81,* 247–258.

Murray, J., (2005). *Social-emotional climate and the success of new teachers: A new look at the ongoing challenge of new teacher retention.* Wellesley Centers for Women, Report WCW 9. Wellesley, MA: Wellesley Centers for Women.

Noddings, N. (1992). *The challenge to care in schools: An alternative approach to education.* New York, NY: Teachers College Press.

Pianta, R. C., Hamre, B., & Stuhlman, M. (2003). Relationships between teachers and children. In W. M. Reynolds, & G. E. Miller (Eds.), *Handbook of psychology: Educational psychology* (vol. 7, pp. 199–234). Hoboken, NJ: John Wiley & Sons.

Pianta, R. C., La Paro, K. M., & Hamre, B. K. (2008). *Classroom Assessment Scoring System™: Manual K–3.* Baltimore, MD: Paul H. Brookes Publishing.

Pianta, R. C., Mashburn, A. J., Downer, J. T., Hamre, B. K., & Justice, L. (2008). Effects of web-mediated professional development resources on teacher-child interactions in pre-kindergarten classrooms. *Early Childhood Research Quarterly, 23,* 431–451.

Pianta, R. C., & Steinberg, M. S. (1992). Teacher–child relationships and the process of adjusting to school. *New Directions for Child Development, 57,* 61–80.

Pianta, R. C., & Walsh, D. J. (1996). *High-risk children in schools: Constructing sustaining relationships.* New York, NY: Routledge.

Raver, C. C., Jones, S. M., Li-Grining, C. P., Metzger, M., Champion, K. M., & Sardin, L. (2008). Improving preschool classroom processes: Preliminary findings from a randomized trial implemented in head start settings. *Early Childhood Research Quarterly, 23,* 10–26.

Retish, P. M. (1973). Changing the status of poorly esteemed students through teacher reinforcement. *Journal of Applied and Behavioral Science, 9,* 44–50.

Rimm-Kaufman, S. E., La Paro, K. M., Downer, J. T., & Pianta, R. C. (2005). The contribution of classroom setting and quality of instruction to children's behavior in kindergarten classrooms. *The Elementary School Journal, 105,* 377–394.

Roeser, R. W., Midgley, C., & Urdan, T. C. (1996). Perceptions of the school psychological environment and early adolescents' psychological and behavioral functioning in school: The mediating role of goals and belonging. *Journal of educational psychology, 88,* 408–422.

Rosenholtz, S. J., & Simpson, C. (1984). Classroom organization and student stratification. *The Elementary School Journal, 85,* 21–37.

Rosenthal, R. J., & Jacobson, L. (1968). *Pygmalion in the classroom: Teacher expectations and pupils' intellectual development.* New York, NY: Holt, Rinehart, & Winston.

Roseth, C. J., Johnson, D. W., & Johnson, R. T. (2008). Promoting early adolescents' achievement and peer relationships: The effects of cooperative, competitive, and individualistic goal structures. *Psychological Bulletin, 134,* 223–246.

Ryan, R. M., Stiller, J. D., & Lynch, J. H. (1994). Representations of relationships to teachers, parents, and friends as predictors of academic motivation and self-esteem. *Journal of Early Adolescence, 14,* 226–249.

Schuncke, G. M. (1978). Social effects of classroom organization. *Journal of Educational Research, 71,* 303–307.

Schunk, D. H., & Zimmerman, B. J. (2006). Competence and control beliefs: Distinguishing the means and ends. In P. A. Alexander, & P. H. Winne (Eds.), *Handbook of educational psychology* (pp. 349–367). Mahwah, NJ: Lawrence Erlbaum.

Silver, R. B., Measelle, J. R., Armstrong, J. M., & Essex, M. J. (2005). Trajectories of classroom externalizing behavior: Contributions of child characteristics, family characteristics, and the teacher–child relationship during the school transition. *Journal of School Psychology, 43,* 39–60.

Simpson, C. H., & Rosenholtz, S. J. (1986). Classroom structure and the social construction of ability. In J. G. Richardson (Ed.), *Handbook of theory and research for the sociology of education* (pp. 113–138). New York, NY: Greenwood Press.

Skaalvik, E. M. (1997). Self-enhancing and self-defeating ego orientation: Relations with task and avoidance orientation, achievement, self-perceptions, and anxiety. *Journal of Educational Psychology, 89,* 71–81.

Stipek, D. J., & Tannatt, L. M. (1984). Children's judgments of their own and their peers' academic competence. *Journal of Educational Psychology, 76,* 75–84.

Taylor, A. R., & Trickett, P. K. (1989). Teacher preference and children's sociometric status in the classroom. *Merrill-Palmer Quarterly, 35,* 343–361.

Trentacosta, C. J., & Shaw, D. S. (2009). Emotional self-regulation, peer rejection, and antisocial behavior: Developmental associations from early childhood to early adolescence. *Journal of Applied Developmental Psychology, 30,* 356–365.

U.S. Department of Education. (2002). The no child left behind act of 2001. Washington, DC: Author. Retrieved from http://www.ed.gov/nclb/overview/intro/execsumm.pdf

Urdan, T., & Midgley, C. (2003). Changes in the perceived classroom goal structure and pattern of adaptive learning during early adolescence. *Contemporary Educational Psychology, 28,* 524–551.

Urdan, T., & Schoenfelder, E. (2006). Classroom effects on student motivation: Goal structures, social relationships, and competence beliefs. *Journal of School Psychology, 44,* 331–349.

Valiente, C., Lemery-Chalfant, K., Swanson, J., & Reiser, M. (2008). Prediction of children's academic competence from their effortful control, relationships, and classroom participation. *Journal of Educational Psychology, 100,* 67–77.

Vondra, J. I., Shaw, D. S., Swearingen, L., Cohen, M., & Owens, E. B. (2001). Attachment stability and emotional and behavioral regulation from infancy to preschool age. *Development and Psychopathology, 13*, 13–33.

Watanabe, M. (2007). Displaced teacher and state priorities in a high-stakes accountability context. *Educational Policy, 21*, 311–368.

Weiner, B. (1974). *Achievement motivation and attribution theory.* Morristown, NJ: General Learning Press.

Weinstein, R. S., Marshall, H. H., Sharp L., & Botkin, M. (1987). Pygmalion and the student: Age and classroom differences in children's awareness of teacher expectations. *Child Development, 58*, 1079–1093.

Wentzel, K. R. (1999). Social-motivational processes and interpersonal relationship: Implications for understanding motivation at school. *Journal of Educational Psychology, 91*, 76–97.

White, K. J., & Kistner, J. (1992). The influence of teacher feedback on young children's peer preferences and perceptions. *Developmental Psychology, 28*, 933–940.

White, K. J., Sherman, M. C., & Jones, K. (1996). Children's perceptions of behavior problem peers: Effects of teacher feedback and peer-reported status. *Journal of School Psychology, 34*, 53–72.

Wigfield, A., Eccles, J. S., Schiefele, U., Roeser, R. W., & Davis-Kean, P. (2006). Development of achievement motivation. In N. Eisenberg, W. Damon, & R. Lerner (Eds.), *Handbook of child psychology: Vol. 3, Social, emotional, and personality development* (6th ed., pp. 933–1002). Hoboken, NJ: Wiley.

Wilson, H. K., Pianta, R. C., & Stuhlman, M. (2007). Typical classroom experiences in first grade: The role of classroom climate and functional risk in the development of social competencies. *The Elementary School Journal, 108*, 81–96.

Zins, J. E., Bloodworth, M. R., Weissberg, R. P., & Walberg, H. J. (2007). The scientific base linking social and emotional learning to school success. *Journal of Educational & Psychological Consultation, 17*, 191–210.

CHAPTER 9

PEER CULTURES
OF ACADEMIC EFFORT
AND ACHIEVEMENT
IN ADOLESCENCE

Why They Matter, and What Teachers Can Do About Them

Jill V. Hamm and Abigail Hoffman
University of North Carolina at Chapel Hill

Thomas W. Farmer
Penn State University

To be academically successful in adolescence, students must navigate complex peer cultures, in which social and academic forces combine to influence their academic dispositions, effort, and achievement. Peer cultures develop among and are maintained by students, but teachers play a significant role in establishing and maintaining peer cultures, through their intentional and unintentional instructional, management, and rela-

Peer Relationships and Adjustment at School, pages 219–250
Copyright © 2012 by Information Age Publishing
All rights of reproduction in any form reserved.

tional practices. Moreover, through developmentally based professional development, teachers can learn how to enhance the peer culture of their classrooms and schools. In this chapter we first review literature that describes the nature of peer cultures of academics. Next, we discuss findings regarding teachers' roles in peer cultures of effort and achievement. Finally, we feature a developmentally based intervention program used with teachers of early adolescents, Project SEALS (Supporting Early Adolescent Learning and School Success), and summarize some of the effects of SEALS from a series of randomized controlled trial experiments conducted in rural schools.

PEER CULTURES OF ACADEMIC BEHAVIORS AND DISPOSITIONS IN ADOLESCENCE

In his seminal book, *The Adolescent Society*, Coleman (1961) portrayed a dominant adolescent culture that rewarded peer more than adult values, and which appeared to value social status over academic accomplishment. What Coleman (1961) described was a peer culture, or a "stable set of activities or routines, artifacts, values, and concerns that children produce and share in interactions with peers" (Corsaro & Eder, 1990, p. 197). Applied to the academic dimension of school, peer cultures communicate, or are perceived to communicate, the acceptability, desirability, and value of effort and achievement. In contemporary studies, there remain findings that as adolescents move into and across middle school, they find classmates who are school-oriented less appealing (Bukowski, Sippola, & Newcomb, 2000) and maintain concerns that their own effort and achievement will compromise their social status (Juvonen & Murdock, 1995). However, a more localized and differentiated view of adolescent peer cultures and their influence on adolescents' own academic behaviors and dispositions is evident, with indications that peer cultures do not necessarily undermine, but instead can, and often do, support effort and achievement.

Adolescents are embedded in numerous collectives of peers. Most adolescents are members of peer groups, which are self-selected collectives of like-minded affiliates who interact with one another on a regular basis (Cairns, Xie, & Leung, 1998; Kindermann, 1993). Peer groups are theorized to be defined by members' shared experiences, including norms, values, and behaviors (Ryan, 2000), that is, by a shared and mutually determined culture. Adolescents use their membership in peer groups to help define their own identity, attitudes, and behaviors (Brown, 1990; Cairns et al., 1998). Although definitions and measurement of peer groups vary, it is generally accepted that through processes of selection and socialization, aspects of the peer group culture hold significant potential to influence members' attitudes and behaviors in a variety of domains including academics and schooling (Cairns et al., 1998; Kindermann, 1993; Ryan, 2000).

Classroom and school student bodies are not self-selected by adolescents, but they provide considerable opportunity for peer contact and interaction, and have features of peer cultures that hold the potential to influence adolescents' academic outcomes (Hamm & Zhang, 2010; Henry, 2008). Although there are other groupings of peers in schools, such as extracurricular activities, research relevant to the peer culture of academic effort and success has focused primarily on peer group, class, and school peer cultures. Among studies focused strictly on peer cultures of effort and achievement, the activities, routines, artifacts, values, and concerns that have received the greatest attention include norms governing effort and achievement, the social costs and benefits of effort and achievement, and peer support for effort and achievement.

Normative Contexts of Peer Cultures

Groups often function as normative contexts that influence the behaviors and dispositions of their members (Lapinski & Rimal, 2005). Groups have *descriptive norms* that are shared behaviors and dispositions that characterize the group. Members adhere to descriptive norms because of the prevalence of the behavior in the group; individuals who do not conform risk social consequences. In studies of peer cultures, descriptive norms are often operationalized as an aggregate of the behaviors or dispositions of the majority of the members of the group (e.g., Hamm, Schmid, Farmer, & Locke, 2011; Kindermann, 1993; Ryan, 2001). Groups can also be characterized by *injunctive* norms, which reflect the standards and expectations for behaviors and values that are perceived to be endorsed by the members of a group. Group norms define peer cultures immediate to adolescents such as peer groups, as well as more intermediate and distal contexts, such as classroom and school groupings.

Peer Group Normative Culture

A significant body of research has investigated the normative context of effort and achievement within and between peers groups, with most studies focused on descriptive norms (Hamm et al., 2011). Findings indicate that peer group normative contexts of effort and achievement can be considerably variable and can be differentiated by their descriptive norms. Moreover, peer group descriptive norms influence members' academic effort and achievement, with most studies assessing peer group descriptive norm influences net of members' prior academic adjustment. For example, Kindermann (1993) reported greater within- than between-group similarity for behavioral engagement among early adolescents, and that the behavioral engagement of the peer group predicted changes to individual members' behavioral engagement over the course of a school year. Ryan (2001) introduced the use of hierarchical linear modeling to partition the variance in student outcomes into within- and between-peer group variance. With an expanded set of academic dispositional and achievement outcomes including achievement and liking and enjoyment of school, this study reported significant similarity within peer groups, between-peer-group variability, and peer group influences over time for both African American and Caucasian early adolescents. More recently, studies have expanded the list of academic outcomes influenced by peer group descriptive norms in diverse samples of adolescents, to include, for example, advanced course-taking in mathematics for girls (Riegle-Crumb, Farkas, & Muller, 2006), dropping out of school (Ream & Rumberger, 2008), time spent on homework and school belonging (Hamm, Schmid, et al., 2011), and educational expectations among girls (Kiuru, Aunola, Vuori, & Nurmi, 2007).

In a study of early adolescents from diverse ethnic groups in rural schools across the United States, Hamm, Schmid, et al. (2011) distinguished injunctive from descriptive peer group norms, finding that within peer groups, members shared beliefs about the group's expectations for effort and achievement and that within-peer-group injunctive norms significantly differentiated peer groups. Moreover, students' perceptions of injunctive norms were significant predictors of members' own effort (time spent on homework) and valuing of school. Descriptive and injunctive norms were correlated for peer groups across various indicators of effort and achievement; for instance, peer groups whose members were characterized by less time spent on homework featured injunctive norms less supportive of effort and achievement. However, the disparity between injunctive and descriptive norms was related to members' academic success: When injunctive norms for effort and achievement were more encouraging than were descriptive norms (actual behaviors of the group), members improved in their effort and valuation of school, net of effects of descriptive norms. This also meant that when injunctive norms were less encouraging of effort and achievement than were descriptive norms, members' time spent on homework and valuing of school suffered across the school year.

The findings from Hamm, Schmid, et al. (2011) demonstrate the value of considering both injunctive and descriptive peer group normative influence, but also signify that students' perceptions of the acceptability of effort and achievement do not align fully with the actual behaviors of their group. Moreover, adolescents are prone to underestimate the acceptability of effort and achievement relative to group members' actual effort and achievement. Findings from a recent study support this conclusion; adolescents underestimated the value that their friends placed on mathematics and English (Bissell-Havran & Loken, 2009). Incorrect estimation of norms is common and provides a natural opportunity for intervention by classroom teachers if they can identify behaviors and dispositions for which the discrepancy occurs and provide feedback to students about the descriptive norms for these targeted behaviors (Henry, 2008).

Coursemate Normative Cultures

Recent research findings that inform an understanding of peer cultures of effort and achievement conceptualize "coursemates" as meaningful collectives of peers that are broader than peer groups and classrooms, yet still immediate to adolescents. In middle and high schools, students enroll in multiple classes with unique combinations of peers; Crosnoe, Frank, and colleagues have drawn on the transcript data from the Add-Health nationally representative dataset of adolescents in high schools to define contexts of students who overlap in their coursework, arguing that these individuals share a "social and academic space in school" that has norms that influence members' academic outcomes (Frank et al., 2008, p. 1648). In one study, Crosnoe, Riegle-Crumb, Field, Frank, and Muller (2008) considered the effects of coursemates' achievement levels as an influence on high school students' enrollment in advanced mathematics and science courses, finding that girls, in particular, were more likely to pursue advanced courses when their coursemates were high achieving. Although strongly predictive, the effects of coursemates' collective achievement were not as powerful as the effects of the peer group's achievement on the courses in which adolescents enrolled. In a related study, Frank and colleagues (2008) found that girls' own course enrollments in mathematics were influenced by the normative course enrollment patterns of girls in their courses; the effect of coursemates' course enrollment decisions was especially pronounced for both male and female students at lower levels of mathematics course enrollment.

Thus, a substantial literature demonstrates the differentiation and influence of normative contexts of peer cultures of effort and achievement. Most studies have focused on local cultures, at the peer group level, but the broader group of students with whom adolescents spend significant aspects of their school day also functions as an influential normative context. This literature focuses primarily on group descriptive norms that define behavioral or dispositional characteristics of groups, although there is evidence that groups have injunctive norms that are influential and that potentially underestimate the acceptability of effort and achievement.

Social Costs and Benefits of Effort and Achievement

Peer cultures of effort and achievement designate valued and desired behaviors, and grant prestigious status such as popularity to individuals who exemplify those values and behaviors (Rubin, Bukowski, & Parker, 2006). Consensual popularity, also known as perceived popularity and reputational popularity, reflects classmates' nominations of peers whom they identify as popular. Students who are perceived by peers to have social power, influence, and admiration are considered to be socially dominant. These dimensions of status are determined through peer nominations from within classrooms, grade levels, or schools; nominations are aggregated and students with disproportionately high numbers of nominations are identified. Likeability and peer admiration also reflects peer consensus, but of the extent to which students are nominated among those liked or admired most in a classroom, grade, or school.

Behavioral and dispositional correlates of these indicators of favorable peer regard signify what is valued by students collectively, and thus represent shared values of the peer culture within school settings. Three inferences about peer cultures of effort and achievement can be drawn from this literature. First, competing values for effort and achievement may be rewarded with social status within school peer cultures. Second, the social costs and benefits of achievement vary by school context. Third, likeability is not compromised by academic success. In addition, research focused specifically on ethnic minority youth allows for similar conclusions, despite theorizing (i.e., Ogbu, 1992) that suggests that academic achievement results in a social cost to ethnic minority youth.

Status Rewards for Academic Success and Lack of Academic Success

Several studies that involve person-centered approaches have helped to elucidate the nuances of popularity and to clarify the regard that school peer cultures hold for academic effort and achievement. Results across studies indicate that academic success is rewarded with status for adolescents who also exhibit prosocial behaviors, but also that pronounced visibility and attention can come to those who exhibit poor achievement. To illustrate, in a study of Dutch early adolescents that used a multi-step process to clarify the heterogeneous nature of consensual popularity among early adolescents, deBruyn and Cillessen (2006) identified and examined two types of popular students. Populistic teens maintained popularity but were not necessarily well liked, whereas prosocial-popular teens maintained both popularity and likeability with their classmates. Based on findings from various methodological approaches (focus group and individual interviews, and sociometric nominations and surveys), the authors concluded that academic effort and achievement was a central point of differentiation between the two types of popular students. Specifically, "antiacademic non-chalance" (p. 620), which reflected an overtly disrespectful attitude toward teachers, minimal effort, and low achievement, was a significant marker that yielded popularity for youth characterized as populistic-populars. Although a certain amount of cheekiness with teachers yielded status for students characterized as prosocial-popular, these students simultaneously maintained greater academic effort and achievement.

Findings from other studies that have used person-centered approaches similarly indicate that both academic success and a poor academic showing can be valued by school peer cultures. A study of rural African American youth identified by teachers as popular revealed a cluster of adolescents who were simultaneously academically engaged and low on aggression as well as a cluster of popular adolescents characterized as minimally engaged and highly aggressive (Estell, Farmer, Irvin, Thompson, Hutchins, & Mc-Donough, 2007). However, in some studies that have employed a person-centered approach to clarify the correlates of high status, a negative academic association is less prominent. For instance, in one study of subtypes of social dominance, the majority of adolescents were in typologies characterized by high achievement and by greater likability (Jonkmann, Trautwein, & Ludtke, 2009).

Social Costs and Benefits of Academic Success Vary Across School Contexts

Despite findings that academic success brings social rewards, results from a handful of studies reveal that academic achievement can compromise peer-nominated popularity (e.g., Gorman, Kim, & Schimmelbusch, 2002; Parkhurst & Hopmeyer, 1998), and in others may be unrelated to status indicators (Vaillancourt, Hymel, & McDougall, 2003). Recent larger-scale studies that involve numerous classrooms or schools have determined that there can be significant variability across settings in the relationship between social status and achievement. Jonkmann et al. (2009) found that the extent to which students with greater GPAs were more likely to be perceived as socially dominant was in part dependent on the academic behavioral norms of the class. In classes in academically oriented academic tracks, more highly achieving students were rewarded with attention and influence, whereas in low academic track classrooms, academic success was not related to social dominance. In a study that used the National Longitudinal Study of Adolescent Health (Add-Health) data, Fuller-Rowell & Doan (2010) examined school achievement level and proportion of students' ethnic group as separate and interacting factors that differentiate the relationship between achievement and status for African American, Asian, Latino, and Caucasian adolescents. Their results indicated that African American and Mexican adolescents experienced significantly worse social costs of achievement when they attended schools that were high achieving and enrolled smaller proportions of same-ethnic peers. However, school contextual factors did not differentiate the relationship between achievement and status for Asian or Caucasian students, or for students of other Latino heritage. Students from these ethnic groups enjoyed a social benefit of achievement, as evidenced by positive relationships between achievement and perceived peer acceptance (Fuller-Rowell & Doan, 2010). These findings suggest a localized nature to peer cultures in terms of their reward systems for academic success, but research on the context of academic success and status is in early stages. Thus far, researchers have focused on the normative level of achievement and school demographic characteristics; other aspects of classroom and school settings, such as teacher behaviors, have been shown to moderate the peer reward system for non-academic behaviors (Chang, Liu, Wen, Fung, Wang, & Xu, 2004) and may be relevant to academic behaviors.

It is also noteworthy that not much attention has been granted to grade-level differences in the relationship between academic success and social status. Many studies have sampled early adolescents or have not investigated grade-level differences. Unlike the results from a number of studies, Gorman et al. (2002) and Parkhurst and Hopmeyer (1998) reported a negative association between academic success and popularity among high school students. Although the normative context may have been different in these studies compared to others, results of research on adolescents suggests that the progression through high school is associated with changes to status markers and other aspects of the peer culture relevant to academic effort and achievement (e.g., Eckert, 1989; Frank et al., 2008). More study is needed to understand developmental and school-contextual variability in the nature and influences of peer cultures of effort and achievement.

Academic Success Does Not Compromise Likeability

A third inference that can be taken from studies of the social costs and benefits of effort and achievement is that although a poor academic showing can be valued by the larger peer group, findings consistently demonstrate that the students who are the most liked by their peers are academically successful. Studies that seek to differentiate types of popularity report that likeable popular students have better academic records (e.g., deBruyn & Cillessen, 2006; Jonkmann et al., 2009). Researchers who have used peer nominations for liked most and liked least to categorize students' sociometric status as "popular" (receiving a disproportionate share of liked most and disproportionately few liked least nominations), "rejected" (receiving a disproportionate share of liked least and disproportionately few liked most), and "neglected" (receiving disproportionately few nominations) indicate either an absence of association between sociometric popularity and academic investment or achievement (i.e., GPA) (Wentzel, 2003) or a positive association, such that peers in general view classmates who work hard, do well, and value school in a favorable light (Wentzel & Asher, 1995). Moreover, poor academic status is associated with peer dislike (sociometric rejection, receiving disproportionately few liked most and many liked least nominations) (Wentzel & Asher, 1995; Wentzel, 2003), indicating that the peer culture finds something distasteful in lower achieving students. However, in these same studies, students classified as sociometrically neglected tend to be higher achieving students, which signifies a potential anonymity within the larger peer group for some higher achieving students.

Social Costs and Benefits of Achievement for Ethnic Minority Students

In a number of studies, scholars have scrutinized the extent to which ethnic minority adolescents, but particularly African American youth, experience a peer culture that opposes academic success and effort. Much of this body of research is a response to Ogbu's (1992; Fordham & Ogbu, 1986) controversial hypothesis that the Black peer group, collectively, opposes and overtly punishes members' effort and achievement. Debate continues over the validity of this hypothesis. For instance, results of one study that used peer nominations for "admired," "respected," and "want to be like" to signify peer cultural values indicated that African American and Latino, but not Caucasian, early adolescent boys who were academically successful or hard-working were less likely to be valued by their male classmates. In contrast, among African American, Latina, and Caucasian girls, girls who were high achieving and perceived to work hard academically were significantly more valued (Graham, Taylor, & Hudley, 1998). In another study, however, Becker and Luthar (2007) reported that urban African American and Latino early adolescent boys and girls expressed greater admiration for higher achieving peers. Findings from a growing body of literature, including studies that have drawn on large-scale, national data sets as well as ethnographic methods, support two inferences. First, African American adolescents (as well as adolescents from other ethnic minority groups) do not appear to experience a pervasive peer culture that opposes academic effort or achievement. Results from a number of studies demonstrate that there is not a social cost (e.g., compromise to popularity) experienced by more highly achieving African American students (Ainsworth-Darnell & Downey, 1998; Cook & Ludwig, 1997, 1998; Downey & Ainsworth-Darnell, 2002; Harris, 2006; Walker, 2006). Some researchers report that African American (and Latino and Caucasian suburban and urban) adolescents enjoy greater peer regard when they are more highly achieving (Becker & Luthar, 2007). Further, there is evidence that social acceptance of achievement is more strongly positive among African American youth than among their Caucasian peers (Ainsworth-Darnell & Downey, 1998).

Second, results of several studies underscore the importance of school variability in the social costs and benefits of achievement for ethnic minority adolescents. In their investigation of adolescents in schools in the Add-Health data set, Fuller-Rowan and Doan (2010) found that if only ethnic group differences are considered, the relationship between GPA and perceived peer acceptance was negative for African American and Native American adolescents and positive for Asian, Latino, and Caucasian adolescents. Once school contextual factors were considered, however, African American and Mexican adolescents perceived a social vulnerability for achievement in high-achieving schools with small proportions of peers of their own ethnic group. Greater proportions of same-ethnic peers in attendance helped to minimize the social costs of achievement for these adolescents in high-achieving schools (Fuller-Rowan & Doan, 2010). Ethnographic research on African American adolescents also leads to the conclusion that that school context must be considered in understanding the extent to which peer cultures reward or punish academic success (Hemmings, 1996; Tyson, Darity, & Castellino, 2005). Tyson et al. maintained that adolescent academic resistance among both African American and Caucasian students is driven more by local school cultures and structures (e.g., socioeconomic disparities, tracking systems) than by a pervasive oppositional peer culture.

Summary

Taken together, studies of the social costs and benefits of effort and achievement indicate that academic success does not tend to compromise early adolescents' social status, nor does it appear to threaten social status specifically for African American adolescents unless they attend high-achieving schools with few African American peers. Researchers have begun to identify contextual variations in the social costs and benefits of effort and achievement; further research is necessary to determine the extent to which differences across studies reflect school and/or developmental differences.

It is also the case that most investigators have focused on the relationship between academic achievement and status, but have not investigated the extent to which peer cultures reward aspects of effort with desirable status. Peer cultures may not hold effort in the same regard as achievement, particularly if academic success does not accompany effort, given that adolescents tend to equate effort with low ability (Juvonen & Murdoch, 1995). Studies of behavioral correlates of peer crowds indicate that students who dedicate themselves to schooling to an extreme, particularly at the expense of participation in other aspects of adolescent culture, may (more likely) attain the undesirable status of outcast or nerd (Brown, 1993).

Peer Support for Effort and Achievement

Although the activities or routines that students engage in together help to define peer cultures (Corsaro & Eder, 1990), far less attention has been granted to what peers actually do, compared to how their collective behaviors translate into normative contexts or status reward systems. Descriptive norms may reflect behavioral similarity within classrooms or within peer groups, but not necessarily peer group activities. For instance, Hamm, Schmid, et al. (2011) found that members of peer groups reported similar amounts of time spent on homework, but this finding does not reveal that members spent that time on homework together as a mutual activity.

One activity of peer cultures that is important to adolescents' academic outcomes is peer support, or the provision of emotional or academic assistance to peers. Students' individual experiences of peer support within peer cultures such as classrooms are associated with desirable academic outcomes, such as interest in school (Wentzel, Battle, Russell, & Looney, 2010); sense of belonging (Hamm & Faircloth, 2005), and academic initiative (Danielsen, Wiium, Wilhelmsen, & Wold, 2010). However, research on peer support as a dimension of peer cultures is limited and focused primarily on individual adolescents' perceptions of peer support and the implications of this perception for their adjustment. Recent studies of peer support at the classroom level have yielded inconsistent results. Wentzel et al. (2010) demonstrated significant classroom-level differences in students' perceptions of peer support, indicating that classrooms can be distinguished by their peer cultures of support, while Danielsen et al. (2010) did not find significant classroom differences in peer support.

Some insight into the provision of peer support within peer groups can be found in two studies of academically successful high school students from ethnic minority groups. One focused exclusively on African American female students (Horvat & Lewis, 2003); the other on African American and Latino male and female students, and mathematics achievement specifically (Walker, 2006). In both studies, students with academically supportive peers described friendly competition among friends that promoted greater effort and achievement for individuals, as well as instances of offering and receiving help for homework, course decisions, and other academic activities. In Horvat and Lewis (2003), female students described peer expectations for effort and achievement and for attending college. Peer affiliates reinforced these expectations through multiple means, including explicit feedback about members' behaviors and dispositions, as well as through "sharing success" (p. 269), a mutual support process of listening and affirming one another's success.

Walker (2006) extended these findings by noting that successful African American and Latino students created peer "intellectual communities" (p. 59) of support for themselves; often these communities included friends, but extended to classmates who shared academic orientations for students whose close peers were less academically inclined. Importantly, students were able to find the peer support that they needed and desired (e.g., encouragement, academic assistance, mutuality of interest) without compromise to their close friendships. Walker (2006) also observed that the peer intellectual community often extended beyond the student's home school, to friends in different schools, as well as to siblings and cousins.

Summary Inferences about Peer Cultures of Effort and Achievement

Taken together, findings suggest that localized peer cultures—those that are immediate to adolescents in terms of contact and opportunity for interaction, as well as shared interests and experience—carry more influence over adolescents' academic effort and achievement than do more distal cultures such as schoolmates or minority group membership. Research on normative peer cultures supports this point; research on status tends to focus on school (or grade-level) peer cultures, but classrooms can vary in behavioral correlates of status, so attention to more localized contexts for this aspect of peer cultures is worthy of attention as well.

Additionally, the literature suggests that peer cultures of effort and achievement tend to be favorable and supportive. Although local cultures of peer groups, coursemates, and classrooms can discourage effort and achievement, and some students may derive social status from being openly defiant toward academic activities, in general, being smart does not compromise social status and does not on the whole seem to put adolescents at risk for exclusion from their peer groups for non-conformity. This finding is encouraging and somewhat counter to stereotypes that adolescents collectively oppose effort and achievement. However, adolescents may not be the best judge of their own peer cultures. They appear to perceive less acceptance and valuing of effort and achievement than is suggested by the behavioral characteristics of their peers. This misperception is worthy of greater attention, as student perceptions of educational contexts can bear greater influence on their behavior than do objective ratings of contexts (Schunk & Meece, 1992). Moreover, discrepancies between real and perceived norms provide opportunities for educators to intervene to promote desirable behaviors (Henry, 2008).

A final point from these studies is that peer cultures of effort and achievement vary within and across classrooms and schools, and are clearly influenced by features of the larger contexts (e.g., classrooms, schools) in which they are embedded. Researchers who study peer contexts in schools have begun to identify contextual influences; we focus specifically on the contributions of teachers' practices to the development of peer cultures.

TEACHERS' CONTRIBUTIONS TO PEER CULTURES
OF EFFORT AND ACHIEVEMENT

Peer cultures, by definition, originate and are perpetuated within collectives of children (Corsaro & Eder, 1990), but the nature of school-based peer cultures can be influenced by features of the school environment (Hamm & Zhang, 2010). Teachers, in particular, are uniquely positioned for influence over local peer cultures of effort and achievement (i.e., classroom and peer group), given that teachers establish the classroom social environment. There are overt efforts teachers can undertake that are directed explicitly toward peer cultures, such as identifying and intervening in problematic peer group or classroom norms for effort and achievement (Henry, 2008). However, much of teachers' role in the development of peer group cultures reflects their "invisible hand," or the unobtrusive, unspoken, and unrecognized ways in which teachers' practices influence aspects of classroom and school social dynamics (Farmer, Lines, & Hamm, 2011). This metaphor, introduced initially by Robert Cairns, reflects an integration of perspectives that consider the development of peer cultures within the boundaries of adult-governed settings such as schools (e.g., Cairns & Cairns, 1994), conceptualize teacher practices that establish a context in which youth more readily adopt and internalize dispositions toward academics (e.g., Wentzel, 2002), and position the teacher as the de facto leader of the peer ecology. Through a variety of means, including their involvement with students, their management of classroom behaviors, the types of academic tasks they assign, and their delivery of curriculum, teachers not only teach academic content, they create social norms and expectations for student interactions, influence students' beliefs about themselves and their classmates, and establish students' role in the learning process (Farmer et al., in press).

Only a handful of studies directly address the intersection of teacher practice and the development of peer cultures for effort and achievement in middle and high schools. Despite origins in diverse disciplines (i.e., psychological, sociological, sociocultural), most of this work has revealed implications of teachers' instructional behaviors for classroom-based peer cultures of mathematics classrooms. In mathematics instruction, distinctions are drawn between reform-oriented and traditional forms of instruction. At a basic level, these orientations reflect a difference between student- versus teacher-oriented instruction, but more specifically involve how teachers use instruction to create classroom communities of mathematics learners, in which students view themselves as competent and capable learners of mathematics and engage in activities similar to those used by mathematicians (National Council of Teachers of Mathematics [NCTM], 1989, 2000). No single set of instructional practices constitute reform-based instruction; scholars highlight practices that emphasize mathematical understanding, allow for discussion of ideas and problem solving, and enable students to assume authority over their own learning and understanding (NCTM, 1989, 2000). Such reform-based instruction stands in contrast to traditional forms of instruction, in which the teacher is the source of information and verification of ideas, and that involve teacher-led formats such as lecture or didactic teaching.

A number of studies illustrate that teachers' use of reform-oriented instructional practices encourage classroom peer cultures that are more hospitable to student effort and achievement, while use of traditional forms of mathematics instruction seems to support peer cultures that are detrimental to student effort and achievement. In an extensive study of mathematics learning in high school, Boaler (2008) observed that social dynamics in classrooms differed in relation to teachers' instruction. Boaler characterized the peer culture of reform-oriented classrooms as having greater "relational equity" than the peer cultures of classrooms taught with a traditional instructional approach. Relational equity is evident in classrooms when students treat one another and their ideas with respect, when they are committed to their peers' as well as to their own learning and academic success, and when they engage in actions that promote others' learning (Boaler, 2008). Boaler speculated that this sense of obligation arose from teachers' continued emphasis on a variety of ways to be smart and to contribute valid mathematical ideas. Finally, students translated these dispositions of obligation for assistance and respect for classmates' ideas into practical means of helping their peers. For example, students in reform-oriented classrooms used questions to probe their classmates when classmates needed assistance, rather than simply telling classmates the answer, which was the more typical peer response in traditional classrooms. Students in reform-oriented classrooms also routinely encouraged struggling peers to remain engaged, whereas students in traditional classrooms were more likely to ignore such classmates.

One of us (Hamm) has investigated the intersection of instruction and peer social dynamics in middle school mathematics classrooms in a large-scale, longitudinal study of students' mathematics learning across the middle grades. One set of findings supported Boaler's conclusion that relational equity was promoted in classrooms characterized by reform-based instruction. Typically there is a strong positive relationship between peer nominations for status as a good student and student grades (e.g., Gest, Domitrovich, & Welsh, 2005). Boaler argued that in traditional mathematics classrooms, students are strongly tied to academic performance as the primary indicator of mathematical competence, and reserve the status of being smart for the highest-achieving students. Classrooms characterized by greater relational equity, she maintained, involve a broader sense among students regarding the multiple ways their peers can be competent and helpful to one another in the learning process, and grant the status of being mathematically able to a wider variety of peers. To investigate these ideas, Hamm and colleagues (Hamm, Malloy, & Meece, 2009) obtained peer nominations of mathematics all-stars and best tutors as indications of who students perceived as the smartest and most able to offer assistance to classmates. One finding was that classrooms identified by trained observers as more strongly reform-oriented had a greater distribution of students in the roles of mathematics all-star and best tutor, signifying that students in the class perceived a broader set of students as smart and efficacious in mathematics. As we noted earlier in this chapter, behavioral or dispositional correlates of students nominated into particular status roles provide valuable insights into the classroom peer culture of effort and achievement. Along the lines of work in this area, we analyzed the strength of the relationship between these types of status and achievement and found a weaker association between students' GPA and the proportion of nominations they received as a math all-star in reform-oriented than traditional classrooms. These results suggested that students used criteria other than grades to make determinations about their classmates' mathematics competence. Taken together, these results support Boaler's findings for high school mathematics classrooms, that teachers' use of reform-based instruction supports a more equitable peer culture of effort and achievement.

In a different study, Hamm, Malloy, and Meece (2006) examined students' perceptions of aspects of mathematics classroom peer cultures in relation to reform- based instruction. The classroom instructional environment was measured by students' perceptions of different types of instruction including the extent to which students were pressed for understanding, engaged in mathematically meaningful activities, taking part in mathematical discourse, and offered opportunities to have mathematical authority over how they learned and over their own understanding. More favorable peer cultures, in terms of greater peer support, less emotional risk, and more favorable peer norms for effort and achievement, developed across the school year in classrooms in which students perceived more strongly that their teachers emphasized learning for understanding. Student perceptions of greater opportunities to engage in mathematical discourse also resulted in improved student perceptions of injunctive peer norms for effort and achievement across the school year.

Thus, the studies by Boaler and by Hamm and colleagues indicate that use of instructional practices that emphasize learning mathematics with understanding, and that allow students to solve problems together and to talk about their mathematical ideas, promotes a more favorable peer culture. Research on how supportive and engaged peer cultures can emerge in mathematics classrooms is particularly valuable given evidence that mathematics classrooms, more so than classrooms of other academic disciplines, are vulnerable to develop peer cultures characterized by disengagement and overt defiance (McFarland, 2001). As noted by Boaler (2008), the instructional practices aligned with reform ideals are not specific to mathematics; they reflect standards developed from research on student learning in general. Enabling students to discuss and substantiate their ideas, to learn deeply for understanding, and to engage in meaningful content and activities is attainable in any academic discipline, and is called for by the professional standards for K–12 instruction in most academic disciplines.

Findings from other studies demonstrate the power of teachers' practice to contribute to classroom peer cultures characterized by behaviors that signified resistance to learning, such as talking out of turn, talking back, sleeping, and engaging in non-academic behaviors. McFarland (2001) integrated ethnographic with survey-based approaches to investigate the development of defiant behavior in relation to teacher instruction and aspects of peer group social dynamics among high school students across a school year. Among many findings, several points expand an understanding of teachers' role in the development of classroom peer cultures. Classrooms can develop and be differentiated by peer cultures of resistance to academic engagement. Although acts of defiance were initially perpetuated by small numbers of students, they spread across peer groups and intensified in frequency to become normative within and characteristic of classrooms. Local peer group cultures within the classroom contributed to classroom cultures of defiance; resistance became more prevalent in classrooms with peer groups in which defiance was more normative early in the school year. Additional findings revealed the role of teachers' instruction, in that acts of defiance were more characteristic of classrooms in which the teacher used student-centered formats such as group work, compared to the peer cultures of classrooms that involved teacher-centered instruction.

This finding may seem counter to Boaler's and Hamm and colleagues' findings that student-oriented instruction aligned with reform-ideals supported positive peer cultures in mathematics classrooms. Several aspects of McFarland's study, as well as findings from an in-depth study of a single mathematics classroom over the course of the school year (Hand, 2010) help to clarify these differences and cast further light on the role of the teacher in the development of peer cultures of effort and achievement. First, unlike the mathematics instruction observed by classrooms characterized as reform-oriented, student-centered instruction as observed by McFarland involved students working together in groups but engaged in superficial tasks that failed to require students to think deeply and develop understanding and competence. Detailing the escalation of oppositional behaviors, Hand (2010) demonstrated how decreasing opportunities to engage in mathematical sense-making and to develop a sense of competence as mathematical learners provoked an increased frequency of oppositional behaviors (e.g., talking to disrupt class, putting one's head down) that originated in individuals but spread and became characteristic for the class peer culture as a whole as the year progressed. Taken together, the findings across the studies suggest that engagement in meaningful interaction with classmates, which offers opportunities for students to develop competence, is a necessary condition for peer cultures to encourage effort and achievement. In the absence of this condition, classrooms are at risk to develop peer cultures that undermine effort and achievement through encouraging behavior that is oppositional to academic effort and success.

A second and related point of clarification is that both McFarland's and Hand's studies highlighted how teachers' classroom management practices can escalate student problem behavior by a few to pervasive, widespread disruptive behavior that becomes "routine practice" within the classroom peer culture (Hand, 2010, p. 123). In both studies, teachers' responses to disruptive or oppositional behavior by individuals became increasingly negative and coercive as the year progressed and defiance ensued, which set the stage for greater rebellion among increasing numbers of students. One issue was that teachers generally failed to bring students back on task once the teacher had declared them to be off-task. Moreover, in Hand's study, the teacher maintained a narrow definition of what constituted legitimate mathematical talk and participation, which excluded much of the students' contributions and established the students as "off-task" instead of actively contributing to the mathematical discussion. The teacher's misinterpretation and mischaracterization of student participation appeared to alienate students and to encourage defiant behavior.

Third, and building on the previous points, McFarland's (2001) and Hand's (2010) studies reveal how instruction and classroom management interact with existing classroom social dynamics and local peer group cultures to contribute to the development of problematic peer cultures of effort and achievement. McFarland found that a key mechanism of the spread of defiance in classrooms with student-centered instruction was tightly knit, established peer groups that provided peer support and insulation from the teacher's wrath for individual members to engage in acts of defiance. In both studies, students with high social status were typically the origins of defiance; instructional formats that were not engaging and tightly controlled by the teacher exacerbated the potential for these students to inspire oppositional behaviors from classmates. In both studies, teachers appeared to fail to realize the power of existing peer dynamics among their students. Teachers' attention to preexisting social dynamics and disruptive behaviors was not addressed by Boaler and Hamm and colleagues; it would be valuable to understand how teachers managed behavioral disruptions and social dynamics in classrooms in which supportive peer cultures evolved. However, McFarland's and Hand's findings suggest that peer cultures are sensitive to teachers' capacity to attend simultaneously to the instructional sphere, to manage developing social dynamics within local peer cultures, and to support students' behavioral competencies.

In conclusion, these findings should encourage a view of classroom-based peer cultures as "co-constructed" (Hand, 2010, p. 124) by students and teachers. This idea is consistent with the invisible hand metaphor, in that many of the teacher actions described were unobtrusive, unspoken, and/or unrecognized by teachers for their contributions to evolving classroom peer cultures. The results of these studies emphasize the need for teachers to be able to coordinate the academic, behavioral, and social aspects of classrooms that involve adolescents. Instructional practices alone are insufficient to engender classroom peer cultures that support learning; teachers must apply classroom management practices that encourage positive interactions and support students' developing competence, in ways that are sensitive to the powerful social dynamics and existing peer cultures that students bring with them into the classroom. Not all teachers capably coordinate the academic, behavioral, and social spheres of the classroom. But, in the absence of this teacher capacity, problematic peer cultures characterized by behavioral disruptions and overt resistance to engagement become routine, academic instruction unravels further, and student learning and achievement is compromised.

HELPING TEACHERS TO SUPPORT POSITIVE PEER CULTURES

Supporting Early Adolescents' Learning and Social Success (SEALS) is a universal intervention program designed to improve teachers' capacity to create supportive learning environments for early adolescents by enhancing students' academic engagement, promoting their use of constructive classroom interpersonal behaviors, and fostering their involvement in positive social relationships with peers who value and are productively engaged in school. We provide a brief overview of the SEALS program prior to describing findings relevant to teachers' role in adolescent peer cultures of effort and achievement; additional detail about SEALS can be found elsewhere (i.e., Farmer, Hamm, Lane, Lee, & Sutherland, 2011, and the articles referenced below).

Overview of SEALS

SEALS is grounded in a developmental science perspective, which maintains that adolescents develop as integrated wholes, in which multiple developmental factors work together as a correlated system (Magnusson & Cairns, 1996). From this perspective, adolescents who develop adjustment difficulties in school tend not to have problems in a single domain such as academics, but rather develop configurations of risk across multiple domains of school functioning (Cairns & Cairns, 1994), which predict adolescent school failure, school dropout, and truncated educational attainment (e.g., Bergman & Magnusson, 1997; Cairns, Cairns, & Neckerman, 1989; Roeser & Peck, 2003). Behavior is central to adaptation and functioning, by coordinating internal (i.e., cognitive, emotional) and external (i.e., ecological, sociological, cultural) aspects of development and experience (e.g., Cairns, 1991; Cairns, Cairns, Neckerman, Ferguson, & Gariépy, 1989). Interventions guided by a developmental science perspective involve a coordinated focus on students' individual attributes and on the naturally occurring contexts in which they are embedded; behavioral change is targeted through a reorganization of internal and external aspects of development, such as individual academic capacities and competencies, beliefs and values, as well as social roles and interactional patterns and social networks and organizational structures (Farmer & Farmer, 2001). Relevant to this chapter, we describe findings related to peer cultures of effort and achievement as a significant adjustment context that reflects both individual and contextual contributions.

The SEALS model is also informed by the person–environment fit hypothesis (Eccles, Lord, & Midgeley, 1991; Eccles et al., 1993), which maintains that many adolescents experience academic, behavioral, and social difficulties during middle school because there is a poor fit between their developmental needs and the demands of the school context. When students' needs and goals are congruent with opportunities afforded by the environment, they will experience positive outcomes (Midgely & Edelin, 1998). However, when students' abilities, characteristics, and aims are not consistent with the resources and demands of the ecology, they are more likely to experience difficulties. Although much of the intervention work that is based on this hypothesis strives to reorganize schools to provide a better fit to student developmental needs, we apply the hypothesis to help teachers develop the capacity to establish a classroom context that is developmentally consistent with the academic, behavioral, and social needs of youth and that enhances their skills, fosters their valuing of new competencies, and promotes their sense of belonging to a supportive community (Farmer, Goforth, Hives, Aaron, Jackson, & Sgammato, 2006; Lipsitz & West, 2006; Midgley & Edelin, 1998).

The SEALS program combines three intervention components (see Figure 9.1). The *academic engagement enhancement* component provides teachers with a structured format for organizing and starting class and instructional activities that are effective at maintaining the attention and involvement of students with learning difficulties. The *competence enhancing behavior management* program centers on proactive classroom behavior management strategies that help teachers teach and reinforce appropriate classroom behavior while providing constructive consequences to reduce problem behavior. Finally, the *social dynamics management* component is designed to enhance teachers' awareness of classroom social dynamics, including peer group affiliations and social roles, and the corresponding impact and applications of peer dynamics to students' academic engagement and classroom behavior.

As illustrated in Figure 9.1, SEALS is theorized to be effective because the professional development associated with each individual component has a collective impact on what teachers do in the classroom (i.e., teacher functioning); teacher functioning influences student functioning and creates a peer and classroom context that supports and reinforces positive student functioning; and in turn, teacher functioning, peer-context conditions, and student functioning contribute to students' academic outcomes. The goal is to help teachers to develop specific understandings, skills, and strategies through a year-long, multiple-format professional development program, and to provide them with a framework for applying this knowledge in a systematic manner that promotes peer contexts that reinforce academic effort and achievement and that teaches early adolescents how to be successful middle school students.

SEALS Effects on School-Based Peer Cultures

Although enhanced academic achievement is an ultimate objective of the SEALS intervention, a central aim of the project is to help teachers promote positive social dynamics, including peer cultures that support students' academic success. In a number of studies, we have demonstrated how teachers who take part in the SEALS program accomplish this aim. These studies are based in Project REAL (Rural Early Adolescent Learning), which is a research intervention project of the National Research Center for Rural Education Support (www.nrcres.org), funded by the Institute for Education Sciences. Project REAL involved delivery of the SEALS intervention to sixth grade teachers in low-resource, rural schools across diverse regions of the United States. The evaluation of the efficacy of SEALS for rural schools is a randomized controlled trials design study of 14 (7 intervention, 7 control) matched pairs of rural, low-resource K–8/K–12 and

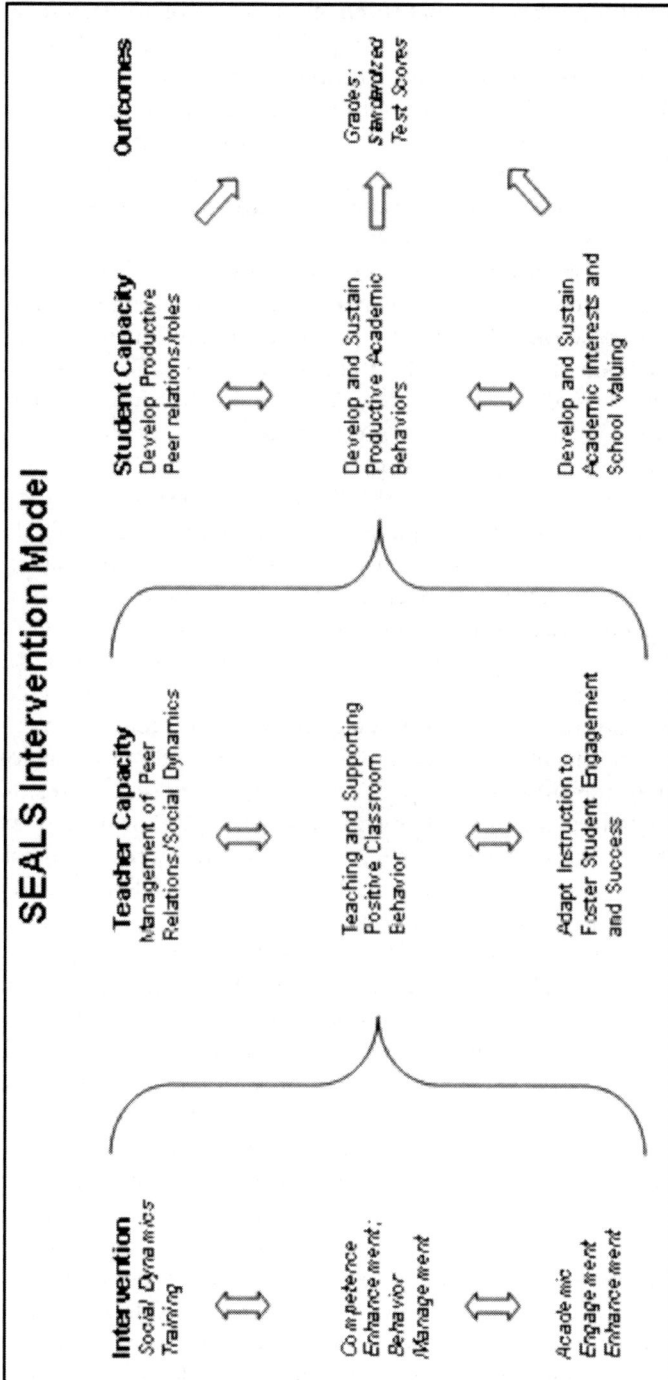

Figure 9.1 Intervention model.

traditional middle schools across seven states. Control schools were "ecological comparisons" (Graesser, 2009, p. 260), in which teachers carried out their daily instructional activities without participation in the SEALS program. We collected data from students at the end of fifth grade (preintervention), the beginning of sixth grade (mid-intervention), and at the end of sixth grade (post-intervention). At some sites, we followed students into the seventh grade to examine potential carry-over effects of the intervention beyond the intervention year.

Results from several studies indicate that students in REAL intervention schools experienced more favorable peer cultures at school following their teachers' participation in the SEALS program than did their counterparts in control schools. In a randomized controlled trial (RCT) that involved two matched pairs of schools in a Northern Plains state, with student bodies composed of Native American and Caucasian early adolescents, we examined intervention effects on students' perceptions of aspects of their school's peer cultures, independently of and interactively with ethnic group and gender, and net of student demographic and baseline controls (Hamm et al., 2010). Students, especially Native American, in intervention schools reported improved injunctive peer norms—that is, perceptions of acceptance of academic effort and achievement—among their peers by the end of the school year in comparison to students' perceptions of peer norms for effort and achievement in control schools. Because we had collected data at multiple time points, we could determine that in intervention schools, student perceptions of peer norms remained stable and positive across the middle school transition year, especially among Native American students, while they declined significantly during the same period in the comparison schools. Moreover, Native American students in intervention schools, compared to students in comparison schools as well as Caucasian students in intervention schools, rated the peer cultures of their schools as involving less emotional risk for academic participation, including perceptions that peers were less likely to make fun of them for participating and making mistakes or for trying hard. These findings suggest that when teachers develop enhanced capacities to coordinate instructional, behavioral, and social dimensions of classrooms, they can offset the declines to classroom peer cultures of effort and achievement that have been demonstrated in early adolescent classrooms and schools (e.g., Hamm & Faircloth, 2005; Roeser, Eccles, & Sameroff, 2000), particularly for Native American students.

Students in intervention compared to control schools also perceived peer cultures less encouraging of bullying. Although norms for encouraging or discouraging bullying are not an obvious dimension of the peer culture of effort and achievement, classroom and school cultures that permit bullying behaviors are at odds with norms favoring academic effort and achievement (Dupper & Meyer-Adams, 2002). Teachers who more effectively discourage peer bullying cultures likely encourage peer cultures that support student effort and achievement.

In a RCT study of two Appalachian schools that received the REAL program and their matched control schools (Farmer, Hamm, et al., 2010), we identified several ways in which teachers who participated in the SEALS program altered the peer cultures of effort and achievement in their schools. First, we found sustained intervention effects on injunctive norms for effort and achievement during and beyond the intervention year. In intervention schools, students' perceived injunctive norms remained supportive across the middle school transition year and into the fall of seventh grade, whereas in control schools, perceived injunctive norms were significantly lower at both the end of the middle school transition year, as well as at the beginning of the seventh grade school year. Only sixth-grade teachers in intervention schools were trained in the SEALS program; thus, the intervention benefit to the peer normative culture of effort and achievement was sufficiently powerful and impervious for students to transfer it to a new school year with different teachers and classroom contexts.

In this same study, we investigated peer group cultures of students identified as at risk for behavioral problems prior to the middle school transition. Prior to the middle school transition, in both intervention and control sites, students identified as at-risk were in peer groups with comparable (and minimally supportive) descriptive norms for effort expended on homework and academic achievement. However, the students who transitioned into SEALS middle schools ended the sixth grade year in peer groups with significantly more favorable descriptive norms for effort and achievement, compared to the students who transitioned into control schools. This finding suggests that following participation in SEALS, teachers created classroom environments that enabled students at risk for significant difficulties during the middle school transition year to find peer group affiliations that supported adaptive academic behaviors.

The findings reported thus far reflect results of analyses with the REAL pilot schools. Recently, we examined peer cultures of effort and achievement within the full cluster randomized controlled trial. Data analyses involve two-level hierarchical linear models estimated for a sample of approximately 1,600 sixth graders nested in intervention schools and their matched controls. All models included level-2 blocking variables to account for matched pairings of schools (see Brown, Jones, LaRusso, & Aber, 2010). Analyses of classroom observation data of the fidelity of implementation of SEALS content indicate that teachers in intervention, compared to control schools, were significantly more likely to use classroom practices aligned with the SEALS program and to create a more supportive learning environment for students. Analyses of students' experiences of aspects of their peer cultures of effort and achievement accounted for student gender and minority status, and included tests for main effects for intervention, as well as for cross-level interaction effects of intervention where appropriate, net of the effects of block variables for matched pairings of schools (Hamm, Farmer, Lambert, & Gravelle, 2012). Results indicate that two aspects of the peer culture of effort and achievement were more favorable at the end of sixth grade, following full implementation of the SEALS program and in comparison to control schools. First, peer group-level injunctive norms for effort and achievement were significantly more supportive of effort and achievement in intervention versus control schools. Second, the social benefits of effort and school valuing to social status were greater in intervention than control schools. That is, overall, students who expended greater effort in schoolwork were viewed as more socially prominent but attained significantly greater social prominence in intervention than control schools. In addition, school valuing compromised nominations for social prominence in general, but significantly less so in intervention than in control schools. These findings from the full sample suggest that teacher capacities targeted in the SEALS program help teachers to create classrooms in which academic effort and success are valued more strongly—or at least, not as strongly devalued—and in which students perceive greater acceptance for effort and achievement within their local peer groups.

The Importance of Teacher Attunement to Peer Group Affiliations

Our findings thus far indicate that teachers who participate in the SEALS professional development program are better able than teachers who lack this training experience to create classroom environments that promote more supportive peer cultures of effort and achievement. SEALS is a multidimensional intervention for which distinct intervention components are intended to have a synergistic effect, and the emphasis is on the coordination of instructional, behavioral, and social dimensions of the classroom. Our intent is not to isolate specific intervention components that most strongly account for effects, but our conceptual model enables us to identify potential mechanisms of change that help to explain why students in intervention schools experience more favorable peer cultures of effort and achievement. As noted in Figure 9.1, changes to teacher functioning are necessary to bring about changes to peer cultures and student adaptation. We have theorized that one reason that peer cultures improve in intervention schools is because teachers have gained a greater understanding of adolescent social dynamics and their implications for student behavioral and academic adjustment.

In multiple studies, we have investigated differences in teacher capacity between intervention and control schools in relation to aspects of the school social environment (Farmer, Hall, Petrin, Hamm, & Dadisman, 2010; Hamm, Farmer, Dadisman, Gravelle, & Murray, 2011). In each study, we examined *teacher attunement,* or teachers' accuracy in identifying the peer group affiliations of their students early in the sixth grade school year, after teachers in intervention schools had completed initial aspects of the SEALS program. We measured teacher attunement based on the accuracy in teacher-generated peer groups relative to student-generated peer group affiliations early in the school year. Teachers who had participated in the initial SEALS professional development program possessed a significantly more accurate understanding of (i.e., greater attunement to) sixth graders' peer group affiliations at this early time point in the school year. We conceptualized teacher attunement as a dimension of teacher involvement that would translate into improved social experiences for students during the middle school transition year (Hamm et al., 2011). None of the studies focused exclusively on the peer culture of effort and achievement; however, the one outcome that explicitly reflected an aspect of peer culture (emotional risk of participation) was improved when teachers had greater attunement. Greater teacher attunement was also related to improvements to students' sense of belonging and perceptions of the school bullying culture (Hamm et al., 2011). These findings suggest that teacher attunement may be a critical dimension of the SEALS training program that enables teachers to use naturally occurring peer group affiliations to promote peer cultures that support student academic achievement and effort.

We considered additional ways in which teachers' functioning was enhanced following participation in the SEALS program. Using ratings of trained observers of teachers' classroom practice late in the school year, following completion of intervention activities, we found that teachers who had experienced the SEALS program more effectively managed classroom social dynamics during instructional time, such as grouping students in relation to evident social dynamics and responding to incidences of social aggression (Hamm et al., 2011). In general, teachers were rated as more effective at managing multiple aspects of the classroom, including social dynamics, instruction, and classroom management (Hamm et al., 2012). Altogether, these findings suggest that the teacher capacities targeted in the SEALS program influence aspects of peer cultures that develop across the sixth grade year and are important in promoting student capacities for academic engagement.

These findings help to clarify a condition under which the SEALS intervention has particularly promotive benefits: When teachers start the school year with an accurate view of student peer group affiliations, they are better positioned to offset declines in peer cultures for academic effort and achievement. More generally, our initial results demonstrate that professional development designed to help teachers to understand how to manage the social, academic, and behavioral forces that combine to affect student adjustment during the middle school transition likely helps teachers guide the development of promotive peer cultures. Without this understanding, teachers may miss opportunities to coordinate their instructional delivery and management of behavioral issues with the local peer group cultures evolving in their classrooms and schools.

CONCLUSION

Peer cultures have been defined as the activities, norms, values, and routines that result from children's sustained interactions (Corsaro & Eder, 1990). In adolescence, academic, social, and behavioral dimensions of development and experience converge to produce peer cultures of academic effort and achievement. Although findings suggest that the entry into and progression through adolescence (and its corresponding school changes) can bring about a devaluing of effort and achievement within the peer group (Bukowski et al., 2000; Juvonen & Murdoch, 1995), there is variability within peer cultures for the acceptability of effort and achievement. Findings are clear that many adolescents experience peer cultures that support effort and achievement, but it is clearly the case that adolescents can experience multiple types of peer cultures that undermine their potential for academic success. Peer cultures of effort and achievement can be found at multiple levels of adolescents' ecologies, including peer group, classroom, coursemate, and school; generally, research suggests that the more immediate the peer culture is to the adolescent, the more influential its features are to members' schooling adjustment. Our intent in this chapter is to feature aspects of peer cultures of effort and achievement that are aligned with Corsaro and Eder's (1990) conceptualization of a peer culture. The dimensions of peer culture portrayed in this chapter and the literature reviewed are not exhaustive. Moreover, the characterization of the studies reviewed as focused on peer culture is our own. Scholars have infrequently invoked this term in their own work; we use the concept to bring together a body of work focused on adolescents and their peers, and to demonstrate the opportunity for teachers to contribute to these influential contexts.

In the past decade in particular, researchers have begun to look for contextual variation in adolescents' experiences. Multiple ways in which features of school contexts influence dimensions of adolescents' peer cultures are increasingly evident. Research findings from diverse literatures demonstrate ways in which teachers, in particular, contribute to the nature of peer cultures that develop within schools and classrooms. Teachers influence the social context, including peer cultures, of their classrooms through often unobtrusive, unintentional, and sometimes unexpected ways. We have characterized their contribution as an invisible hand, to capture the idea that much of what teachers do to shape the peer environment is not explicit, and it is not obvious, sometimes even to teachers themselves (Farmer et al., in press). Little research attention has been focused on the implications of teachers' practice for the evolution of adolescent peer cultures; the studies we identified converge in finding that peer cultures are not only a product of adolescents' interactions, but of teachers' coordinated efforts to manage instructional, social, and behavioral demands of their classrooms. Teachers are likely to find successful coordination of these demands to be daunting, and a challenge for which they are typically ill-prepared from preservice course work and in-service professional development.

The SEALS intervention was developed to help teachers understand how academic, social, and behavioral domains of adjustment converge for their adolescent students, and how to coordinate their instructional and classroom management practices with evolving social dynamics to create classroom environments that support students' academic competence, positive behavioral adaptation, and productive social relationships. Our initial findings from a large-scale randomized controlled trials intervention project with low-resource rural schools indicate that participation in the SEALS program helps teachers to promote supportive peer cultures, which in turn are expected to enhance students' academic success. Our future efforts to evaluate the efficacy of the SEALS program will involve attention to additional aspects of adolescent peer culture, and to the extent to which teachers can promote student achievement through altering dimensions of the peer culture.

There is not strong alignment between the literature that focuses on dimensions of peer culture and the literature that focuses on teachers' contribution to peer cultures. Moreover, there is a vast literature on teacher influences on the classroom environment that extends beyond a mathematics instructional focus. There are likely many ways in which teachers enact an invisible hand to contribute to the evolving peer cultures of peer groups within their classrooms and for their classrooms and schools more generally. We hope that this review inspires additional attention to ways that teachers and students co-construct supportive peer cultures for effort and achievement in middle and high schools.

REFERENCES

Ainsworth-Darnell, J. W., & Downey, D. B. (1998). Assessing the oppositional culture explanation for racial/ethnic differences in school performance. *American Sociological Review, 63,* 536–553.

Becker, B. E., & Luthar, S. S. (2007). Peer-perceived admiration and social preference: Contextual correlates of positive peer regard among suburban and urban adolescents. *Journal of Research on Adolescence, 17,* 117–144.

Bergman, L. R., & Magnusson, D. (1997). A person-oriented approach in research on developmental psychopathology. *Developmental Psychopathology, 9,* 291–319.

Bissell-Havran, J. M., & Loken, E. (2009). The role of friends in early adolescents' academic self-competence and intrinsic value for math and English. *Journal of Youth and Adolescence, 38,* 41–50.

Boaler, J. (2008). Promoting 'relational equity' and high mathematics achievement through an innovative, mixed-ability approach. *British Educational Research Journal, 34,* 167–194.

Brown, B. B. (1990). Peer groups and peer cultures. In S. S. Feldman & G.R. Elliott (Eds.), *At the threshold: The developing adolescent* (pp. 171–196). Cambridge, MA: Harvard University Press.

Brown, B. B. (1993). School culture, social politics, and the academic motivation of U.S. students. In T. M. Tomlinson (Ed.), *Motivating students to learn* (pp. 63–98). Berkeley, CA: McCutchan.

Brown, J. L., Jones, S. M., LaRusso, M. D., & Aber, J. L. (2010). Improving classroom quality: Teacher influences and experimental impacts of the 4Rs program. *Journal of Educational Psychology, 102,* 153–167.

Bukowski, W. M., Sippola, L. K., & Newcomb, A. F. (2000). Variations in patterns of attraction of same- and other-sex peers in early adolescence. *Developmental Psychology, 36,* 147–154.

Cairns, R. B. (1991). Multiple metaphors for a singular idea. *Developmental Psychology, 27,* 23–26.

Cairns, R. B., & Cairns, B. D. (1994). *Lifelines and risks: Pathways of youth in our time.* New York, NY: Harvester Wheatsheaf.

Cairns, R. B., Cairns, B. D., & Neckerman, H. J. (1989). Early school dropout: Configurations and determinants. *Child Development, 60,* 1437–1452.

Cairns, R. B., Cairns, B. D., Neckerman, H. J., Ferguson, L. L., & Gariépy, J. L. (1989). Growth and aggression: Childhood to early adolescence. *Developmental Psychology, 25,* 320–330.

Cairns, R., Xie, H., & Leung, M. C. (1998). The popularity of friendship and the neglect of social networks: Toward a new balance. *New Directions for Child Development, 80,* 25–53.

Chang, L., Liu, H., Wen, Z., Fung, K., Wang, Y., & Xu, Y. (2004). Mediating teacher liking and moderating authoritative teachering on Chinese adolescents' perceptions of antisocial and prosocial behaviors. *Journal of Educational Psychology, 96,* 369–380.

Coleman, J. S. (1961). *The adolescent society: The social life of the teenager.* Santa Barbara, CA: Greenwood Press.

Cook, P. J., & Ludwig, J. (1997). Weighing the 'burden' of 'acting White': Are there race differences in attitudes toward education? *Journal of Policy Analysis and Management, 16,* 256–278.

Cook, P. J., & Ludwig, J. (1998). The burden of 'acting White': Do Black adolescents disparage academic achievement? In C. Jencks & M. Phillips (Eds.), *The*

Black–White test score gap (pp. 375–400). Washington, DC: Brookings Institution Press.

Corsaro, W. A., & Eder, D. (1990). Children's peer cultures. *Annual Review of Sociology, 16,* 197–220.

Crosnoe, R., Riegle-Crumb, C., Field, S., Frank K., & Muller, C. (2008). Peer group contexts of girls' and boys' academic experiences. *Child Development, 79,* 139–155.

deBruyn, E., & Cillessen, A. H. (2006). Popularity in early adolescence: Prosocial and antisocial subtypes. *Journal of Research on Adolescence, 21,* 1–21.

Danielsen, A. G., Wiium, N., Wilhelmsen, B. U., & Wold, B. (2010). Perceived support provided by teachers and classmates and students' self-reported academic initiative. *Journal of School Psychology, 48,* 247–267.

Downey, D. B., & Ainsworth-Darnell, J. W. (2002). The search for oppositional culture among black students. *American Sociological Review, 67,* 156–164.

Dupper, D.R., & Meyer-Adams, N. (2002). Low-level violence: A neglected aspect of school culture. *Urban Education, 37,* 350–364.

Eccles, J. S., Lord, S., & Midgley, C. (1991). What are we doing to early adolescents? The impact of educational contexts on early adolescents. *American Journal of Education, 99,* 521–542.

Eccles, J. S., Midgley, C., Wigfield, A., Buchanan, C. M., Reuman, D., Flanagan, C., & Maciver, D. (1993). Development during adolescence: The impact of stage–environment fit on young adolescents' experiences in schools and families. *American Psychologist, 48,* 90–101

Eckert, P. (1989). *Jocks and burnouts: Social categories and identities in the high school.* New York, NY: Teachers College Press.

Estell, D. B., Farmer, T. W., Irvin, M. J., Thompson, J. H., Hutchins, B. C., & McDonough, E. M. (2007). Patterns of middle school adjustment and ninth grade adaptation of rural African American youth: Grades and substance use. *Journal of Youth and Adolescence, 36,* 477–487.

Farmer, T. W., & Farmer, E. M. Z. (2001). Developmental science, systems of care, and prevention of emotional and behavioral problems in youth. *American Journal of Orthopsychiatry, 71,* 171–181.

Farmer, T. W., Goforth, J. B., Hives, J., Aaron, A., Jackson, F., & Sgammato, A. (2006). Competence Enhancement Behavior Management. *Preventing School Failure, 50,* 39–44.

Farmer, T. W., Hall, C. M., Petrin, R. A., Hamm, J. V., & Dadisman, K. (2010). Evaluating the impact of a multicomponent intervention model on teachers' awareness of social networks at the beginning of middle school in rural communities. *School Psychology Quarterly, 25,* 94–106.

Farmer, T. W, Hamm, J. V., Petrin, R.A, Robertson, D., Murray, R.A., Meece, J.L., & Brooks, D.S. (2010). Supporting early adolescent learning and social strengths: Promoting productive contexts for students at-risk for EBD during the transition to middle school. *Exceptionality, 18,* 94–106.

Farmer, T. W., Hamm, J. V., Lane, K., Lee, D., & Sutherland, K. (2012). *Conceptual foundations and components of a contextual intervention to promote student engagement during early adolescence: The SEALS model.* Manuscript under review.

Farmer, T. W., Lines, M. M., & Hamm, J. V. (2011). Revealing the invisible hand: The role of teachers in children's peer experiences. *Journal of Applied Developmental Psychology, 32,* 247–256.

Fordham, S., & Ogbu, J. U. (1986). Black students' school success: Coping with the 'burden of acting White.' *Urban Review, 18,* 176–206.

Frank, K. A., Muller, C., Schiller, K., Riegle-Crumb, C., Mueller, A. S., Crosnoe, R., & Pearson, J. (2008). The social dynamics of math coursetaking in high school. *American Journal of Sociology, 113,* 1645–1696.

Fuller-Rowell, T., & Doan, S. (2010). The social costs of academic success across ethnic groups. *Child Development, 81*(6), 1696–1713.

Gest, S. D., Domitrovich, C. E., & Welsh, J. A. (2005). Peer academic reputation in elementary schools: Associations with changes in self-concept and academic skills. *Journal of Educational Psychology, 97,* 337–346.

Gorman, A. H., Kim, J., & Schimmelbusch, A. (2002). The attributes adolescents associate with peer popularity and teacher preference. *Journal of School Psychology, 40,* 143–165.

Graesser, A. C. (2009). Inaugural editorial for *Journal of Educational Psychology. Journal of Educational Psychology, 101,* 259–261.

Graham, S., Taylor, A. Z., & Hudley, C. (1998). Exploring achievement values among ethnic minority early adolescents. *Journal of Educational Psychology, 90,* 606–620.

Hamm, J. V., & Faircloth, B. S. (2005). Peer context of mathematics classroom belonging in early adolescence. *The Journal of Early Adolescence, 25,* 345–366.

Hamm, J. V., & Farmer, T. W. (2011, March). *Enhancing the effects of teacher attunement to student peer group affiliations on the school social-affective context: Promotive effects of the SEALS intervention.* Paper presented at the annual meeting of the Society for Research on Educational Effectiveness, Washington, D.C.

Hamm, J. V., Farmer, T. W., Dadisman, K., Gravelle, M., & Murray, A. (2011). Teachers' attunement to students' peer group affiliations as a source of improved student experiences of the school social context following the middle school transition in rural schools. *Journal of Applied Developmental Psychology, 32,* 267–277.

Hamm, J. V., Farmer, T. W., Lambert, K., & Gravelle, M. (2012). *Enhancing peer cultures of effort and achievement in early adolescence: Benefits of the SEALS Program.* Manuscript under review.

Hamm, J. V., Farmer, T. W., Robertson, D., Dadisman, K., Murray, A. R., Meece, J., & Song, S. (2010). Effects of a developmentally-based intervention with teachers on Native American and White early adolescents' schooling adjustment in rural settings. *Journal of Experimental Education, 78,* 343–377.

Hamm, J. V., Malloy, C., & Meece, J. L. (2006, April). *The social context of mathematics education reform.* Symposium paper presented at the annual meetings of the research pre-session of the National Council of Teachers of Mathematics, St. Louis, MO.

Hamm, J. V., Malloy, C. E., & Meece, J. (2009). *Correlates and consequences of growth in conceptual understanding across middle and high school.* Final Report submitted to the Spencer Foundation.

Hamm, J. V., Schmid, L., Farmer, T. W., & Locke, B. (2011). Injunctive and descriptive peer group norms and the academic adjustment of rural early adolescents. *Journal of Early Adolescence, 31,* 1–33.

Hamm, J. V., & Zhang, L. (2010). The schooling context of adolescents' peer relations. In J. Meece & J. Eccles (Eds.), *The handbook of schooling effects on development* (pp. 518–554). Mahwah, NJ: Erlbaum.

Hand, V. M. (2010). The co-construction of opposition in a low-track mathematics classroom. *American Educational Research Journal, 47,* 97–132.

Harris, A. L. (2006). I (don't) hate school: Revisiting oppositional culture theory of blacks' resistance to schooling. *Social Forces, 85,* 797–834.

Hemmings, A. (1996). Conflicting images? Being Black and a model high school student. *Anthropology and Education Quarterly, 27,* 20–50.

Henry, D. (2008). Changing classroom social settings through attention to norms. In M. Shinn & H. Yoshikawa (Eds.), *Toward positive youth development: Transforming schools and community programs* (pp. 40–57). New York, NY: Oxford University Press.

Horvat, E. M., & Lewis, K. S. (2003). Reassessing the 'Burden of Acting White': The importance of peer groups in managing academic success. *Sociology of Education, 76,* 265–280.

Jonkmann, K., Trautwein, U., & Ludtke, O. (2009). Social dominance in adolescence: The moderating role of the classroom context and behavioral heterogeneity. *Child Development, 80,* 338–355.

Juvonen, J., & Murdoch, T. B. (1995). Grade-level differences in the social value of effort: Implications for self-presentation tactics of early adolescents. *Child Development, 66,* 1694–1705.

Kindermann, T. A. (1993). Natural peer groups as contexts for individual development: The case of children's motivation in school. *Developmental Psychology, 29,* 970–977.

Kiuru, N., Aunola, K., Vuori, J., & Nurmi, J. E. (2007). The role of peer groups in adolescents' educational expectations and adjustment. *Journal of Youth and Adolescence, 36,* 995–1009.

Lapinski, M. K., & Rimal, R. N. (2005). An explication of social norms. *Communication Theory, 15,* 127–147.

Lipsitz, J., & West, T. (2006). What makes a good school? Identifying excellent middle schools. *Phi Delta Kappan, 88*(1), 57–66.

Magnusson, D., & Cairns, R. B. (1996). Developmental science: Toward a unified framework. In R. B. Cairns, G. H. Elder Jr., & E. J. Costello (Eds.), *Developmental Science* (pp. 7–30). Cambridge, UK: Cambridge University Press.

McFarland, D. (2001). Student resistance: How the formal and informal organization of classrooms facilitate everyday forms of student resistance. *American Journal of Sociology, 107,* 612–678.

Midgley, C., & Edelin, K. C. (1998). Middle school reform and early adolescent well-being: The good news and the bad. *Educational Psychologist, 33,* 195–206.

National Council of Teachers of Mathematics. (1989). *Curriculum and evaluation standards for school mathematics.* Reston, VA: Author.

National Council of Teachers of Mathematics. (2000). *Principles and standards for school mathematics.* Reston, VA: Author.

Ogbu, J. U. (1992). Adaptation to minority status and impact on school success. *Theory into Practice, 31,* 287–295.

Parkhurst, J. T., & Hopmeyer, A. (1998). Sociometric popularity and peer-perceived popularity: Two distinct dimensions of peer status. *Journal of Early Adolescence, 18,* 125–144.

Ream, R. K., & Rumberger, R. W. (2008). Student engagement, peer social capital, and peer dropout among Mexican American and non-Latino White students. *Sociology of Education, 81,* 109–139.

Riegle-Crumb, C., Farkas, G., & Muller, C. (2006). The role of gender and friendship in advanced course taking. *Sociology of Education, 79,* 206–228.

Roeser, R. W., Eccles, J. S., & Sameroff, A. J. (2000). School as a context of early adolescents' academic and social-emotional development: A summary of research findings. *The Elementary School Journal, 100,* 443–471.

Roeser, R. W., & Peck, C. P. (2003). Patterns and pathways of educational achievement across adolescence: A holistic-developmental perspective. *New Directions for Child and Adolescent Development, 101,* 39–62.

Rubin, K. H., Bukowski, W. M., & Parker, J. G. (2006). Peer interactions, relationships, and groups. In N. Eisenberg, W. Damon, & R. M. Lerner (Eds.), *Handbook of child psychology, 5th ed.: Vol 3. Social, emotional, and personality development* (pp. 619–700). Hoboken, NJ: John Wiley & Sons, Inc.

Ryan, A. (2000). Peer groups as a context for the socialization of adolescents' motivation, engagement, and achievement in school. *Educational Psychologist, 35,* 101–111.

Ryan, A. (2001). The peer group as a context for the development of young adolescent motivation and achievement. *Child Development, 72,* 1135–1150.

Schunk, D., & Meece, J. L. (1992). *Student perceptions in the classroom.* Hillsdale, NJ: Erlbaum.

Tyson, K., Darity, W., Jr., & Castellino, D. R. (2005). It's not 'a Black thing': Understanding the burden of acting White and other dilemmas of high achievement. *American Sociological Review, 70,* 582–605.

Vaillancourt, T., Hymel, S., & McDougall, P. (2003). Bullying is power: Implications for school-based intervention strategies. *Journal of Applied School Psychology, 19,* 157–176.

Walker, E.N. (2006). Urban high school students' academic communities and their effects on mathematics success. *American Educational Research Journal, 43,* 43–73.

Wentzel, K. R. (2002). Are effective teachers like good parents? Teaching styles and student adjustment in early adolescence. *Child Development, 73,* 287–301.

Wentzel, K. R. (2003). Sociometric status and adjustment in middle school: A longitudinal study. *Journal of Early Adolescence, 23,* 5–27.

Wentzel, K. R., & Asher, S. R. (1995). The academic lives of neglected, rejected, popular, and controversial children. *Child Development, 66,* 754–763.

Wentzel, K. R., Battle, A., Russell, S. L., & Looney, L. B. (2010). Social supports from teachers and peers as predictors of academic and social motivation. *Contemporary Educational Psychology, 35,* 193–202.

CHAPTER 10

THE COPING POWER PROGRAM FOR AT-RISK AGGRESSIVE STUDENTS

John E. Lochman, Caroline Boxmeyer, Nicole Powell, and Joan Barth
The University of Alabama

Edward D. Barker
Birkbeck University of London

Children's aggressive behavior is a concerning issue for schools, not only in terms of maintaining order and safety, but also in regard to students' academic achievement. For school-aged children, aggression rarely exists independently of other maladaptive behaviors. Indeed, aggressive-disruptive behavior has a strong association with poor academic performance and dropping out of school (e.g., Farrington, 1989). The need to address antisocial aggressive behaviors as well as intellectual factors in students at risk for dropping out of school is underscored by the fact that the majority of students who drop out have IQs in the normal range (French & Conrad, 2001). However, the relation between aggression and academic problems is somewhat complex.

Peer Relationships and Adjustment at School, pages 251–278
Copyright © 2012 by Information Age Publishing

251

RELATION BETWEEN AGGRESSION
AND ACADEMIC PROBLEMS

Children with aggressive and disruptive behavior frequently have co-existing academic problems, including low academic achievement and a lack of school connectedness and involvement (e.g., Bennett, Brown, Boyle, Racine, & Offord, 2003). Children with both academic and behavioral problems are at heightened risk for negative adolescent outcomes, including school failure, substance use, violence, and delinquency (Loeber, 1990). In early to middle childhood, disruptive children can experience peer rejection and highly negative reactions from teachers. Children's academic progress and their bond to school weakens around this time, and by early adolescence they become more susceptible to deviant peer influences (Dishion & Andrews, 1995). Children who have low commitment to and dislike school, who are frequently truant, who have low levels of achievement, who have high rates of school failure, and who spend little time on homework and perceive school work to be irrelevant experience earlier onset of delinquency and adolescent drug use (e.g., Coie, 1996).

Externalizing behaviors have been associated with achievement in multiple academic areas including reading (e.g., Cornwall & Bawden, 1992) and mathematics (e.g., Pagani, Fitzpatrick, Archambault, & Janosz, 2010). Negative associations also exist between aggressive behavior and skills important to academic achievement such as motivation (Wentzel, 1993), on-task behavior (Coie, Lochman, Terry, & Hyman, 1992), academic engagement (Stipek & Miles, 2008), and self-control (Krueger, Caspi, Moffitt, White, & Stouthammer-Loeber, 1996). Furthermore, the relation between aggression and academic problems holds for elementary school aged children (e.g., Chen, Huang, Chang, Wang, & Li, 2010; Miles & Stipek, 2006), middle school students (French & Conrad, 2001), adolescents (e.g., Bartholemy & Lounsbury, 2009; Lounsbury, Sundstrom, Gibson, & Loveland, 2003; Loveland, Lounsbury, Welsh, & Buboltz, 2007; Schwartz, Gorman, Nakamoto, & McKay, 2006), and college students (e.g., Balkin, 1987). However, aggression and academic problems are not consistently linked in kindergarten and first grade (e.g., Duncan et al., 2007; Jorm, Share, Matthews, & Maclean, 1986; Loveland et al., 2007; Miles & Stipek, 2006), suggesting that the relation strengthens over time.

Externalizing behaviors and academic problems appear to be related for both boys and girls (e.g., Duncan et al., 2007; Masten et al., 2005). However, the relation may be stronger for girls. Interestingly, Loveland et al. (2007) found that aggression accounted for twice as much variance in girls' grade point averages than those of boys. The authors proposed that teachers' reactions to student aggression may explain the stronger association between grades and aggression for girls. For example, because aggressive girls' behavior violates gender norms, girls may elicit harsher penalties from teachers, which could result in a disruption of their learning. Teachers might also be more aware of boys' aggression, which tends to be more overt than that of girls, and this increased teacher attention might lead to more access to remediation opportunities for aggressive boys than for aggressive girls.

A somewhat different approach to examining the relations between aggression and academic behavior and achievement creates student profiles based on peer or teacher ratings of peer relationships and academic performance. Farmer, Estell, Hall, Pearl, Van Acker, and Rodkin (2008) explain that academic, behavioral, and social competencies influence each other and over time become organized as "packages of correlated constraints" (p. 196) that support the continuity of behavior problems. Much of this work is an outgrowth of peer sociometric research showing that children with a combination of aggression and low peer social acceptance are at risk for dropping out of school (Parker & Asher, 1987). However, aggressive children are often not socially isolated (Pellegrini, Bartini, & Brooks, 1999) and sometimes are even identified as being "popular" at school, suggesting that aggressive children are heterogeneous in their social relationships. Farmer et al. (2008) have found two distinct groups of aggressive children as early as fourth grade. The "tough" children (1) have many positive characteristics, including athletic ability, social skills and popularity; (2) are average in their school performance; but (3) are also rated high in aggression. The second group, "troubled," (1) have few positive characteristics, (2) experience problems in a several social and academic areas, and (3) are also described as being aggressive and disruptive. Both "tough" and "troubled" children are at risk for later academic problems, although perhaps for different reasons. "Tough" students may feel that they need to disengage from school to maintain their popularity (Farmer et al., 2008). In contrast, "troubled" children may lack more basic cognitive and social skills which cause a greater range of problems and academic risk.

The student profile approach suggests that the predictive relations between aggression and academic problems are complex and most likely bidirectional.

Prediction of Academic Problems from Aggression

Longitudinal research provides evidence that conduct problems are predictive of future academic problems in the later elementary grades, middle school, and high school (see Miles & Stipek, 2006, for a review). For example, in a study spanning 20 years, Masten et al. (2005) found that children's externalizing behavior problems in elementary school were predictive of academic problems in adolescence, which subsequently predicted internalizing problems in adulthood. Chen, Rubin, and Li (1997) found that aggressive and disruptive behaviors in a sample of Chinese fourth graders predicted lower academic achievement in sixth grade, but the inverse relation was not found. Similarly, McIntosh, Flannery, Sugai, Braun, and Cochrane (2008) measured discipline referrals, GPA, and standardized achievement scores in eighth graders and reexamined these variables one year later. They found that discipline referrals in eighth grade related to ninth grade standardized test scores as well as ninth grade discipline referrals. Although academic achievement indicators and discipline referrals were negatively related in eighth grade, McIntosh et al. did not find a significant relation between eighth grade academic achievement and discipline referrals in eighth grade after controlling for the direct effects.

Several hypotheses have been proposed to explain the negative impact of aggression on achievement. First, students who engage in aggressive behaviors during instructional time are not engaged in the learning process; further, if disciplinary measures remove them from the classroom, the loss of instructional time may be extended (e.g., Arnold, 1997). Aggressive behavior also serves to disrupt relationships with teachers and peers, possibly to the detriment of achievement. Students who do not feel connected to their teachers may lack motivation to gain teacher approval by engaging in academic assignments. Support for this hypothesis was provided by Stipek and Miles (2008), who followed students from kindergarten and first grade through fifth grade and found a negative effect for aggression on academic achievement over time. Examination of mediating processes indicated that children's aggressive behavior led to more conflict in teacher–child relationships and subsequently reduced engagement in academic tasks. Ultimately, this pathway resulted in a detrimental effect on academic achievement.

Not surprisingly, aggressive students are also likely to have conflicted relationships with their peers. It follows that aggressive students may lack socially reinforcing peer experiences connecting them to the school environment, leading to feelings of alienation and disengagement that can generalize to academic tasks (O'Farrell, Morrison, & Furlong, 2006). Problematic peer relationships are associated with a desire to avoid school and with decreases in school liking (e.g., Ladd, Kochenderfer, & Coleman, 1997), and students whose peers perceive them as aggressive are at risk for negative educational outcomes, including school dropout (Risi, Gerhardstein, & Kistner, 2003). Aggressive children who have problems with the general peer group may also gravitate toward deviant peers who may engage in behaviors that interfere with the educational process, such as truancy (Schwartz et al., 2006).

To summarize, this research suggests that several mechanisms could account for the ability of aggression to predict later academic problems. However, there is also evidence that school aggression predicts later academic problems.

Prediction of Aggression from Academic Problems

The predictive power of poor academic skills has been demonstrated across a number of developmental time points. For example, Miles and Stipek (2006) conducted a five-year longitudinal study of low-income children, starting when the children were between four and six years old. Results indicated that poor literacy achievement in lower grades predicted aggression in higher grades. Similarly, McIntosh, Horner, Chard, Boland, and Good (2006) found that both reading and behavior variables measured in kindergarten predicted discipline referrals in fifth grade. In an extensive longitudinal study, Farrington (1989) identified school failure at age eight as one of six major factors with a strong predictive relationship to later aggression. Studies have also examined these relations during transitions to middle, junior, or high school. In one such study of seventh and ninth graders, Herrenkohl, Catalano, Hemphill, and Toumbourou (2009) found that academic achievement and school commitment predicted physical and relational aggression over a one year period. Interestingly, the school variables had more extensive relations to aggression and substance use than family attachment after one year.

It has been hypothesized that the predictive relation between academic functioning and aggression may be explained in part through mediating emotional processes. Children who struggle academically may become frustrated in the classroom, and these feelings of frustration may spill over into negative interactions with teachers and peers (Miles & Stipek, 2006). Awareness of poor academic skills might also elicit feelings of embarrassment and anxiety in students; as a result, students might attempt to hide their academic problems behind an oppositional or hostile demeanor.

Interrelatedness of Aggression and Academic Skills: Implications for Intervention

The current body of research contains findings supporting aggression as a predictor of academic problems, as well as support for academic problems predicting aggression; the relationship is likely reciprocal and influenced by a multitude of factors (Stipek & Miles, 2008). At the heart of either pathway, students may experience negative school relationships, frustration at school, and a weakened school bond. Regardless of the direction of the relationship, it is clear that students who struggle academically or have externalizing behaviors would stand to benefit from developing self-regulation, anger management, and prosocial and social problem solving skills. Improvements in these areas may lead to more positive interactions with teachers and peers in the school environment and, subsequently, to experiences that support learning, such as increased assistance from teachers and peers, increased engagement in the learning process, and greater motivation to meet teacher and peer expectations.

Improving self-regulation, anger management, and prosocial and social problem solving skills are main objectives of the Coping Power program, a multi-component intervention targeting school-aged children with aggressive behavior problems. Coping Power is designed to address problems in emotion regulation as well as social-cognitive deficiencies and distortions that often accompany aggressive behavior in children.

THE COPING POWER PROGRAM

Coping Power (Lochman, Wells, & Lenhart, 2008; Wells, Lochman, & Lenhart, 2008) was designed to address social-cognitive deficiencies that contribute to aggressive children's behavioral problems. Designed for implementation in schools, the program addresses several areas relevant to students' school functioning including goal setting, organizational and study skills, emotion awareness, anger management, perspective taking, social problem solving, and promoting positive peer relationships. A corresponding parent component also addresses school-related issues including parental support in academics and monitoring of peer relationships.

Coping Power Program Child Component

The Coping Power Program Child Component is a 34-session, group-based preventive intervention that targets aggressive students in the fourth through sixth grades. With modifications, the program can be delivered individually and to slightly younger or older students. Coping Power typically spans a 15- to 18-month period, taking place across two academic years (e.g., spring of fourth grade and all of fifth grade). Ideally, the school guidance counselor, psychologist, or social worker and a paraprofessional co-leader meet weekly with groups of four to seven students. Meetings are 45–60 minutes in duration and are highly structured. Each session comprises a consistent set of opening and closing activities as well as specific exercises that target the program's main content areas. In addition to group sessions, participating students meet individually with leaders each month to promote the student–leader bond and to individualize the program as needed.

Behavior Management

The Coping Power Child Component includes a behavior management plan, incorporating positive reinforcement for prosocial behavior and consequences for disruptive and off-task behaviors. Based on their positive participation in activities and compliance with group rules, students can earn points during each session. Points can be saved or spent each week on prizes assembled by the leaders. The prizes usually include small, low-point value items (e.g., stickers) as well as larger, more desirable items (e.g., video games) that promote students' emerging abilities to work toward a goal and to delay gratification. For variety and to limit expenditures, leaders often include intangible rewards such as homework passes and special school privileges (e.g., reading announcements over the school PA system).

Often, students' interest in earning points is sufficiently motivating to encourage appropriate behavior during group meetings. However, disruptive behaviors do arise, and the program outlines a plan for managing such problems. Minor disruptive behaviors are addressed through strategies such as selective ignoring and differential reinforcement of appropriate behaviors. However, when behavior problems persist and/or require more direct intervention, students are given a verbal warning or "strike." After accruing three strikes for disruptive, noncompliant, and/or off-task behaviors, students can fail to earn points for the meeting. Should behavior problems continue or escalate after this consequence is imposed, students may be asked to leave the group to process with one of the leaders or to return to their classroom.

Opening Activities

To promote retention of information across sessions, each Coping Power meeting opens with a review of the previous session's content. Each student is asked to recall one concept from the last group meeting, giving leaders the opportunity to assess students' retention and understanding of the material and to review and correct as needed.

Next, the group engages in a review of students' progress toward weekly behavioral goals. Each student produces a goal sheet that specifies the goal that he or she has been working on during the previous week, along with the teacher's daily feedback on the student's progress. Leaders process any successes or problems with the goal, and, taking the students' progress or lack thereof into account, the leaders and students work together to develop a goal for the coming week. A major function of the goal-setting process is to enhance generalization of treatment gains into the classroom through daily monitoring and feedback to students. Also, the process serves to involve teachers more closely in the treatment process and encourages students to develop independent responsibility for keeping track of a daily assignment.

Closing Activities

Each Coping Power session closes in the same way, with a series of three activities. First, students are asked to provide positive feedback to one other student, commenting on his or her behavior during the meeting or on an episode of good coping or prosocial behavior that occurred during the week. Such feedback, coming from peers, tends to be meaningful and reinforcing to students. Next, leaders review points earned by students during the session and offer them the opportunity to spend their points in the prize box. Finally, if time permits, students who have earned at least one point during the meeting are permitted to spend the last five to ten minutes in free-time activities, which may include games, drawing, or visiting with peers. Free time serves as an additional reinforcer for appropriate behavior during the meeting and allows leaders time to process and problem-solve with students who did not earn free time.

Goal Setting

The main focus of the initial Coping Power sessions is on goal setting and, as noted above, the goal-setting process continues as an opening activity for the duration of the program. Students learn to define the term "goal" and to apply the concept to their own desires for improvements and achievements. This includes instruction on breaking long-term goals down into discrete behavioral steps that can be accomplished on a daily basis. For example, a student who sets a long-term goal of being promoted to the sixth grade might identify short-term goals of completing homework, working productively on classroom assignments, studying for tests, and using appropriate language in the classroom. The short-term goals can then be transferred to the weekly goal-setting process, serving as individual goals for the students' goal sheets.

Organization and Study Skills

A session on organization and study skills is included early in the Coping Power curriculum to address the deficits in academic meta-skills that frequently coincide with aggressive behavioral problems. The topic is reviewed in the second year of the program to address the increasing demands for independence and responsibility for academic tasks that occur as students progress into higher grades. Activities in this component focus on helping students to recognize how organizational skills impact their academic success and their relationships with teachers. In one exercise, students are challenged to find common items in their backpacks as quickly as possible; the winners of this game then share how they have organized their belongings and all students are given the opportunity to clean out and reorganize their bags. Another game-type activity involves students being given a set of cards, each with the name of a common word. The students are timed while they look for words announced by the leader, and then the students are given time to organize the cards as they wish. Next, the word-finding activity is repeated, and students who have used a functional strategy (e.g., alphabetizing the cards; organizing them by category) demonstrate substantial increases in their speed, highlighting the benefits of good organization. Additional exercises, role-plays, and discussions underscore the importance of fully understanding the requirements of assignments, developing effective study habits, and planning for long-term projects.

Emotion Awareness

Sessions devoted to emotion awareness help students recognize and label their internal experiences of arousal. The concept that "all feelings are acceptable, but some behaviors are not" is emphasized throughout this unit, and students are encouraged to recognize their anger at its earliest, most manageable stages. Through discussion, visual stimuli, and games, students learn to identify behavioral, cognitive, and physiological cues that accompany the expression of different feelings, with a particular emphasis on anger. Leaders point out that students can self-monitor for their personal anger cues as signals to use coping strategies to control their emotions. Students are further encouraged to recognize the situations or "triggers" that lead to different levels of anger. A final set of activities focuses on the identification of varying degrees of anger, introducing a thermometer analogy to illustrate the concept. As a between-sessions homework assignment, students keep a daily anger log, indicating on a thermometer the level of anger they experience and the trigger that led to their anger.

Anger Management

After gaining experience with recognizing anger cues and triggers, students are taught cognitive self-control strategies to manage their anger. First, students learn to distract themselves from anger-inducing stimuli by focusing their attention elsewhere. In-session activities involve several group members taunting a target student, who is instructed to engage in a challenging memorization or construction task. Through guided discussion, the target students recognize that they were able to control rising anger by immersing themselves in the task. Next, the impact of self-talk on increasing or decreasing the experience of anger is explored, and students develop an individualized list of coping self-statements to use when angry. Active practice with coping self-statements takes place in a hierarchy of structured taunting activities that range from puppet plays to group members directly teasing one another. Other anger control strategies taught and practiced include breathing, visualization, and muscle relaxation.

Perspective Taking

Children with aggressive behavior problems commonly display characteristic distortions and deficiencies in their social-cognitive processing, including increased attention to hostile environmental cues and a tendency to attribute hostile intent to others' actions. Because these processing problems can contribute to conflicts in social relationships, several sessions are devoted to improving students' abilities to accurately infer others' thoughts and intentions and to enhance their understanding of others' feelings. Discussion and role-plays involve students generating a range of explanations for others' actions in hypothetical and actual situations. Several activities directly focus on correcting students' faulty perceptions of teachers' goals and intentions. Through exercises such as conducting a teacher interview and a "family feud" game, students are encouraged to recognize that teachers assign work and discipline students with the students' best interests in mind.

Social Problem Solving

Students are also taught adaptive strategies to effectively negotiate social problem situations. The problem-solving, or "PICC," process is structured around three steps, which include accurately describing the problem situation (Problem Identification), generating a list of possible solutions to the problem (Choices), and evaluating the potential outcomes of these solutions (Consequences). The PICC model encourages students to inhibit impulsive responding during social problem situations and to consider whether a particular behavioral choice will help them to meet their short-term and long-term goals. The PICC model also serves as a framework by which leaders can help students to broaden their often limited repertoire of responses to social conflicts. Behavioral choices involving discussion, compromise, and negotiation are introduced by leaders when students provide less effective strategies (e.g., direct actions, aggression). Sessions include opportunities for practice with the PICC model through role-plays of both hypothetical situations and real-life problems elicited from students. Students solidify their problem-solving abilities through a video-making activity in which they create a commercial describing and depicting effective use of the PICC model.

Developing Positive Peer Relationships

A final set of sessions addresses the difficulties in peer relationships commonly displayed by children with aggressive behavior. The goals of this unit are to both promote the development of positive peer relationships and to discourage students' participation in deviant peer activities. Students learn to recognize the prosocial qualities in themselves and in others that are important in friendships, practice successful group entry and negotiation skills, and identify positive peer groups with which they would like to affiliate. Peer pressure is defined and discussed, and students practice using refusal skills in role-plays that may include topics such as substance abuse and delinquent activities.

Coping Power Program Parent Component

The Coping Power Parent Component is a 16-session intervention offered to parents of students participating in the Coping Power Child Component at their schools. Typically run in groups of six to eight parents or pairs of parents, sessions are approximately 90 minutes in length and are run by the school guidance counselor, school psychologist, or school social worker. The curriculum is designed to span the same 15- to 18-month period as the Child Component, with certain topic areas covered in both components at the same time. Parents receive information about the skills their children are learning in Coping Power and are encouraged to provide modeling, guidance, and reinforcement of children's use of these skills at home. The Coping Power Parent Component also covers unique content areas, including parent involvement in academics; management of parental stress; management of children's problem behaviors; and promoting family cohesion, communication, and problem-solving.

Session Structure

Coping Power Parent Component sessions follow a structured format, including opening activities, an interactive content-based presentation, and a closing period. Following an unstructured visiting period, meetings open with a recap of the previous session and a review of completed homework. Topics are introduced in didactic presentations, with parents being encouraged to share personal examples and to practice skills through role-play exercises. Each session closes with a homework assignment designed to increase parents' awareness of their children's behaviors and/or to practice effective parenting skills.

Parent Involvement in Academics

Leaders and parents discuss the importance of parental involvement in children's academic success, focusing on parent–teacher communications and parent supervision of homework completion. Leaders provide information on communication and collaboration between parents and teachers, and parents role-play parent–teacher conferences. Parents also develop a structure for monitoring their children's homework completion and are encouraged to implement the plan with their children on a daily basis.

Management of Parental Stress

Activities included in the parent stress management component are designed to promote parents' recognition of stressful events and circumstances in their lives and to assist parents in developing plans for effectively dealing with their stress. Parents learn skills to cope with stress such as time management strategies, relaxation exercises, scheduling positive activities, and using adaptive cognitive self-statements.

Behavior Management

The majority of the Coping Power Parent Component focuses on developing strategies for effective management of children's behaviors. Sessions cover a variety of techniques designed to promote children's positive behaviors and correct inappropriate behaviors. Parents first focus on enhancing their relationships with their children by scheduling one-on-one time to engage in positive activities. Parents also discuss and practice techniques including praising the prosocial opposites of problem behaviors, ignoring minor disruptive behaviors, delivering effective instructions, and establishing house rules and expectations. Discipline strategies including time out, privilege removal, and work chores are also reviewed.

Building Positive Family Practices

A final set of sessions encourages parents to explore their thoughts and feelings about future parenting challenges and discuss strategies that promote long-term family functioning. Parents discuss ways to remain positively involved with their children through adolescence such as scheduling family outings and enjoyable activities at home. Parents also develop a communication system for family conflicts and issues and learn to apply the PICC model to family problem situations. Finally, the importance of parent supervision of children's peer outings is emphasized, and parents are encouraged to set up a communication system in which their children keep them informed of their whereabouts and activities.

Anger Coping and Coping Power Programs: Behavioral Outcomes

Effects of the Anger Coping Program

Coping Power grew out of earlier intervention research on Anger Coping, a briefer, child-only version of the intervention (Larson & Lochman, 2002). After positive behavioral changes were found in an uncontrolled pilot study of Anger Coping (Lochman, Nelson, & Sims, 1981), a controlled trial was undertaken in which 76 aggressive and disruptive fourth to sixth grade boys (53% African American, 47% Caucasian) were randomly assigned to: Anger Coping (AC), goal setting (GS), Anger Coping plus goal setting (AC+GS), or untreated control (UC) cells (Lochman, Burch, Curry, & Lampron, 1984). At the one-month post-intervention follow-up, in comparison to UC and GS, aggressive boys in the Anger Coping conditions (AC, AC+GS) displayed less parent-reported aggression and were observed to engage in less disruptive classroom behavior . The addition of a goal-setting component in the AC+GS cell tended to enhance treatment effects (Lochman et al., 1984).

In a study of follow-up effects, Lochman, Coie, Underwood, and Terry (1993) found that a school-based social relations program derived from Anger Coping had significant impact at post-intervention and at a one-year follow-up with aggressive-rejected children (aggressive children who have many negative and few positive peer relationships), but not with rejected-only children. A three-year follow-up study of the program's preventive effects found that compared to an untreated aggressive group, Anger Coping boys had significantly lower rates of marijuana and drug involvement and lower rates of alcohol use, and they maintained their improvements in self-esteem and in social problem-solving skills (Lochman, 1992). In all of these areas, Anger Coping boys were functioning in the same range as nonaggressive boys at follow-up. However, there were no longer-term preventive effects on delinquency, and the classroom behavioral improvements had faded. Only a subset of Anger Coping boys who had received a second-year booster intervention maintained reductions in passive off-task classroom behavior, suggesting that a longer intervention might be necessary to maintain overt classroom behavioral changes. This series of studies suggested the need for a broader, multi-component intervention to have a more lasting effect on serious antisocial outcomes, leading to the development of Coping Power.

Efficacy and Effectiveness Studies of the Coping Power Program

Several studies have examined the efficacy and effectiveness of Coping Power, as well as factors affecting program dissemination. In a first study (Lochman & Wells, 2004), 183 boys (61% African American; 39% Caucasian) who had high rates of teacher-rated aggression in fourth or fifth grades were randomly assigned to either a school-based Coping Power child component, to a combination of Coping Power child and parent components, or to an untreated control condition. Intervention took place over two academic years (4th and 5th grades for some children, 5th and 6th grades for others). Outcome analyses indicated that Coping Power produced lower rates of delinquent behavior and parent-rated substance use at a one-year follow-up than did the control condition, and these intervention effects were most apparent for the combined child and parent Coping Power program. Boys also displayed teacher-rated behavioral improvements in school during the follow-up year, and these effects were evident in both intervention conditions and appeared to be primarily influenced by the Coping Power child component. The intervention effect on substance use was stronger with moderate income boys than boys from low-income families, and the intervention-produced improvements in school behavior were more apparent for Caucasian boys than for African American boys. Normative comparison analyses with a non-risk sample of 63 boys from the same schools indicate that the intervention moved at-risk boys into normative ranges for substance use, delinquency, and school behavior, in contrast to at-risk control boys who significantly differed from the normative group on the latter two outcomes.

Subsequent studies continued to examine the effectiveness of the core Coping Power program while experimenting with different delivery approaches that might make the program more amenable as a school-based intervention. One such study examined whether the effects of Coping Power, offered as an indicated prevention intervention for high-risk aggressive children, could be enhanced by adding a universal prevention component (Lochman & Wells, 2002b). The universal intervention was randomly offered to half of the fifth grade teachers and consisted of in-service training for teachers and large-scale parent meetings for all parents of children in universal intervention classrooms. The sample consisted of 245 male (66%) and female (34%) aggressive fourth graders (78% African American; 20% Caucasian) who randomly assigned to one of four conditions: (1) indicated intervention + universal intervention, (2) indicated intervention only (the traditional Coping Power program), (3) universal intervention only, and (4) a no intervention comparison group. Intervention began in the fall of fifth grade and continued midway through sixth grade. Analyses of post-intervention effects comparing intervention to control conditions (Lochman & Wells, 2002b) indicate that the combined Coping Power plus universal intervention produced lower rates of self-reported substance use and lower teacher-rated aggression, indicating the value of nesting Coping Power within a universal prevention program. Coping Power by itself produced reduced ratings of parent-rated proactive aggression and lower activity level by children. At a one-year follow-up, Coping Power produced reductions in substance use, delinquency, and aggressive behavior in the school setting (Lochman & Wells, 2003), thus replicating the follow-up effects of the Lochman & Wells (2004) efficacy study.

Two randomized controlled trials have examined outcomes of an abbreviated version of Coping Power that can be implemented in one school year (24 child and 10 parent sessions). In a study of 240 fifth graders rated in the at-risk range for aggression, the program produced significant reductions in teacher-rated externalizing behavior for children who had a caregiver attend at least one parent session (Lochman, Boxmeyer, Powell, Roth, & Windle, 2006) in comparison to children randomly assigned to a control condition. In a randomized controlled trial with 119 students, an independent research team in Oregon found that the 24-session Coping Power child component alone produced significant teacher-rated behavioral improvements (Peterson, Hamilton, & Russell, 2009) in comparison to controls. Other research groups are currently evaluating the use of Coping Power in after-school settings (Cowell, Horstmann, Linebarger, Meaker, & Aligne, 2008).

Coping Power has also been adapted for use with special populations and in non-school settings. For example, a modification for aggressive deaf children (Lochman et al., 2001) led to reductions in aggression among those who received Coping Power, in comparison to a randomly assigned control condition. In addition, a briefer Dutch version of Coping Power was evaluated in a clinic study in which children with disruptive behavior disorders ($N = 77$) were randomly assigned to Coping Power or to clinic care-as-usual (including behavioral and cognitive behavioral therapy, family therapy, psychoanalytic therapy, and social skills training). Participants in both conditions improved significantly on disruptive behavior post-treatment and at a six-month follow-up, but the Coping Power group had significantly greater reduction in overt aggression by post-treatment (van de Wiel, Matthys, Cohen-Kettenis, & van Engeland, 2007) compared to the care-as-usual condition. Coping Power clinicians had significantly less experience than care-as-usual therapists, indicating Coping Power was more cost-effective in producing similar types of effect sizes (van de Wiel et al., 2003). At the four-year follow-up, Coping Power children had significantly lower marijuana and tobacco use than did care-as-usual children, although the conditions did not differ in alcohol use (Zonneyville-Bender, Matthys, van de Wiel, & Lochman, 2007). The Coping Power children were using marijuana and tobacco within the range of a normative comparison group at the time of this long-term follow-up, indicating long-lasting, preventive effects of the intervention (Zonneyville-Bender et al., 2007).

Controlled Dissemination Study of the Coping Power Program

The majority of the research sited has used trained clinical professionals in the delivery of the program. Thus, a significant hurdle for effective dissemination the Coping Power program is for it to be successfully implemented by school staff. A controlled dissemination study of Coping Power was recently conducted in 57 schools in Alabama. School counselors were randomly assigned to be trained to implement Coping Power with high-risk aggressive fourth and fifth graders ($N = 351$) or to a care-as-usual control condition ($N = 180$). Half of the counselors in the dissemination condition received a basic form of training that included three days of initial training and monthly supervision meetings while implementation was underway. The other counselors in the dissemination condition received a more intensive form of training that included the above components as well as monthly feedback on implementation fidelity and quality based on review of recorded sessions. The intensity of training had a notable impact on child outcomes. In comparison to the control condition, significant reductions in child externalizing behavior (from teacher, parent, and child ratings) only occurred when the more intensive form of training was provided (i.e., when counselors received immediate supervisory feedback based on recorded sessions; Lochman, Boxmeyer, Powell, Qu, Wells, & Windle, 2009). School-level factors and counselor personality traits were associated with quality of program implementation, with counselors with more agreeable and conscientious personality traits demonstrating the best program implementation. Counselors who were high on cynicism and who were in schools with low staff autonomy and high managerial control had particularly poor quality of implementation and child and parent engagement (Lochman, Powell, Boxmeyer, Qu, Wells, & Windle, 2009).

Anger Coping and Coping Power Programs: Academic and Social Outcomes

The research above indicates that the Coping Power program is generally successful in reducing aggressive and antisocial behaviors including substance use. The next set of studies further examined specific academic and social outcomes.

Academic Outcomes

In a dissemination study of Anger Coping, program developers provided training to school staff and assisted with the evaluation, but the program was completely implemented by school staff. As part of a Safe Schools grant, the Wake County (North Carolina) Public School System provided Anger Coping training to all school counselors and psychologists in the system (Larson & Lochman, 2002). The training consisted of three full-day training sessions in the spring and summer prior to the implementation of the program, monthly two-hour large-group consultation sessions during program implementation, and two telephone "hotline" hours per week during program implementation. The ongoing consultation and hotline hours were believed to be essential in assisting staff in handling both routine and unexpected problems encountered by school staff during the implementation of the program.

Children were referred for Anger Coping by teacher ratings of aggressive and disruptive behavior. Children in self-contained special education classes were excluded, but mainstreamed special education students were eligible. Forty-one Anger Coping groups were begun at 40 schools, providing service to 200 children. The 161 students with at least partial post data had an average age of 9.8 years. Although there was no control group in this dissemination study, changes in children's academic, behavioral, and social adjustment were assessed. The Anger Coping children had a 12% improvement at the one-year follow-up in their grade-level achievement in mathematics and reading as assessed by a state achievement measure, and this improvement was significantly higher than the system-wide improvement rate over the same period. These children were also found to have a significantly lower rate of increased in-school suspensions in comparison to other children their age in this school system. The academic gains after one year suggest that behavioral improvements by the end of the intervention may have contributed to improved attention and motivation in class work, which may in turn have led to increased academic achievement. The relative improvement in suspension rate suggests that the children's behavioral improvements had generalized over time.

Because of the lack of a control group in the Anger Coping dissemination study, the academic gains cannot be conclusively linked to the program. However, in subsequent controlled studies, intervention children have improved on academically related variables, supporting the conclusion that social-cognitive preventive interventions can influence children's academic functioning. Lochman, Boxmeyer et al. (2009) found that Coping Power, led by intensively trained school counselors, led to improvements in children's study skills compared to randomly assigned control students. Coping Power's focus on organizational and study skills and the weekly goals that are often academically focused (e.g., completing homework) have facilitated improvement in children's abilities to engage in more sustained and diligent study behaviors in the classroom and to purposefully attend to and study academic assignments.

Social Outcomes

The contextual social-cognitive model underlying Coping Power and Anger Coping (Lochman & Wells, 2002a) is based in part on Crick and Dodge's (1994) social information processing (SIP) model. Variables associated with children's social competency include their SIP skills, social skills, level of peer acceptance, and ability to avoid involvement with deviant peers. Children's poor peer relations and their involvement with deviant peers lead aggressive elementary school children to initiate more serious antisocial behavior, such as substance use, in middle school (Fite, Colder, Lochman, & Wells, 2007, 2008).

Pre–post analyses in the previously noted dissemination study of Anger Coping indicated that Anger Coping had effects on the relevant SIP mediating variables that should have been affected by the program (Larson & Lochman, 2002). Anger Coping children displayed significant improvements in their ability to generate competent solutions to social problems. By post-intervention, they evidenced a higher rate of verbal assertion, compromise, and bargaining strategies. They also showed a reduction in their rate of irrelevant problem solutions, indicating that they had improved their cause–effect reasoning in social situations. This improvement in generating positive problem solutions and the reduction in irrelevant problem solutions parallels problem-solving outcomes found in randomized controlled trials of Coping Power with aggressive deaf children (Lochman et al., 2001) and in the earlier three-year follow-up study of Anger Coping outcomes (Lochman, 1992). These findings indicate that the problem-solving training in Anger Coping and Coping Power appears to be producing an anticipated effect.

Besides program effects on the generation of competent problem solutions (Step 4 in the SIP model), Coping Power has assisted aggressive children in reducing their expectation that aggression will lead to positive outcomes (Step 5 in the SIP model). In a randomized, controlled effectiveness trial, Coping Power children tended reduce their expectations that aggression can be successfully used to reduce aversive reactions from others, in comparison to control children (Lochman & Wells, 2002b). Similarly, in the dissemination trial of Coping Power, intensively trained counselors produced significant improvements in children's expectations about the negative consequences of aggression (relative to comparison children's increases in these maladaptive expectations; Lochman, Boxmeyer, et al., 2009). Thus, the program's focus on children's awareness of consequences of their behavior in the social problem-solving sessions, in the weekly behavioral goal-setting, in the structured feedback and consequences provided for children's adherence to group rules during sessions, and in the parent training sessions on consistent parenting practices have assisted children to better anticipate consequences for their behavior, and thereby to better regulate their socially problematic behaviors.

Improvements in SIP skills would be expected to lead to intervention-produced changes in children's school social behaviors. Children in the Anger Coping dissemination study demonstrated significant improvements in self- and teacher-reported social competence (Larson & Lochman, 2002). Teachers rated the children as being better able to calm down when upset, to recognize their feelings, to handle conflict in more adaptive ways, and to cooperate and interact in fair ways with peers. The children themselves, on a measure of perceived competence, perceived that they had become more competent in their interactions with peers and more accepted by their peers. Similar effects have been noted in randomized control trials of Coping Power providing intensive training to staff. Relative to children in control groups, children receiving Anger Coping (Lochman, Lampron, Gemmer, Harris, & Wyckoff, 1989) and Coping Power (Lochman & Wells,

2002b) have perceived that they are better accepted by their classmates by the end of intervention. Coping Power children have also been rated by their teachers as having more social skills (Lochman & Wells, 2002b) and as having more leadership and positive peer relations (Lochman, Boxmeyer et al., 2009) at the end of intervention in comparison to control children.

A key assumption of this form of preventive intervention is that if the intervention can target key processes within the contextual social cognitive model that serve as the basis for the program, then the program should be able to affect key problem behavior outcomes. Several of the key social-cognitive processes targeted by Coping Power are (1) children's hostile attribution biases (Step 2 in the SIP model), which lead children to incorrectly infer that other children and adults intentionally provoke and antagonize them, and (2) children's outcome expectations for aggression (Step 5 in the SIP model), which lead children to expect that they will be likely to gain consequences that they perceive as rewarding when they engage in aggressive behaviors with others. Path analyses using the sample from the Lochman and Wells (2004) efficacy study indicate that the intervention effects were at least partly mediated by changes in boys' social-cognitive processes, schemas, and parenting processes (Lochman & Wells, 2002a). Changes in social-cognitive appraisal processes, involving boys' hostile attributions and resulting anger, and decision-making processes, involving reductions in the boys' expectations that aggressive behavior would lead to good outcomes for them, reduced the risk for antisocial behavior. In addition to these mediational effects for children's SIP processes, changes in boys' schemas involving their beliefs about their degree of internal control over successful outcomes and the complexity of their internal representations of others and changes in their perceptions of the consistency of their parents' discipline efforts were found to contribute to the mediation of reductions in delinquency, substance use, and school behavioral problems. Consistent with the assumptions of the contextual social-cognitive model, boys' engagement in serious problem behavior in the year following their involvement in Coping Power was affected in part by the improvements in the ways that they perceived and processed their social world and in their expectations of more consistent and predictable responses from their parents.

In the absence of intervention, aggressive children who have excessive, pervasive attributions about others' hostile intentions are likely to emit more toxic social behaviors. In addition, increases in hostile attributions, following perceived provocations, have been found to be directly linked to increases in physiological arousal (Williams, Lochman, Phillips, & Barry, 2003). Anger and associated arousal can flood the information-processing abilities of individuals, leading children to be progressively less able to competently perceive others' intentions and to think about adaptive responses to difficult social problems. An angry, aroused child is also more likely to use automatic information processing; to then impulsively and quickly re-trieve salient, often incompetent responses from memory (Rabiner, Len-hart, & Lochman, 1990); and to respond with reactive aggression (Dodge, Lochman, Harnish, Bates, & Pettit, 1997). In contrast, as children, even at-risk children, begin to have more tolerant and accurate perceptions of others' intentions during social encounters, they are likely to respond less angrily to others, emit more prosocial behaviors, and have increased pos-sibilities for developing satisfying social relationships over time.

Children who are less aroused are able to use more deliberate informa-tion processing, to more carefully review the available solutions in their memory, and to select more competent solutions to enact. Progressive posi-tive changes in attributions and anger during social encounters may con-tribute, over time, to changes in youths' social affiliation patterns and in their beliefs and expectations, including: (1) turning to less deviant peer groups, thus reducing the risk for delinquency and substance use; (2) as youth begin to react less impulsively, focusing more on outcomes requiring long-term goals, such as successful attainment of academic goals, and en-gaging in productive behaviors at school to attain these goals; (3) as youth become less impulsively aggressive, beginning to expect that aggressive strategies are not as likely to lead to satisfying outcomes for them as will oth-er, less antisocial, strategies; and (4) as youth become less impulsively ag-gressive, having enhanced beliefs that they have an internal locus-of-control over their ability to attain positive outcomes. It appears that Coping Power, by influencing targeted SIP active mechanisms, has influenced children's longer-term outcomes (Lochman & Wells, 2002a).

IMPLICATIONS FOR EDUCATIONAL POLICY AND FOR INTERVENTION DISSEMINATION

Attention to the Implementation Process

One of the most important implications of this line of research is that the dissemination of evidence-based preventive interventions into regular school and agency settings is not as straightforward as it is typically attempt-ed. Successful translation of promising programs into community settings is not likely to occur with the often-used simple approach of just providing a one-day workshop to the counselors or clinicians. Instead, the current find-ings suggest that careful attention must be provided to the intensity of the training that is required and to the characteristics of the counselors and the settings in which the intervention will be provided.

In our research, we have found that a complex cognitive-behavioral program requires more training than just an initial workshop, and even than a workshop plus monthly follow-up consultation. Counselors who received this level of training were not able to produce reliable and consistent reductions in the externalizing behavior of aggressive children in their schools (Lochman, Boxmeyer et al., 2009). Instead, counselors needed to have these training elements plus ongoing, readily available technical assistance and feedback about the quality of the implementation of their program drawn from audiotaped sessions. The coders for implementation quality rated counselor variables such as their ability to capitalize on teaching moments, to give proper consequences to behavior in the session, to provide relevant examples of concepts, and to interact with the children in positive ways. We speculate that counselors who know that they will receive feedback about their audiotaped sessions are more likely to carefully structure their sessions and to monitor students' behavior and their own behavior more closely. The degree of intensity of training is likely to vary depending on the prior experience of the trainees. For counselors with limited experience with structured, manualized, evidence-based interventions, as was the case for our field trial study, a high level of intensity of training will likely be required. If the trainees have already received extensive training in cognitive-behavioral theories and techniques, then somewhat less intensive training may be necessary. Similarly, if an intervention is brief and less complex, less intense training may be necessary.

Dissemination of interventions must also account for individual differences in counselors and settings that will be involved. In our research, we have found that counselors who are more conscientious and agreeable are more likely to implement an intervention with a high level of quality (Lochman, Powell, Boxmeyer, Qu, Wells, & Windle, 2009). Counselors who are adept at self-regulation are likely to model that coping style to students and to handle frustrations in their clinical work with greater aplomb and equanimity. In addition, the organizational climate of the school or clinic may serve as a protective factor or exacerbate the risks to implementation quality associated with certain personality features of counselors. Counselors who are highly cynical about organizational change, and who tend to be skeptical that innovations will make a difference, are more likely to implement an evidence-based intervention with high quality if they are in schools that validate staff as professionals, reinforce professional autonomy, and permit less hierarchical decision-making. An effective organizational climate is a protective factor in the implementation process.

Attention to Possible Iatrogenic Effects of Group Interventions

Before widespread dissemination of interventions occur, it is critical to understand who the interventions successfully influence and whether there are intervention characteristics that can produce iatrogenic effects or subgroups of youth who are vulnerable to iatrogenic effects of a program (Matthys & Lochman, 2010). Within the youth violence prevention field, a critical concern that has arisen is the potential iatrogenic effect due to working with antisocial children in groups where their behavior problems may escalate. Research results are sufficiently alarming to lead some researchers to recommend that practitioners must be cautious in how they provide group-based interventions (Dishion, McCord, & Poulin, 1999).

In one of the seminal articles on this form of iatrogenic effects, youth who had received intervention sessions in seventh grade had higher rates of tobacco use and of teacher-rated delinquent behaviors than did the control children after one year, and these iatrogenic effects were evident even if the parents had also received intervention in the combined condition. At a three-year follow-up, the teen intervention conditions continued to have more tobacco use and delinquency (Poulin, Dishion, & Burraston, 2001), partially due to deviancy training among group members.

A recent meta-analysis (Weiss, Caron, Ball, Tapp, Johnson & Weisz, 2005) concluded that the overall risk for iatrogenic effects is sometimes overstated (group effect size of .79, individual effect size of .68), but that there are developmental periods of sensitivity to peer deviancy. Groups are at risk for having worse effects as children approach adolescence, consistent with prior concerns that group iatrogenic effects may be most noticeable as children move into early adolescence. This meta-analysis suggests that iatrogenic effects of group interventions are not universal effects and that it is critically important to further research the potential iatrogenic effects of group interventions at key developmental points. In addition to developmental issues, the therapists' behaviors may play a key role in whether deviancy training emerges in cognitive-behavioral groups. Carefully managed and supervised groups may avoid iatrogenic effects (Dishion & Dodge, 2006). The leaders' abilities to manage and structure peer interactions can assist in redirecting or stopping peers' reinforcement of deviant behaviors.

Although we have not found overall iatrogenic effects for group-delivered Coping Power, a group delivery format may limit the degree of positive gains. We are currently engaged in a randomized controlled trial comparing group versus individual administration of the Coping Power child component to address this question. This study will also examine the role of leader behaviors in minimizing deviancy training effects in group-based intervention with aggressive youth. Preliminary analyses of a prior small-scale randomized controlled trial indicated that intervention formats may have differential effects on different types of outcomes, as individual administration of Coping Power appeared to have stronger post-intervention effects on parent-rated aggression, while group administration of Coping Power appeared to yield greater improvements in social-cognitive and self-regulation outcomes, including increased value placed on affiliation social goals over dominance and revenge social goals. Clearly, because of the ubiquity of group delivery of interventions, extensive research will be necessary on factors contributing to negative effects of groups and on mechanisms for moderating these negative effects.

Attention to Intervening at Key Developmental Transitions

The programmatic research on Anger Coping and Coping Power suggests that cognitive behavioral interventions can have significant and lasting effects on children's delinquency, substance use, and school aggression. For these programs, timing the intervention just before entry into middle school may have been important to the program's utility. At this time, parents and children are concerned about the transition to a new school setting and the associated risks. During this period, a set of risk factors appear to co-occur and to increase the rate of youths' antisocial behavior. Risk factors include a looser and more impersonal school context in middle school, youths' movement into puberty, and greater opportunity to interact with deviant peers. Intervening with children just before exposure to these risks may lead to better coping. Also, screening children for targeted prevention programs near the end of elementary school has the advantage of occurring when children with childhood-limited conduct problems are desisting from their behavior problems (Matthys & Lochman, 2010), potentially increasing the precision of screening. Prevention programs can be successfully provided at times of other developmental transitions, such as entry into preschool, elementary school, and high school.

REFERENCES

Arnold, D. H. (1997). Co-occurrence of externalizing behavior problems and emergent academic difficulties in young high-risk boys: A preliminary evaluation of patterns and mechanisms. *Journal of Applied Developmental Psychology, 18*(3), 317–330.

Balkin, J. (1987). Psychological correlates of success in college. *Educational and Psychological Measurement, 47*(3), 795–798.

Barthelemy, J. J., & Lounsbury, J. W. (2009). The relationship between aggression and the Big Five personality factors in predicting academic success. *Journal of Human Behavior in the Social Environment, 19*(2), 159–170.

Bennett, K. J., Brown, K. S., Boyle, M., Racine, Y., & Offord, D. (2003). Does low reading achievement at school entry cause conduct problems? *Social Science and Medicine, 56,* 2443–2448.

Chen, X., Huang, X., Chang, L., Wang, L., & Li, D. (2010). Aggression, social competence, and academic achievement in Chinese children: A 5-year longitudinal study. *Development and Psychopathology, 22*(3), 583–592.

Chen, X., Rubin, K. H., & Li, D. (1997). Relation between academic achievement and social adjustment: Evidence from Chinese children. *Developmental Psychology, 33*(3), 518–525.

Coie, J. D. (1996). Prevention of violence and antisocial behavior. In R. Dev. Peters & R. J. McMahon (Eds.), *Preventing childhood disorders, substance abuse, and delinquency* (pp. 1–18). Thousand Oaks, CA: Sage.

Coie, J. D., Lochman, J. E., Terry, R., & Hyman, C. (1992). Predicting early adolescent disorder from childhood aggression and peer rejection. *Journal of Consulting and Clinical Psychology, 60*(5), 783–792.

Cornwall, A., & Bawden, H. N. (1992). Reading disabilities and aggression: A critical review. *Journal of Learning Disabilities, 25*(5), 281–288.

Cowell, K., Horstmann, S., Linebarger, J., Meaker, P., & Aligne, C. A. (2008). Pediatrics in the community a "vaccine" against violence: Coping Power. *Pediatrics in Review, 29,* 362–363.

Crick, N. R., & Dodge, K. A. (1994). A review and reformulation of social information-processing mechanisms in children's social adjustment. *Psychological Bulletin, 115,* 74–101.

Dishion, T. J., & Andrews, D. W. (1995). Preventing escalation in problem behaviors with high-risk young adolescents: Immediate and 1 year outcomes. *Journal of Consulting and Clinical Psychology, 63,* 538–548.

Dishion, T. J., & Dodge, K. A. (2006). Deviant peer contagion in interventions and programs: An ecological framework for understanding influence mechanisms. In K. A. Dodge, T. J. Dishion, & J. E. Lansford (Eds.), *Deviant peer influences in programs for youth* (pp. 14–43). New York, NY: Guilford.

Dishion, T.J., McCord, J., & Poulin, F. (1999). When interventions harm: Peer groups and problem behavior. *American Psychologist, 54,* 755–764.

Dodge, K. A., Lochman, J. E., Harnish, J. D., Bates, J. E., & Pettit, G. S. (1997). Reactive and proactive aggression in school children and psychiatrically impaired chronically assaultive youth. *Journal of Abnormal Psychology, 106,* 37–51.

Duncan, G. J., Dowsett, C. J., Claessens, A., Magnuson, K., Huston, A. C., Klebanov, P., et al. (2007). School readiness and later achievement. *Developmental Psychology, 43*(6), 1428–1446.

Farmer, T.W., Estell, D. B., Hall, C. M., Pearl, R., Van Acker, R., & Rodkin, P. C. (2008). Interpersonal competence configurations, behavior problems, and social adjustment in preadolescence. *Journal of Emotional and Behavioral Disorders, 16,* 195–212.

Farrington, D. P. (1989). Early predictors of adolescent aggression and adult violence. *Violence and Victims, 4*(2), 79–100.

Fite, P.J., Colder, C.R., Lochman, J.E., & Wells, K.C. (2007). Pathways from proactive and reactive aggression to substance use. *Psychology of Addictive Behaviors, 21,* 355–364.

Fite, P.J., Colder, C.R., Lochman, J.E., & Wells, K.C. (2008). The relation between childhood proactive and reactive aggression and substance use initiation. *Journal of Abnormal Child Psychology, 36,* 261–271.

French, D. C., & Conrad, J. (2001). School dropout as predicted by peer rejection and antisocial behavior. *Journal of Research on Adolescence, 11,* 225–244.

Herrenkohl, T. I., Catalano, R. F., Hemphill, S. A., & Toumbourou, J. W. (2009). Longitudinal examination of physical and relational aggression as precursors to later problem behaviors in adolescents. *Violence and Victims, 24,* 3–19.

Jorm, A., Share, D. L., Matthews, R., & Maclean, R. (1986). Behaviour problems in specific reading retarded and general reading backward children: A longitudinal study. *Journal of Child Psychology and Psychiatry, 27*(1), 33–43.

Krueger, R. F., Caspi, A., Moffitt, T. E., White, J., & Stouthamer-Loeber, M. (1996). Delay of gratification, psychopathology, and personality: Is low self-control specific to externalizing problems? *Journal of Personality, 64,* 107–129

Ladd, G. W., Kochenderfer, B. J., & Coleman, C. C. (1997). Classroom peer acceptance, friendship, and victimization: Distinct relational systems that contribute uniquely to children's school adjustment? *Child Development, 68*(6), 1181–1197.

Larson, J., & Lochman, J. E. (2002). *Helping school children cope with anger: A cognitive-behavioral intervention.* New York, NY: Guilford.

Lochman, J. E. (1992). Cognitive-behavioral interventions with aggressive boys: Three-year follow-up and preventive effects. *Journal of Consulting and Clinical Psychology, 60,* 426–432.

Lochman, J. E., Boxmeyer, C. L., Powell, N. P., Qu, L., Wells, K. C., & Windle, M. (2009). Dissemination of the Coping Power program: Importance of intensity of counselor training. *Journal of Consulting and Clinical Psychology, 77,* 397–409.

Lochman, J. E., Boxmeyer, C. L., Powell, N. P., Roth, D., & Windle, M. (2006). Masked intervention effects: Analytic methods for addressing low dosage of intervention. *New Directions for Evaluation, 110,* 19–32.

Lochman, J. E., Burch, P. P., Curry, J. F., & Lampron, L. B. (1984). Treatment and generalization effects of cognitive-behavioral and goal setting interventions with aggressive boys. *Journal of Consulting and Clinical Psychology, 52,* 915–916.

Lochman, J. E., Coie, J. D., Underwood, M., & Terry, R. (1993). Effectiveness of a social relations intervention program for aggressive and nonaggressive rejected children. *Journal of Consulting and Clinical Psychology, 61,* 1053–1058.

Lochman, J.E., FitzGerald, D.P., Gage, S.M., Kannaly, M.K., Whidby, J.M., Barry, T.D., et al. (2001). Effects of social-cognitive intervention for aggressive deaf children: The Coping Power Program. *Journal of the American Deafness and Rehabilitation Association, 35,* 39–61.

Lochman, J. E., Lampron, L. B., Gemmer, T. C., Harris, S. R., & Wyckoff, G. M. (1989). Teacher consultation and cognitive behavioral interventions with aggressive boys. *Psychology in the Schools, 26,* 179–188.

Lochman, J. E., Nelson, W. M. III & Sims, J. P. (1981). A cognitive behavioral program for use with aggressive children. *Journal of Clinical Child Psychology, 10,* 146–148.

Lochman, J. E., Powell, N. P., Boxmeyer, C. L., Qu, L., Wells, K. C., & Windle, M. (2009). Implementation of a school-based prevention program: Effects of counselor and school characteristics. *Professional Psychology: Research & Practice, 40,* 476–482.

Lochman, J. E., & Wells, K. C. (2002a). Contextual social-cognitive mediators and child outcome: A test of the theoretical model in the Coping Power Program. *Development and Psychopathology, 14,* 971–993.

Lochman, J.E., & Wells, K.C. (2002b). The Coping Power Program at the middle school transition: Universal and indicated prevention effects. *Psychology of Addictive Behaviors, 16,* S40–S54.

Lochman, J. E., & Wells, K. C. (2003). Effectiveness study of Coping Power and classroom intervention with aggressive children: Outcomes at a one-year follow-up. *Behavior Therapy, 34,* 493–515.

Lochman, J. E., & Wells, K. C. (2004). The Coping Power program for preadolescent aggressive boys and their parents: Outcome effects at the one-year follow-up. *Journal of Consulting   and Clinical Psychology, 72,* 571–578.

Lochman, J.E., Wells, K.C., & Lenhart, L.A. (2008). *Coping Power child group program: Facilitator guide.* New York, NY: Oxford.

Loeber, R. (1990). Development and risk factors of juvenile antisocial behavior and delinquency. *Clinical Psychology Review, 10,* 1–42.

Lounsbury, J. W., Sundstrom, E., Gibson, L. W., & Loveland, J. M. (2003). Broad versus narrow personality traits in predicting academic performance of adolescents. *Learning and Individual Differences, 14,* 65–75.

Loveland, J. M., Lounsbury, J. W., Welsh, D., & Buboltz, W. C. (2007). The validity of physical aggression in predicting adolescent academic performance. *British Journal of Educational Psychology, 77*(1), 167–176.

Masten, A. S., Roisman, G. I., Long, J. D., Burt, K. B., Obradović, J., Riley, J. R., et al. (2005). Developmental cascades: Linking academic achievement and externalizing and internalizing symptoms over 20 years. *Developmental Psychology, 41*(5), 733–746.

Matthys, W., & Lochman, J.E. (2010). *Oppositional defiant disorder and conduct disorder in childhood.* Oxford, England: Wiley-Blackwell.

McIntosh, K., Flannery, K. B., Sugai, G., Braun, D., & Cochrane, K. L. (2008). Relationships between academics and problem behavior in the transition from middle school to high school. *Journal of Positive Behavior Interventions, 10,* 243–255.

McIntosh, K., Horner, R. H., Chard, D. J., Boland, J. B., & Good, R. H. (2006). The use of reading and behavior screening measures to predict nonresponse to school-wide positive behavior support: A longitudinal analysis. *School Psychology Review, 35*(2), 275–291.

Miles, S. B., & Stipek, D. (2006). Contemporaneous and longitudinal associations between social behavior and literacy achievement in a sample of low-income elementary school children. *Child Development, 77*(1), 103–117.

O'Farrell, S. L., Morrison, G. M., & Furlong, M. J. (2006). School engagement. In G. G. Bear & K. M. Minke (Eds.), *Children's needs III* (pp. 45–58). Bethesda, MD: National Association of School Psychologists.

Pagani, L. S., Fitzpatrick, C., Archambault, I., & Janosz, M. (2010). School readiness and later achievement: A French Canadian replication and extension. *Developmental Psychology, 46*(5), 984–994.

Parker, J. G., & Asher, S. R. (1987). Peer relations and later personal adjustment: Are low accepted children "at risk"? *Psychological Bulletin, 102,* 357–389.

Pellegrini, A. D., Bartini, M., & Brooks, F. (1999). School bullies, victims, and aggressive victims: Factors relating to group affiliation and victimization in early adolescence. *Journal of Educational Psychology, 91*(2), 216–224.

Peterson, M. A., Hamilton, E. B., & Russell, A. D. (2009). Starting well: Evidenced-based treatment facilitates the middle school transition. *Journal of Applied School Psychology, 25*(2), 183–196.

Poulin, F., Dishion, T. J., & Burraston, B. (2001). 3-year iatrogenic effects associated with aggregating high-risk adolescents in cognitive-behavioral interventions. *Applied Developmental Science, 5,* 214–224.

Rabiner, D. L., Lenhart, L., & Lochman, J. E. (1990). Automatic vs. reflective social problem solving in relation to children's sociometric status. *Developmental Psychology, 26,* 1010–1026.

Risi, S., Gerhardstein, R., & Kistner, J. (2003). Children's classroom peer relationships and subsequent educational outcomes. *Journal of Clinical Child and Adolescent Psychology, 32*(3), 351–361.

Schwartz, D., Gorman, A. H., Nakamoto, J., & McKay, T. (2006). Popularity, social acceptance, and aggression in adolescent peer groups: Links with academic performance and school attendance. *Developmental Psychology, 42*(6), 1116–1127.

Stipek, D., & Miles, S. (2008). Effects of aggression on achievement: Does conflict with the teacher make it worse? *Child Development, 79*(6), 1721–1735.

van de Wiel, N. M. H., Matthys, W., Cohen-Kettenis, P. T., Maassen, G. H., Lochman, J. E., & van Engeland, H. (2007). The effectiveness of an experimental treatment when compared with care as usual depends on the type of care as usual. *Behavior Modification, 31,* 298–312.

van de Wiel, N. M. H., Matthys, W., Cohen-Kettenis, P. T., & van Engeland, H. (2003). Application of the Utrecht Coping Power Program and care as usual to children with disruptive behavior disorders: A comparative study of cost and course of treatment. *Behavior Therapy, 34,* 421–436.

Weiss, B., Caron, A., Ball, S., Tapp, J., Johnson, M., & Weisz, J. R. (2005). Iatrogenic effects of group treatment for antisocial youths. *Journal of Consulting and Clinical Psychology, 73,* 1036–1044.

Wells, K.C., Lochman, J.E., & Lenhart, L.A. (2008). *Coping Power parent group program: Facilitator guide.* New York, NY: Oxford.

Wentzel, K. R. (1993). Does being good make the grade? Social behavior and academic competence in middle school. *Journal of Educational Psychology, 5,* 357–364.

Williams, S. C., Lochman, J. E., Phillips, N. C., & Barry, T. D. (2003). Aggressive and nonaggressive boys' physiological and cognitive processes in response to peer provocations. *Journal of Clinical Child & Adolescent Psychology, 32,* 568–576.

Zonnevylle-Bender, M. J. S., Matthys, W., van de Wiel, N. M. H., & Lochman, J. (2007). Preventive effects of treatment of DBD in middle childhood on substance use and delinquent behavior. *Journal of the American Academy of Child and Adolescent Psychiatry, 46,* 33–39.

CHAPTER 11

KiVa ANTI-BULLYING PROGRAM

Implications for School Adjustment

Christina Salmivalli
University of Turku, Finland
University of Stavanger, Norway
Edith Cowan University, Western Australia

Claire F. Garandeau
University of Turku, Finland

René Veenstra
University of Groningen, the Netherlands
University of Turku, Finland

Bullying is a common problem in schools worldwide (Smith, Morita, Junger-Tas, Olweus, Catalano, & Slee, 1999). It is usually defined as repeated aggressive behavior against a victim who cannot readily defend him- or herself (Olweus, 1999). The prevalence of bullied children varies considerably across countries (from 5% in Sweden to over 30% in Lithuania), being on

Peer Relationships and Adjustment at School, pages 279–307
Copyright © 2012 by Information Age Publishing
All rights of reproduction in any form reserved.

average 11% across the 35 countries involved in WHO's Health Behavior in School-aged Children survey (Craig & Harel, 2004). Bullies represent another 11% of school-aged children. Children who report both bullying others and being bullied by others (i.e., bully-victims) were not identified in the HBSC study above, but other research has shown that approximately 2 to 6 % of schoolchildren can be classified as bully-victims (Haynie et al., 2001; Nansel, Overpeck, Pilla, R. Ruan, Simon-Morton, & Scheidt, 2001; Solberg, Olweus, & Endresen, 2007).

The need for effective antibullying interventions is motivated first of all by the multitude of psychosocial problems documented among victimized children and youth. Victims of bullying tend to experience insecurity, depression, and anxiety, and they are often highly rejected by their classmates (Card, 2003; Card & Hodges, 2008; Hawker & Boulton, 2000). For a number of victims, their experiences continue to affect their lives later on in adulthood (Isaacs, Hodges, & Salmivalli, 2008; Sourander et al., 2007).

Probably the most tragic incidents related to victimization are school shootings, which have during the past few years taken place in several countries, including Finland. There is evidence that most school shooters have experienced marginalization and victimization by their peers, these experiences often being accompanied by interest in firearms, ideological factors, or mental health problems (Leary, Kowalski, Smith, & Phillips, 2003). Even apart from the most serious tragedies, victimization is clearly a threat to the well-being of children and youth who are directly involved, and by reducing victimization, a lot of suffering among vulnerable children and adolescents can be avoided.

In the present chapter, we focus on one possible negative consequence of peer victimization, which is lowered academic functioning, and on the possibility that antibullying programs might, as their "side-effect," improve students' school liking, academic motivation, and actual performance. We first discuss the effectiveness of antibullying programs in general, review evidence concerning the association between victimization and school adjustment, and provide an overview of the KiVa antibullying program. Finally, we provide empirical findings about the impact of KiVa on the school adjustment of students in schools implementing the program and discuss the findings in the broader context of antibullying intervention research.

ANTIBULLYING PROGRAMS AND SCHOOL ADJUSTMENT

Effectiveness of School-Based Programs to Reduce Bullying

School-based programs to prevent and tackle bullying have been developed and evaluated in many countries across the world (Smith, Pepler, & Rigby, 2004), and several meta-analyses on the effectiveness of such programs have been published during the past decade (Baldry & Farrington, 2007; Ferguson, San Miguel, Kilburn, & Sanchez, 2007; Merrell, Gueldner, Ross, & Isava, 2008; Smith, Schneider, Smith, & Ananiadou, 2004; Ttofi & Farrington, 2010; Ttofi, Farrington, & Baldry, 2008; Vreeman & Carroll, 2007). Together, these meta-analyses reveal that the effects are overall modest in size and show great variability, some of them being negative and thus indicating undesirable outcomes (increases in bullying and/or victimization). In the most recent meta-analysis in the area, Ttofi and Farrington (2010) concluded, however, that *school-based antibullying programs are effective*. They reported average reductions of 17–23% and 17–20% for bullying others and being bullied, respectively. In other words, after the implementation of an antibullying program, there were on average 17–23% fewer bullies and 17–20% fewer victims in intervention schools than in schools in the control condition. The authors pointed out that even effect sizes that are considered small from a statistical point of view correspond to a substantial amount of bullying and victimization prevented and thus to huge amounts of suffering among children and youth avoided. Antibullying programs are clearly worth investing in and developing further.

Much further work is needed in the area of bullying intervention evaluations. Although some programs work better than others, it is not well understood why that is the case. Thus, the challenges involve the investigation of both mediators and moderators, in addition to main effects of antibullying programs. The important questions yet to be answered are how the programs produce their effects and on which children, but also what kind of classrooms and schools benefit most from the interventions. Another related issue is the quality of implementation and its association with the effects obtained. We argue that in addition to these relatively often discussed issues, looking at the "side effects" of intervention programs is important, for both theoretical and practical reasons that will be discussed later on in this chapter.

"Side Effects" of Antibullying Programs

As most intervention evaluations have limited their outcome variables to bullying and victimization, possible "side effects" of interventions have received less attention. We use the term *side effects* to refer to positive outcomes of antibullying interventions that go beyond the initially intended or desired results of the program. For instance, Olweus (1991) reported that the Olweus Bullying Prevention Program reduced antisocial behavior (e.g., vandalism, theft, and truancy) and increased school satisfaction. Fekkes, Pijpers, and Verloove-Vanhorick (2006) found a trend for a decrease in reported depression in schools implementing an antibullying program. Williford and colleagues (Williford, Boulton, Noland, Little, Kärnä, & Salmivalli, 2012) found reductions in anxiety, depression, and negative peer perceptions in schools implementing the KiVa anti-bullying program. There are several possible explanations for such effects (see Figure 11.1).

First, and most obviously, the effects might be mediated by decreases in experienced victimization. If victimization leads to dissatisfaction and depression, decreases in victimization experiences should lead to better adjustment over time (indirect path "a" in Figure 11.1). The study by Williford and colleagues (2012) found evidence for such effects, showing that decreases in victimization in schools implementing the KiVa program were associated with decreases in depression and anxiety, as well as more positive perceptions of peers in general.

Second, positive side effects might be mediated through decreases in bullying others (indirect path "b" in Figure 11.1). If bullies understand that their practices are no more tolerated and must stop, this might lead to overall reductions in negative behaviors and better adjustment. The reductions in antisocial behavior in general reported by Olweus (1991) might be examples of such effects, although this was not tested in his study.

Third, the effects might be mediated by reductions in witnessed bullying/victimization (indirect path "c" in Figure 11.1). Simply witnessing peers being harassed has been linked to heightened daily anxiety and school dislike (Nishina & Juvonen, 2005) as well as elevated levels of mental health problems and substance use (Rivers, Poteat, Noret, & Ashurst, 2009). Moreover, Huitsing, Veenstra, Sainio, and Salmivalli (2010) found that in addition to classroom average level of victimization, the classroom specificity of victims (referring to a situation in which a few children are constantly targeted by several bullies) was related to higher average levels of depression and lower levels of self-esteem reported by all children in the classroom. Together, these findings suggest that children witnessing victimization, especially when it is

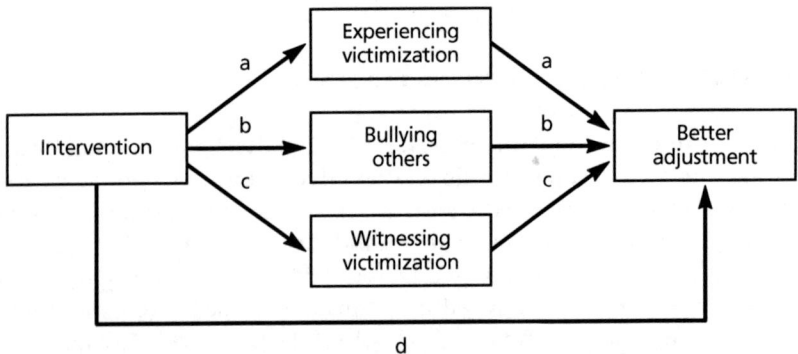

Figure 11.1 Possible pathways of the "side-effects" of antibullying programs.

selectively targeted at a few children in a classroom, are more maladjusted than their age-mates not witnessing such negative interactions within the peer group. Such effects can be tested by asking students directly about the victimization they have witnessed before and after the implementation of a program, and examining the relation between this observed victimization (while controlling for the victimization targeted at students themselves) and changes in adjustment. Other approaches are also plausible. Intervention effects mediated by witnessed victimization might be indicated by elevated levels of well-being and better adjustment at the classroom level in those classrooms where victimization has been reduced. In other words, children in classrooms where the level of bullying or victimization decreases over time would become better adjusted—even children who were not victimized themselves.

Fourth, the side-effects of an antibullying program might be completely independent of changes in bullying or victimization. A program might involve elements (such as social skills training, empathy training, group work) that result in more positive interactions among children and youth in general, regardless of the presence of bullying practices. It might thus be possible for an antibullying program to enhance school well-being while not even being effective in—or in addition to—reducing victimization. In Figure 11.1, path "d" displays such a direct effect.

One potential side effect of antibullying programs that has received little attention—perhaps none—in program evaluations is *improvement in school adjustment.* Positive impacts on school adjustment, including not only school well-being but also academic motivation and achievement, have rarely been included in the evaluations of such programs. Documenting such effects would be highly important for several reasons. First, they may help justify the use of the programs, as school personnel are sometimes more concerned about students' academic performance than their interpersonal relationships. Second, showing that decreases in victimization are related to better academic adjustment over time would provide the most stringent test of causal effects between victimization and school-related outcomes. Finally, potential influences of antibullying programs on the academic adjustment of the wider peer community can shed light on the impact of victimization on peers who are not victimized themselves (e.g., classroom-level benefits that are related to decreases in victimization would suggest that academic adjustment can be negatively affected among children who are merely witnessing victimization).

Victimization and School Adjustment

School adjustment is a broad construct reflecting students' overall resources for school work. It includes school satisfaction, engagement, and motivation, as well as learning and academic achievement (Wentzel, 2009). Victimization is an obvious threat to school adjustment, as it can be assumed to reduce victimized students' liking of (and presence at) school as well as their motivation and achievement. Although the effects of systematic victimization on school adjustment and especially academic competence have rarely been studied, a plethora of research indicates that the quality of peer relations, especially emotional support (or lack of it) from peers, has significant consequences for school motivation, engagement, and achievement (for a review, see Wentzel, 2009, pp. 536–538).

To date, most studies investigating the link between victimization and academic achievement have been concurrent. In their recent meta-analysis, Nakamoto and Schwartz (2010) included 33 studies from Asia, Europe, and North America. The negative association between peer victimization and academic achievement was statistically significant (average effect size = –.12 with 95% confidence interval ranging from –.15 to –.09) but not very strong. Three things should be taken into consideration, however. First, academic achievement is only one aspect of school adjustment. Students may enjoy going to school, feel well-adjusted in the school environment, and be motivated to learn without being high-achievers. Second, an examination of concurrent associations between measures of victimization and measures of academic functioning reveals only a little about the nature of the link between the two phenomena. Importantly, such correlations do not provide information on whether victimization at one point is related to higher academic difficulties later in time, without the two being strongly correlated concurrently. Thus, they do not shed light on the direction of effects—does victimization lead to difficulties in school adjustment or the other way around? Third, there is a possibility that students with very high as well as those with very low academic achievement are at risk for victimization, which might make the average effects vanish.

Longitudinal studies on the victimization–school adjustment link suggest that peer victimization has an impact on various aspects of children's school adjustment. Nansel, Haynie, and Simons-Morton (2003) studied the relationship between victimization in the first year of middle school and later school adjustment, including doing well on schoolwork, following rules, doing homework, and getting along with classmates. They found that children classified as victims during grade six reported poorer school adjustment in the spring of that same year and in the spring of the seventh grade compared to children who were not involved in bullying, even after controlling for their baseline scores. Surveying a sample of kindergartners in the fall and the spring of the school year, Kochenderfer and Ladd (1996) found not only that being victimized was associated with a dislike of and a desire to avoid school, but also that early victimization predicted increases in school avoidance. Children's feelings about their school environment grew worse only after they had been exposed to maltreatment from their peers. Similarly, a long-term longitudinal investigation of two forms of chronic peer maltreatment, abuse, and exclusion showed that school avoidance behaviors were likely to increase for chronically abused children, whereas classroom disengagement was likely to increase for chronically excluded children between kindergarten and fifth grade (Buhs, Ladd, & Herald, 2006).

In addition to school avoidance and classroom participation, being subjected to peer abuse may also affect victims' ability to focus on their school work. In a two-year longitudinal study of first-, second-, and fourth-graders, it was found that prior victimization was associated with attention difficulties, among other symptoms, at time 2, after controlling for time 2 victimization and initial attention difficulties (Hanish & Guerra, 2002). Recently, it was also demonstrated that victimization was related to disrupted concentration on class work (Boulton, Trueman, & Murray, 2008) and uniquely predicted lower levels of academic competence, whereas friendships were related to school liking as well as better academic competence (Erath, Flanagan, & Bierman, 2008). Unfortunately, the cross-sectional design of these two studies did not allow inferences about causal effects.

Victimization by peers may not affect lack of concentration on schoolwork, school avoidance, or academic failure directly. The hypothesis that the role of victimization in school adjustment difficulties is due, at least partly, to its influence on internalizing problems is supported by the literature. Children who are victimized at school tend to experience increases in loneliness, social withdrawal, anxiety, and depression (Boivin, Hymel, & Bukowski, 1995; Hodges & Perry, 1999; Hanish & Guerra, 2002; Kochenderfer & Ladd, 1996). In turn, those internalizing problems may jeopardize successful school adjustment (e.g., Needham, Crosnoe, & Muller, 2004). It has been shown that psychological distress, including depressive symptoms, social anxiety, low self-worth and loneliness, mediate the association between perceived peer victimization and academic functioning, namely grades and absences (Nishina, Juvonen, & Witkow, 2005). Peer harassment at the beginning of sixth grade predicted increases in internalizing symptoms in the spring, which were associated with school functioning in the spring. Consistent with these findings, Schwartz, Gorman, Nakamoto, and Tobin (2005) demonstrated in an elementary school sample that high initial levels of victimization predicted low levels of academic functioning a year later, and these changes were explained by both initial levels of depression and increases in depression between the two waves of assessment.

The negative impact of peer harassment on children's well-being is not limited to those who are the targets of bullying behaviors (Huitsing et al., in press; Nishina & Juvonen, 2005; Rivers et al., 2009). Witnessing other children being victimized may increase one's feelings of insecurity and fear of becoming a target of bullying behaviors in the future. Fear of future victimization has actually been found to be associated with disrupted concentration on class work (Boulton et al., 2008). Furthermore, even if most children's attitudes are against bullying (Boulton, Trueman, & Flemington, 2002; Rigby & Johnson, 2006; Rigby & Slee, 1991; Whitney & Smith, 1993), their actual behaviors are not in accordance with their private sentiments. Namely, students witnessing victimization rarely publicly intervene on behalf of the victim, but instead tend to react in ways that are socially rewarding to the bully (O'Connell, Pepler, & Craig, 1999; Salmivalli, Lagerspetz, Björkqvist, Österman, & Kaukiainen, 1996; Salmivalli & Voeten, 2004). Feelings of guilt or shame induced by this dissonance might therefore undermine the academic adaptation of children witnessing high levels of bullying in their environment.

Overall, victimization in a classroom is likely to promote a climate that is damaging to the academic adjustment not only of victimized children but of all other classmates. As far as we know, no longitudinal study has been done to test the influence of victimization on children who are in classes with high levels of victimization although not necessarily targets of harassment themselves. If changes in school adjustment are related to classroom-level reductions in victimization, this would strongly suggest that merely *being in a classroom with high levels of victimization* has a negative impact on school adjustment. Changes that are independent of either individual- or classroom-level victimization, on the other hand, would suggest that the intervention program contains elements that directly influence the classroom/school climate and thus the academic adjustment of all children.

KIVA ANTI-BULLYING PROGRAM: EFFECTS ON SCHOOL ADJUSTMENT

KiVa in a Nutshell

KiVa is a new anti-bullying program developed in the University of Turku with funding from the Finnish Ministry of Education and Culture. After the evaluation period, the diffusion of KiVa to Finnish comprehensive schools started in 2009, and after the first three years, 82% of all schools in the country are currently implementing it.

The name of the program, KiVa, is an acronym of the expression *KiusaamistaVastaan*, Against Bullying, but the word *kiva* also means in Finnish *nice* or *good*. It is often used to refer to a person who is considered nice or kind. The KiVa antibullying program includes both universal actions to prevent the occurrence of bullying and indicated actions to address individual bullying cases coming to the attention of the school staff. The program has a multifaceted theoretical background (e.g., Salmivalli, Kärnä, & Poskiparta, 2010). It is based on research on participant roles in bullying that started over a decade ago (Salmivalli et al., 1996) as well as on recent studies on the social standing of aggressive children in general (e.g., Cillessen & Mayeux, 2004; Rodkin, Farmer, Pearl, & Van Acker, 2000) and bullies in particular (Juvonen, Graham, & Schuster, 2003). More specifically, the program is predicated on the idea that bystanders often contribute to the emergence and maintenance of bullying by assisting and reinforcing the bully (Salmivalli & Peets, 2009; Salmivalli, Voeten, & Poskiparta, 2011), which in turn provides bullies with the status and power that they seek (Salmivalli, 2010; Sijtsema, Veenstra, Lindenberg, & Salmivalli, 2009). It is thus assumed that a positive change in the behaviors of classmates can reduce the social rewards gained by bullies and consequently their motivation to bully.

The KiVa program has several features that, when taken together, differentiate it from other antibullying programs. First, KiVa includes a broad and encompassing array of concrete and professional materials for students, teachers, and parents. Rather than offering "guiding principles" to school personnel, it provides them with a whole range of activities to be carried out with students. Second, KiVa harnesses the powerful learning media provided by the Internet and virtual learning environments. Third, while focusing on the bystanders, or witnesses of bullying, KiVa goes beyond "emphasizing the role of bystanders," mentioned in the context of several intervention programs, and actually provides ways to enhance empathy, self-efficacy, and efforts to support the victimized peers.

In the lower-level elementary school, or primary school (grades 1–6 in the Finnish school system) the *universal actions* include a series of *student lessons* given by classroom teachers in grades 1 and 4: there are specific, age-appropriate versions for the two grade levels. During the evaluation of KiVa, the student lessons were implemented in all grade levels in the intervention schools: the first-graders' version was used in grades 1–3, whereas the fourth-graders' version was implemented in grades 4–6. In secondary school (in Finland, grades 7–9), the program involves four *themes*. The latter are targeted at seventh-graders who start in secondary school. The program manual gives recommendations regarding how much time should be devoted to working on each theme, but the schools themselves decide how they organize the school year around the themes (as a sequence of lessons, several theme days, and so on). The topics of each student lesson and theme are presented in Table 11.1.

The student lessons and themes aim at increasing children's empathy toward victimized peers, raising their awareness of the role that the group plays in maintaining bullying, raising their awareness of the various strategies that can be put into practice to support victims, and promoting their self-efficacy to do so. They involve discussions, group work, role-play exercises, and showings of short films about bullying. In the primary school ver-

TABLE 11.1   The Contents of the Student Lessons (Grades 1 and 4) and Themes (Grade 7)

Grade 1 (10 double lessons)	Grade 4 (10 double lessons)	Grade 7 (4 themes)
1. Let's get to know each other!	1. Respect is for everyone	1. Group interaction Motto: *Resist the pressure*
2. Emotions	2. In a group	
3. Our class—everyone is included!	3. Recognize bullying	2. Me and the others Motto: *Me, you, us*
4. Difference is a richness	4. Hidden forms of bullying	3. Forms of bullying Motto: *No-one deserves to be bullied*
5. No bullying in KiVa school	5. Consequences of bullying	
6. We won't join in bullying!	6. Group involvement in bullying	4. The consequences and counterforces of bullying Motto: *It's up to us!*
7. Your support is needed	7. Confronting bullying as a group	
8. I will not be bullied!	8. What to do if I get bullied?	
9. Literature lesson	9. KiVa school—let's do it together!	
10. KiVa contract	10. How are we doing?	

sions of the program, class rules based on the central topic of each lesson are successively adopted one at a time.

A unique feature of the KiVa-program is an antibullying computer game included in the primary school version of the program, with different versions for grade levels 1 and 4. The students play the game during and between the lessons described above. The game involves five levels that can be played as soon as particular lessons have been given in the classroom. Additionally, students who have access to Internet can also play the game at home in their free time. Each level of the KiVa game includes three components that have been named "I know," "I can," and "I do."

In the "I know" component, the students learn new facts about bullying but also examine what they have learned from the lessons thus far. They are asked questions about the content of the lessons in game-like tasks, and they can test themselves with respect to different characteristics (e.g., how well you can resist the group pressure; what kind of classmate you are).

In the "I can" component, the students move around in a virtual school and face different challenging situations in the school corridors, playgrounds, and lunchrooms. They make decisions regarding how to respond in these situations, what to say and what to do, and get feedback based on the choices they make. They can also have access to and thus reflect on the feelings and thoughts of other characters in the game before and after their own actions.

The third component, "I do," is designed to encourage students to make use of their knowledge and skills in real-life situations. This happens by asking them to report—at each level of the game—which learned skills they have put into practice, for instance, whether they have treated others with respect, whether they have resisted group pressure, or whether they have supported someone who was victimized. Again, the students get feedback based on their reports.

For secondary school students, there is a virtual learning environment called KiVa Street. After signing in, the students can go around in the street visiting different places. For instance, they can go to a library and find information about bullying, or they can enter a movie theater and watch short films about bullying.

The main aim of the universal actions, such as the student lessons and the computer game, is to make bystanders aware of the role they play in the bullying process, to make them show that they are against bullying, and to provide them with safe strategies to support the victim instead of encouraging the bully. Research has shown that self-efficacy is an important predictor of supporting and defending victimized classmates (Pöyhönen, Juvonen, & Salmivalli, 2010). It should be noted, however, that although the emphasis of student lessons is clearly on counteracting bullying, they contain many elements that are likely to promote the understanding of others' emotions, engagement in positive interactions, and resisting peer pressure.

The *indicated actions* of KiVa refer to the handling of acute cases of bullying. In each school, a team of three teachers (or other school personnel), along with the classroom teacher, addresses each case of bullying that has come to their attention. All cases in which bullying is suspected (for instance, when a student or a parent contacts school personnel concerning bullying, or a teacher observes interactions signaling bullying) go through a screening procedure after which it is decided whether the case is systematic bullying and should be handled by the school's KiVa team or whether it is something else, such as a quarrel/conflict between two or more students. If it fulfills the criteria of bullying, it is handled through a set of individual and small-group discussions with the victims and with the bullies, organized by the members of the KiVa team. Follow-up meetings take place in each case, typically one or two weeks after the first meetings. In addition, the classroom teacher always discusses the issue with two to four prosocial and high-status classmates of the victim, encouraging them to support the classmate who is having a difficult time.

So far, research on the effectiveness of KiVa has shown that the program reduces bullying and victimization substantially (Kärnä, Voeten, Little, Poskiparta, Kaljonen, & Salmivalli, 2011). The effects vary across grade levels, being strongest among fourth-graders and weakest among secondary school students, that is, in grades 7–9 in the Finnish school system (Kärnä et al., 2011; Kärnä, Alanen, Voeten, Little, Poskiparta, & Salmivalli, submitted). KiVa seems to impact many different forms of victimization, from physical acts to cybervictimization (Salmivalli et al., 2010). In a recent meta-analysis, Ttofi and colleagues (2008) concluded that KiVa was among the one third of programs evaluated so far that were clearly effective in reducing bullying problems in schools.

As already shown by the first evaluation study of KiVa (Kärnä et al., 2011), the program had a positive effect on fourth-to-sixth-grade students' school well-being, besides its ability to reduce bullying as well as being bullied significantly. However, such main effects do not tell anything about whose school well-being can be improved, and in which classrooms such changes are most likely to happen. In addition, the school well-being construct used by Kärnä and colleagues did not distinguish between different aspects of school adjustment; it was created by collapsing across items originally developed to assess perceived classroom and school climate, school liking, academic motivation, and self-perceived academic achievement. Even if the variables are interrelated, it seems reasonable, conceptually, to treat the two latter scales (motivation and achievement) as independent from the ones measuring school well-being more generally.

Despite its focus on bullying and constructive bystander reactions, there are many elements in KiVa that might influence peer interactions and relations more generally, thus making the school a more pleasant environment to everyone. During the student lessons, topics such as respectful communication, emotions, emotion regulation, group interaction, and group pressure are handled. Even the awareness of the school personnel being committed to preventing bullying and to intervening to stop it can be assumed to increase feelings of safety among children.

AIMS OF THE STUDY

The first aim of the study reported here was to evaluate the effects of the KiVa antibullying program on three distinct aspects of school adjustment: school well-being, academic motivation, and academic achievement. Second, we tested whether declines in victimization were associated with increases in school adjustment over time at the individual level. Given the deleterious effects of peer abuse on academic adaptation, we expected to see positive changes in the school adjustment of students whose victimization was reduced during the academic year. Third, we tested the effect of a decline in victimization on school adjustment at the classroom level. We expected that decreases in victimization at the classroom level would be associated with higher school functioning within the classroom, after controlling for individual-level effects. The presence of such an effect could be taken as an indication that merely being in a classroom where a lot of victimization is going on (i.e., witnessing victimization) is related to maladjustment. Finally, it is also possible that potential positive changes in one or more aspects of school adjustment in schools implementing KiVa are unrelated to changes in victimization. This would imply that the KiVa program contains elements that affect the school adjustment of children regardless of their influence on the levels of victimization children either experience or witness. Thus, we tested the potential direct effects (not mediated by decreases in victimization at either individual or classroom level) of intervention on school adjustment.

METHOD

Participants and Procedure

KiVa anti-bullying program has been evaluated with a randomized controlled trial involving more than 30,000 participants from over 200 schools in different parts of Finland. The data for the present study come from the first phase of the evaluation (Kärnä et al., 2011). Data collection for the evaluation of the KiVa program was conducted in two phases, the first phase (2007–2008) including students who were in Grades 3–5 at the time of the pre-test, and in Grades 4–6 (being on average 10 to 12 years of age) during the intervention year. The present study is based on this first-phase sample described in more detail below.

To recruit schools, letters describing the study were sent in the fall of 2006 to all schools giving comprehensive education in mainland Finland (at that time, 3,444 schools). The letter included information about the goals and content of KiVa and an enrollment form. The 279 volunteering schools were stratified by their province, and in the first phase, 78 of them were randomly assigned to intervention (39 schools) and control (39 schools) conditions. In twelve schools (six in each group), instruction is given in Swedish, the second official language of Finland. The students in these schools mostly (but not exclusively) belong to the Swedish-speaking minority living in Finland. In order to ensure a good response rate, schools giving special education only were excluded from the sample. However, the sample includes children with special education status who are integrated in mainstream schools.

The 78 participating schools represent all five provinces of mainland Finland. The target sample at Wave 1 included 429 classrooms and a total of 8,237 students in grades 3–5 (mean age: 9–11 years). To recruit the children, their parents were sent information letters including a consent form. A total of 7,564 students (91.7% of the target sample) received active consent to participate in the study. One whole school dropped out before the data collection started because of problems related to their school facilities.

By the time Waves 2 and 3 were collected, some changes in the student composition had taken place, with the departure of 251 students and the arrival of 463 new students. Between Waves 1 and 2, two control schools (51 students) dropped out, and five more (640 students) between Waves 2 and 3. Thus, the final sample included 7,360 students from 426 classrooms in 70 schools. Altogether, 49.8% of the respondents were girls and 50.2 % were boys. Most students were native Finns (i.e., Caucasian), with the proportion of immigrants being 2.4%.

The school year in Finland lasts from mid-August to the end of May. Student data were collected at three time points: in May 2007, in December 2007–January 2008, and in May 2008. The implementation of KiVa started in mid-August, in the beginning of the new school year. Students filled out Internet-based questionnaires in the schools' computer labs during regular school hours. The process was administered by the teachers, who received detailed instructions about two weeks prior to data collection. In addition, the teachers had the possibility to get support by phone or e-mail before and during the data collection. They were given individual passwords for all the students who had obtained parental permission to participate in the study. They distributed the passwords to the students, who used them to log in to the questionnaire. The order of questions, individual items, and scales was extensively randomized, so that the order of presentation of the questions could not have any systematic effect on the results. The students were assured that their answers would remain strictly confidential and would not be revealed to teachers or to parents.

Measures

At the beginning of the questionnaire, students were asked information about several background variables. In the present study, only gender, age, and family composition (i.e., whether the child lived with both parents, a single parent, one parent and one step-parent, or with some other adults) were used. The language of instruction of the schools (Finnish or Swedish) was determined on the basis of information provided by the schools.

To measure victimization, we used the global item from the revised Olweus' Bully/Victim questionnaire (Olweus, 1996): "How often have you been bullied at school in the last couple of months?" Students answered on a five-point scale (0 = *Not at all*, 4 = *Several times a week*).

Students' school adjustment was operationalized as their school well-being, academic motivation, and academic achievement. School *well-being* included several subscales developed by Metsämuuronen and Svedlin (2004): general liking of school (3 items, e.g., "My school days are generally nice"), classroom climate (3 items, e.g., "There is a good climate in our class"), and school climate (5 items, e.g., "I feel safe at school"). Students responded to all items on a five-point Likert-type scale (0 = I disagree completely, 4 = I agree completely). The subscales were all internally consistent (Cronbach's alphas ranging from .77 to .79 at time 1, .72 to .80 at time 2, and .82 to .91 at time 3) and their intercorrelations were relatively high (rs between .59 and .74 at time 1, .60 and .77 at time 2, and .67 and .84 at time 3). The average of the three subscales formed the school well-being variable (α = .84, .85, and .90 at times 1, 2, and 3 respectively).

Academic motivation consisted of an average of two items initially developed in the Finnish National Board of Education (Metsämuuronen & Svedlin, 2004):"Learning brings me joy" and "I want to know and learn many different things." The responses were given on a five-point scale (0 = I disagree completely, 4 = I agree completely). The internal consistency was .75, .79, and .84 at times 1, 2, and 3 respectively.

Academic achievement was assessed by a single item: "I am performing well at school," with the same five-point scale that was used for the other scales. In addition, students responded to four items regarding their difficulties in the following areas: reading, reading comprehension, mathematics, and foreign languages. The four-point scale used to evaluate difficulties in each of these areas ranged from 0 = no difficulties to 3 = a lot of difficulties. The single item we used to assess academic achievement was negatively correlated with each of these items (rs between –.23 and –.30), as expected. We decided to use only the single general item in the present study, as many students have difficulties only in one or other area, and thus the items capturing difficulties in different areas do not form a reliable scale.

RESULTS

Descriptive Statistics and Mean Differences

The correlations between all study variables are presented in Table 11.2. The school adjustment variables were all positively related to each other (rs ranging from .24 to .64). Victimization was negatively associated with all school adjustment variables at the three times of assessment, being most strongly correlated with school well-being.

Table 11.3 shows the mean scores and standard deviations of students from KiVa schools and control schools on the three adjustment variables. Only students whose responses were available at each assessment point were included in computation of the means. On average, school adjustment tended to decrease as a function of time: at each assessment point, students from both intervention and control schools scored lower on each adjustment variable than they did in the previous assessment.

TABLE 11.2 Correlations Among All Measures at the Three Times of Testing

Measure	1	2	3	4	5	6	7	8	9	10	11	12	13	14
1. School well-being T1	—													
2. Academic motivation T1	.64	—												
3. Academic achievement T1	.56	.46	—											
4. Self-reported victimization T1	-.33	-.09	-.17	—										
5. Peer-reported victimization T1	-.22	-.06	-.10	.40	—									
6. School well-being T2	.56	.36	.34	-.25	-.18	—								
7. Academic motivation T2	.39	.45	.29	-.06	-.03^b	.63	—							
8. Academic achievement T2	.33	.27	.43	-.15	-.09	.57	.50	—						
9. Self-reported victimization T2	-.24	-.07	-.14	.45	.31	-.35	-.08	-.08	—					
10. Peer-reported victimization T2	-.19	-.06	-.10	.33	.70	-.23	-.06	-.12	.37	—				
11. School well-being T3	.46	.31	.29	-.20	-.15	.57	.39	.67	-.25	-.17	—			
12. Academic motivation T3	.36	.39	.24	-.09	-.07	.43	.51	.92	-.11	-.07	.75	—		
13. Academic achievement T3	.31	.27	.36	-.12	-.07	.39	.34	.58	-.12	-.07	.70	.63	—	
14. Self-reported victimization T3	-.20	-.04^a	-.10	.39	.27	-.29	-.07	-.09	.47	.32	-.31	-.13	-.16	—
15. Peer-reported victimization T3	-.17	-.05	-.10	.28	.59	-.21	-.05	-.10	.32	.72	-.20	-.08	-.09	.37

Note: All correlations are significant at $p < .001$, except correlations with subscripts [a] ($p < .01$) and [b] ($p < .05$).

TABLE 11.3 Means and Standard Deviations for School Adjustment Variables in Intervention and Control Schools

	Intervention schools (*N* = 2,964)	Control Schools (*N* = 1,930)	*t*
Academic motivation at T1	3.26 (0.85)	3.23 (0.85)	1.431
Academic motivation at T2	3.07 (0.88)	3.01 (0.95)	2.319*
Academic motivation at T3	2.92 (1.01)	2.84 (1.04)	2.708**
Academic achievement at T1	3.18 (0.90)	3.16 (0.92)	0.609
Academic achievement at T2	3.05 (0.95)	3.06 (0.96)	−0.100
Academic achievement at T3	3.01 (1.03)	2.92 (1.07)	2.807**
School well-being at T1	3.00 (0.71)	2.96 (0.71)	2.356*
School well-being at T2	2.95 (0.73)	2.86 (0.76)	4.089***
School well-being at T3	2.90 (0.84)	2.75 (0.86)	5.881***

*$p < .05$; ** $p < .01$; *** $p < .001$

The pattern of mean differences between KiVa schools and control schools at the three assessment points suggests that KiVa had an impact on each aspect of school adjustment. Whereas KiVa schools and control schools did not differ significantly in academic motivation and achievement at pretest, they differed in both dimensions at time 3, when students in KiVa schools reported higher motivation and better achievement than students in control schools. With respect to school well-being, students in KiVa schools had slightly higher scores already at time 1, but this difference became increasingly larger as the intervention continued (being the largest at the third assessment point).

Effects of KiVa on School Adjustment

We used multilevel modeling with MLwiN 2.0 (Rasbash, Charlton, Browne, Healy, & Cameron, 2005) to estimate the effects of the KiVa program on our outcome variables of interest. We analyzed data of 5,010 students within 318 classes from 70 schools who participated in the pre- and posttest of KiVa. All these students were in classrooms that contained at least eight students. Thus, students from very small classes were excluded from the analyses.

The differences between KiVa schools and control schools were examined after controlling for baseline levels of several background variables: gender, language of instruction at school (Finnish vs. Swedish), family breakup, and both absolute and relative (i.e., age in comparison to classmates) age of the student.

The results of the first models concerning effects at time 2, that is, seven months after the pretest and four months after the beginning of the implementation of KiVa, are presented in Table 11.4a. The results from models concerning effects at time 3, one year after the pretest and after nine months of implementing KiVa, are displayed in Table 11.4b. In all models, the effects of the control variables showed that boys tended to score lower on school adjustment. Students in Swedish-speaking schools reported higher school adjustment than students in Finnish-speaking schools. The "family breakup" variable seen in the table was coded as 0 = child living with both biological parents and 1 = child not living with both biological parents. Thus, children living with both parents reported better school adjustment than those with some other kind of family composition. Although the absolute age of the student was negatively associated with academic motivation and achievement at time 2 and time 3 (i.e., older students being less motivated and reporting lower achievement), the relative age was related to

TABLE 11.4a Effects of the KiVa Intervention Program on School Well-Being, Academic Motivation, and Academic Achievement After Four Months of Implementation

	School well-being T2	Academic achievement T2	Academic motivation T2
Intercept	1.522 (0.042)	1.841 (0.049)	1.801 (0.050)
School well-being T1	0.462 (0.012)**	—	—
Academic achievement T1	—	0.388 (0.013)**	—
Academic motivation T1	—	—	0.403 (0.012)**
KiVa intervention	**0.059 (0.025)***	**0.008 (0.029)**	**0.049 (0.029)**
Being a boy	−0.079 (0.019)**	−0.046 (0.026)	−0.175 (0.024)**
Being in a Swedish-speaking school	0.129 (0.040)**	0.157 (0.048)**	0.105 (0.047)*
Family breakup	−0.042 (0.024)	−0.087 (0.033)**	−0.067 (0.030)*
Age	−0.017 (0.016)	−0.072 (0.019)**	−0.094 (0.019)**
Relative age	−0.011 (0.014)	0.044 (0.018)*	0.035 (0.017)*
Variance			
School level	0.001 (0.001)	0.000 (0.000)	0.000 (0.000)
Class level	0.014 (0.003)	0.009 (0.005)	0.016 (0.005)
Student level	0.379 (0.009)	0.741 (0.016)	0.613 (0.014)

Note: $N = 5{,}010$ students, $N = 318$ classes, $N = 70$ schools.
** $p < .01$; * $p < .05$ (two-tailed)

TABLE 11.4b   Effects of the KiVa Intervention Program on School Well-Being, Academic Motivation, and Academic Achievement After Nine Months of Implementation

	School well-being T3	Academic achievement T3	Academic motivation T3
Intercept	1.767 (0.050)	1.973 (0.053)	1.909 (0.053)
School well-being T1	0.360 (0.011)**	—	—
Academic achievement T1	—	0.319 (0.012)**	—
Academic motivation T1	—	—	0.327 (0.012)**
KiVa intervention	**0.119 (0.046)****	**0.087 (0.042)***	**0.085 (0.040)***
Being a boy	−0.176 (0.022)**	−0.121 (0.028)**	−0.274 (0.027)**
Being in a Swedish-speaking school	0.130 (0.066)*	0.111 (0.063)	0.086 (0.061)
Family breakup	−0.072 (0.028)**	−0.104 (0.035)**	−0.080 (0.034)*
Age	−0.003 (0.020)	−0.066 (0.022)**	−0.075 (0.023)**
Relative age	−0.005 (0.017)	0.037 (0.020)	0.040 (0.020)*
Variance			
School level	0.017 (0.006)	0.010 (0.005)	0.006 (0.005)
Class level	0.033 (0.006)	0.020 (0.007)	0.034 (0.008)
Student level	0.552 (0.012)	0.925 (0.026)	0.845 (0.018)

Note: $N = 5,010$ students, $N = 318$ classes, $N = 70$ schools.
** $p < .01$; * $p < .05$ (two-tailed)

higher academic achievement at time 2 and academic motivation at time 2 and time 3. This means that students who were older than their classmates tended to be more academically motivated and, at time 2, were more likely than their relatively younger classmates to report that they performed well at school. Most of the variance in academic adjustment (especially in achievement) was between individual students. Variation at the classroom level was small, and variation between schools almost nonexistent.

After controlling for the above variables, the KiVa program had a significant effect on school well-being already at time 2, that is, after the first four months of implementation. The effects on school motivation and achievement were in the same positive direction, but not yet significant (Table 11.4a). At time 3, at the end of the school year when the KiVa program had been implemented for nine months, the effect on school well-being had become stronger. Furthermore, KiVa then had a positive and significant effect on academic motivation as well as academic achievement (Table 11.4b).

Are Changes in School Adjustment Related to Reduced Victimization?

As the KiVa program had positive effects in terms of improved school adjustment, we next wanted to test whether reductions in victimization could explain the improvements in the different aspects of school adjustment. Thus, we examined whether changes in school well-being, motivation, and achievement were associated with changes in victimization either at the individual or at the classroom level. In these analyses, we decided to use the whole sample for two reasons. First, we wanted to avoid losing any power (even though our sample was huge in terms of the number of students, the number of classrooms was of course much more modest, and we were interested in both individual and classroom-level effects). Second, we had no reason to believe that the association between victimization and school adjustment would be different in the intervention and in the control schools. In other words, we believed that if reduced victimization led to heightened school adjustment, this would happen regardless of the reason for such a reduction.

Change scores for each variable (change in victimization from time 1 to time 3, change in each school adjustment variable from time 1 to time 3) were calculated for each student in our sample. Furthermore, we calculated change scores in mean level of victimization for each classroom from time 1 to time 3. Change scores for school adjustment were then regressed on change scores in victimization. The findings are presented in Table 11.5.

As shown in the second row of Table 11.5, individual-level reduction in victimization led to significant changes in all three school adjustment variables, indicating that the students whose level of victimization was reduced reported positive changes in their school well-being and academic motivation, as well as academic achievement. Not surprisingly, the effect was strongest for school well-being, the variable that initially had the strongest concurrent correlation with victimization. However, the classroom-level reduction in victimization was also significantly related to the increase in school well-being, after controlling for the effects at the individual level. In other words, school well-being improved in classrooms where the level of victimization decreased. This classroom effect is an effect beyond changes in individual levels of victimization and supports the idea that decreases in witnessed victimization lead to improved school functioning.

We also tested whether potential positive changes in one or more aspects of school adjustment were related to the KiVa intervention, but not to the changes in victimization. The positive effect of the KiVa intervention presented in Table 11.5 implies that the KiVa program contains elements that affect the school adjustment of students regardless of the influence of the intervention on the levels of victimization students either experience or witness. This effect was the same for all three outcomes. A comparison between a model

TABLE 11.5   Individual and Classroom-Level Associations Between Changes in Victimization and Changes in School Adjustment Variables from T1 (May 2007) to T3 (May 2008)

	Change in school well-being T3 – T1	Change in achievement T3 – T1	Change in motivation T3 – T1
Intercept	–0.240 (0.024)	–0.249 (0.028)	–0.426 (0.027)
Change in victimization T3 – T1	–0.156 (0.013)**	–0.115 (0.017)**	–0.071 (0.015)**
Change in classroom level victimization T3 – T1	–0.148 (0.053)**	0.025 (0.066)	–0.095 (0.063)
KiVa intervention	0.071 (0.030)*	0.071 (0.030)*	0.071 (0.030)*
Variance			
Random slope (change in school adjustment on change in victimization) T3 – T1	0.008 (0.003)**	0.012 (0.006)*	0.005 (0.005)
Class level	0.027 (0.006)	0.027 (0.009)	0.025 (0.008)
Student level	0.620 (0.014)	1.168 (0.026)	1.065 (0.023)

Notes: $N = 5{,}010$ students, $N = 318$ classes, $N = 70$ schools.
** $p < .01$; * $p < .05$ (two-tailed)

with three separate parameters for the effect of the KiVa intervention versus a model with one common parameter revealed that the difference in deviance between the two models was 0.65 ($df = 2$), $p = 0.72$. This suggests that the model with one common parameter was more parsimonious.

Finally, we tested whether the effect of change in victimization on change in school adjustment differed between students in a classroom. Do all students benefit to the same extent from the change in victimization, or does the school adjustment of some students improve much more than that of others? Including such random effects in the model led to a better fit with the data; the decrease in deviance was 35.85 ($df = 3$), $p < 0.01$. To what extent are these random effects important? The average effect of change in victimization on change in school well-being is –0.156 and the random slope is 0.008. The random slope can be seen as the variance of the average effect, and the standard deviation is then equal to $\sqrt{0.008}$, which is 0.089. The 95% confidence interval of the average effect of change in victimization on change in school well-being is thus –0.156 ± 1.96 * .089, which is –0.331 to 0.019. Thus, the effect for some students is much larger than for others. The 95% confidence interval of the average effect of change in victimization on change in school achievement, the other random effect in Table 11.5, is –0.115 ± 1.96 * .110 and ranges from –0.330 to 0.100. Thus, there are clearly differential effects for students. A decrease in victimization is clearly related to an increase in achievement for some students, but not for others.

CONCLUSIONS

Tackling bullying effectively is a necessity for numerous reasons. Reducing victims' suffering, which sometimes persists long after their school years are over (Card, 2003; Hawker & Boulton, 2000; Isaacs et al., 2008; Sourander et al., 2007), is the main goal of antibullying intervention programs. Interventions are essential from the bullies' perspective as well: They need to get a strong message that their behavior is unacceptable in order to develop into adults with healthy and supportive interpersonal relationships (about the problems many bullying children face later in their life, see Sourander et al., 2007). To date, many antibullying programs have been evaluated (Baldry & Farrington, 2007; Ferguson et al., 2007; Merrell et al., 2008; Smith et al., 2004; Ttofi & Farrington, 2010; Ttofi et al., 2008; Vreeman & Carroll, 2007). These evaluation studies have often focused on showing that "the program works" (in terms of reducing bullying or victimization) rather than trying to capture the underlying mechanisms of change or possible side effects of the interventions. In addition to easing the victims' plight, antibullying programs may impact the adjustment of much wider group of children and youth. Showing effects on academic motivation and achievement might be especially important in order to convince the stakeholders about the necessity to develop and implement such programs.

We examined the influence of KiVa, a new antibullying program developed at the University of Turku and now widely implemented in Finnish schools, on different aspects of school adjustment among children in grades 4–6. Our findings indicate, first, that the KiVa program had positive effects on each of the three types of school adjustment assessed: school well-being, academic motivation, and academic achievement. Thus, not only did students like school more and perceive the classroom and school climates more positively after the intervention, but they also reported a higher motivation to learn and even performed better at school. The effect on school well-being emerged early, being significant already after the first four months of implementation of the program (the fall semester), and it became larger after nine months of implementation. The effects on school motivation and academic achievement took longer to manifest, being significant after nine months (i.e., the whole academic year) of implementation. Furthermore, they were weaker than the effects obtained for school well-being.

Changes in school adjustment were related to reductions in victimization both at the individual and at the classroom level. The school adjustment of students whose individual level of victimization decreased improved over time, as reflected in changes in their well-being and, to a somewhat lesser extent, their school motivation and academic performance. However, improved school well-being was also evidenced more generally in classrooms where the average level of victimization was reduced. Thus, the positive impact of reduced victimization extended beyond victimized children to benefit also other children in classrooms in which victimization was successfully reduced. Further research is needed to investigate the mechanisms of such beneficial effects. There is already some literature about potential mediators among children merely witnessing the harassment of their classmates, such as reduced anxiety (Nishina & Juvonen, 2005) as well as depression and low self-esteem (Huitsing et al., 2010). In addition to the fear of becoming the next victim, students may also feel guilty for witnessing frequent victimization: It is known that most of them do not intervene on behalf of the victim (Salmivalli et al., 1996), although they believe that would be the right thing to do.

Although untested in our study, it is also plausible that changes in former bullies' school adjustment partly account for the positive effects observed in classrooms where victimization went down. Being a bully is associated with low academic achievement (Ma, Phelps, Lerner, & Lerner, 2009). A decrease in victimization at the classroom level implies that at least some bullies in those classrooms reduced their aggressive behaviors and ceased to receive the peer popularity that often accompanies antisocial behaviors (e.g., Cillessen & Mayeux, 2004; Rodkin et al., 2000). Former bullies may therefore devote more time and energy to school work and seek approval or recognition through greater academic achievement.

Interestingly, the effects of KiVa were not completely mediated by changes in victimization, but the program also had a direct influence on the school adjustment of the students. Over and above the effects that were associated with individual- and classroom-level reductions in victimization, children targeted by KiVa reported increases in school well-being, motivation, and achievement during the school year in which the program was implemented. One explanation of such a direct effect is that some elements of the program (such as the student lessons, where important topics related to social interaction with peers are brought up, discussed, and worked on) alter the peer interactions overall into more constructive and positive ones. Furthermore, the values and norms promoted in KiVa in order to discourage bullying may extend to the academic domain and thereby benefit academic functioning. For instance, teaching children that they should provide help to a peer who is being victimized may encourage them to offer work-related assistance to classmates experiencing academic difficulties. Similarly, KiVa lessons incite children to perceive differences among classmates as richness and to be careful that no one in the class is being left out. This may facilitate effective collaboration during academic group tasks, especially by increasing the participation of low-status students who might otherwise stay quiet and not benefit from the activity (see Cohen & Lotan, 1995). Encouraging children to resist group pressure and fostering the idea that the majority is not always right may also convince children of the necessity to think for themselves and question what they are taught. Understanding the value of developing their own thoughts may in turn prove particularly useful in their academic endeavors.

Alternatively, it can be the case that victims of peer harassment—even if their victimization had not stopped—received more support from their peers as a consequence of the KiVa program and were therefore better adjusted in the school context. Kärnä and colleagues (2011) provided evidence that KiVa increased the empathy towards victimized peers as well as self-efficacy to support them and reduced the bystanders' likelihood of reinforcing the bullies' mean acts. In light of the evidence showing that victims who are defended and supported by their peers are better adjusted than undefended victims (Sainio, Veenstra, Huitsing, & Salmivalli, 2011), it is plausible that the negative effects of victimization might be attenuated by the intervention even in cases in which the victimization continues.

An obvious limitation of the study reported here is that all school adjustment variables were self-reported by children. This critique is most justified with respect to academic achievement, which was not only self-reported but also assessed by a single item ("I am performing well at school"). Although this variable was significantly related to children's self-reported performance on four academic subjects, more objective measures of academic achievement (such as GPA or teacher reports on performance) would have been preferable. Our results show, however, that at least children's own perceptions of their performance were positively influenced by KiVa.

KiVa is not meant to be a short-lived project starting and ending in the schools implementing it, but it is rather meant to become a permanent part of their antibullying work. During the program evaluation, the student lessons included in the universal actions of KiVa were implemented in each grade level. In the following years, all first- and fourth-graders in KiVa schools will be involved in the lessons, meaning that there will be a time when all children in grades 1–6 will have gone through them twice (and after secondary school, three times). In addition, individual cases of bullying coming to the attention of school personnel are effectively handled by the KiVa teams and classroom teachers, regardless of the grade level of the students. Thus, it is possible that the program effects on victimization as well as general school adjustment will be even stronger in the years to come, when KiVa will have been systematically implemented for a longer period of time.

In conclusion, the findings reported in the present chapter are important as they (1) provide strong evidence of the impact of victimization on school adjustment, both at the individual and at the classroom level, and

(2) are helpful in justifying the worthiness of antibullying work for school personnel and stakeholders, as well as politicians. Antibullying interventions are valuable not only because they benefit a relatively small minority of students who are repeatedly tormented by their peers at school, but also because they increase the well-being, school motivation, and possibly even academic performance of a much wider group of students.

ACKNOWLEDGEMENTS

We wish to express our gratitude to the Finnish Ministry of Education and Culture for funding the development and initial evaluation of the KiVa program (www.kivakoulu.fi). Besides the funding from the Ministry, the present study was supported by the Academy of Finland grant (project number 134843) to the first author. We are thankful to all schools participating in the evaluation study and for all people working on the KiVa project in the University of Turku, as well as our national and international collaborators.

REFERENCES

Baldry, A., & Farrington, D. (2007). Effectiveness of programs to prevent school bullying. *Victims & Offenders, 2,* 183–204.

Boivin, M., Hymel, S., & Bukowski, W. M. (1995). The roles of social withdrawal, peer rejection, and victimization by peers in predicting loneliness and depressed mood in childhood. *Development and Psychopathology, 7,* 765–785.

Boulton, M. J., Trueman, M., & Flemington, I. (2002). Associations between secondary school pupils' definitions of bullying, attitudes towards bullying, and tendencies to engage in bullying: Age and sex differences. *Educational Studies, 28,* 353–370.

Boulton, M. J., Trueman, M., & Murray, L. (2008). Associations between peer victimization, fear of future victimization and disrupted concentration on class work among junior school pupils. *British Journal of Educational psychology, 78,* 473–489.

Buhs, E. S., Ladd, G. W., & Herald, S. L. (2006). Peer exclusion and victimization: Processes that mediate the relation between peer group rejection and children's classroom engagement and achievement? *Journal of Educational Psychology, 98,* 1–13.

Card, N. A. (2003, April). *Victims of peer aggression: A meta-analytic review.* Paper presented at the Society for Research in Child Development biennial meeting, Tampa, FL.

Card, N. A., & Hodges, E. V. E. (2008). Peer victimization among schoolchildren: Causes, consequences, and considerations in assessment and intervention. *School Psychology Quarterly, 23,* 451–461.

Cillessen, A. H. N., & Mayeux, L. (2004). From censure to reinforcement: Developmental changes in the association between aggression and social status. *Child Development, 75,* 147–163.

Cohen, E. G., & Lotan, R. A. (1995). Producing equal-status interaction in the heterogeneous classroom. *American Educational Research Journal, 32,* 99–120.

Craig, W., & Harel, Y. (2004). Bullying, physical fighting, and victimization. In C. Currie et al. (Eds.), *Young people's health in context: International report from the HBSC 2001/02 survey.* WHO Policy Series: Health policy for children and adolescents Issue 4. Copenhagen, Denmark: WHO Regional Office for Europe.

Erath, S., Flanagan, K., & Bierman, K. (2008). Early adolescent school adjustment: Associations with friendship and peer victimization. *Social Development, 17,* 853–870.

Fekkes, M., Pijpers, F. I., Verloove-Vanhorick, S.P. (2006). Effects of antibullying school programs on bullying and health complaints. *Archives of Pediatrics & Adolescent Medicine, 160,* 638–644.

Ferguson, C., San Miguel, C., Kilburn, J., & Sanchez, P. (2007). The effectiveness of school-based anti-bullying programs: A meta-analytic review. *Criminal Justice Review, 32,* 401– 414.

Hanish, L. D., & Guerra, N. G. (2002). A longitudinal analysis of patterns of adjustment following peer victimization. *Development and Psychopathology, 14,* 69–89.

Hawker, D. S. J., & Boulton, M. J. (2000). Twenty years' research on peer victimization and psychosocial maladjustment. A meta-analytic review of cross-sectional studies. *Journal of Child Psychology and Psychiatry, 41,* 441–455.

Haynie, D., Nansel, T., Eitel, P., Crump, A., Saylor, K., Yu, K., & Simons-Morton, B. (2001). Bullies, victims, and bully-victims: Distinct groups of at-risk youth. *Journal of Early Adolescence, 21,* 29–49.

Hodges, E. V. E., & Perry, D. G. (1999). Personal and interpersonal antecedents and consequences of victimization by peers. *Journal of Personality and Social Psychology, 76,* 677–685.

Huitsing, G., Sainio, M., Veenstra, R., & Salmivalli, C. (2010, August 31). "It must be me" or "It could be them?" The impact of the social network position of bullies and victims on victims' adjustment. *Social Networks.* Advance online publication DOI: 10.1016/j.socnet.2010.07.002.

Isaacs, J., Hodges, E. V. E., & Salmivalli, C. (2008) Long-term consequences of victimization by peers: A follow-up from adolescence to young adulthood. *European Journal of Developmental Science, 2,* 387–397.

Juvonen, J., Graham, S., & Schuster, M. (2003). Bullying among young adolescents: The strong, weak, and troubled. *Pediatrics, 112,* 1231–1237.

Kochenderfer, B. J., & Ladd, G. W. (1996). Peer victimization: Cause or consequence of school maladjustment? *Child Development, 67,* 1305–1317.

Kärnä, A., Alanen, E., Voeten, M., Little, T., Poskiparta, E., & Salmivalli, C. (submitted). Effectiveness of the KiVa antibullying program: Grades 1–3 and 7–9. *Journal of Educational Psychology.*

Kärnä, A., Voeten, M., Little, T., Poskiparta, E., Kaljonen, A., & Salmivalli, C. (2011). A large-scale evaluation of the KiVa antibullying program: Grades 4–6. *Child Development, 82,* 311–330.

Leary, M. R., Kowalski, R. M., Smith, L., & Phillips, S. (2003). Teasing, rejection, and violence: Case studies of the school shootings, *Aggressive Behavior,* 29, 202–214.

Ma, L., Phelps, E., Lerner, J., & Lerner, R. (2009). The development of academic competence among adolescents who bully and who are bullied. *Journal of Applied Developmental Psychology, 30,* 628–644.

Merrell, K., Gueldner, B., Ross, S., & Isava, D. (2008). How effective are school bullying intervention programs? A meta-analysis of intervention research. *School Psychology Quarterly, 23,* 26–42.

Metsämuuronen, J., & Svedlin, R. (2004). Kouluviihtyvyyden muuttuminen peruskoulussa ja lukiossa iän funktiona [Change in perceived well-being in primary and secondary schools as a function of age]. Manuscript submitted for publication.

Nakamoto, J., & Schwartz, D. (2010). Is peer victimization associated with academic achievement? A meta-analytic review. *Social Development, 19,* 221–242.

Nansel, T. R., Haynie, D. L., & Simons-Morton, B. G. (2003). The association of bullying and victimization with middle school adjustment. *Journal of Applied School Psychology, 19,* 45–51.

Nansel, T., Overpeck, M., Pilla, R., Ruan, W., Simon-Morton, B., & Scheidt, P. (2001). Bullying behaviors among U.S. youth: Prevalence and association with psychosocial adjustment. *Journal of the American Medical Association, 285,* 2094–2100.

Needham, B., Crosnoe, R., & Muller, C. (2004). Academic failure in secondary school: The inner-related role of health problems and educational context. *Social Problems, 57,* 569–586.

Nishina, A., & Juvonen, J. (2005). Daily reports of witnessing and experiencing peer harassment in middle school. *Child Development, 76,* 435–450.

Nishina, A., Juvonen, J., & Witkow, M. R. (2005). Sticks and bones may break my bones, but names will make me feel sick: The psychosocial, somatic, and scholastic consequences of peer harassment. *Journal of Clinical Child and Adolescent Psychology, 34,* 37–48.

O'Connell, P., Pepler, D., & Craig, W., (1999) Peer involvement in bullying: Insights and challenges for intervention. *Journal of Adolescence, 22,* 437–452.

Olweus, D. (1991). Bully/victim problems among schoolchildren: Basic facts and effects of a school based intervention program. In D. Pepler & K. Rubin (Eds.), *The development and treatment of childhood aggression* (pp. 411–448). Hillsdale, NJ: Erlbaum.

Olweus, D. (1996). *The revised Olweus bully/victim questionnaire.* Bergen, Norway: Research Center for Health Promotion (HEMIL Center), University of Bergen.

Olweus, D. (1999). Sweden. In P. K. Smith, Y. Morita, J. Junger-Tas, D. Olweus, R. Catalano, & P. Slee (Eds.), *The nature of school bullying: A cross-national perspective* (pp. 7–27). London, UK: Routledge.

Pöyhönen, V., Juvonen, J., & Salmivalli, C. (2010). What does it take to defend the victimized peer? The interplay between personal and social factors. *Merrill-Palmer Quarterly, 56,* 143–163.

Rasbash, J., Charlton, C., Browne, W.J., Healy, M., & Cameron, B. (2005). *MLwiN Version 2.02.* Bristol, UK: Centre for Multilevel Modelling, University of Bristol.

Rigby, K., & Johnson, B. (2006). Expressed readiness of Australian schoolchildren to act as bystanders in support of children who are being bullied. *Educational Psychology*, 26, 425–440.

Rigby, K., & Slee, P. T. (1991). Bullying among Australian school children: Reported behavior and attitudes toward victims. *Journal of Social Psychology*, *131*, 615–627.

Rivers, I., Poteat, V., Noret, N., & Ashurst, N. (2009). Observing bullying at school: The mental health implications of witness status. *School Psychology Quarterly*, *24*, 211–223.

Rodkin, P., Farmer, T., Pearl, R., & Van Acker, R. (2000). Heterogeneity of popular boys: Antisocial and prosocial configurations. *Developmental Psychology*, *36*, 14–24.

Sainio, M., Veenstra, R., Huitsing, G., & Salmivalli, C. (2011). Victims and their defenders: A dyadic approach. *International Journal of Behavioral Development*, *35*, 144–151. DOI: 10.1177/0165025410378068.

Salmivalli, C. (2010). Bullying and the peer group: A review. *Aggression and Violent Behavior*, *15*, 112–120.

Salmivalli, C., Kärnä, A., & Poskiparta, E. (2010). From peer putdowns to peer support: A theoretical model and how it translated into a national anti-bullying program. In S. R. Jimerson, S. M. Swearer, & D. L. Espelage (Eds). *Handbook of Bullying in Schools: An International Perspective* (pp. 441–454). New York, NY: Routledge.

Salmivalli, C., Kärnä, A., & Poskiparta, E. (2011) Counteracting bullying in Finland: The KiVa program and its effects on different forms of being bullied. *International Journal of Behavioral Development*, *35*, 405–411.

Salmivalli, C., Lagerspetz, K., Björkqvist, K., Österman, K., & Kaukiainen, A. (1996). Bullying as a group process: Participant roles and their relations to social status within the group. *Aggressive Behavior*, *22*, 1–15.

Salmivalli, C., & Peets, K. (2009). Bullies, victims, and bully–victim relationships in middle childhood and early adolescence. In K.H.Rubin, W.M.Bukowski, & B. Laursen (Eds.), *Handbook of Peer Interactions, Relationships and Groups* (pp. 322–340). NY: Guilford.

Salmivalli, C., & Voeten, M. (2004). Connections between attitudes, group norms, and behaviors associated with bullying in schools. *International Journal of Behavioral Development*, *28*, 246–258.

Salmivalli, C., Voeten, M., & Poskiparta, E. (2011). Bystanders matter: Associations between defending, reinforcing, and the frequency of bullying in classrooms. *Journal of Clinical Child and Adolescent Psychology*, *40*, 1–9.

Schwartz, D., Gorman, A., Nakamoto, J., & Toblin, R. (2005). Victimization in the peer group and children's academic functioning. *Journal of Educational Psychology*, *97*, 425–435.

Sijtsema, J., Veenstra, R., Lindenberg, S., & Salmivalli, C. (2009). An empirical test of bullies' status goals: Assessing direct goals, aggression, and prestige. *Aggressive Behavior*, *35*, 57–67.

Smith, P. K., Morita, J., Junger-Tas, D., Olweus, D., Catalano, R., & Slee, P. (1999). *The nature of school bullying: A cross-national perspective*. London, UK: Routledge.

Smith, P., Pepler, D., & Rigby, K. (2004). *Bullying in schools: How successful can interventions be?* New York, NY: Cambridge University Press.

Smith, J. D., Schneider, B. H., Smith, P. K., & Ananiadou, K. (2004). The effectiveness of whole-school antibullying programs: A synthesis of evaluation research. *School Psychology Review, 33,* 547–560.

Solberg, M., Olweus, D., & Endresen, I. (2007). Bullies and victims at school: Are they the same pupils? *British Journal of Educational Psychology, 77,* 441–464.

Sourander, A., Jensen, P., Rönning, J. A., Niemelä, S., Helenius, H., Sillanmäki, L., et al. (2007). What is the early adulthood outcome of boys who bully or are bullied in childhood? The Finnish "From a Boy to a Man" study. *Pediatrics, 120,* 397–404.

Ttofi, M., & Farrington, D.P. (2011). Effectiveness of school-based programs to reduce bullying: A systematic and meta-analytic review. *Journal of Experimental Criminology, 7,* 27–56. DOI: 10. 1007/s11292-010-9109-1.

Ttofi, M., Farrington, D.P., & Baldry, A.C. (2008). *Effectiveness of programmes to reduce school bullying: A systematic review.* Report prepared for The Swedish National Council for Crime Prevention. Västerås, Sweden: Edita Norstedts.

Vreeman, R. C., & Carroll, A. E. (2007). A systematic review of school-based interventions to prevent bullying. *Archives of Pediatrics & Adolescent Medicine, 161* 78–88.

Wentzel, K. (2009). Peers and academic functioning at school. In K. Rubin, W. Bukowski, & B. Laursen (Eds.), *Handbook of peer interactions, relationships, and groups* (pp. 531–547). New York, NY: Guilford.

Whitney, I., & Smith, P.K. (1993). A survey of the nature and extent of bullying in junior/middle and secondary schools. *Educational Research, 35,* 3–25.

Williford, A., Boulton, A., Noland, B., Little, T. Kärnä, A., & Salmivalli, C. (2012). Effects of the KiVa anti-bullying program on adolescents' depression, anxiety, and perception of peers. *Journal of Abnormal Child Psychology, 40,* 289–300.

Lightning Source UK Ltd.
Milton Keynes UK
UKOW030623120413

209107UK00003B/33/P